ORGANIZATION DEVELOPMENT IN HEALTHCARE: CONVERSATIONS ON RESEARCH AND STRATEGIES

ADVANCES IN HEALTH CARE MANAGEMENT

Series Editors: John D. Blair, Myron D. Fottler, Grant T. Savage and Leonard Friedman

Recent Volumes:

Volume 1: Advances in Healthcare Management, Edited by John D. Blair, Myron D. Fottler, and Grant T. Savage

Volume 2: Advances in Healthcare Management, Edited by Myron D. Fottler, Grant T. Savage, and John D. Blair

Volume 3: Advances in Healthcare Management, Edited by Grant T. Savage, John D. Blair, and Myron D. Fottler

Volume 4: Bioterrorism, Preparedness, Attack and Response, Edited by John D. Blair, Myron D. Fottler, and Albert C. Zapanta

Volume 5: International Healthcare Management, Edited by Grant T. Savage, Jon A. Chilingerian, and Michael Powell

Volume 6: Strategic Thinking and Entrepreneurial Action in the Health Care Industry, Edited by John D. Blair, Myron D. Fottler, Eric W. Ford, and G. Tyge Payne

Volume 7: Patient Safety and Health Care Management, Edited by Grant T. Savage and Eric. W. Ford

Volume 8: Biennial Review of Health Care Management: Meso Perspectives, Edited by Grant T. Savage and Myron D. Fottler

Volume 9: Strategic Human Resource Management in Health Care, Edited by Grant T. Savage, Myron D. Fottler, and Naresh Khatri

ADVANCES IN HEALTH CARE MANAGEMENT
VOLUME 10

ORGANIZATION DEVELOPMENT IN HEALTHCARE: CONVERSATIONS ON RESEARCH AND STRATEGIES

EDITED BY

JASON A. WOLF
The Beryl Institute, USA

HEATHER HANSON
Kaiser Permanente, USA

MARK J. MOIR
Sanford Health, USA

LEN FRIEDMAN
The George Washington University, USA

GRANT T. SAVAGE
University of Missouri School of Medicine, USA

Emerald

United Kingdom – North America – Japan
India – Malaysia – China

Emerald Group Publishing Limited
Howard House, Wagon Lane, Bingley BD16 1WA, UK

First edition 2011

British Library Cataloguing in Publication Data
A catalogue record for this book is available from the British Library

ISBN: 978-0-85724-709-4
ISSN: 1474-8231 (Series)

Printed and bound by CPI Group (UK) Ltd, Croydon, CR0 4YY

CONTENTS

PART V: INFORMATION TECHNOLOGY

PART VI: SYSTEMS ISSUES

LIST OF CONTRIBUTORS

Henk Akkermans	Tilburg School of Economics & Management, Tilburg University, Tilburg, The Netherlands
Mona Al-Amin	Department of Health Services Research, Management and Policy, University of Florida, Gainesville, FL, USA
Margarete Arndt	Graduate School of Management, Clark University, Worcester, MA, USA
Philip L. Bailin	Cleveland Clinic, Cleveland, OH, USA
Neal R. Barshes	Surgery Education, Brigham and Women's Hospital, Boston, MA, USA
Luciano Bedoya Corazzo	Divisiόn de Planeamiento, Procesos y Tecnología, Pacifico Peruano Suiza, Lima, Peru
Barbara Bigelow	Graduate School of Management, Clark University, Worcester, MA, USA
Yvonne Brunetto	Southern Cross Business School, Southern Cross University, Coolangatta, Australia
Stefano Calciolari	Univerità della Svizzera italiana, Lugano, Switzerland, and Bocconi University, Milan, Italy
Hal S. Currey	College of Medicine, Medical University of South Carolina, and Medical University Hospital Authority, SC, USA

Sebastian Desmidt	Faculty of Business Administration and Public Administration, University College Ghent, Ghent, and Faculty of Economics and Business Administration, Ghent University, Ghent, Belgium
Rodney Farr-Wharton	Innovation and Entrepreneurship, University of the Sunshine Coast, Maroochydore, Australia
Kathleen FitzSimons	Organisational Consultant, Cleveland, OH, USA
Arie Franx	Division Women and Baby, University Medical Centre Utrecht, The Netherlands
Eric W. Ford	Department of Business Administration and Marketing, Bryan School of Business and Economics, University of North Carolina Greensboro, Greensboro, NC, USA
Andrew N. Garman	Health Systems Management, National Center for Healthcare Leadership, Rush University, Chicago, IL, USA
Jim Goes	School of Advanced Studies, University of Phoenix, AZ, USA
Barry Halm	School of Public Health, University of Minnesota, Saginaw, MN, USA
Corinne Haviley	Central Dupage Hospital, Winfield, IL, USA
Elizabeth Holloway	Leadership and Change Program, Antioch University, Yellow Springs, OH, USA
Margaret M. Hopkins	Department of Management, University of Toledo, Toledo, OH, USA
Irwin B. Horwitz	Cameroon School of Business, University of St. Thomas, Houston, TX, USA

Sujin K. Horwitz — Cameroon School of Business, University of St. Thomas, Houston, TX, USA

Jonathan King — College of Business, Oregon State University, Corvallis, OR, USA

Mitchell Kusy — Leadership and Change Program, Antioch University, Yellow Springs, OH, USA

Christy Lemak — Department of Health Management and Policy, University of Michigan, Ann Arbor, MI, USA

Nir Menachemi — Health Care Organization and Policy, University of Alabama at Birmingham School of Public Health, Birmingham, AL, USA

Robyn Y. Nishimi — National Quality Forum, Washington, DC, USA

Deborah A. O'Neil — Department of Management, Bowling Green State University, Bowling Green, OH, USA

Debra E. Orr — Organizational Leadership, Roosevelt University, Chicago, IL, USA

Patrick Albert Palmieri — División de Negocios de Salud, Pacifico Peruano Suiza, and Center for American Education, Universidad San Ignacio de Loyola, Lima, Peru

Victoria A. Parker — Health Policy & Management, Boston University School of Public Health, Boston, MA, USA

Karen L. Pellegrin — College of Pharmacy, University of Hawaii Hilo, HI, USA

Lori T. Peterson	Department of Management and Labor Relations, Nance College of Business, Cleveland State University, Cleveland, OH, USA
Angèle Pieters	Tilburg University, Tilburg, The Netherlands
Anita A. Prinzie	Manchester Business School, Manchester, UK; Ghent University, Ghent, Belgium
Cynthia Roberts	College of Business, Purdue University North Central, Westville, IN, USA
Carolyn Roper	College of Business, Purdue University North Central, Westville, IN, USA
Irwin M. Rubin	Temenos Inc., Honolulu, HW, USA
Fatema Salam	The Center for Health Care Quality, The George Washington University, Washington, DC, USA
Kate Shacklock	Griffith Business School, Griffith University, Gold Coast campus, Australia
James K. Stoller	Cleveland Clinic, Cleveland, OH, USA
Robert Weech-Maldonado	Department of Health Services Administration, University of Alabama at Birmingham, AL, USA
Jason A. Wolf	Public Administration and Policy, The Beryl Institute, Bedford, TX, USA, and School of Public Administration, American University, Washington, DC, USA

LIST OF REVIEWERS

Margarete Arndt
Graduate School of Management, Clark University, Worcester, MA, USA.

Barbara Bigelow
Graduate School of Management, Clark University, Worcester, MA, USA

Andrew N. Garman
Rush University, Chicago, IL, USA

Jim Goes
School of Advanced Studies, University of Phoenix, AZ, USA

Jonathan King
Oregon State University, Portland, OR, USA

Christy Lemak
Department of Health Management and Policy, University of Michigan, Ann Arbor, MI, USA

Nir Menachemi
University of Alabama, Birmingham, AL, USA

Victoria A. Parker
Boston University, Boston, MA, USA

Eric W. Ford
University of North Carolina Greensboro, Greensboro, NC, USA

*This book is dedicated in honor and memory of
one of our contributors,
Dr. Barry J. Halm,
a visionary healthcare leader,
husband, father, friend and mentor to so many
making a difference in healthcare every day.
He will be missed.*

PREFACE

Advances in Health Care Management (*AHCM*) is a research annual that publishes state-of-the-art reviews and research on special topics in the field of health care management. As conceived by the founding coeditors, John D. Blair (Texas Tech University), Myron D. Fottler (University of Central Florida), and Grant T. Savage (University of Alabama at Birmingham), and as originally commissioned by JAI Press, *AHCM* provides a forum for leading research on health care management. Volumes 1–3 offer reviews of the field, research on selected topics, and best papers from the Health Care Management Division of the Academy of Management. In contrast, volumes 4–7 focus on a range of special topics, from bioterrorism to international health care management to entrepreneurship to patient safety.

Under Emerald Publishing Group, state-of-the-art review volumes were introduced to complement the *AHCM* volumes on topics of special interest. Volume 8 published in 2009 is devoted entirely to the review of health care management research. Continuing the tradition of special topics, volume 9, published in 2010, focuses on strategic human resource management in health care management.

Three guest editors, who combine scholarship with practice, were the impetus for this volume on organizational development in health care: Jason A. Wolf (The Beryl Institute), Heather A. Hanson (Kaiser Permanente), and Mark Moir (Sanford Health). These guest editors have both contributed to and facilitated contributions by others in the field of health care organizational development. As with many other volumes in the series, this volume of *AHCM* has a strong set of international authors. Moreover, volume 10 introduces a new coeditor for the *AHCM* series, Leonard Friedman, professor, associate chair, and program director at George Washington University.

Significantly, Len Friedman's participation as a coeditor for the *AHCM* series represents an inflection point in the development of this publication. From this point forward, *AHCM* will produce two volumes a year, alternating between special topic volumes and state-of-the-art reviews. Volume 11, to be published later in 2011, will be devoted to state-of-the-art reviews. And in 2012, volume 12 will be focused on international health information technology, while volume 13 will focus on macrolevel theory and applications in its review of the state of the art in health care management.

When *AHCM* was launched, we believed there was a need for a publication that provided a forum for scholarship that not only made important contributions to the field but was also capable of illuminating the bridges from theory to practice and from practice to theory. With volume 10 of *ACHM*, scholarship and practice are intertwined; we hope you, the reader, find this unique perspective both valuable and insightful.

Grant T. Savage
Leonard Friedman

INTRODUCTION

A PERSPECTIVE ON ORGANIZATIONAL WELL-BEING

Health care organizations provide a unique and insightful microcosm of the many larger challenges health care systems face around the world. To improve our health care industry, one has to first improve the internal health and well-being of the organizations that deliver care every day. In other words, to become a high-functioning industry, the organization has to become healthy first (Lovey, Nadkarni, & Erdelyi, 2007). This book has been crafted to catalyze this journey of creating healthy and vibrant health care organizations through proven strategies and evidence-based practices and in doing so have some part in transforming our global health care industry.

As one looks at the foundation of health care, care providers (physicians, nurses, support staff, etc.) are educated and trained to heal and improve the health of individuals in their care. The field of organization development (OD) takes on a very similar positioning. Scholars and practitioners of OD are educated and trained to improve the health of organizational systems, specifically by focusing on individual, team, and organizational strategies. To improve and potentially transform health care, we believe it is necessary to connect these two distinct, yet related fields to foster personal and organization health and well-being from the inside out. This book provides an opportunity to learn from many exceptional scholar-practitioners in the field who have taken bold and courageous steps to explore and improve the internal conditions within health care organizations.

Fostering health in health care and reconnecting the industry with its humanness will require rigorous focus and an unwavering commitment to systemic change. Watson (2009) avows, "radical change from within is an essential and necessary requirement to reverse the non-caring trend many experience or witness in hospitals and health care today" (p. 467). The culture within health care has been described as one "which has lost its way: a culture void of humanity and authentic human caring relationships, and void of meaningful communication and connections" (Watson, 2009, p. 468). With these daunting challenges ahead, this book begins to reveal the interrelated nature of the critical elements necessary to improve health care and organizational well-being overall.

As the content for the work unfolded and the contributions came together, a framework for the integrated elements of organizational well-being began to emerge. While we do not suggest one is more important than the other, these elements of organizational well-being seemed to mirror the critical elements of health care success itself. This framework is built on the interrelated nature of culture, change, leadership, relationships, technology, and systems. It begins, to tell through the contributions of our authors, an intricate and powerful story of how OD plays a critical role in health care performance (Fig. 1).

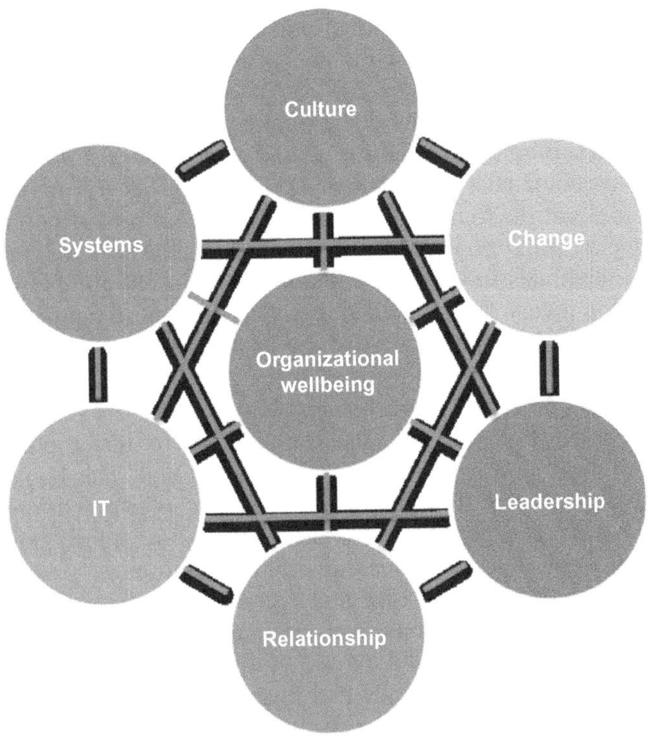

Fig. 1. A Framework for Organization Development in Health care and Organizational Well-Being.

PART I: CULTURE

As Section I unfolds, authors begin by providing context to the underlying nature of organizations and the often invisible influences that drive behaviors and actions. Understanding culture and how to influence cultural change is a critical element to improving our health care systems. The three chapters in this section include

- Demystifying and Improving Organizational Culture in Health care
- The Organization's Mission Statement: Give Up Hope or Resuscitate? A Search for Evidence-Based Recommendations
- Enhancing the Cultural Competency of Health care Organizations

Each chapter highlights evidence-based strategies to understand and transform organizations. These strategies begin by generating awareness of cultural dynamics and then identifying and creating actionable steps and lived experiences to shift and leverage the underlying conditions to strategically improve the culture.

PART II: CHANGE

Section two builds on the foundation of culture and focuses on the nature of change in health care systems. The two chapters in this section include

- Employee Engagement: A Prescription for Organizational Transformation
- The Relationship between the Survey-Guided Assessment of Culture within Specific Nursing Work Groups and Readiness for Change

The chapter on employee engagement provides a rich narrative of the transformation occurring within health care and the resulting need to build engagement into the culture of organizations to ensure survival. Building on the focus of engagement, the next chapter begins to examine change in health care seen through new models of care delivery systems and physical structures. This chapter ties the concepts of culture, change, and leadership together in a meaningful way that highlight the potential within change.

PART III: LEADERSHIP

Edgar Schein, author of *Organizational Culture and Leadership*, has often said leadership and culture are two sides of the same coin. In a similar vein, this section begins to make explicit the need for purposeful leadership development strategies to support culture and change. The following two chapters begin to highlight these strategies:

- The Four C's of Leadership Development
- Leadership and Organization Development in Health Care: Lessons from the Cleveland Clinic

The first chapter develops a method for leadership development that focuses on competency, connections, creation of shared understanding, and the capacity for change. As this clearly depicts, the interrelated nature of these elements are essential to creating wholeness and health in the organization. The second chapter dives more deeply into specific strategies for physician leadership development. Physicians are being recognized as critical leaders and members of high-performing care teams, and this chapter highlights a case study and outcomes from these efforts at Cleveland Clinic.

PART IV: RELATIONSHIPS AND TEAMS

Relationships and teams becomes the point at which the three previous topics – culture, change, and leadership – become manifest. This section begins to uncover one of the more challenging factors of organizational life – how we behave and interact at work. These chapters highlight the damage of dysfunction among teams and within individuals that create toxic environments in organizations. However, the authors provide evidence-based strategies for improving team dynamics, calling out unacceptable behaviors, and implementing best practices for building workplace relationships. The following four chapters guide you through this section:

- Addressing Dysfunctional Relations among Health care Teams: Improving Team Cooperation through Applied Organizational Theories
- Characteristics of Positive Working Relationships between Nursing and Support Service Employees
- The Impact of Supervisor–Subordinate Relationships upon Nurses' Ability to Solve Workplace Problems: Implications for Their Commitment to the Organization
- Systems Approach to Address Incivility and Disruptive Behaviors in Health care Organizations

PART V: INFORMATION TECHNOLOGY

As one looks at the landscape for health care, it is impossible to ignore the implications from an information technology (IT) standpoint. As organizations implement and continuously upgrade systems for electronic medical records and other technology implementations, the need for IT integration has never been more critical. The following two chapters begin this dialogue:

- IT and Organization: A Delicate Partnership
- Technological Iatrogenesis: The Manifestation of Inadequate Organizational Planning and the Integration of Health Information Technology

The critical message carried in each of these chapters is the articulation of the incredible need for integration of IT within the health care system. This integration is not only from a mechanistic standpoint but also from the nature of how the IT partnership is a part of and influences the larger system outlined in this book. Organizations that are successful need to rethink how to build IT into the culture, meaningful change efforts, leadership, and team operations to create the most effective and efficient use of technology.

PART VI: SYSTEMS ISSUES

The final section in this book includes the following three chapters:

- E Pluribus Unum: Using Group Model Building with Many Interdependent Organizations to Create Integrated Health Care Networks
- Health care Organizations as "Patients": Transforming the Fundamental OD Paradigm
- Sustaining High-Performance: Dynamic Balancing in an Otherwise Unbalanced System

These chapters are instrumental in defining the systems elements to improving the well-being of health care organizations. The success of this industry is dependent on the ability to understand how systems operate and designing organizations that have alignment, balance, and coherence. These chapters provide the linkages between the six elements or sections detailed in this book and provide readers with proven practices and strategies for redesigning organizations to achieve high performance.

A CALL TO ACTION

As you begin your exploration of this book, remember that there is not simply one path through. Pick a topic that speaks to your interest or one that touches the nerves of an organizational challenge you are currently facing. From that experience, see what grabs you next. The careful weaving of OD practice in health care is not a linear exercise, but rather it is the continuous ebb and flow of challenges and solutions, opportunities and action. If at the end of this work, you see the true value of OD as a resource for creating greater outcomes in health care performance, then our general message was received. But if you take this information and are inspired to act in helping transform health care from the inside out, then our hopes will have been realized.

> Far better it is to dare mighty things, to win glorious triumphs even though checkered by failure, than to rank with those poor spirits who neither enjoy nor suffer much because they live in the gray twilight that knows neither victory nor defeat. – Theodore Roosevelt

REFERENCES

Lovey, I., Nadkarni, M., & Erdelyi, E. (2007). *How healthy is your organizations? The leaders guide to curing corporate diseases and promoting joyful cultures*. Westport, CT: Praeger Publishers.

Watson, J. (2009). Caring science and human caring theory: Transforming personal and professional practices of nursing and health care. *Journal of Health and Human Services Administration*, *31*(4), 466–483.

Jason A. Wolf
Heather Hanson
Mark J. Moir

PART I
CULTURE

DEMYSTIFYING AND IMPROVING ORGANIZATIONAL CULTURE IN HEALTH CARE

Karen L. Pellegrin and Hal S. Currey

ABSTRACT

Organizational culture is defined as the shared values and beliefs that guide behavior within each organization, and it matters because it is related to performance. While culture is generally considered important, it is mysterious and intangible to most leaders. The first step toward understanding organizational culture is to measure it properly. This chapter describes methods for measuring culture in health care organizations and how these methods were implemented in a large academic medical center. Because of the consistent empirical link between the dimension of communication, other culture dimensions, and employee satisfaction, special attention is focused in this area. Specifically, a case study of successful communication behaviors during a major "change management" initiative at a large academic medical center is described. In summary, the purpose of this chapter is to demystify the concept of culture and demonstrate how to improve it.

Keywords: Organizational culture; performance improvement; communication; change management; safety climate; measurement; survey methodology; work environment scale

Organization Development in Healthcare: Conversations on Research and Strategies
Advances in Health Care Management, Volume 10, 3–23

ISSN: 1474-8231/doi:10.1108/S1474-8231(2011)0000010007

INTRODUCTION

While most leaders believe "organizational culture" has an important impact on performance and employee satisfaction, they view culture as amorphous, intangible, and mysterious. To the organizational scientist, culture is simply a collection of behaviors; all meaningful behaviors are measurable, and what is measurable can be changed. The purpose of this chapter is to demystify the concept of culture and demonstrate how to improve it. Proper methods for measuring culture in health care organizations are described, and how these methods were implemented in a large academic medical center is presented. Because of the consistent empirical link between the dimension of communication, other culture dimensions, and employee satisfaction, special attention is focused in this area. Specifically, a case study of successful communication behaviors during a major "change management" initiative at a large academic medical center is described. While some argue that there are differences between the terms "organizational culture," "climate," and "work environment," they are used interchangeably in this chapter.

WHAT IS ORGANIZATIONAL CULTURE AND DOES IT MATTER?

While no one definition exists, organizational culture is generally accepted to be the shared values and beliefs that guide behavior within each organization. And culture is generally assumed to be related to performance and to the success or failure of attempts to improve performance (Detert et al., 2000). Detert and colleagues synthesized the existing literature on organizational culture and identified eight general dimensions:

1. *The basis of truth and rationality in the organization*: This dimension is the extent to which organizations value science and data for problem solving and decision making or other variables such as personal experience and intuition.
2. *The nature of time and time horizon*: This dimension reflects orientation toward the future versus the present, which is manifested in the extent to which organizations plan for and invest in the future and the importance placed on short-term versus long-range performance.
3. *Motivation*: This dimension reflects beliefs about human nature and the extent to which humans are internally versus externally motivated and

inherently good or bad; these beliefs are manifested in the incentives, rewards, and punishments within an organization.

4. *Stability versus change/innovation/personal growth*: This dimension is the extent to which an organization values and seeks to maintain the status quo versus constantly seeking to innovate and improve.
5. *Orientation to work, task, and coworkers*: This is the extent to which an organization is focused on productivity and results versus other factors such as process and social aspects of work.
6. *Isolation versus collaboration/cooperation*: This dimension is the extent to which work in an organization is completed individually or in teams.
7. *Control, coordination, and responsibility*: This is the extent to which work is controlled and decision making is concentrated or shared. This dimension is manifested by formal rules and procedures and the extent of worker autonomy.
8. *Orientation and focus – internal and/or external*: This reflects the nature of the relationship between an organization and its environment. Organizations differ in the extent to which they focus internally and externally, such as on customers and competitors, the community, and suppliers.

There is evidence to support the notion that organizational culture matters in terms of performance. For example, strong cultures generally predict better performance. A "strong" culture is one in which the values and beliefs are intensely held by a large number of employees throughout the organization, which increases behavioral consistency. The research has demonstrated that culture strength, defined as the degree of agreement with and commitment to organizational values and norms, generally predicts positive performance across industries, particularly in highly competitive markets and in relatively stable environments (Sorensen, 2002).

There is also evidence to support the importance of culture in mergers, acquisitions, and joint ventures. In general, organizational culture differences predict negative outcomes in mergers and acquisitions. In fact, in international joint ventures, organizational culture similarity matters more than national culture similarity in the success of the venture. In these ventures, the most important organizational culture dimension appears to be the communication climate. That is, similarities in the extent to which organizations tend to be more open or closed in information sharing predict success (Pothukuchi, Damanpour, Choi, Chen, & Park, 2002).

In addition to looking at culture generally, specific dimensions predict performance. For example, employee perceptions of safety practices and attitudes toward safety reflect the "safety climate" within an organization.

A meta-analysis of research in this area found that safety climate influences involvement in and adherence to safety procedures. This analysis supports the conclusion that improving safety climate will enhance employee safety performance and accident prevention (Clarke, 2006).

Similar links between organizational culture and performance have also been found in the health care industry. For example, a recent study found that hospitals with better safety climate scores had lower rates of patient safety events. Safety climate was measured via employee survey at 91 hospitals, and patient safety risk was measured using the Agency for Health care Research and Quality Patient Safety Indicators. These indicators are derived from available inpatient administrative data and can be used to help identify potential adverse events occurring during hospitalization. Of particular interest, while frontline personnel's perceptions of better safety climate (especially perceptions of lower fear of shame) predicted lower risk, senior manager perceptions did not. This finding underscores the importance of measuring culture through employee perceptions, not just senior managers whose views may or may not be in synch with those of the employees in the trenches (Singer, Lin, Falwell, Gaba, & Baker, 2009).

Research has also demonstrated that, in the health care industry, organizations with a "high-performance work environment" are more likely to have employee perceptions of higher service quality. And service quality predicts customer satisfaction. A "high performance" work environment is represented by core characteristics including involvement, empowerment, trust, goal alignment, training, teamwork, communication, and performance-based rewards. This study was conducted at 147 Veterans Health Administration medical facilities using employee and patient surveys (Scotti, Harmon, & Behson, 2007).

In a nutshell, organizational culture matters.

CASE STUDY: LEVERAGING COMMUNICATION BEHAVIORS TO CHANGE CULTURE

As shown above, research indicates that communication is a key element in high-performance cultures and is significantly related to the success or failure of joint ventures. During any major organizational change, communication is likely to matter even more. However, few studies have been conducted on organizational change communication (Frahm & Brown, 2005). Therefore, leaders have little evidence-based guidance in this area. This section describes a major successful "change management" initiative at the Medical University of South Carolina Medical Center (MUSC-MC) and how specific communication behaviors were orchestrated before, during, and after the changes were implemented to reduce risk and promote a healthy, stronger culture.

In 1993, the looming crisis that triggered the need for significant change was a rapid deterioration in financial performance due to changing reimbursements and increased competition. These changes threatened both patient care and teaching missions of the MUSC-MC. An organizational overhaul was necessary for survival, and it was determined that all 200 members of the management team (including senior managers) would be removed from their positions and invited to apply for any of the 100 restructured positions that would comprise the new management team. A total of 400 employees were laid off, many of whom competed for new or existing positions at the MUSC-MC.

A communication plan was developed by the change management team with the advice and direction of a local nationally known marketing and public relations firm Rawle Murdy. Eight weeks prior to the beginning of the restructuring of management and subsequent layoffs, the following communications were implemented:

- Letters describing the reason for the reorganization and the process were sent to politicians, community leaders, and opinion makers throughout the state. Follow-up letters were sent to these stakeholders to keep them apprised and remind them of the critical need.
- Weekly letters describing the process and updates were sent to all faculty of all the colleges.
- A weekly newsletter describing the process, rationale, and schedule for replacement of the management was sent to all employees.

The new team was selected over a three-week period. A new executive director was named, who selected six administrators during the first week. During the second week, the administrators selected approximately 30 directors. During the third week, the directors selected approximately 70 managers.

Although it was a stressful time in the history of the MUSC-MC, no formal grievances were filed by any existing or former employees, and no other adverse outcomes were noted. The MUSC-MC emerged a financially strong organization. The communication plan worked so well that the administrative team decided to continue some of the processes into the future, including

- Weekly administrative team meetings
- Weekly meetings of the entire new management team (format included information dissemination, answers to questions and comment period, brief weekly address by the executive director, and occasional speakers on important topics), later renamed "Communications" meeting
- Weekly publication of highlights from the management team meetings sent via e-mail throughout the university
- Weekly paper copies of the highlights distributed to each work unit

> Our experience with communication during the mid-1990s led us to embrace communication at all levels as an organizational priority. In today's competitive and transparent health care arena, we have to continually improve service and quality of care. Every employee needs to understand our metrics-based goals and specifically how their performance moves us in the right direction. A comprehensive communication program is essential.
>
> Betts Ellis, Administrator for Institutional Relations, Medical University Hospital Authority, Charleston, South Carolina

While this example does not constitute scientific evidence of the critically important role of communication during times of change, it is consistent with the existing literature that this clear and comprehensive communication plan greatly enhanced the successful transformation of the MUSC-MC. Senior management support for these communication activities is reflected in the fact that they continue today.

MEASURING ORGANIZATIONAL CULTURE

Given the importance of culture, organizations can benefit significantly from measuring it. The foundation of sound culture measurement is sound survey methodology. This means

1. Reliable and valid survey instrument
2. Standardized, unbiased survey administration process
3. Clear, constructive report of results

The Survey

The survey(s) chosen should have demonstrated reliability and validity. Reliability refers to the accuracy or preciseness of the instrument. Is your bathroom scale reliable? If it measures in meaningfully small increments (e.g., ounces or pounds rather than tons), and you get the same reading if you step on the scale repeatedly, and that reading closely approximates your true weight, your scale is reliable. Validity refers to the extent to which the instrument measures the construct you think measures. This is generally more complicated to demonstrate than reliability, but is important. What is your bathroom scale measuring? It measures only heaviness. It does not measure the healthiness of your weight, which is determined by additional factors such as height, level of hydration, and percent body fat. To establish the validity of your bathroom scale in measuring weight or heaviness, you could compare its readings with other instruments known to measure this construct (e.g., your doctor's office scale). Given that we lose body tissue by eating fewer calories than we burn, the validity of your bathroom scale for measuring weight would be further supported by decreased weight readings following a month of consistent calorie deficits.

One important principle of sound instruments is that reliability is a requirement for validity. That is, an instrument can be reliable without being valid (i.e., without knowing what it is measuring). But an instrument cannot be valid without being reliable. Therefore, a sound organizational culture survey is one that reliably measures the shared values and beliefs that guide behavior within an organization. Surveys that reflect one or more of the eight general dimensions of culture identified by previous theory and research (as described in the previous section) are more likely to be valid instruments.

Survey Administration

As mentioned previously, organizational culture surveys should not be administered only to managers or executives. Espousing values is not the same as living them. In organizations where leaders give lip service to organizational values, there will likely be a discrepancy between what leaders say is important and what the employees say is actually reinforced or discouraged by leaders' behaviors.

Ideally, all employees in an organization will receive the survey. Because of available technology and Web-based services, administering large volumes of surveys is now very inexpensive. Paper response forms can be quickly scanned by a computer rather than having each survey hand-entered into a database. With the availability of online survey services, such as Survey Monkey (http://www.surveymonkey.com/), paperless surveys can be administered in a very user-friendly, cost-effective way.

While different technologies can be used to administer the survey, what is most important is that the administration process be standardized and unbiased. Standardization means that the survey be administered at the same time and in the same manner throughout the organization. For example, if all employees have and use e-mail at work, an e-mail with a link to the Web-based survey could be sent to all employees with instructions that the survey be completed by a certain date. To increase response rate, be sure to have the senior executive send a cover letter or e-mail explaining the importance of the survey and publicly committing to use results from the survey to improve the organization. In addition, employees should be given time during work hours to complete the survey.

To ensure unbiased results, the survey must be administered in a way that allows employees to respond anonymously. Employees will be more likely to answer honestly if they are confident their individual responses will not be linked to them either directly or through identifiers. The process for collecting surveys is also important to ensure unbiased responses. With paper surveys, the employee response forms should *not* be turned in to the employee's supervisor, even if enclosed in a sealed envelope. There is no need to introduce this temptation for the supervisor to "peek" or in any way manipulate the survey data. Instead the survey should identify a neutral and independent party, preferably external to the entity undergoing the survey, to minimize the potential for biased results.

Survey Results

Once the survey responses have been collected and are in a database, the scale and/or subscales of the instrument need to be calculated according to the scoring instructions. Then descriptive and analytical statistics can be extracted to describe the results and identify opportunities for improvement. A summary report should be presented to all employees, including the action items that will be taken by the leadership team to improve the culture. Individual reports should be generated for the manager of each major work unit within the organization. Executives should support and provide assistance to their managers to implement actions to improve the cultures within these units.

BENEFITS OF THE WORK ENVIRONMENT SCALE IN HEALTH CARE ORGANIZATIONS

The Work Environment Scale (WES) (Moos, 2008) is one of the most rigorously tested and validated measures of organizational culture. Dr. Rudolf Moos is a psychologist and Professor of Psychiatry and Behavioral Sciences at Stanford University School of Medicine. He has published extensively in the peer-reviewed literature and published the first edition of the WES in 1981. The WES has several benefits that make it very appealing for measuring organizational culture in health care settings:

1. *Reliability*: The WES subscales generally have adequate internal consistency (a measure of reliability), including in samples of health care workers. In addition, acceptable one-month test-retest reliability of the WES subscales has been documented.
2. *Validity*: The WES subscales fit well conceptually with the general dimensions of culture discussed previously. Only two of the eight general dimensions (i.e., basis of truth and rationality, internal versus external orientation) is not represented by the WES subscales, and there is 1 of the 10 WES subscales that does not fit with the 8 general dimensions (i.e., Physical Comfort). The alignment between these subscales and dimensions is shown in Table 1. Numerous studies reported in the peer-reviewed literature have documented the validity of the WES across industries, including in health care settings. For example, significantly different WES profiles were produced by Hospital Corpsmen assigned to four different military work settings. In addition, Hospital Corpsmen who reported their work environment as more supportive and well-organized were more willing to volunteer for additional duty. Several studies of health care workers have demonstrated a link between WES subscales and symptoms of burnout and job dissatisfaction. Among nurses working in specialized and general hospital units, stress was associated with high work pressure and low autonomy, coworker cohesion, and supervisor support as measure by the WES. In a state psychiatric hospital, employees in lower staff-to-patient ratio areas reported lower support, autonomy, and clarity and higher work pressure as measured by the WES. Among nursing home employees, the WES was strongly associated with institutional loyalty. WES subscales were predictors of retention among acute care nurses in a county hospital. Finally, several studies in health care organizations documented positive changes in the work environment after implementing changes designed to improve it.

Table 1. Alignment between the General Dimensions of Organizational Culture and the WES Subscales.

General Dimensions Identified by Detert, Schroeder, and Mauriel (2000)	Work Environment Scale (Moos, 2008) Subscales
The basis of truth and rationality in the organization	
The nature of time and time horizon	*Work pressure*: The degree to which high work demands and time pressure dominate the job milieu
Motivation	*Involvement*: The extent to which employees are concerned about and committed to their jobs
Stability versus change/innovation/personal growth	*Innovation*: The emphasis on variety, change, and new approaches
Orientation to work, task, and coworkers	*Task orientation*: The emphasis on good planning, efficiency, and getting the job done
Isolation versus collaboration/cooperation	*Coworker cohesion*: How much employees are friendly and supportive of each other
	Supervisor support: The extent to which management is supportive of employees and encourages employees to be supportive of one another
Control, coordination, and responsibility	*Autonomy*: How much employees are encouraged to be self-sufficient and to make their own decisions
	Clarity: Whether employees know what to expect in their daily routine and how explicitly rules and policies are communicated
	Managerial control: How much management used rules and procedures to keep employees under control
Orientation and focus – internal and/or external	
	Physical comfort: The extent to which the physical surroundings contribute to a pleasant work environment

3. *Normative data*: The *WES Manual* includes normative data so that organizations using the WES can compare their data to the normative sample. These data are updated with each new edition of the manual. The *WES Manual* includes separate normative data for the health care industry, which makes this tool extremely valuable for use in health care organizations. The normative samples in the current (fourth) edition of

the *WES Manual* include over 5,000 employees in the general work sample and over 8,600 employees in the health care and social service work sample. This health care sample includes employees from outpatient medical and psychiatric clinics, patient care staff in hospital settings, staff not involved in patient care, and administrative and supervisory staff from a variety of community, public, and academic health care organizations. There are significant differences between the general work sample and the health care work sample on most subscales, demonstrating the importance of a separate normative sample for the health care industry. Finally, in general, scores on 8 of the 10 subscales are positively correlated with employee satisfaction. Work pressure is negatively associated with employee satisfaction, and managerial control is not correlated with employee satisfaction.

In summary, the WES is a rigorously tested measure of organizational culture, and the only one with a large health care normative sample. Compared to the other culture measures that might be considered for use in health care organizations, the WES appears to be the best overall choice. For a comparison of other available culture instruments used in health care, see Scott, Mannion, Davies, and Marshall (2003). For additional information on finding culture surveys, see the appendix.

CUSTOMIZING CULTURE ASSESSMENT METHODS TO UNIQUE ORGANIZATIONAL NEEDS

Once an appropriate tool has been identified for the measurement of culture, overall assessment methodology should be considered and customized to the unique needs of the organization. That is, rather than just measuring culture in isolation, consideration should be given to the measurement of other variables of interest to the organization as part of an overall organizational assessment. Thinking through the following issues will help the organization develop a more meaningful assessment designed to answer specific questions that are of interest to the organization.

What additional instruments might be beneficial to administer with the general culture measure? By considering current priorities and activities within the organization, there could be significant added value to including an additional instrument. For example, if the organization is launching efforts to improve safety, including a measure of safety climate would allow examination of correlations between safety and general organizational culture. These analyses could help guide the safety improvement efforts by identifying dimensions of culture that best predict safety climate.

What "anchor items" might be beneficial to administer with the general culture measure? An anchor item is a single, general question of interest to the organization. For example, anchor items might include

- Overall, are you satisfied with your job?
- Overall, how would you rate the work environment here?
- Would you recommend this medical center to friends or family seeking health care?
- Would you recommend this medical center to friends or family seeking employment?

Analyses can be performed to identify the culture dimensions that are the best predictors of these anchor items. Knowing the predictors can help guide improvement efforts in these areas.

What level of detail is of interest to the organization? Identifying the level of granularity is important in designing an assessment. If the survey is administered with no defining details about the employees, there will be only one total organizational profile, which will limit its use in understanding and improving culture within subgroups. If too many identifying details are included, anonymity is threatened, which may introduce bias. The following are items to consider for inclusion based on the goals and objectives of the organizational assessment:

- work unit level
- clinician type
- demographics
- supervisor vs. non-supervisor
- day shift vs. night shift
- full-time vs. part-time employee
- number of years working in the health care industry
- number of years working at this organization

What organizational performance measures could be examined in conjunction with organizational culture? Depending on how large the organization is and how many work units will be identified on the survey, additional variables can be examined and analyzed in relationship to the culture dimensions and other items from the survey. For example, it may be of value to measure financial performance and/or quality indicators within each work group. This can help the organization determine which culture dimensions best predict performance.

It is important to keep in mind that correlations from variables measured at the same time do not permit conclusions about cause and effect. Rather they tell us which variables predict other variables. While not as rigorous as experimental methods, a correlational design can be a very cost-effective way of generating hypotheses that can inform the prioritization and design of improvement efforts.

CASE STUDY: USING CULTURE DATA TO IMPROVE LEADERSHIP

The methods described in this chapter were implemented at the MUSC-MC in 1998, several years after the reorganization described above. The purpose of this assessment was to identify strengths and weaknesses and key leverage points (i.e., predictors of variables important to the organization) by surveying the medical center employees, faculty, and house staff about the organizational culture and practices. Quality management and human resources practices were of particular interest given changes implemented in these areas. The assessment was repeated four years later in 2002 to allow comparison of results to the baseline survey. One of the major changes that occurred between baseline and follow-up surveys was a change in the organizational status of the MUSC-MC, which had been a traditional state entity. In 2000, the Medical Center became a public benefit corporation, officially named the Medical University Hospital Authority. This allowed the adoption of more competitive and efficient human resources and procurement policies.

The survey was comprised of the following elements:

1) The *WES* (Moos, 2008) was selected as the instrument to measure general organizational culture.
2) The *Total Quality Management Practices & Culture (TQM)* scale (Zeitz, Johannesson, & Ritchie, 1997) was selected as the instrument to measure the implementation of TQM within the organization as preliminary reliability and validity of this tool were available. This instrument was designed to measure the extent to which an organization has adopted the beliefs and practices that are consistent with a quality management philosophy. Normative data, which are not specific to the health care industry, are categorized according to three distinct types of organizations: those with no quality program in place, those with a beginning program in place, and those with a moderate-to-advanced program in

place. The dimensions included from this instrument in the assessment survey were

a. *Management support*: Leadership commitment to quality and improvement
b. *Employee suggestions*: Frequency and use of suggestions from employees
c. *Use of data*: Use of data to monitor performance at the individual and work unit level
d. *Supplier relationships*: Availability and adequacy of needed parts, materials, supplies, and equipment
e. *Supervision*: Feedback and recognition from immediate supervisor
f. *Improvement*: Work unit's commitment to and focus on improvement efforts
g. *Customers*: Work unit's understanding of and focus on customers and their needs
h. *Communication*: Effectiveness of organization's communication (including recognition and conflict resolution)

3) Six *"anchor items"* were designed and added to this survey to measure overall satisfaction with the work environment. These items permit the identification of leverage points through analyses that show which of the subscales in the above two survey tools are the best predictors of overall satisfaction.
4) Other *miscellaneous* items were included to assess targeted areas of interest to the medical center administration, particularly those pertaining to human resources practices.

Over 1,600 employees, faculty, and house staff completed both baseline and follow-up surveys. Baseline results indicated that, on two of the 10 WES subscales, the medical center was significantly better than the normative health care sample. The other subscales were not significantly different from the health care normative sample. On the TQM subscales, results were somewhat consistent with an organization with a beginning TQM program in place.

Four years later, the follow-up survey was conducted. These results showed significant improvement from baseline and that the medical center was significantly different from the health care normative sample on all 10 subscales, and in the positive direction for those nine subscales generally found to be correlated with employee satisfaction. On the TQM scale, there were significant improvements in three of the dimensions and a significant decline in one of the dimensions. Given these improvements in the organizational culture and practices, it is not surprising that there were significant improvements in three of the six anchor items measuring overall satisfaction. In particular, improvements were seen in supervision, leadership, and recommendations of the medical center as a place to work. These changes are shown in Figs. 1–3.

The most consistent predictors of the anchor items pertaining to overall satisfaction were the effectiveness of the organization's communications (i.e., TQM Communication subscale), leadership's commitment to quality and improvement (i.e., TQM Management Support subscale), and employee's perception of the link between job performance and compensation (one of the miscellaneous items of interest to administrators). Thus, these three areas were identified as the "leverage points" for improving employee satisfaction.

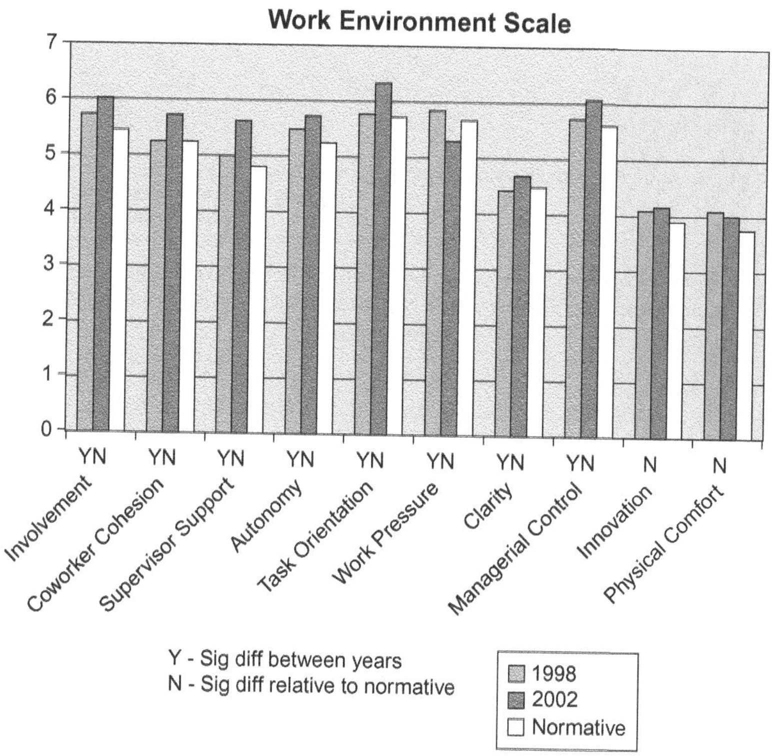

Fig. 1. Mean Scores on Work Environment Scale Dimensions: MUSC Medical Center 1998 and 2002 versus Normative Sample.

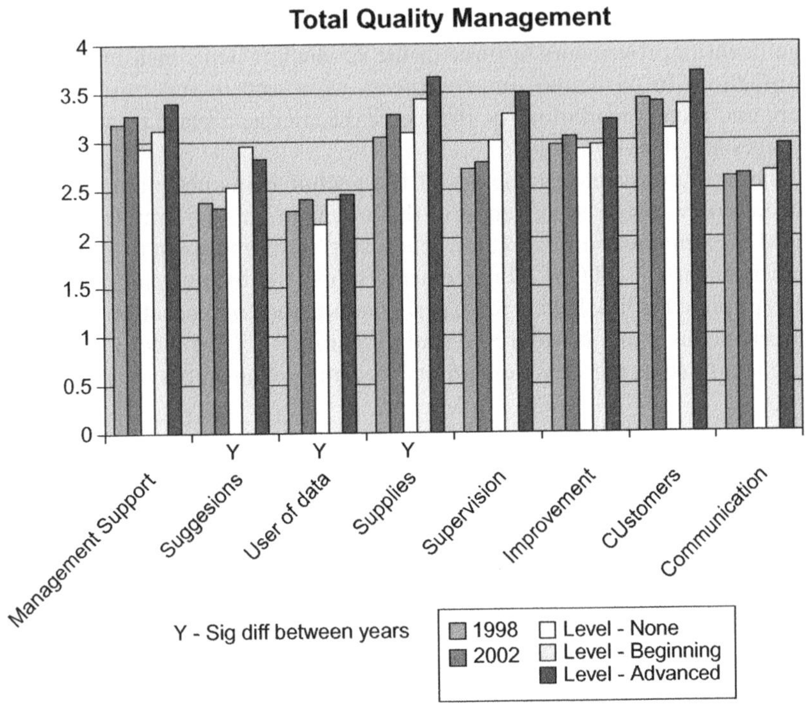

Fig. 2. Mean Scores on TQM Scale Dimensions: MUSC Medical Center 1998 and 2002 versus Normative Samples with No, Beginning, or Advanced TQM Program Implemented.

While it cannot be concluded that these three areas cause employee satisfaction, these are good areas to invest improvement efforts as they are at least strong predictors of employee satisfaction. Thus, for these subscales, drill-down descriptive statistics for each item were presented so that leaders could identify specific areas to target improvements.

In addition to these overall results, analyses were broken out by type of staff (i.e., employee, faculty, house staff) and by work unit. Each manager was given his/her work unit's profiles with item-level analysis where there were opportunities for improvement. Overall, this assessment showed significant improvements within the organization relative to baseline and identified areas most appropriate for investing future improvement efforts.

It has been well established that employee and patient satisfaction are positively correlated. We have learned that it's important to designate employee satisfaction as an

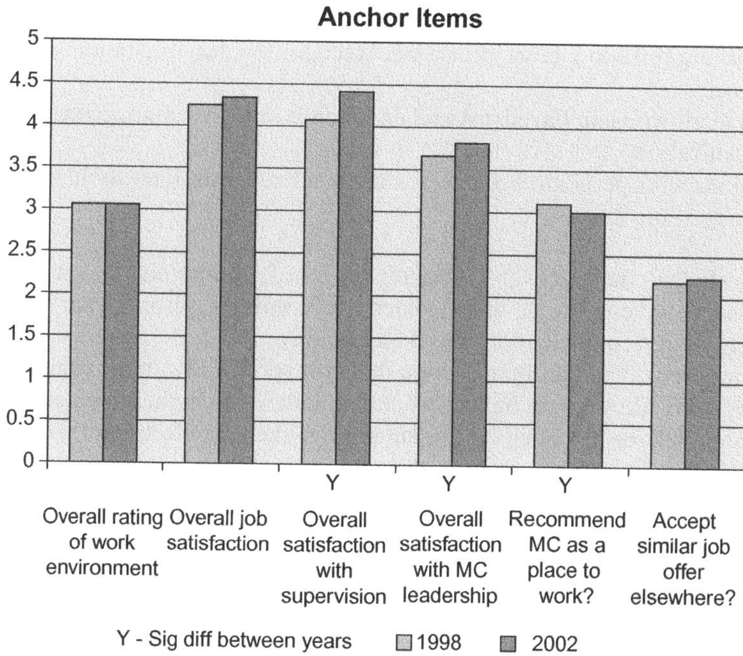

Fig. 3. Mean Scores on Anchor Items: MUSC Medical Center 1998 and 2002.

organizational goal and to measure progress through use of a reputable survey tool. Managers are expected to work collaboratively with their staff to develop specific action plans for continued improvement in satisfaction results, and our leadership team is responsible for preparation of an organization-wide action plan. All managers' performance evaluations include progress made on employee satisfaction scores.

W. Stuart Smith, MUSC Vice President and Executive Director of the MUSC Medical Center, Charleston, South Carolina

THE COMMUNICATION DIMENSION OF CULTURE

In the case study described above, the communication subscale was the most consistent predictor of general employee satisfaction. The following are the items (the second one is reverse-scored) from this subscale (Zeitz et al., 1997):

- Management here does a good job of communicating with employees.
- There is poor communication between departments in this organization.

- Around here, conflicts are resolved to the satisfaction of those concerned.
- This organization gives praise and recognition for outstanding performance.
- All in all, you can have trust and confidence in higher management in this organization.
- People who perform well receive financial rewards such as higher pay, bonuses, or awards.

These few items cover a broad range of communication variables, including audience (e.g., management to employee, cross-departmental), content (e.g., conflict and praise), and nonverbal (i.e., rewards for performing well). The fact that the one item not specifically about communication ("All in all, you can have trust and confidence in higher management in this organization") loaded on this subscale is likely a reflection of the critical importance of communication in the relationship between executives and the rest of the organization. Thus, employees who perceive good communication within the organization are more likely to have trust and confidence in the leadership. Of course, the reverse is also true.

Several other studies provide additional support for the importance of communication within organizations. For example, trust in top management is positively related to satisfaction with and quality of information shared by management (Byrne & LeMay, 2006). In addition, good communication is one of the strongest predictors of a healthy work environment. In turn, a healthy work environment is significantly correlated with higher job satisfaction, commitment, and morale and with lower absenteeism and intent to quit (Lowe, Schellenberg, & Shannon, 2003).

If organizational culture is defined as "shared values and beliefs that guide behavior within each organization," then communication is critical by definition. The sharing of values and beliefs occurs daily in verbal and nonverbal, formal and informal communications. Words and behaviors that encourage and reward performance are particularly important. Bowen and Ostroff (2004) emphasize the importance of this in their examination of the "strength" of the HRM system. They view HRM practices as "communications from the employer to employee" (p. 207) and the strength of the HRM system as its effectiveness in conveying the types of information needed to create conformity rather than ambiguity. They also propose that the strength of the HRM system facilitates the emergence of organizational culture and can enhance organizational performance by promoting organizational behaviors that are consistent with strategic goals. These proposals build nicely on the research demonstrating that strong cultures (in which values and beliefs are intensely held by a large number of employees) generally predict better performance (Sorensen, 2002), likely due to behavioral consistency (i.e., "conformity").

THE FUTURE OF ORGANIZATIONAL CULTURE RESEARCH

As practitioners work to implement best practice based on the research to date, what can scientists do to further the knowledge in this area? The study of organizational culture is vast and complex with many questions unanswered. First, more information is needed about what factors affect culture. For example, what types of communication are most effective in getting to shared values and beliefs and consistent performance? How does organizational structure and type shape culture (e.g., centralized versus decentralized; private versus public; for-profit versus nonprofit)? Second, more information is needed about the relationship between culture and performance. For example, while strong cultures generally lead to improved performance, what are the circumstances in which a strong culture leads to bad performance (e.g., Enron)? Of the eight general dimensions of culture, which are most predictive of performance under what circumstances? Third, more information is needed about potential "treatments" for dysfunctional cultures. In studies of psychiatric conditions such as anxiety and depression, the research shows that psychotherapy generally works. However, cognitive–behavioral treatments have generally been shown to be most effective. What is the organizational equivalent of cognitive–behavioral therapy? Finally, more information is needed about unique factors in the health care industry pertaining to culture. As demonstrated by Moos (2008), the culture in health care organizations is significantly different than in other organizations in a way that is generally perceived as more negative. Can this be changed? Or is it inherent in the nature of the services delivered? Until these questions are answered, organizational culture can be demystified and improved through sound measurement, analysis, and action.

REFERENCES

Bowen, D. E., & Ostroff, C. (2004). Understanding HRM-firm performance linkages: The role of the "strength" of the HRM system. *Academy of Management Review*, *29*(2), 203–221.

Byrne, Z. S. & LeMay, E. (2006). Different media for organizational communication: Perceptions of quality and satisfaction. *Journal of Business and Psychology*, *21*(2), 149–173.

Clarke, S. (2006). The relationship between safety climate and safety performance: A meta-analytic review. *Journal of Occupational Health Psychology*, *11*(4), 315–327.

Detert, J. R., Schroeder, R. G., & Mauriel, J. J. (2000). A framework for linking culture and improvement initiatives in organizations. *Academy of Management Review*, *25*(4), 850–863.

Frahm, J. A. & Brown, K. A. (2005). Building an organizational change communication theory. Academy of Management Best Conference Paper. OCIS: C1–C6.

Lowe, G. S., Schellenberg, G., & Shannon, H. S. (2003). Correlates of employees' perceptions of a healthy work environment. *American Journal of Health Promotion*, *17*(6), 390–399.

Moos, R. H. (2008). *Work environment scale manual: Fourth edition*. Mind Garden, Inc. Available at www.mindgarden.com

Pothukuchi, V., Damanpour, F., Choi, J., Chen, C. C., & Park, S. H. (2002). National and organizational culture differences and international joint venture performance. *Journal of International Business Studies*, *33*(2), 243–265.

Scott, T., Mannion, R., Davies, H., & Marshall, M. (2003). The quantitative measurement of organizational culture in health care: A review of the available instruments. *Health Services Research*, *38*(3), 923–945.

Scotti, D., Harmon, J., & Behson, S. J. (2007). Links among high-performance work environment, service quality, and customer satisfaction: An extension to the healthcare sector. *Journal of Healthcare Management*, *52*(2), 109–124.

Singer, S., Lin, S., Falwell, A., Gaba, D., & Baker, L. (2009). Relationship of safety climate and safety performance in hospitals. *Health Services Research*, *44*(2 pt. I), 399–421.

Sorensen, J. B. (2002). The strength of corporate culture and the reliability of firm performance. *Administrative Science Quarterly*, *47*, 70–91.

Zeitz, G., Johannesson, R., & Ritchie, J. E. (1997). An employee survey measuring total quality management practices and culture. *Group and Organization Management*, *22*(4), 414–444.

APPENDIX. HOW TO FIND CULTURE SURVEYS

The best place to find a sound organizational culture survey is in peer-reviewed journals. These are academic journals that publish research findings that have been systematically reviewed by experts for scientific rigor and impact. If you do not have access to specialized library-based search engines that include peer-reviewed journals in business management, social sciences, and health care, an effective free search tool is Google Scholar (http://scholar.google.com/).

Another potential source of organizational culture surveys is management consultants or firms. Some consultants have developed their own proprietary surveys that might have been rigorously tested. However, without a rigorous independent review process, it is difficult to be certain of the survey validity, which means you will be vulnerable to misuse and misinformation. Some consultants who use their own survey to measure culture have a business model based on an inherent conflict of interest. Their "black box" survey is used to demonstrate the need for the organization to purchase additional consulting services.

The authors of this chapter are aware of a consultant who charged a six-figure fee to measure an organization's culture using a proprietary survey. Not surprisingly, the consultant used the survey results to diagnose the organizational culture as "unhealthy" and offered to "treat" the organization for another six-figure fee. This is the kind of questionable behavior that led two editors of *The Economist* to publish the book *The Witch Doctors* in 1996. This book is a scathing critique of the unfounded management fads driven by management gurus and consultants. Since then, there has been a welcome and growing movement toward "evidence-based management" to improve organizational performance based on science rather than fad.

The WES is copyrighted (i.e., not in the public domain). However, the fees for permission to use it are very reasonable, especially given the many benefits of using this instrument and relative to the costs of proprietary tools used by some consultants and consulting firms. Information on purchasing the WES manual, bibliography, scoring, and reproduction permission are available at the following web site: http://mindgarden.com/products/wes.htm.

THE ORGANIZATION'S MISSION STATEMENT: GIVE UP HOPE OR RESUSCITATE? A SEARCH FOR EVIDENCE-BASED RECOMMENDATIONS

Sebastian Desmidt and Anita A. Prinzie

ABSTRACT

The increasing complexity and dynamicity of their environment compels health care managers to search relentlessly for effective management instruments. One strategic tool that both academics and practitioners have deemed critical to the success of any health care organization is the development of a meaningful mission statement. However, despite the seemingly omnipresence of the concept, studies indicate that creating an effective mission statement seems to be extremely difficult, if not downright frustrating for a lot of health care managers. This inability to create an effective mission statement roots for the greater part in the fact that the previous literature has provided little practical guidance on how health care administrators should formulate and deploy mission statements. Given the increasing pressure on health care organizations to develop an effective mission statement, this chapter (1) provides a detailed analysis of the mission statement concept based on a thorough

Organization Development in Healthcare: Conversations on Research and Strategies
Advances in Health Care Management, Volume 10, 25–41

ISSN: 1474-8231/doi:10.1108/S1474-8231(2011)0000010008

literature analysis and (b) offers empirically based recommendations on how to successfully formulate and implement a mission statement within a health care organization based on a systematic analysis of relevant empirical research. These analyses and the derived evidence-based recommendations will help health care managers to revive their mission statement and make it more than a piece of paper.

Keywords: Mission statement; literature analysis; evidence-based recommendations

The increasing complexity and dynamicity of their environment compels health care managers to search for strategic tools that enable them to not only address these changes but also improve organizational performance and motivate organizational members to perform at the highest possible level (Forehand, 2000).

One strategic tool that both academics and practitioners have deemed critical to the success of any health care organization is the development of a meaningful mission statement (Bart & Tabone, 2000; Desmidt & Heene, 2007). However, despite the seeming omnipresence of the concept, studies indicate that mission statements do not often appear to deliver the promised benefits (Piercy & Morgan, 1994). Moreover, in reality, creating an effective mission statement seems to be extremely difficult, if not downright frustrating (Bart & Tabone, 1999; Vandijck, Desmidt, & Buelens, 2007).

This inability to create an effective mission statement roots for the greater part in the fact that the previous literature has provided little practical guidance on how health care administrators should formulate and deploy mission statements (Bart & Tabone, 1999). The majority of the literature discusses the potential advantages of a well-crafted mission statement but rarely provides any clues or advice on how to realize these benefits in practice.

Given the increasing pressure on health care organizations to develop an effective mission statement (e.g., Flemish hospitals are since 2003 compelled by law to have a strategic plan containing a mission statement), on the one hand, and the difficulties encountered by health care administrators to do so, on the other, this chapter (1) provides a detailed analysis of the mission statement concept based on a thorough literature analysis and (b) offers empirically based recommendations on how to successfully develop a mission statement within a health care organization based on a systematic analysis of relevant empirical research.

THE ESSENCE OF MISSION STATEMENTS

The Historical Roots of the Mission Statement Concept

Although mission statements have become one of the most applied and discussed management instruments, it is very difficult to uncover the exact genesis of the concept. Most likely the concept of mission statements is historically rooted in the larger concept of organizational goals. The concept of organizational goals postulates the existence of an overriding goal or purpose, over and above the goals of the organizational members (Simon, 1964), which is critical to the successful functioning of an organization (Boyd & Levy, 1966).

The interest in the concept of "organizational goals" increased significantly in the 1960s due to the growing attention for the notion of strategic planning. The rise of organized or strategic planning elbowed out a more intuitive approach of business planning in favor of a formalized style of planning to translate the goals of the organization into action (Mockler, 1970; Steiner, 1970). The first, and crucial step, of this rational and phased process is the development of a clear definition of the organizational purpose and aspirations. Newman (1967), for example, stressed that formulating an organizational purpose is a "way to delve in the core of the organization [and] to ask: 'What business are we in or do we want to be in? Why should society tolerate our existence?'"

In line with this perspective, Jones (1960) stressed that organizations need a much more dependable philosophical pattern that will challenge organizational members and make them proud. Without using the term "mission statement," Jones defined as one of the first the core of the mission statement concept by stating that every organization needs a framework that encompasses two main ideas: (a) the idea of big, long-term, permanent goals or objectives and (b) an idea of the means of achieving them.

The following step in the elaboration and popularization of the notion "mission statement" was triggered by the agenda-setting work of Peter Drucker in the early 1970s. Drucker stressed the importance of business missions and addressed the issue of developing mission statements as a management tool for focusing attention on organizational goals and purposes (Klemm, Sanderson, & Luffman, 1991; Piercy & Morgan, 1994). Pivotal in the work of Drucker is the proposition that an organization is not defined by its name, statutes, or articles of incorporation but by its mission. In the 1980s, various authors (Band, 1985; McGuire & Chamberlain, 1984; Truskie, 1984) took forward Drucker's ideas and helped the concept of mission statements penetrate the academic world. Lundberg (1984, p. 31), for example, stated already in 1984 that "everyone agrees that [mission statements] are necessary [and that] it is a commonplace in management literature that statements of mission are the cornerstones upon which objectives, policies, and plans should be laid."

In the following decades, mission statements conquered the world of the practitioners and became one of the most popular management tools in both profit and nonprofit organizations. Studies indicate that over 85% of the North American profit organizations have developed a mission statement (Rigby, 2001), while the majority of public and nonprofit organizations (including health care providers (Bart & Tabone, 1999), nursing homes (Kalis, van Delden, & Schermer, 2004), public agencies (Weiss & Piderit, 1999), nonprofit youth and recreation service organizations (Brown & Yoshioka, 2003), and libraries (Kuchi, 2006)) seem to have joined "the herd" of organizations issuing a formal mission statement (Rainey & Steinbauer, 1999).

The key to the increasing popularity of mission statements most probably lies in a myriad of mutually reinforcing factors. We propose that at least five factors have contributed to the popularity of mission statements.

First of all, the seemingly low "entry barrier" to engage in the process of developing and implementing a mission statement. At first glance the conception and implementation of an effective mission statement seems to be neither too time consuming nor resource consuming and within the reach of every management team (Bart, 2002).

Second, there is a profusion of academic literature supporting the claim that mission statements can produce a host of organizational benefits and consequently contribute to the overall performance of an organization (Bart & Baetz, 1998; Ireland & Hitt, 1992).

Third, the virtues of having a well-articulated mission statement are extolled in almost every current management textbook, thus contributing to the reputation and face credibility of the concept (Bart & Tabone, 1998).

Fourth, mission statements are a vital building block of numerous management concepts and models such as strategic planning, strategic management, and the Balanced Scorecard. Organizations intending to implement these management techniques will first have to tackle the challenge of developing a mission statement.

And last but not least, mission statements have become one of the favorite subjects of the "management fashion setters." Management fashion setters (for example, consulting firms, management gurus, business mass media publications, and business schools) disseminate the transitory collective beliefs that certain management techniques are at the forefront of management progress and have to be implemented without lingering (Abrahamson, 1996).

Defining the "Mission Statement" Concept

Given (a) the collective enthusiasm with which academics and practitioners have embraced the concept of mission statements and (b) the growing body of research, it is surprising that there is still a lot of confusion about the definition and structure of the concept. Terms such as mission statement, business mission, statement of purpose, and value statement are often used to underpin overlapping and interchangeable concepts (Schwartz, 2001). Some even speak of a "terminological jungle" (Haberberg & Rieple, 2001).

One of the most succinct and earliest definitions of mission statements is provided by Ackoff (1984), who subscribes mission statements as "a broadly defined, enduring statement of purpose that distinguishes a business from others of its type." This definition probably contains the vital DNA of mission statements, i.e., that mission statements are both enduring and specific to the individual organization (Hooley, Cox, & Adams, 1992). Ireland and Hitt (1992, p. 35), on the other hand, state that mission statements "indicate what the organization intends to accomplish, identifies the market(s) in which the firm intends to operate, and reflects the philosophical premises that are to guide actions," while Jones and Kahaner (1995, p. 17) define mission statements as "the operational, ethical, and financial guiding lights of companies. They are not simply mottoes or slogans: they articulate the goals, dreams, behaviour, culture and strategies of companies."

The tendency to expand on the succinct definition provided by Ackoff thickened the conceptual mist surrounding the concept. Campbell and Yeung (1991a, 1991b) tried to address this issue by distinguishing two schools of thought on mission statements: (a) the strategic school and (b) the cultural school.

The strategic school emphasizes the pivotal role mission statements play in the strategic processes of every organization. The mission statement represents the strategic blueprint of the organization and acts as the starting point of the intended strategy. Ideally the mission statement delivers the building blocks to (a) define the organization's goals for value creation and distribution, and (b) to design the way the organization will be composed, structured, and coordinated in pursuing its goals for value creation and distribution (Sanchez & Heene, 2004). "Strategic mission statements" focus on components such as the distinctive competence of the organization, the desired competitive position, the specific customers/markets served, the specific products/services offered, performance objectives, and/or a definition of the technology.

In contrast, the cultural or psychological school of mission statement stresses the emotional rationale a mission statement should address: "A mission is the cultural glue which enables an organization to function as a collective unity. This cultural glue consists of strong norms and values that influence the way in which people behave, how they work together and how they pursue the goals of the organization" (Campbell & Yeung, 1991b, p. 15). The underpinning element in this approach is the importance of organizational core values. "Core values [...] are the organization's basic precepts about what is important in business and life, how business should be conducted, its view of humanity, its role in society, the way the world works, and what is to be held inviolate" (Collins & Porras, 1995, p. 82). The cultural school emphasises mission statement components such as values, beliefs, philosophy, specific behavior standards and policies, one clear and compelling goal, and the cultural identity of the organization.

In order to overcome the limitations and univocal focus of both schools, several authors proposed an integrative view on mission statements (Pearce II & David, 1987; Stone, 1996). One of the most respected attempts

Fig. 1. The Ashridge Model.

(Hooley et al., 1992) to integrate both schools is the Ashridge model (Campbell & Yeung, 1991a). According to the Ashridge model, a mission statement should consist of four reinforcing elements: purpose, values, strategy, and behavior standards (Fig. 1).

THE MISSION OF MISSION STATEMENTS

Now that we have gained more insight into the concept of mission statements, this raises the simple question why mission statements enjoy such popularity in both the academic world as well as the world of practitioners. The answer is as simple as the question itself: a host of literature, testimonials, and growing body of research offer validity to the assumption that creating a mission statement generates organizational benefits (Bart & Baetz, 1998; Bart, Bontis, & Taggar, 2001; Weiss & Piderit, 1999). Frequently cited benefits include

1. Mission statements clarify the organization's direction and purpose. A clear definition of the organizational mission is a prerequisite to formulate realistic, coherent short- and long-range goals and to choose between strategies (Bart et al., 2001).
2. Mission statements focus the allocation of organizational resources. By providing a common direction that transcends individual, departmental, and transitory needs (Kemp & Dwyer, 2003), the mission statement acts as a strategic framework or standard for allocating organizational resources (Bartkus, Glassman, & McAfee, 2000). The strategic boundaries established by the mission statement will facilitate organizational decision-making processes. Hence, the mission statement provides an antidote for "the most common degenerative disease of organizations, especially large ones; splintering their always limited resources on things that are 'interesting' or look 'profitable' rather than concentrating them on a very small number of productive efforts" (Drucker, 1992, p. 112).
3. Mission statements stimulate communication with important internal and external stakeholders. The mission statement can be an effective vehicle for communicating with internal and external stakeholders (Bartkus et al., 2000). By clarifying the organization's goals and methods for value creation and distribution, the organization can convince the stakeholders of her legitimacy and persuade them to provide the essential (tangible or intangible) resources needed to sustain the activities of the organization (Sanchez & Heene, 2004).

4. Mission statements describe the values that will guide and inspire organizational members. Consequently, the mission statement serves as a focal point for individuals to identify with the organization's purpose and direction (Bart et al., 2001). The resulting shared sense of purpose or "sense of mission" is the cultural glue that will, if carefully crafted and implemented, excite, inspire, and motivate those who are expected to participate in the pursuit of the organizational goals (Campbell & Yeung, 1991a, 1991b). The "sense of mission" hereby acts as cultural control and coordinating mechanism that focuses employee efforts on the achievement of strategic goals based on goal internalization and emotional commitment.

In the specific case of health care managers, research indicated that health care managers primarily develop mission statements with the aim of (1) providing the organization with a common purpose, (2) defining the scope of the hospital's activities, and (3) promoting shared values (Bart & Tabone, 1998).

MISSION STATEMENTS: THE HARSH REALITY

However, despite the profusion of academic literature supporting the claim that mission statements can produce a host of organizational benefits and consequently contribute to the overall performance of an organization (Bart & Baetz, 1998; Bart et al., 2001; Campbell & Yeung, 1991b; Weiss & Piderit, 1999), some studies indicate that mission statements do not often appear to deliver the promised benefits (Piercy & Morgan, 1994). Bart (1997), for example, enquired the senior managers of 88 leading North American corporations and came to the conclusion that (a) only 8% of the managers stated that they thought their current mission statements were fully clear or self-evident to the rest of the organization, (b) only 28% claimed that they were making significant strides toward achieving their mission statement, and (c) most managers reported that the organizational understanding, commitment, and support necessary for mission statement acceptance was less than forthcoming. Furthermore, research by Vandijck et al. (2007) pointed out that Flemish not-for-profit health care managers feel that their mission statement has no significant positive influence on the day-to-day behavior of their organizational members nor that members throughout the organization are committed to the mission statement.

Findings like these are grist to the mill of the mission statement skeptics who view mission statements as fruitless compositions of apple-and-pie statements. These skeptics argue that mission statements are often unreadable, uninspiring, and largely composed of pious platitudes (Cochran & David, 1986). Even well-written and unique mission statements are considered to be not more than a literary exercise with limited practical value. Ackoff (1984), for example, stated that mission statements can be labeled effective only if they change or influence the behavior of the organization that crafted it. If not, they have no value. According to Bartkus et al. (2000), mission statements will always fail this Litmus test of effectivity. Moreover, they argue that mission statements can sometimes even be counterproductive. Mission statements that are empty public relations initiatives and disconnected from the true capabilities and strengths of the organization can generate cynicism rather than pride (O'Gorman & Doran, 1999). In other situations, hollow mission statements may serve as a constant reminder to organizational members of how few resources they have been given to accomplish the mission statement. In such cases, mission statements are an indication of "symbolic management." Rather than to provide "the needed resources or make the necessary changes that are more likely to motivate and inspire, the organization develops a mission statement to help win support of constituents, with no intention of providing those resources or making those changes" (Bartkus et al., 2000, p. 26).

MISSION STATEMENTS: GIVE UP HOPE OR RESUSCITATE?

The profusion of rational- and logical-sounding arguments of both advocates and skeptics make it impossible to see the wood for the threes. Are mission statements a valuable management instrument or just another management fad? A difficult question to answer.

Despite the growing body of literature supporting the value of mission statements, one has to acknowledge that in many organizations, mission statements do not deliver the promised benefits. The central question, however, is if this "mission statement failure" can be attributed to the instrument itself or rather roots in the way the instrument is used by health care managers. It is no secret that in many organizations, mission statements are mere window dressing and are not developed with the intention to generate any real organizational change or to function as an actual management instrument. These mission statements are not the result of a carefully crafted formulation and implementation process but rather the product of half-hearted attempts to copy other successful organizations (what the institutionalists call "mimetic isomorphism") or to comply with legislation (coercive isomorphism) (DiMaggio & Powell, 1983). It is obvious that such "file drawer mission statements" are not more than a mere literary exercise with limited practical value and organizational impact.

But what if the management team is willing to invest the necessary time and resources to bring the organization's mission to life? What are in this case the factors that drive mission statement success? In order to answer this question, we conducted a state of the art literature review in order to develop a set of empirical-based recommendations on how to successfully develop a mission statement within a health care organization. More specific, based upon the systematic literature review process for management research initialized by Tranfield, Denyer, and Smart (2003), we scanned 7 electronic in order to identify all empirical articles addressing the concept of mission statements within a health care-related setting. By identifying and analyzing all empirical studies focusing on the factors that contribute to the effectiveness of mission statements within a health care setting, it was possible to distinguish 10 evidence-based recommendations for developing and implementing successfully a mission statement (Table 1).

The following paragraphs discuss our findings.

Developing a Mission Statement

The formulation or reformulation process of a mission statement should start with a careful deliberation of its organizational function. Worded differently, Why do you want to write a mission statement? Study results indicate that not all mission statement drivers or rationales are positively correlated with the selected performance indicators. Only 5 (out of 10) rationales seem to lead to success. These rationales (ranked) are: (a) to motivate/inspire hospital members, (b) to promote shared values, (c) to provide a common direction, (d) to guide resource allocation, and (e) to include the interest of key external stakeholders (Bart & Baetz, 1998). The rationales "enabling the CEO to assert control" and "refocus during a crisis," on the other hand, did not correlate with the outcome measures to any great extent. Identifying and elucidating the purpose of the mission statement is thus an essential first step as it will set the outlines for the rest of the development

Table 1. Empirically Based Recommendations for Developing and Implementing a Mission Statement.

Developing your mission statement:

1. Contemplate what you want to achieve with your mission statement (Bart & Baetz, 1998);
2. Do not only involve specific stakeholder groups in the development process but stimulate high levels of participation (Bart & Tabone, 2000);
3. The development process should not be a top–down but a joint effort (Bart & Tabone, 2000);
4. Be creative. Rigid and formal processes have been proved to be less effective (Bart & Tabone, 2000).

Formulating your mission statement:

5. Articulate your distinctive competence/strengths, unique identity, the specific customers (patients) served, and how you satisfy them. Do not include specific financial outcomes and nonfinancial objectives (Bart & Tabone, 1999);
6. Draft and redraft until you are satisfied with how the various mission statement components are written and what they express (Bart & Tabone, 1999);
7. Avoid passive constructions, relational process verbs, and nominalization as such linguistic structures make a mission statement impersonal (Smythe, et al., 2006).

Implementing your mission statement:

8. The more the merrier. Use various methods to communicate the mission statement. Especially (a) using posters/plaques and (b) stimulating word of mouth have proven to be effective (Bart & Tabone, 2000);
9. Include middle and lower managers in the communication process. By virtue of their organizational position they can help you communicate and clarify the mission statement (Butcher, 1994);
10. Try to align virtually every organizational dimension or structure with your mission statement (Bart & Tabone, 1998).

and formulation process. Research by Bart & Tabone (1999), for example, indicated that health managers need to consider the "goal" of their mission statement (e.g., influence behavior or provide inspiration) since not all mission components were found to influence all performance measures uniformly. Consequently, health care managers should strive for congruence between the behind-the-mission-statement intention and its specific wording and content (Smythe, Malloy, Hadjistavropoulos, Martin, & Bardutz, 2006).

Once the mission statement rationales are clearly defined, the actual mission statement drafting process can begin. Empirical research within the health care sector indicates that such a process is more likely to be successful and satisfying if it has the following three characteristics (Bart & Tabone, 2000):

- The development process style should not be a top–down process but a joint organizational effort in order to resolve disagreements and to craft a unique and enduring mission statement. Especially the involvement of senior managers, middle managers, nonmanagers, and customers (patients) in the creation process was seen to have a significantly positive relationship with performance. The study results furthermore indicate that higher levels of participation by almost all stakeholders contribute to better performance outcomes.

- The development process should not be rigid and formal. The mission architects should be allowed to take whatever steps are judged to be necessary to arrive at a suitable mission.
- An effective mission statement is distinguished by creativity. It seems to be far more beneficial for a hospital's mission leadership team to follow an original (or homemade) process rather than one simply taken from a text book and forced on the organization.

The Content of the Mission Statement

Health care managers should carefully select their mission statement components as the research findings demonstrate that certain components are more important than others. Some components appear to have little or no association with performance outcomes (i.e., "specific financial outcomes" and "non-financial objectives"), while others exhibit a significant positive correlation with all of the selected outcome measures (i.e., "distinctive competence/strength," "specific customers (patients) served," "unique identity," and "concern or satisfying customers/patients") (Bart & Tabone, 1999). Additionally, the research findings indicate that some components (i.e., "competitive strategy," "desired competitive position," and "concern for shareholders"), which appear to matter, are not always the most popular (Bart & Tabone, 1999). Moreover, although empirical results demonstrate that hospital executives believe that their mission statement has a positive impact on performance when they include the content addressed by (a) the grand inspiration (purpose and values), (b) benefactors (general concern for the organization's stakeholders), (c) competitive orientation (distinctive competences, position, and strategy of the organization), and (d) business definition factor (description of the core services and identity of the organization) (Bart & Hupfer, 2004), most health care mission statements focus predominantly on describing rather succinctly (a) the purpose, (b) the general goal of the organization, and (c) which services/products the organization offers to which customers (patients) (Bart & Tabone, 1999;

Williams, Smythe, Hadjistavropoulos, Malloy, & Martin, 2005). Furthermore, it is important to pay attention not only to the selection of the mission statement components but also to how these components are written. Study results indicate that a higher level of satisfaction with how specific mission statement components are worded leads to higher positive correlations with the selected performance indicators (Bart & Tabone, 1999; Williams et al., 2005). In addition, more "traditional" or unclear phrasing could also give the impression that the component is simply thrown in out of convention rather than attempting to truly articulate the importance of certain stakeholders or goals (Bart & Tabone, 1999). Smythe et al. (2006) consequently suggest avoiding the use of passive constructions, relational process verbs, and nominalization as these linguistic structures conceal or deemphasize the agent of action (e.g., "Health care is provided to patients" versus "We provide health care to patients").

Implementing the Mission Statement

If you think that drafting the mission statement was a difficult exercise, you are in for a treat: communicating the mission statement effectively is even harder. Research indicates that a lot of managers hold the false assumption that mere transmission equates to communication (Desmidt & Heene, 2007). Managers often invest a considerable amount of time and resources in formulating the mission statement but neglect the fact that a mission statement needs to be communicated and clarified in order to become effective. Blinded by their own positive perception and understanding of the mission statement, many executives believe that the "salute and execute" mode still operates. Confident that everyone will march to the new orders, they do not think additional communication is necessary (Lippitt, 1997).

However, in reality, the mere presence of a mission statement does not imply that all organizational members are aware of it, let alone motivated by it (Butcher, 1994). First of all, mission statement messages are often changed, misinterpreted, or lost entirely as they travel to layers of supervisors and employees. Secondly, to be relevant to the miscellaneous components of a large organization, mission statements are necessarily abstract and free of references to a specific work context (Leiter & Harvie, 1997). This level of abstractness makes it very difficult for non-management staff members to recognize the link between the mission statement and their day-to-day activities. Most non-management staff members consequently do not see how his or her objectives are driven by the mission statement and how they contribute to the overall goals of the organization. As a result, it is of utmost importance that health care managers try to increase the quality of the communication process in order to stimulate employee buy-in.

Research indicates that there are at least three factors that enhance the quality of the mission statement communication process and could therefore strengthen the effectiveness of mission statements. First is the selection of appropriate communication channels. Empirical findings indicate that (a) some communication instruments have more wide-range influence than others ("word of mouth" and "poster/plaques," in particular, correlate strongly with all of the selected performance outcomes while publishing the mission statement in the annual report seemed to have no effect), and (b) there is a positive relationship between the total number of communication channels used and the six performance measures (Bart & Tabone, 2000). Diversity and creativity thus seem to pay off.

Second, include middle and lower managers in the communication process. By virtue of their organizational position, first-line supervisors, such as nurse managers, can provide an interface between executives and front-line staff, which makes them an essential partner in (a) communicating the mission statement and (b) integrating the broad mission statement values into day-to-day work activities (Leiter & Harvie, 1997). First-line supervisors interact with subordinates on a daily basis and have ample opportunities to communicate their knowledge of the mission statement and to become not only monitors and coaches, but also role models for translating knowledge into behavior (Butcher, 1994). The resulting face-to-face communication will stimulate interaction and feedback about the mission statement, and help to transform the mission statement from a mere piece of paper to an effective management instrument.

Third is strengthening the level of mission–organization alignment. Besides mere communicating the mission statement, it is of vital importance to make the mission statement tangible and visible by aligning the organization with the mission statement components. Study results provide overwhelming support for the importance of aligning virtually every organizational dimension (e.g., organizational structure, types of rewards, objectives and targets, and job descriptions) with the mission statement (Bart & Tabone, 2000). Aligning organizational components with the mission statement will also avoid that the mission statements become a "paper tiger" with limited practical relevance.

CONCLUSION

Although some authors question the effectiveness of mission statements, we believe that mission statements can generate added value within an organization. However, managers have to be aware of the fact that the conception and implementation of a mission statement is not an easy task. In order to generate any benefits, mission statements have to be backed up by a carefully crafted development and implementation plan. If not, the mission statement of your organization will have no more value than the paper it is written on.

REFERENCES

Abrahamson, E. (1996). Management fashion. *Academy of Management Review, 21*(1), 254–285.

Ackoff, R. (1984). Mission statements. *Planning Review, 15*(4), 30–32.

Band, W. (1985). Defining your business mission. *Sales and Marketing Management in Canada, 26*(April), 32–33.

Bart, C. K. (1997). Industrial firms and the power of mission. *Industrial Marketing Management, 26*(4), 371–383.

Bart, C. K. (2002). Creating effective mission statements. Recapturing the power and the glory of mission. *Health Progress, 83*(5), 42–55.

Bart, C. K., & Baetz, M. (1998). The relationship between mission statements and firm performance: An exploratory study. *Journal of Management Studies, 35*(6), 823–853.

Bart, C. K., Bontis, N., & Taggar, S. (2001). A model of the impact of mission statements on firm performance. *Management Decision, 39*(1), 19–35.

Bart, C. K., & Hupfer, M. (2004). Mission statements in Canadian hospitals. *Journal of Health Organization Management, 18*(2/3), 92–110.

Bart, C. K., & Tabone, J. (1998). Mission statement rationales and organizational alignment in the not-for-profit health care sector. *Health Care Management Review, 23*(4), 54–69.

Bart, C. K., & Tabone, J. (1999). Mission statement content and hospital performance in the Canadian not-for-profit health care sector. *Health Care Management Review, 24*(3), 18–29.

Bart, C. K., & Tabone, J. (2000). Mission statements in Canadian not-for-profit hospitals: Does process matter? *Health Care Management Review, 25*(2), 45.

Bartkus, B., Glassman, M., & McAfee, B. (2000). Mission statements: Are they smoke and mirrors? *Business Horizons, 43*(6), 23–28.

Boyd, H., & Levy, S. (1966). What kind of corporate objectives? *Journal of Marketing, 30*(4), 53–58.

Brown, W., & Yoshioka, C. (2003). Mission attachment and satisfaction as factors in employee retention. *Nonprofit Management & Leadership, 14*(1), 5–18.

Butcher, A. H. (1994). Supervisors matter more than you think: Components of a mission-centered organizational climate. *Hospitals & Health Services Administration, 39*(4), 505–519.

Campbell, A., & Yeung, S. (1991a). Creating a sense of mission. *Long Range Planning*, *42*(4), 10–20.

Campbell, A., & Yeung, S. (1991b). Mission, vision, and strategy intent. *Long Range Planning*, *24*(4), 145–147.

Cochran, D., & David, F. (1986). The communication effectiveness of organizational mission statements. *Applied Journal of Communication Research*, *14*(4), 108–118.

Collins, J., & Porras, J. (1995). Building a visionary company. *California Management Review*, *37*(2), 80–100.

Desmidt, S., & Heene, A. (2007). Mission statement perception: Are we all on the same wavelength? A case study in a Flemish hospital. *Health Care Management Review*, *32*(1), 77–87.

DiMaggio, P. J., & Powell, W. W. (1983). The iron cage revisited: Institutional isomorphism and collective rationality in organizational fields. *American Sociological Review*, *48*, 147–160.

Drucker, P. (1992). *Managing for the future*. New York: Truman Talley Books.

Forehand, A. (2000). Mission and organizational performance in the healthcare industry. *Journal of Healthcare Management*, *45*(4), 267–277.

Haberberg, A., & Rieple, A. (2001). *The strategic management of organisations*. New Jersey: Prentice Hall.

Hooley, G., Cox, A., & Adams, A. (1992). Our five year mission – to boldly go where no man has gone before. *Journal of Marketing Management*, *8*(1), 35–48.

Ireland, R., & Hitt, M. (1992). Mission statements: Importance, challenge and recommendations for development. *Business Horizons*, *3*, 34–42.

Jones, M. (1960). Evolving a business philosophy. *Journal of the Academy of Management*, *3*(2), 93–98.

Jones, P., & Kahaner, L. (1995). *Say it and live it: The 50 corporate mission statements that hit the mark*. New York: Doubleday.

Kalis, A., van Delden, J., & Schermer, M. (2004). "The good life" for demented persons living in nursing homes. *International Psychogeriatrics*, *16*(4), 429–439.

Kemp, S., & Dwyer, L. (2003). Mission statements of international airlines: A content analysis. *Tourism management*, *24*(6), 635–653.

Klemm, M., Sanderson, S., & Luffman, G. (1991). Mission statements: Selling corporate values to employees. *Long Range Planning*, *24*(3), 73–78.

Kuchi, T. (2006). Communicating mission: An analysis of academic library web sites. *Journal of Academic Librarianship*, *32*(2), 148–154.

Leiter, M. P., & Harvie, P. (1997). Correspondence of supervisor and subordinate perspectives during major organizational change. *Journal of Occupational Health Psychology*, *2*(4), 343–352.

Lippitt, M. (1997). Say what you mean, mean what you say. *Journal of Business Strategy*, *19*(4), 18–20.

Lundberg, C. (1984). Zero-In: A technique for formulating better mission statements. *Business Horizons*, *27*(5), 30–33.

McGuire, T., & Chamberlain, P. (1984). Mission effectiveness study identifies, reinforces values. *Health Progress*, *65*(10), 57–58.

Mockler, R. (1970). Theory and practice of planning. *Harvard Business Review*, *48*(2), 73–80.

Newman, W. H. (1967). Shaping the master strategy of your firm. *California Management Review*, *9*(3), 77–88.

O'Gorman, C., & Doran, R. (1999). Mission statements in small and medium-sized businesses. *Journal of Small Business Management*, *37*(4), 59–66.

Pearce II, J., & David, F. (1987). Corporate mission statements: The bottom line. *Academy of Management Executive*, *1*(2), 109–114.

Piercy, N., & Morgan, N. (1994). Mission analysis: An operational approach. *Journal of General Management*, *19*(3), 1–19.

Rainey, H., & Steinbauer, P. (1999). Galloping elephants: Developing elements of a theory of effective government organizations. *Journal of Public Administration Research and Theory*, *9*(1), 1–32.

Rigby, D. (2001). Putting tools to the test: Senior executives rate 25 top management tools. *Strategy & Leadership*, *29*(3), 4–12.

Sanchez, R., & Heene, A. (2004). *The new strategic management: Organization, competition, and competence*. London: Wiley.

Schwartz, M. (2001). The nature of the relationship between corporate codes of ethics and behaviour. *Journal of Business Ethics*, *32*(3), 247–262.

Simon, H. (1964). On the concept of organizational goal. *Administrative Science Quarterly*, *9*(1), 1–21.

Smythe, W., Malloy, D., Hadjistavropoulos, T., Martin, R., & Bardutz, H. (2006). An analysis of the ethical and linguistic content of hospital mission statements. *Health Care Management Review*, *31*(2), 92–98.

Steiner, G. A. (1970). Rise of the corporate planner. *Harvard Business Review*, *48*(5), 133–139.

Stone, R.A. (1996). Mission statements revisited. *SAM Advanced Management Journal*, *6*(1), 31–37.

Tranfield, D., Denyer, D., & Smart, P. (2003). Developing an evidence-informed approach to management knowledge by means of systematic review. *British Journal of Management*, *14*(3), 207–222.

Truskie, S. (1984). The driving force of successful organizations. *Business Horizons*, *27*(4), 43–48.

Vandijck, D., Desmidt, S., & Buelens, M. (2007). Relevance of mission statements in Flemish not-for-profit healthcare organizations. *Journal of Nursing Studies*, *15*(2), 131–141.

Weiss, J., & Piderit, S. (1999). The value of mission statements in public agencies. *Journal of Public Administration Research & Theory*, *9*(2), 193–223.

Williams, J., Smythe, W., Hadjistavropoulos, T., Malloy, D., & Martin, R. (2005). A study of thematic content in hospital mission statements: A question of values. *Health Care Management Review*, *30*(4), 304–314.

ENHANCING THE CULTURAL COMPETENCY OF HEALTH CARE ORGANIZATIONS

Robert Weech-Maldonado, Mona Al-Amin, Robyn Y. Nishimi and Fatema Salam

ABSTRACT

According to the Census, racial/ethnic minority populations are growing at such a fast rate that by 2050 more than 50% of the population will belong to a minority group (US Census, 2001). The increasing diversity of the U.S. population is one of the many changes that health care delivery organizations need to proactively address in order to better serve their community and improve their performance. In this paper, we argue that cultural competency not only is important from a societal perspective, i.e., reducing health disparities, but can also be a strategy for health care organizations to improve quality, lower cost, and attract customers. We provide detailed recommendations for health care leaders and managers to adopt in order to successfully serve a diverse patient population.

Keywords: Cultural competency; diversity management; racial/ethnic minorities

Organization Development in Healthcare: Conversations on Research and Strategies
Advances in Health Care Management, Volume 10, 43–67

ISSN: 1474-8231/doi:10.1108/S1474-8231(2011)0000010009

INTRODUCTION

Given the changing demographics of the US population, specifically the projected growth of minority groups in the next 40 years, health care providers should adapt their practices in order to be more responsive to the increasing diversity of the American population. The Office of Minority Health's standards for culturally and linguistically appropriate services (CLAS) for health care organizations (HCOs) (2001), the National Quality Forum's (NQF) recent publication of preferred practices for measuring and reporting cultural competency, and the Joint Commission's proposed standards on cultural competency for hospital accreditation are some examples of the growing recognition of the importance of cultural competency in health care (Siegel, Haugland, & Chambers, 2003; The Lewin Group, 2002; NQF, 2009).

This chapter aims at familiarizing health care leaders with the importance of cultural competency by exposing them to current demographic trends and their potential impact on health care delivery organizations. This chapter also reviews research on how to enhance the cultural competency of the HCO as a whole and health care workforce specifically. The cultural competency of health care workers is crucial for the success and even survival of health care delivery organizations and has implications on quality of care and access for different ethnic and racial groups. In this chapter we present a framework that can guide HCOs' leaders in their efforts to enhance the cultural competency of their organizations and consequently be better equipped to face the continuously changing health care environment.

DIVERSITY AND HEALTH CARE ORGANIZATIONS

It has been widely documented that the United States is witnessing a rapid growth in minority populations. According to the Census, minority populations are growing at such a fast rate that by 2050 more than 50% of the population will belong to a minority group (US Census, 2001). The groups that are contributing the most to this growth are Hispanics and Asians. As documented by the Census (2001), from 1980 until 2000, the white population grew by only 9% while Hispanics by 122% and the Asians by approximately 190%. If this trend continues, by 2050, around 25% of the U.S. population will be Hispanic. Thus, about one out of every two patients admitted to a hospital or seen by a physician will belong to a minority group and about one out of every four patients will be Hispanic.

In addition to the increasing diversity at home, leaders should also be aware of the "international patients" market that is likely to grow with the continuously expanding global economy. It is estimated that around 400,000 foreign patients travel each year to the United States to receive inpatient medical care (Deloitte Center for Health Solutions, 2008). These patients benefit not only the admitting hospitals and their medical professionals but also the local community through money spent in hotels, restaurants, shopping, etc. The international patients' market is very lucrative, given that hospitals are not subject to cost containment restrictions while providing services and also because patients from foreign countries who seek care in the United States are usually well-off financially and require complicated procedures and treatments.

Thus, health care leaders and managers have to be strategic thinkers and adopt practices in their organizations that will enable them to be successful providers of care to a diverse population of patients. One of the main characteristics of a successful leader is his or her ability to observe trends and take the necessary actions to benefit from these trends. Strategies developed by health care leaders to address the issue of demographic changes occurring in the United States should focus on reorganizing organizational processes and training and expanding the health care workforce to meet the needs of our "diverse" future.

CULTURAL COMPETENCY AND ORGANIZATIONAL PERFORMANCE

Culture can be viewed as an "integrated pattern of learned beliefs and behaviors" shared by individuals of a group that can affect styles of communication, interpersonal relationships, values, and customs (Betancourt, Green, & Carrillo, 2002). Various sociocultural factors, such as race/ethnicity, nationality, language, gender, socioeconomic status (SES), physical and mental ability, sexual orientation, and occupation, can influence the cultural background of an individual.

Culture is central in the delivery of health care services, since it can influence patients' health beliefs, medical practices, attitudes toward medical care, and levels of trust (Office of Minority Health, 2001; Betancourt, Green, & Carrillo, 2003). Cultural differences can ultimately impact how health information is received, understood, and acted upon (Anderson et al., 2003). Clinical barriers occur when cultural differences are not adequately addressed in health care delivery, resulting in lower access and quality of care for culturally diverse populations. As such, addressing cultural differences becomes imperative, and HCOs are espousing cultural competency as an organizational strategy.

Brach and Fraser (2000) have proposed a model whereby cultural competency practices can ultimately result in a reduction in health disparities. In this model, cultural competency practices can influence the behavior of clinicians and patients, and bridge cultural gaps. This, in turn, can improve the likelihood of diverse populations receiving appropriate services and experiencing improved outcomes and a reduction in health disparities. For example, cultural competency can reduce barriers in clinician–patient communication, which in turn can improve access to care and ultimately outcomes of care (Anderson et al., 2003).

One of the major organizational barriers for cultural competency is the perceived impact it may have on costs. However, Brach and Fraser (2002) have argued the business care for cultural competency. In their view (Fig. 1), HCOs have four interrelated financial incentives for cultural competency. First, by becoming culturally competent, HCOs can increase their appeal to diverse populations, and increase their market share. This is particularly critical as the population becomes increasingly diverse. Second, cultural competency can improve the performance of HCOs in quality measures that are monitored by private purchasers, which can be particularly important in competitive markets with a large diverse population. Third, increasingly public purchasers, such as Medicaid and Medicare, are instituting cultural competency requirements in their contracts. HCOs must comply with these requirements to maintain their contracts with said public purchasers. Fourth, cultural competency has the potential to reduce costs by reducing unnecessary diagnostic testing, inappropriate use of services, and medical errors.

Fig. 1. Cultural Competency and Organizational Performance.

Toward a Definition of Cultural Competency

While the case has been made for cultural competency from a clinical and business standpoint, the major challenge remaining is how to define and assess cultural competency. Various definitions exist of cultural competency. One distinguishing characteristic of these definitions is the unit of analysis. While some definitions have focused on the individual or clinician level (Cooper & Roter, 2003; Sanders & Ewart, 2005), others have focused on the organizational level (Office of Minority Health, 2001; Betancourt et al., 2002; Romeo, 2007). Yet other definitions recognize both individual and organizational aspects of cultural competency (Office of Minority Health, 2001; Romeo, 2007; NQF, 2008).

All the definitions seem to agree on an ultimate outcome for cultural competency: to improve health care delivery for diverse populations. However, some of these definitions focus on the structural aspects of cultural competency, such as having the capacity or ability to address the health care needs of diverse patient populations (Office of Minority Health, 2001; Betancourt et al., 2002), while others describe cultural competency as a process (Romeo, 2007). Yet other definitions use a combination of structural and process aspects, describing it as a set of behaviors, or attitudes, or both (Cross, Bazron, Dennis, & Isaacs, 1989).

In its definition of cultural competency, the NQF addresses both individual and organizational aspects of cultural competency as well as the structural and process elements of cultural competency:

> Cultural competency is the ongoing capacity of health care systems, organizations and professionals to provide for diverse patient populations high quality care that is family- and patient-centered, evidence based, and equitable. (NQF, 2008)

Cultural competency is achieved through policies, learning processes, and structures by which organizations and individuals develop the attitudes, behaviors, and systems that are needed for effective cross-cultural interactions, including but not limited to sociocultural factors such as race/ethnicity, nationality, language, gender, SES, immigrant status, physical and mental ability, sexual orientation, religion, health literacy, age, and occupation (Betancourt et al., 2003). These factors can be conceptualized as cultural group identities. Individuals' affiliations to cultural groups are complex, with individual differences based on the group identity profile and strength of the group identities (Cox, 1994). For example, a second-generation Hispanic of higher SES will differ from a recent immigrant Hispanic of lower SES in terms of its group identity profile as well as the strength of the group identities. These differences will affect an individual's interactions with the health care system.

High-quality care implies state-of-the-art care based on evidence-based clinical practices. According to the Institute of Medicine's (IOM) "equity" aim for health system improvement (2001), quality of care should not differ because of sociocultural factors. Family centeredness implies respecting the desire of culturally diverse groups to include their family members in health care decision making (Brach & Fraser, 2000). The care is patient-centered when clinicians treat each patient as an individual, within the context of his or her care (Carrillo, Green, & Betancourt, 1999). This requires a partnership among clinicians, patients, and families to ensure that health care decisions take into account patient preferences.

Guiding Principles for Cultural Competency

Guiding principles for measuring and reporting cultural competency quality provide broad themes and direction that promote standardized measurement and reporting, drive practice improvement and measure development, and support implementation. The guiding principles are intended to be overarching and/or cross-cutting all (or multiple) domains of the framework presented in the next section. There are five principles that guide the development of the proposed cultural competency framework.

Principle 1. Multilevel Approach

Cultural competency should be viewed as a multilevel approach with assessments and interventions needed at the system, provider organization, group, and individual levels.

Cultural competency has generally been viewed as pertinent to individual clinical interactions. However, this view fails to recognize that "clinicians will become culturally competent only with the support and/or encouragement of the health systems in which they participate" (Brach & Fraser, 2000). "Cultural competence should be considered as much of a function of the organization as it is a result of the interactions between providers and patients" (California Pan-Ethnic Health Network, 2001).

Four levels of care can be identified with each requiring a different set of measures of and interventions for cultural competency: (1) system – as represented by a health care or managed care entity that oversees a number of owned or affiliated provider organizations; (2) provider organization – the entities that provide direct services to the patient, such as clinics, hospitals, and nursing homes; (3) group – includes formal departmental and cross-departmental teams; (4) individual – people involved directly or indirectly in the delivery of care (Siegel et al., 2003; Shortell & Kalunzy, 1999).

Principle 2. Viewed as a Process and Continuum

Cultural competency should be viewed as an ongoing process of organizational transformation in a continuum from early to later stages of development.

For HCOs to become more culturally competent, they will need to engage in a change process of organizational transformation. This entails an organizational culture change from a monoculture, or culture that "accepts only one way of doing things and one set of values and beliefs," to a pluralistic environment, or an environment that accepts and integrates people from diverse cultural backgrounds (Daft & Marcic, 2005).

This change process has been described as a continuum from early to later stages of development. For example, Tirado (1998) proposes a five-stage model of organizational change: culturally resistant, culturally unaware, culturally conscious, culturally insightful, and culturally versatile. Similarly, Dreachslin (1996) proposes a five-stage change model from affirmative action to valuing diversity: discovery, assessment, exploration, transformation, and revitalization.

Principle 3. Systems Approach

Successful implementation of cultural competency initiatives to achieve high-quality, culturally competent care requires an organizational commitment toward a systems approach.

Successful implementation of cultural competency requires an organizational commitment toward a systems approach (Curtis, Dreachslin, & Sinioris, 2007; Dreachslin & Myers, 2007). In this approach, the HCO is viewed as a system comprised of interrelated and interdependent subsystems, such as patient care, ancillary services, professional staff, and financial, informational, physical, and administrative subsystems (Longest, Rakich, & Darr, 2000).

Related to systems thinking is the open systems perspective that views organizations interacting with their environment to secure resources, process them, and produce some type of output. To survive, it is critical that organizations respond to the demands of their environment to ensure a continuous inflow of resources (Scott & Davis, 2007). For HCOs, the community is the major resource supplier. Therefore, HCOs have to adapt to the changing community needs to ensure their survival.

Cultural competency should not be conceived as a standalone, point-in-time effort pertinent only to clinical interactions. Rather, HCOs should strive toward a systems approach where cultural competency practices are integrated throughout their management and clinical subsystems. Furthermore, HCOs should engage their communities in meaningful participation in the organization's decision making and power structures.

Principle 4. Diversity Management
Addressing both organizational and clinical aspects in managing diversity and the needs of both a diverse workforce and patient population are important factors in culturally competent care.

The cultural competency and diversity management literatures have had different focuses with respect to diversity issues. The cultural competency literature has had a clinical orientation with a focus on patient–clinician interactions, while the diversity management literature has had an organizational orientation with a focus on workforce issues. However, these differences are becoming increasingly less distinct as both camps agree on the importance of both to cultural competency (Weech-Maldonado, Dreachslin, Dansky, De Souza , & Gatto, 2002). For example, it is increasingly recognized that organizations need strategies aimed at recruiting and retaining a diverse workforce, as well as staff training and development in cross-cultural communication skills to enhance cultural competency.

Principle 5. Continuous Improvement
Cultural competency should not be viewed as an endpoint, but rather organizations should strive for continuous improvement (Campinha-Bacote, Yahle, & Langenkamp, 1996).

Continuous improvement in cultural competency represents an ongoing process whereby organizations (1) determine cultural competency goals in the context of its strategic plan; (2) assess individual, group, and organizational baseline performance to determine gaps in performance; (3) develop interventions to close the gaps in performance; and (4) reassess performance to determine the effectiveness of the interventions. For example, in designing cultural competency training, the organization should determine goals for its training in the context of its strategic plan, measure current performance against needs, design training to address the gap, implement the training, assess training effectiveness, and strive for continuous improvement (Curtis et al., 2007).

FRAMEWORK FOR ENHANCING ORGANIZATIONAL CULTURAL COMPETENCY

Restructuring your organization and patient care processes to better serve a diverse patient population requires the adoption of a holistic framework that not only ensures higher quality and patient satisfaction but also incorporates the means to continuously monitor and evaluate the level of your organization's cultural competency. The framework presented in this chapter consists of seven core competencies or domains of cultural competency and their respective subdomains (Fig. 2).

Organizational development focuses on guiding organizations in their change initiatives and in structuring work processes in a manner that ensures their long-term viability and competitiveness (Jones, 2009). Transforming into a culturally competent HCO takes more than just a top management decision. It is an organizational shift that should involve all employees and work processes. In this chapter, we propose seven main competencies (domains) that should be developed by organizations striving to be more culturally competent. Each of the seven proposed domains also includes specific subdomains that further articulate the core competencies of high-quality, culturally competent care. The main domains include leadership, integration into management systems and operations, patient–provider communication,

Fig. 2. Framework for Enhancing Organizational Cultural Competency.

care delivery and supporting mechanisms, workforce diversity and training, community engagement, and finally, data collection and quality improvement.

Leadership

Successful HCOs recognize that organizational leaders, including clinical leaders, administrative leaders, and the Board of Trustees, play an essential role in developing and implementing cultural competency activities, in setting organizational policy and strategy, and in monitoring organizational performance. Leaders in HCOs need to work on the following subdomains in order to successfully execute their transformational roles: (1) commitment to diversity, (2) organizational culture, (3) leadership diversity, (4) dedicated staff and resources, (5) policies, and (6) training and development.

One of the most important steps leaders have to take is to show employees, patients, and the community that they are highly committed to diversity. Cultural competency activities are most effective when the organization's governing board and top management embraces cultural competency and communicates this support throughout the organization (Brach, Paez, & Fraser, 2006; Dansky, Weech-Maldonado, De Souza, & Dreachslin, 2003). Moreover, leaders should be aware that one of their most important and challenging roles is creating an organizational culture that is inclusive and values cultural differences. Organizational culture is usually defined as the shared values, beliefs, assumptions, and symbols that determine the manner in which the organization carries out its business (Smircich, 1983). Culture is critical to organizations because it shapes how they interact with their employees, customers, suppliers, and competitors (Louis, 1983). Organizational leaders are instrumental in setting organizational culture (Muller & Haase, 1994). An inclusive culture signifies that the organization's decision-making processes include diverse points of views from within and outside the organization. When an organization values diversity, it is shown through its practices, structures, and policies. Without an organizational culture that values and encourages diversity, organizations are unlikely to achieve cultural competency.

However, leadership commitment and an organizational culture that values diversity are ineffective if the leadership composition lacks the diversity it attempts to propagate. Leadership at all levels of the organization, including the Board of Trustees, should reflect the community diversity (The Lewin Group, 2002). Leadership diversity increases the likelihood that the needs of a diverse workforce and patient population are taken into account in organizational decision-making processes (Anderson et al., 2003). Yet minorities have traditionally faced barriers, or a "glass ceiling" effect, that have excluded them from upper management positions (Cox, 1994). As such, HCOs need proactive human resource strategies aimed at diversifying the leadership ranks and breaking the glass ceiling.

Moreover, an organization shows its commitment to cultural competency by dedicating resources and designating staff for cultural competency activities. Dedicated resources can be shown by budgeting resources for cultural competency activities (The Lewin Group, 2002; Wilson-Stronks & Galvez, 2007). Dedicated staff can include an executive-level staff member, and department or office that focuses on multicultural and/or linguistic issues. This can be instrumental in coordinating organization-wide initiatives and monitoring progress toward cultural competency goals (Brach et al., 2006; Wilson-Stronks & Galvez, 2007).

All of the above subdomains need to be supported by organizational policies. Formal policies need to address cultural competency issues, such as recruitment and retention of a diverse workforce, language services, and training and development (The Lewin Group, 2002; Wilson-Stronks & Galvez, 2007). Policies "express an organization's intentions and provide a blueprint for action" (Dreachslin & Hobby, 2008). These internal policies should be in conformity with external regulatory and statutory policies. Finally, training and development of leaders at all levels of the organization, including the Board of Trustees, on cultural competency issues is essential (The Lewin Group, 2002). Leadership participation in training and development sends a signal to organizational members of its commitment to cultural competency.

Integration into Management Systems and Operations

Cultural competence needs to be integrated throughout all management practices of the organization: (1) strategic planning, (2) performance evaluation, (3) reward systems, (4) service planning, (5) marketing, and (6) public relations. The strategic planning process includes environmental scanning, asset and needs assessment of the communities served, and formulation of goals related to cultural competency (Office of Minority Health, 2001). Strategic goals reflect the organizational priorities for resource use and deployment. Therefore, organizational strategies need to account for the diverse population the organization serves and also the diverse staff it employs.

Successful organizations rely on performance evaluation in their decisions. Performance evaluation including job descriptions and performance evaluation systems should include criteria related to cultural competency (Office of Minority Health, 2001; The Lewin Group, 2002). This evaluation process should include assessments of patient and family experiences with care. This results in accountability for meeting cultural competency goals. However, it is not enough to incorporate cultural competency in performance evaluation; managers and staff should also be rewarded for meeting cultural competency goals (The Lewin Group, 2002). Incentives help align the organizational members' goals with those of the organization. Thorndike's law of effect states that behavior or performance that is reinforced tends to be repeated (Hrebiniak & Joyce, 1984).

When organizations are undergoing service planning, they should design their services taking into account the needs of their diverse patient populations. This includes all elements of the health care encounter from admission to discharge with the ultimate goal of improving access to care for all patients (Betancourt et al., 2003). Examples include expanding clinical hours to accommodate community work patterns, adapting to ethnic or religious dietary preferences, and allowing for large families visiting or staying with hospitalized patients (Betancourt et al., 2003; Wilson-Stronks & Galvez, 2007).

Finally, two important management practices that can help organizations garner from their cultural competency efforts are marketing and public relations. Organizations should promote and market their services through a variety of media that reaches out to diverse populations, including ethnic newspapers, television news programs, and radio stations (Wilson-Stronks & Galvez, 2007). Marketing should also emphasize the availability of language services, such as interpretation and translation services. Organizations should also raise public awareness of cultural competency activities and progress in meeting goals (Office of Minority Health, 2001; The Lewin Group, 2002). This can include a statistical annual report on patient demographics, interpreter use and availability, translated materials, staff training in cultural competency, and survey results of patient experiences with care. This can serve as a marketing tool while enhancing the organization's image among diverse communities.

Patient–Provider Communication

Patient–provider communication addresses all communication between the patient and clinicians as well as support staff. We view the following services and competencies as very important for a good patient–provider communication: interpreter services, translation services, health literacy strategies, knowledge of culture and social context, cultural awareness, cross-cultural communication skills, and family centeredness.

High-quality interpreter services are needed at all points of patient contact to improve provider and staff communication with patients of limited English proficiency. Accurate communication increases the likelihood of receiving appropriate care (Office of Minority Health, 2001; Anderson et al., 2003; Wilson-Stronks & Galvez, 2007). Language concordant encounters have better communication, interpersonal processes, and outcomes than language discordant encounters (Clark, Sleath, & Rubin, 2004; Grant Makers in Health, 2003; Seijo, Gomez, & Freidenberg, 1991; Perez-Stable, Napoles-Springer, & Miramontes, 1997; Fernandez, Schillinger, & Grumbach et al., 2004). However, the limited supply of bilingual providers has led HCOs to use interpreter services to bridge language gaps. When evaluating the quality of interpreter services, it is important to distinguish between professional and ad hoc interpreters (Ngo-Metzger, Telfair, & Sorkin, 2006). Ad hoc interpreters are "individuals whose primary job function in the health care setting is something other than interpretation and includes the patient's family members, friends, clinic staff, or even fellow patients." On the other hand, professional interpreters are "those individuals whose sole function in the health care setting is to interpret" (Grant Makers in Health, 2003). Prior research has shown the effectiveness of professional interpreters compared to ad hoc interpreters (Jacobs, Launderdale, & Meltzer, 2001; Tocher & Larson, 1999; Enguidanos & Rosen, 1997). Professional interpreter services may be in person or remote. Remote interpreter services include telephone language lines, video links, and other remote systems. Regardless of the type of interpreter used, interpreters should have proficiency in both languages, mastery of medical terminology in both languages, memory skills, ability to negotiate a three-way conversation, and basic knowledge of cultural aspects that can influence health. Bilingual providers should be proficient in the target language, including knowledge of medical terminology (Ngo-Metzger et al., 2006).

In addition to interpreter services, patient-related written materials should be translated into the most common languages of the patient population (Office of Minority Health, 2001; The Lewin Group, 2002). Examples of relevant patient-related materials include applications, consent forms, preventive and treatment instructions, and patient education materials. Translated materials should be evaluated for linguistic and cultural appropriateness with respect to both content and context (Weech-Maldonado, Weidmer, Morales, & Hays 2001). Linguistically appropriate translated materials are conceptually and technically equivalent to the source language. Technical equivalence refers to similarity in grammar and syntax, while conceptual equivalence refers to the absence of differences in meaning and content between the source and translated documents. Weidmer, Hurtado, Weech-Maldonado, Ngo-Metzger, and Bogen (2006) have proposed a translation process that involves (1) obtaining two independent forward translations; (2) conducting a review of translation by a separate bilingual reviewer; and (3) reconciling translations by committee (forward translators and bilingual reviewer) consensus. Culturally appropriate translated materials reflect the cultural assumptions, norms, values, and expectations of the target population (Marin & Marin, 1991). Qualitative methods, such as focus groups and cognitive interviews, are particularly useful in assessing the cultural appropriateness of translated materials (Weech-Maldonado et al., 2001).

Health literacy is very important for HCOs for many reasons, the most important of which is its effect on quality. Patients' inabilities to comprehend instructions can have effect on their compliance with physicians' recommendations and thus can negatively affect the outcome of their care. HCOs should address the literacy needs of the patient in both oral and written communication (Ngo-Metzger et al., 2006). Healthy People 2010 defines health literacy as the "degree to which individuals can obtain, process, and understand the basic health information and services they need to make appropriate health decisions" (Department of Health & Human Services [DHHS], 2008). People with low health literacy tend to have more problems with both written and oral communication (Center for Health care Strategies, 2005a, 2005b). Several strategies have been suggested for health care professionals to improve oral and written communication with low literacy patients (Ad Hoc Committee on Health Literacy, 1999; Williams, Davis, Parker, & Weiss, 2002; (Center for Health care Strategies, 2005a, 2005b): (1) avoid use of medical jargon, and instead use commonly understood words; (2) use audiovisual aids to supplement oral and written instructions; (3) include interactive instructions by making patients do, write, say, or show something to demonstrate their understanding (teach back method); (4) write materials at a sixth-grade level or lower; and (5) pretest materials to evaluate whether materials are suitable for the intended audience.

HCOs should also proactively engage in obtaining knowledge of culture and social context of the populations they serve and plan to target. This could be attained by having the knowledge base of cultural groups with respect to traditional healing practices; health-related beliefs and cultural values; disease incidence, prevalence, and outcomes; as well as health disparities (Lavizzo-Mourey, 1996; Campinha-Bacote, 2002; Kim-Godwin, Clarke, & Barton, 2001; DeRosa & Kochurka, 2006). It should include also an awareness of the historical context that may explain the way different groups interact with the health care system (Betancourt et al., 2003). One example is the relationship between the Tuskegee Syphilis Study and mistrust of health care professionals among African Americans. However, care must be exercised that this cultural knowledge does not lead to or reinforce stereotyping (Betancourt et al., 2003). Rather this knowledge should be used in the context of patient-centered care and effective cross-cultural communication skills (Galanti, 2004).

It is common knowledge in the diversity management literature that for individuals and organizations to be culturally competent, they should be aware of their own culture. Cultural awareness is about self-examination and exploration of one's own cultural background. This includes an awareness of one's own assumptions, biases, stereotypes, and prejudices with respect to individuals from other cultures (Campinha-Bacote, 2002; Kim-Godwin et al., 2001; DeRosa & Kochurka, 2006). Being aware of one's own cultural influences and the key elements of other cultures is, however, not enough to ensure a good patient–provider communication. Health care providers should also have cross-cultural communication skills. This includes skills to obtain culturally relevant data, such as those used in conducting cultural assessments and culturally based physical assessments (Campinha-Bacote, 2002; Kim-Godwin et al., 2001; DeRosa & Kochurka, 2006; Hobgood, Sawning, Bowen, & Savage, 2006). It also includes skills needed in "identifying and negotiating different styles of communication, decision-making preferences, roles of family, sexual and gender issues, and issues of mistrust, prejudice, and racism" (Betancourt et al., 2003). Patient-centered cross-cultural communication makes the patient a primary source of cultural knowledge and an active participant in the patient–doctor negotiation. Finally, HCOs should ensure that the care provided is family centered. Family centeredness is respecting the desire of culturally diverse groups to include their family members in health care decision making (Brach & Fraser, 2000).

Care Delivery and Supporting Mechanisms

This encompasses the delivery of care, the physical environment of where the care is delivered, and links to supportive services and providers.

Organizations need to incorporate cultural competency into their physical environment, assessment tools, coordination of care, linkages with alternative medicine provider, linkages with community-based organizations, and health information technology.

The physical environment should include culturally sensitive design and architecture, where the décor, artwork, posters, and literature reflect the diversity of the service area (The Lewin Group, 2002). It also includes appropriate signage in the major languages spoken in the service area (Office of Minority Health, 2001). Moreover, during the delivery of care, assessment tools should elicit culturally relevant information on health beliefs, behaviors, and practices (The Lewin Group, 2002). These data can be used to assist with establishing a physical environment and care delivery that are culturally appropriate for the community served. HCOs should be equipped to coordinate the care of its diverse population. This includes documenting and tracking referrals to other health care services in the continuum of care (from ambulatory to long-term care) and ensuring that information on patients' cultural and linguistic needs is shared with other health care providers. Coordination of care includes managing the transition back to home, nursing home or other institutional care, and supporting palliative and end-of-life care. HCOs should also establish linkages with alternative medicine providers by identifying patients' use of alternative providers and coordinating with these providers to augment allopathic treatments and avoid complications due to incompatible therapies (Brach & Fraser, 2000).

In addition to coordination of care and linkages with alternative medicine providers, HCOs should ensure a sustainable relationship with community-based organizations. It is important to identify community-based organizations, such as human, social service, and religious organizations, and coordinate with them to assist with care delivery, as understanding and addressing the context of the patient (e.g., SES, supports/stressors, environmental hazards) is an important element of cultural competency (The Lewin Group, 2002; Betancourt et al., 2003). Finally, health information technology, such as electronic and personal medical records, should be used to enhance and promote the delivery of culturally competent care.

Workforce Diversity and Training

Workforce diversity and training can be viewed as a means to providing more effective services for culturally diverse populations via proactive human resource recruitment and retention strategies to ensure diversity at all levels of the organization, and it also relates to whether training and development activities include state-of-the-art content in cultural competency and reflect organizational commitment toward cultural competency. HCOs should specifically be aware of the following sub-domains: (1) recruitment, (2) retention, (3) training commitment, and (4) training content.

HCOs should develop recruitment practices aimed at diversifying the workforce at all levels of the organization (The Lewin Group, 2002). Racial/ethnic and language concordance between patient and provider has been associated with better patient experiences with care and satisfaction (Ngo-Metzger et al., 2006; Betancourt et al., 2003). However, the current demographics of the health professions do not correspond to the composition of the general workforce. For example, while African Americans and Hispanics account for about 25% of the workforce, fewer than 12% of physicians and therapists, and only 15% of registered nurses, are from these two racial/ethnic groups (Dreachslin & Hobby, 2008). This calls for proactive recruitment strategies that will result in a more diverse applicant pool. As such, organizations "need to find alternatives to generic newspaper advertisements, search firms, and other mainstream recruiting methods. Community-based and national health organizations and networks as well as publications and search firms that target diverse populations may provide better channels for recruiting and advertising vacancies" (Office of Minority Health, 2001). Furthermore, organizational efforts aimed at improving the diversity of the workforce pipeline are needed. This may include partnerships with local elementary and secondary schools, particularly those with a high percentage of racial/ethnic minorities, to increase their interest in the health care professions.

Organizational efforts need to go beyond recruitment strategies and should also include retention strategies; otherwise organizations can become a "revolving door" for diverse employees, as they leave the organization in pursuit of better opportunities or a more welcoming environment. Retention strategies include efforts to create a welcoming climate for diverse populations, identifying barriers that prevent employees from achieving their full potential, and providing equitable promotional opportunities (Office of Minority Health, 2001; Anderson et al., 2003). Formal mentoring programs, professional development and training, work–life balance and flexible benefits, and affinity groups are among the human resource retention strategies that can be used (Dreachslin & Hobby, 2008).

Human resource practices should ensure training commitment to cultural competency. Organizations need to ensure that managers and staff at all levels of the organization receive appropriate and ongoing training in cultural competency (Office of Minority Health, 2001; The Lewin Group, 2002). Finally, staff training curriculum should emphasize the knowledge and skills as outlined under the (a) patient–provider communication and the (b) care delivery and supporting domains (The Group, 2002; Anderson et al., 2003). In addition, staff training should include strategies to assist a diverse staff with relating to each other. Leadership training should include content from all seven domains of cultural competency. Cultural competency training can be delivered as a standalone program, or it can be integrated into other training programs. Formal training can be complemented with less formal activities that develop staff knowledge about cultures and languages in their hospital, such as cultural fairs and reading clubs focused on specific cultures or languages (Wilson-Stronks & Galvez, 2007). These trainings should be conducted by qualified staff that are trained in cultural competency, and should be periodically updated and repeated. The trainings should be assessed for effectiveness and relevance in meeting the cultural needs of patients.

Community Engagement

This refers to active outreach, as well as community inclusion and partnership in organizational decision making. Community outreach includes collaborative relationships and partnerships with community entities to understand and address the cultural and linguistic needs of the communities served (Wilson-Stronks & Galvez, 2007; Weech-Maldonado & Merrill, 2000). It may also include liaisons, such as community health workers where members of minority communities are used to reach out to those communities (The Lewin Group, 2002; Brach & Fraser, 2000); for example, using community health workers that are trained to teach others with the same chronic conditions about disease self-management.

In addition to community outreach, it is important especially for academic centers to encourage community-based participatory research (CBPR). CBPR has been defined as a "collaborative research approach that is designed to ensure and establish structures for participation by communities affected by the issue being studied, representatives of organizations, and researchers in all aspects of the research process to improve health and well-being through taking action, including social change" (Viswanathan et al., 2004). By engaging in CBPR, HCOs enable the generation of actionable knowledge that can be used to address the most pressing health needs of the populations served (Cook, 2008).

Community engagement can be facilitated by having meaningful representation in organizational decision making using formal and informal mechanisms for community involvement, such as community advisory groups or committees in service planning and implementation (Office of Minority Health, 2001; The Lewin Group, 2002). Finally, organizations should invest in both infrastructure and human capital of the communities served, and should take into account the community assets in its outreach, education, and information-gathering activities.

Data Collection and Quality Improvement

This means whether the organization collects data necessary to assess its cultural competency, or performs routine self-assessments in this regard, or integrates cultural competency into its quality improvement activities. With respect to data collection, HCOs need mechanisms for routine data collection and documentation of patient and community cultural competency related information, assessments of patient experiences with care, cross-cultural complaints and resolutions, and organizational cultural competency practices. Patient cultural competency–related information includes data on cultural subgroups, such as race/ethnicity, language preferences, education, and income of patients, and integrating these data into the information systems (Office of Minority Health, 2001; The Lewin Group, 2002). These data are important for strategic and service planning, and can be used to monitor health care disparities as well as for quality improvement (Betancourt et al., 2002). The Joint Commission now requires collection of patients' language and communication needs in the patient record (Wilson-Stronks & Galvez, 2007). Community cultural competency related information includes current demographic, cultural, socioeconomic, and epidemiological profile and needs assessment of the communities served and using the data for strategic planning purposes, quality improvement, and public reporting initiatives (Office of Minority Health, 2001; The Lewin Group, 2002; Wilson-Stronks & Galvez, 2007).

Patient experiences with care should be assessed in the patient's first language using qualitative and quantitative methods. Patient assessments of care are critical since they capture firsthand experiences as patients interact with the health care system. The Consumer Assessments of Health care

Providers and Systems (CAHPS) is a set of standardized survey instruments that assess patient experiences with care across provider settings. Prior research using CAHPS data has shown racial/ethnic and language differences in patients' experiences with care (Weech-Maldonado et al., 2003; Weech-Maldonado et al., 2004). Focus groups and personal interviews are qualitative methods that can complement quantitative assessments, such as CAHPS, by providing more in-depth information on the observed cultural differences in patient experiences with care. These data can be used for quality improvement purposes (Betancourt et al., 2002).

HCOs need mechanisms in place to identify and resolve cross-cultural conflicts or complaints by patients (Office of Minority Health, 2001). Individuals from diverse backgrounds are more vulnerable to face experiences where their cultural differences are not accommodated or respected by the HCOs. Some of the mechanisms that HCOs can adopt to identify and resolve cross-cultural conflicts are "providing cultural competence training to staff who handle complaints and grievances or other legal or ethical conflict issues; providing notice in other languages about the right of each patient/consumer to file a complaint or grievance; providing the contact name and number of the individual responsible for the disposition of a grievance; and offering ombudsperson services" (Office of Minority Health, 2001).

HCOs should document the delivery of culturally competent care services, such as the provision and timeliness of language services, workforce diversity, referrals to alternative medicine providers, and community-based organizations. This information is important for ongoing self-assessments of cultural competency, as well as for public reporting of such activities.

In addition to data collection, HCOs need to conduct ongoing self-assessments to assess their progress in meeting cultural competency goals (Office of Minority Health, 2001). Assessments are needed at all four levels of care: system, provider organization, group, and individual (Betancourt et al., 2003). System and provider organizational-level assessments provide a picture of the organization's readiness toward cultural competency by examining its structures, policies, and practices. Group-level assessments can provide a gauge of organizational culture and climate. Individual-level assessments can assess cultural competency and cross-cultural skills at the individual level.

To facilitate the process of self-assessment, HCOs should include cultural competency–related measures in the organizational performance management systems, such as balanced score cards, organizational climate surveys, adverse events reports, and outcomes-based evaluations (Office of Minority

Health, 2001; Wilson-Stronks & Galvez, 2007). Examples of metrics that can be incorporated are patient and human resource outcomes for different cultural groups. Including these measures in performance management systems elevates their importance for the institution (Dreachslin & Myers, 2007).

Finally, HCOs need to integrate cultural competency into their quality improvement (QI) activities. QI can be viewed as an organization-wide approach to planning and implementation of continuous improvement in performance. As such, QI "emphasizes continuous examination and improvement of work processes by teams of organizational members trained in basic statistical techniques and problem solving tools and empowered to make decisions based on the analysis of data" (Weiner et al., 2006). HCOs can use QI activities to address health disparities in access, outcomes, or patient experiences with care.

CONCLUSION

Given the importance of cultural competency for the long-term viability of HCOs, it is very important for HCOs to engage in proactive steps to ensure their leadership in this domain. Changing population demographics and specifically the growth of minority populations can be viewed as either a threat or an opportunity for HCOs. By becoming more culturally competent, organizations can develop the strengths needed to benefit from diversity and treat it as an opportunity to enhance performance, improve current patient satisfaction, and increase market share. Moreover, as we discussed in the introduction of this chapter, globalization is becoming increasingly evident in the health care industry. Whether in medical tourism, immigration of health care professionals, and outsourcing, cultural competency will prepare HCOs to better garner from the changing face of health care.

The framework proposed in this chapter delineates the core competencies that comprise high-quality, culturally competent care and guides health care leaders on the manner through which these competencies could be achieved and maintained. This chapter achieved three major goals. First, we proposed a definition of cultural competency that addresses both individual and organizational aspects of cultural competency, as well as the structural and process elements of cultural competency in health care. Second, we established five guiding principles that are intended to be overarching and/or cross-cutting all (or multiple) domains of the proposed framework. Finally, we proposed a framework consisting of seven core competencies or domains of cultural competency: (1) leadership; (2) integration into management systems and operations; (3) patient–provider communication; (4) care delivery and supporting mechanisms; (5) workforce diversity; (6) community engagement; and (7) data collection, public accountability, and quality improvement. Each of the seven proposed domains also includes specific subdomains that further articulate the core competencies of high-quality, culturally competent care.

REFERENCES

Ad Hoc Committee on Health Literacy for the Council of Scientific Affairs Health Literacy (1999). Report of the council on scientific affairs. *Journal of American Medical Association*, *281*(6), 552–557.

Anderson, L. M., Scrimshaw, S. C., Fullilove, M. T., Fielding, J. E., Normand, J., & The Task Force on Community Preventive Services. (2003). Culturally competent healthcare systems: A systematic review. *American Journal of Preventive Medicine*, *24*(3), 68–79.

Betancourt, J. R., Green, A. R., & Carrillo, J. E. (2002). *Cultural competence in health care: Emerging frameworks and practical approaches*. New York: The Commonwealth Fund.

Betancourt, J. R., Green, A. R., & Carrillo, J. E. (2003). Defining cultural competence: A practical framework for addressing racial/ethnic disparities in health and health Care. *Public Health Reports*, *118*(4), 293–302.

Brach, C., & Fraser, I. (2000). Can cultural competency reduce racial and ethnic health disparities? A review and conceptual model. *Medical Care Research and Review*, *57*, 187–217.

Brach, C., & Fraser, I. (2002). Reducing disparities through culturally competent health care: An analysis of the business case. *Quality Management in Health Care*, *10*(4), 15–28.

Brach, C., Paez, K., & Fraser, I. (2006). *Cultural competence California style*. Rockville, MD: Agency for Healthcare Research and Quality.

California Pan-Ethnic Health Network. (2001). *Diverse patients, disparate experience: The use of standardized patient satisfaction surveys in assessing the cultural competence of health care organizations*. Oakland: California Pan-Ethnic Health Network.

Campinha-Bacote, J. (2002). The process of cultural competence in the delivery of healthcare services: A model of care. *Journal of Transcultural Nursing*, *13*(3), 181–184.

Campinha-Bacote, J., Yahle, T., & Langenkamp, M. (1996). The challenge of cultural diversity for nurse educators. *Journal of Continuing Education in Nursing*, *27*(2), 59–64.

Carrillo, J. E., Green, A. R., & Betancourt, J. R. (1999). Cross-cultural primary care: A patient-based approach. *Annals of Internal Medicine*, *33*(10), 829–834.

Center for Healthcare Strategies. (2005a). *Strategies to Assist Low-Literate Health Care Consumers*. Available at www.chcs.org/publications3960/publications_show.htm?doc_id=291711. Last accessed December 2005.

Center for Healthcare Strategies. (2005b). What is health literacy? Fact sheet 1 to 9. Available at www.chcs.org/publications3960/publications_show.htm?doc_id=291711. Last accessed December 2005.

Clark, T., Sleath, B., & Rubin, R. H. (2004). Influence of ethnicity and language concordance on physician-patient agreement about recommended changes in patient health behavior. *Patient Education and Counseling*, *53*(1), 87–93.

Cook, W. K. (2008). Integrating research and action: A systematic review of community-based participatory research to address health disparities in environmental and occupational health in the USA. *Journal of Epidemiology and Community Health*, *62*(8), 668–676.

Cooper, L. A., & Roter, D. L. (2003). Patient-provider communication: The effect of race and ethnicity on process and outcomes of healthcare. In: B. D. Smedley, A. Y. Stith, & A. R. Nelson (Eds), *Institute of Medicine. Unequal Treatment: Confronting Racial and Ethnic Disparities in Healthcare*. Washington, DC: The National Academic Press.

Cox, T. (1994). *Cultural diversity in organizations: Theory, research & practice*. San Francisco, CA: Berrett-Koehler.

Cross, T. L., Bazron, B. J., Dennis, K. W., & Isaacs, M. R. (1989). *Towards a culturally competent system of care. Vol I: A monograph on effective services for minority children who are severely emotionally disturbed*. Georgetown: National Technical Assistance Center for Children's Mental Health, Georgetown University Child Development Center.

Curtis, E. F., Dreachslin, J. L., & Sinioris, M. (2007). Diversity and cultural competency training in health care organizations: Hallmarks of success. *The Health Care Manager*, *26*(3), 255–262.

Daft, L. R., & Marcic, D. (2005). *Understanding management*. Chula Vista, CA: South-Western College Publication.

Dansky, K. H., Weech-Maldonado, R., De Souza, G., & Dreachslin, J. (2003). Organizational strategy and diversity management: Diversity sensitive orientations as a moderating influence. *Health Care Management Review*, *28*(3), 243–253.

Deloitte Center for Health Solutions. (2008). Medical tourism: Consumers in search of value. Available at http://www.deloitte.com/assets/Dcom-UnitedStates/Local%20Assets/Documents/us_chs_MedicalTourismStudy(3).pdf. Last accessed April 2011.

Department of Health & Human Services. (2008). *Healthy people 2010*. Available at www.healthypeople.gov. Last accessed October 2008.

DeRosa, N., & Kochurka, K. (2006). Implement culturally competent care in your workplace. *Nursing Management*, *37*(10), 18–26.

Dreachslin, J., & Hobby, F. (2008). Racial and ethnic disparities: Why diversity leadership matters. *Journal of Healthcare Management*, *53*(1), 8–13.

Dreachslin, J. L. (1996). *Diversity leadership*. Chicago, IL: Health Administration Press.

Dreachslin, J. L., & Myers, V. L. (2007). A systems approach to culturally and linguistically competent care. *Journal of Healthcare Management*, *42*(4), 220–226.

Enguidanos, E. R., & Rosen, P. (1997). Language as a factor affecting follow-up compliance from the emergency department. *Journal of Emergency Medicine*, *15*(1), 9–12.

Fernandez, A., Schillinger, D., Grumbach, K., et al. (2004). Physician language ability and cultural competence. An exploratory study of communication with Spanish-speaking patients. *Journal of General Internal Medicine*, *19*(2), 167–174.

Galanti, G. A. (2004). *Caring for patients from different cultures*. Pennsylvania, PA: University of Pennsylvania Press.

Grant Makers in Health. (2003). *In the right words: Addressing language and culture in providing health care*. San Francisco: Grant Makers in Health.

Hobgood, C., Sawning, S., Bowen, J., & Savage, K. (2006). Teaching culturally appropriate care: A review of educational models and methods. *Academic Emergency Medicine, 13*(12), 1288–1295.

Hrebiniak, L. G., & Joyce, W. (1984). *Implementing strategy*. New York: Macmillan Publishing Company.

Institute of Medicine. (2001). *Crossing the quality chasm: A new health system for the 21st century*. Washington, DC: Institute of Medicine, Committee on Quality Health Care in America.

Jacobs, E. A., Launderdale, D. S., Meltzer, D., et al. (2001). Impact of interpreter services on delivery of health care to limited English-proficient patients. *Journal of General Internal Medicine, 16*(7), 468–474.

Jones, L. (2009). Organization development. In: Borkowski N. (Ed.), *Organizational bevahior, theory, and design in health care*. Sudbury, MA: Jones and Bartlet Publishers.

Kim-Godwin, Y. S., Clarke, P. N., & Barton, L. (2001). A model for the delivery of culturally competent community care. *Journal of Advanced Nursing, 35*(6), 918–925.

Lavizzo-Mourey, R. (1996). Cultural competence: Essential measurements of quality for managed care organizations. *Annals of Internal Medicine, 124*(10), 919–921.

Lewin Group. (2002). *Indicators of cultural competence in health care delivery organizations: An organizational cultural competence: Assessment profile*. Falls Church: The Lewin Group.

Longest, B. B., Rakich, S. J., & Darr, K. (2000). *Managing health services organizations and systems*. Baltimore, MD: Health Professions Press.

Louis, M. (1983). Culture: Yes. Organization: No. Paper Presented at the annual meeting of the Academy of Management, Dallas.

Marin, G., & Marin, B. V. (1991). *Research with Hispanic populations*. Newbury Park, CA: Sage Publications.

Muller, H. J., & Haase, B. E. (1994). Managing diversity in health services organizations. *Hospital & Health Services Administration, 39*(4), 415–434.

National Quality Forum. (2009). *A comprehensive framework and preferred practices for measuring and reporting cultural competency*. Washington, DC: National Quality Forum.

Ngo-Metzger, Q., Telfair, J., Sorkin, D. L., et al. (2006). *Cultural competency and quality of care: Obtaining the patient's perspective*. New York: The Commonwealth Fund.

Office of Minority Health. (2001). *National standards for culturally and linguistically appropriate services in health care: Final report*. Washington, DC: US Department of Health and Human Services; Office of Minority Health.

Perez-Stable, E. J., Napoles-Springer, A., & Miramontes, J. M. (1997). The effects of ethnicity and language on medical outcomes of patients with hypertension or diabetes. *Medical Care, 35*(12), 1212–1219.

Romeo, C. (2007). Caring for culturally diverse patients: One agency's journey toward cultural competence. *Home Healthcare Nurse, 25*(3), 206–213.

Sanders, J., & Ewart, B. (2005). Developing cultural competence for healthcare leaders through work based learning. *Work-Based Learning in Primary Care, 3*, 99–105.

Scott, W. R., & Davis, G. F. (2007). *Organizations and organizing: Rational, natural and open system perspective*. Upper Saddle River, NJ: Pearson/Prentice Hall.

Seijo, R., Gomez, H., & Freidenberg, J. (1991). Language as a communication barrier in medical care for Hispanic patients. *Hispanic Journal of Behavioral Sciences, 13*(4), 363–376.

Shortell, S. M., & Kalunzy, D. A. (1999). *Health care management: Organization design & behavior*. New York: Thomson Delmar Learning.

Siegel, C., Haugland, G., & Chambers, E. D. (2003). Performance measures and their benchmarks for assessing organizational cultural competency in behavioral health care service delivery. *Administration and Policy in Mental Health*, *31*(2), 141–170.

Smircich, L. (1983). Concepts of culture and organizational analysis. *Administrative Science Quarterly*, *28*, 339–358.

Tirado, M. (1998). *Monitoring the managed care of culturally and linguistically diverse populations*. Washington, DC: The National Clearinghouse for Primary Care Information.

Tocher, T. M., & Larson, E. B. (1999). Do physicians spend more time with non-English-speaking patients? *Journal of General Internal Medicine*, *14*(5), 303–309.

Viswanathan, M., Ammerman, A., Eng, E., Gartlehner, G., Lohr, K. N., Griffith, D., Rhodes, S., Samuel-Hodge, C., Maty, S., Lux, L., Webb, L., Sutton, S. F., Swinson, T., Jackman, A., & Whitener, L. (2004). *Community-based participatory research: Assessing the evidence*. Rockville, MD: Agency for Healthcare Research and Quality.

Weech-Maldonado, R., Dreachslin, J. L., Dansky, K. H., De Souza, G., & Gatto, M. (2002). Racial/ethnic diversity management and cultural competency: The case of Pennsylvania hospitals. *Journal of Healthcare Management*, *47*(2), 111–124.

Weech-Maldonado, R., Elliot, M. N., Morales, L. S., Spritzer, K., Marshall, G., Grant, N., & Hays, R. D. (2004). Health plan effects on patient assessments of Medicaid managed care among racial/ethnic minorities. *Journal of General Internal Medicine*, *19*(2), 136–145.

Weech-Maldonado, R., & Merrill, S. B. (2000). Building partnerships with the community: Lessons from the Camden Health Improvement Learning Collaborative. *Journal of Healthcare Management*, *45*(3), 189–205.

Weech-Maldonado, R., Morales, L. S., Elliot, M. N., Spritzer, K., Marshall, G., & Hays, R. D. (2003). Race/Ethnicity, language and patient's assessments of care in Medicaid managed care. *Health Services Research*, *38*(3), 789–808.

Weech-Maldonado, R., Weidmer, B. O., Morales, L. S., & Hays, R. D. (2001). Cross-cultural adaptation of survey instruments: The CAHPS experience. In: M. Cynamon & R. Kulka (Eds), *Seventh Conference on Health Survey Research Methods* (pp. 75–82). Hyattsville, MD: DHHS. Available at www.cdc.gov/nchs/data/conf/conf07.pdf. Last accessed October 2008.

Weidmer, B., Hurtado, M., Weech-Maldonado, R., Ngo-Metzger, Q., & Bogen, K. (2006). *Guidelines for translating CAHPS surveys*. Rockville: Agency for Healthcare Research and Quality.

Weiner, B. J., Alexander, J. A., Shortell, S. M., Baker, L. C., Becker, M., & Geppert, J. J. (2006). Quality improvement implementation and hospital performance on quality indicators. *Health Services Research*, *42*(2), 307–334.

Williams, M. V., Davis, T., Parker, R. M., & Weiss, B. D. (2002). The role of health literacy in patient-physician communication. *Family Medicine*, *34*(5), 383–389.

Wilson-Stronks, A., & Galvez, E. (2007). *Hospitals, language and culture: A snapshot of the nation. exploring cultural and linguistic services in the nation's hospitals*. Joint Commission on Accreditation of Healthcare Organizations. Oakbrook Terrace.

THE ROLE OF MISSION, ORGANIZATIONAL CULTURE, AND CULTURAL COMPETENCY IN FURTHERING THE DEVELOPMENT OF HEALTH CARE ORGANIZATIONS: A COMMENTARY

Margarete Arndt and Barbara Bigelow

INTRODUCTION

We appreciate the editors' invitation to comment on these three papers, and we thank the authors for giving us so much food for thought. The papers linked together well conceptually. We can see an organization's mission necessitating cultural competency in service delivery and an organization's culture enhancing or hindering fulfillment of a mission or the commitment to cultural competency. In this commentary we will look at these papers from three different lenses – the nature of evidence, the role of normative admonitions in health care literature, and historical context – as a way to raise questions that link these papers to broader issues that affect health care

Organization Development in Healthcare: Conversations on Research and Strategies
Advances in Health Care Management, Volume 10, 69–74

ISSN: 1474-8231/doi:10.1108/S1474-8231(2011)0000010010

research. Since we are commenting on the chapters "blind," we cannot refer to the authors by name. For brevity's sake we will refer to the chapters as the Culture paper, the Mission paper, and the Competency paper.

THE NATURE OF EVIDENCE

Health care organizations operate in a climate where the expectations, for better or worse, are that managers use evidence as the basis for practice; that evidence can be developed as it is in medicine, i.e., through systematic reviews and meta-analyses; and that it can be applied rationally to management decisions. We have raised a cautionary note about these assumptions, pointing out, for example, that health care management practice often is influenced by politics and power and that in such a context evidence itself can take on multiple meanings (Arndt & Bigelow, 2009). In this connection we find the work of Tranfield, Denyer, and Smart (2003), which is cited in the *Mission* paper useful. Tranfield et al. (2003) lay out why systematic reviews and meta-analyses as they are conducted in medicine are not likely approaches in management: Management studies are often qualitative, do not usually ask identical research questions or measure variables the same way, and do not usually provide raw data for meta-analyses.

Tranfield et al. (2003) suggest an alternative in the form of a "narrative review" (p. 217) that relies on interpretation rather than quantitative re-analysis and provides a broad description of the field. While at first glance this sounds like a thorough traditional literature review, Tranfield et al. (2003) see it as going further through well-developed categories of information that constitute an "audit trail" (p. 218). This approach allows readers to make their own assessment about the quality of the evidence authors use to support a point and illustrate their reasoning. If we apply Tranfield et al.'s (2003) approach to these three papers, we could envision a narrative that explicates categories including the industries in which cited research took place (e.g., health care, nuclear energy, transportation, banking, manufacturing), the nature of articles (e.g., theoretical, empirical, practitioner anecdote, consultant's prescription), or the location where the research was conducted (e.g., the United States or other countries). This would allow researchers to clarify what is already known and agreed upon in the field (Tranfield et al., 2003) and provide evidence to support their own contributions to the field. Evidence from such a narrative review would also be helpful to practitioners who gain insight into what worked where, for whom, and under what circumstances as they assess the extent to which practices from other organizations might be applicable to their own organization. For example, it may be important for a health care manager to know when studies cited in an article come from research in other countries with different health care or reimbursement systems.

The three papers differ in how they present information. The *Culture* paper provides the results of a survey but without sufficient context to assess the application of the evidence beyond this institution. The *Mission* paper expressly refers to Tranfield et al. (2003) as it promises a "systematic review" of empirical literature in health care (p. 34) as the basis for "evidence-based" recommendations to managers around mission statements. Yet the authors fall short of their ambition. The paper does not identify the "7 electronic [databases]" that were searched and provides no systematic information on what the search yielded. For another, the section on findings draws on a small number of articles, and many of those had already been cited earlier in the paper. In our estimation, this does not create a satisfactory audit trail that lets the readers assess the quality of the evidence underlying the recommendations.

The *Competency* paper provides the most thorough literature review. While it was not designed by the authors to follow the Tranfield et al. (2003) approach, it nonetheless created an overall impression that knowledge has been accumulating in the field and was ready to be translated into a proposed framework for consideration by managers. It will remain an empirical question what outcomes are achieved by managers who adopt this framework. Only empirical research along those lines will create "evidence" about what factors are associated with what results under what conditions, and in what health care organizations.

NORMATIVE ADMONITIONS

We have noted over the years that material from the private sector is often included in health care research (be it the literature review, framing of research questions, or discussion) without qualification, revealing an underlying assumption that practices and behaviors in the not-for-profit sector are (or should be) the same as in the private sector, and that management practices from the latter can be readily transferred into the not-for-profit sector (Arndt & Bigelow, 2000). The three papers avoid this to varying degrees.

In the case of the *Mission* paper, we wonder whether its broad framing adequately distinguishes between health care organizations and firms in other industries. Organizations in the private sector operate under a mandate for profitability, which must influence organizational decisions at all levels. We believe that this may include consideration of what mission statement the organization can "afford." In contrast, in a not-for-profit organization the mission statement itself is the overall mandate (Rangan, 2004).

The *Culture* paper offers a limited literature review that does include material from the private sector, but the authors are careful in the methods and discussion sections to point out differences between health care workers and the general workforce. Thus, this chapter brackets the assumption that findings from the private sector are equally applicable to health care and can be translated directly into prescriptions for health care managers. Finally, the *Competency* paper draws overwhelmingly on writings from the health care sector in its extensive literature survey. The question of whether business practices are directly applicable to health care remains an empirical question, mostly because it has received so little attention, given the widespread enthusiasm about viewing health care organizations as just another "business."

In our work we have noted that despite the pervasive concern with evidence, normative admonitions absent evidence still play a central role in the literature when attention is turned to implications for managers. Based on these three chapters, health care managers should measure their organizational culture, develop seven core competencies with respect to cultural competency, and develop a mission statement using a carefully crafted development and implementation plan. In reality it is unlikely that many health care managers would be able to follow these admonitions, especially when they are combined with the myriad other admonitions managers are told to follow in order to survive in an increasingly hostile environment.

The *Culture* paper begins with an overview of culture based on the conceptual framework of Detert, Schroeder, and Mauriel (2000) and moves to a brief summary of how communication "enhanced the successful transformation of MUSC-MC." The link between communications in MUSC-MC and the need for health care organizations in general to measure culture is unclear, leaving the normative prescription that health care organizations should commit time and resources to the dissemination and analysis of the survey. *Mission* comes closest to providing a compelling argument for developing a mission statement but the audit trail needs strengthening before claiming that "the success of any health care [*sic*] organization is the development of a meaningful mission statement."

Most dramatic are the normative prescriptions in the *Competency* paper where the term "should" occurs dozens of times. The paper begins with the statement that cultural competency is "crucial for the success and even survival of health care delivery organizations." We do not wish to argue that being patient centered is bad or unnecessary for a health care organization, but the leap to the large number of normative requirements embedded in the seven core competencies raises concerns. Is it necessary to the survival of health care organizations that they do all of this? Warnings like this have been attached to many normative admonitions in the past, and if there is empirical evidence that failure to incorporate any or all of these practices has led to the demise of health care organizations, it should be cited.

HISTORICAL CONTEXT

We would like to return now to the topics of mission, organizational culture, and cultural competency from a historical perspective. The *Mission* paper implies that there could be something faddish about the interest in mission statements, and we resonate to that with respect to the private sector. In the not-for-profit sector, however, the concept of a larger societal purpose for health care organizations goes back very far. Looking at hospitals, for example, conversations about their purpose arose at the very beginning of the hospital movement in this country. It encompassed not only the care for acutely ill patients, but also a role as the "chief factor in the process of remolding and remaking the modern social fabric" (Modern Hospital, 1913, p. 32), guardian of public health with respect to "garbage disposal, smoke elimination, pure water, housing conditions ..." (Modern Hospital, 1915, p. 345), and aid in the "Americanization" of foreign-born patients and employees (Modern Hospital, 1919, p. 46).

As to the need for cultural competency, we know that hospitals in urban areas dealt with large numbers of foreigners and that they approached them very differently. For example, the superintendent of one hospital described them as "aliens" with "little ambition" and "inclined to become dependent" (Sanborn, 1914, p. 7). In contrast, another institution employed a teacher to teach convalescing patients reading, writing, and arithmetic. It was described as part of an effort to "[win] every immigrant, man and woman, with whom there is a chance, for America" (Modern Hospital, 1919, p. 46).

These three papers made us reflect on what is different now. One difference is how societal expectations of hospitals ostensibly focus on their role as a business while implicitly still adhering to the older definition of the hospital as a charitable institution with wide-ranging purposes. There is no doubt in our mind that this must put stress on internal organizational cultures. Another difference is that cultural competency is a topic in many more institutions as a result of geographic changes. The authors of the *Competency* paper link it to "better patient care." While one can see this as a part of a continuing quest for hearts and minds, we are concerned that such a specific goal could become equated with socializing patients into current concepts of "good" patient care and compliance with today's favored treatment regimens to satisfy organizational goals.

On that note, let us say thank you again to the editors and authors.

REFERENCES

Arndt, M. & Bigelow, B. (2000). The transfer of business practices into hospitals: History and implications. In: J. Blair, M. Fottler, & G. Savage (Eds), *Advances in health care management* (Vol. 1, pp. 339–368). Bingley, UK: Emerald.

Arndt, M., & Bigelow, B. (2009). Evidence-based management in health care organizations: A cautionary note. *Health Care Management Review*, *34*(3), 206–213.

Detert, J. R., Schroeder, R. G., & Mauriel, J. J. (2000). A framework for linking culture and improvement initiatives in organizations. *Academy of Management Review*, *25*, 850–863.

Modern Hospital. (1913). Salutatory. *1*, 32–33.

Modern Hospital. (1915). Hospitals and the public health. *5*, 345–346.

Modern Hospital. (1919). Americanization work in hospitals. *12*, 46.

Rangan, V. K. (2004). Lofty missions, down-to-earth plans. *Harvard Business Review*, *82*(3), 112–119.

Sanborn, C. F. (1914). The value of convalescent labor in hospital work. *Modern Hospital*, *3*, 7–10.

Tranfield, D., Denyer, D., & Smart, P. (2003). Towards a methodology for developing evidence-informed management knowledge by means of systematic review. *British Journal of Management*, *14*, 207–222.

PART II
CHANGE

EMPLOYEE ENGAGEMENT: A PRESCRIPTION FOR ORGANIZATIONAL TRANSFORMATION

Barry Halm

ABSTRACT

Ivanitskaya, Glazer, and Erofeev (2009) suggest that "the most fundamental element of any organization that helps the organization to survive is the individual person" (p. 109). It is the motivation of human capital that makes a health care organization come to life. Health care is a unique industry; its accomplishments are directly dependent upon the competencies and technical skills of its employees. "When people in the workplace fulfill their organizational roles, then the organization thrives" (Ivanitskaya et al., 2009, p. 110). Health care systems will require organizations that thrive and exhibit characteristics of continuous growth, expressing excessive levels of energy and an immense capacity for flourishing. Anticipating the challenges of the next decade, health care organizations must achieve a higher degree of employee engagement to enhance organizational performance and profitability. The data analyzed for this chapter indicate that employees who are engaged are more enthusiastic and aspired to achieve both individual and organizational success. The chapter concludes by suggesting five operating practices to

Organization Development in Healthcare: Conversations on Research and Strategies
Advances in Health Care Management, Volume 10, 77–96

ISSN: 1474-8231/doi:10.1108/S1474-8231(2011)0000010011

establish an employee engagement culture – defining the employee's role in fulfilling the organization's purpose, selecting employees with capability and passion, supporting and valuing the employee, creating sustainable reward systems, and developing feedback and reinforcement mechanisms.

Keywords: Employee engagement; motivation; organization change; transformational change

OVERVIEW OF THE HEALTH CARE DELIVERY SYSTEM

Since the inception of the American health care system, the system has been in a continual state of transformation as it sought to find balance between the cost effectiveness in the delivery of health care, providing equal access for all citizens, and affirming the highest quality provided within a safe environment. This increased mandate for high-quality, cost-effective health care that is accessible to all citizens has generated a process of continuous improvement, implemented across the health care industry. Cummings and Worley (2005) defined continuous improvement as "designing and managing all aspects of an organization in a never-ending quest for quality" (p. 662). Throughout the decades the health care system has been challenged by declining reimbursement, increasing competition, escalating mandated regulation, and an ever advancing evolution in the science of medicine. In addition, government is demanding a reduction in the escalating cost of health care, but simultaneously desiring the same or higher levels of care for its citizens. A transformational response to these environmental factors can only be accomplished through an organizational culture that requires full engagement of an organization's workforce.

This evolution of change has escalated through the twentieth century, with Medicare and Medicaid legislation in the 1960s, which expanded the availability of health benefits to the elderly and society's poor. The 1970s brought expansion of facilities and services requiring a mandate for health planning and Certificate of Need laws. The 1980s generated escalated health care costs driven by enhanced levels of competition and expansion of select clinical services in the disciplines of cardiology and oncology. Price controls were enacted, and Prospective Payment was created to deal with this ever increasing cost of health care delivery. The 1990s brought a new dimension to the delivery of health care by generating new technology that allows for less invasive and safer clinical practice, which led to the growth of ambulatory care services and outpatient surgery.

The twenty-first century introduced new pressures of cost containment, concepts of managed care, and a complexity of the integrated delivery organization. The first decade of the twenty-first century found the American health care system in an economic crisis. In November 2008, the American Hospital Association released the results of a "rapid response survey" that represented data gathered from 736 hospitals in 30 states. This survey reported that in the quarter ended September 30, 2008, hospitals posted negative profit margins of 1.6% in comparison to the same quarter a year earlier reflecting a positive 6.1% margin. It was during March 2009 that Moody's Investment Services and in July 2009 that Standard & Poors Investment Services each issued a report that identified the declining financial health of "not-for-profit" hospitals. Both Moody's and Standard & Poors revised their outlook for the acute hospital sector to negative from stable due to weakening profitability and a deterioration of balance sheet strength. It is clearly evident that today's health care system is dramatically different from those of generation ago.

RESPONSE TO A CHANGING ENVIRONMENT

The economic downturn of 2008 through 2009 has impacted the financial health of hospitals and health care systems, eroding the financial viability of those organizations and threatening the stability of the total health care system. As the general economy falters and unemployment rises hospitals find themselves impacted by falling revenues, declining admissions, and negative investment earnings. These factors (driven by a recession) confirm significant financial challenges and economic pressures being placed upon the health care system, which will require most organizations to consider reducing operational costs in an effort to achieve profitability. The most prevalent method to reduce overhead costs is staff reductions and program elimination; both impacting job security and employee self-esteem.

Private and public sectors have collectively increased their mandate demanding higher-quality, cost-effective health care that is accessible to all citizens. These demands coupled with the current economic environment has placed the U.S. health care system at the juxtaposition of responding to the changing patterns of health care and medical delivery, while at the same time reducing the costs associated with providing health care services – forcing hospitals into a state of radical adjustment and organized transformation. Such modification will have a profound impact upon an organization's culture, the morale of its employees, and the functional role of employees within these newly designed health delivery organizations and systems.

The health care system is confronted with two critical external events – an escalating mandate for a new method in the way health care is delivered (i.e., expansion of coverage for all citizens and enhancing the efficacy for the care being delivered) and initiating a permanent process of cost containment that slows the rapid increases in health care costs. Simultaneous to these external events, new economic limitations are forcing internal adaptations with the way health care organizations operate. Health care workers are confronted with changing roles and responsibilities that are modifying both the way care is delivered and the means by which patients are receiving treatment. The increasing complexity in the delivery of health care has required organizations to become less structured and more adaptive, flexible, and responsive. These organizational dynamics impact the role, functions, and duties of each health care worker.

In times past, a proficient nurse was one that took physician orders without questioning, documented the patient's condition in a written medical record, and provided a regional standard of clinical competence. Today, that same professional nurse must have both clinical and managerial proficiency to be a member of a multidisciplinary care team, possess critical thinking skills responsive to the changing science of medicine, and able to provide a national standard of clinical competence. Work is much more demanding – blending the complexity of medicine with the compassion demanded by patients, the stress of delivering technology-based medicine, and the anxiety created by increasing expectations for cost-effective services delivered in a safe atmosphere.

These environmental characteristics have reshaped the way work is deployed, requiring looser supervision and creating a greater need for employees to be totally engaged in the performance of their work (Thomas, 2009). This new world of health care delivery requires employees to have a new set of professional skills and competencies, a deep sense of personal satisfaction in the service to others, and the ability to operate in a chaotic and rapidly changing environment. In today's economic climate, health care organizations will require greater employee involvement, which demands individual empowerment, the delegation of authority, and the freedom that allows employees to make intelligent decisions.

CREATING A PLATFORM FOR EMPLOYEE INVOLVEMENT

Ivanitskaya, Glazer, & Erofeev (2009) suggest that "the most fundamental element of any organization that helps the organization to survive is the individual person" (p. 109). It is the motivation of human capital that makes a health care organization come to life. Health care is a unique industry; its accomplishments are directly dependent upon the competencies and technical skills of its employees. "When people in the workplace fulfill their organizational roles, then the organizations thrives" (Ivanitskaya et al., 2009, p. 110). Health care systems will require organizations that thrive and exhibit characteristics of continuous growth, expressing excessive levels of energy and an immense capacity for flourishing.

Anticipating the challenges of the next decade, health care organizations must achieve a higher degree of employee engagement to enhance organizational performance and profitability. Cameron, Dutton, and Quinn (2003) wrote that "today employee empowerment is viewed as an essential element in the management of change, or the ability of an organization to adjust to internal and external factors and to hone and improve upon the services or products of the organization" (p. 347). Since human capital is an essential component and represents the greatest economic cost to a health care organization, the effective and efficient use of human capital can improve productivity, enhance patient quality, and generate greater economic returns.

Thomas (2009) suggests that "organizations need workers to take an active responsibility for handling more and more of the uncertainties involved in the accomplishment of their purpose" (p. 19). Fulfillment of the organization's purpose or mission is the collective responsibility of the employed workers. An organization's success is directly related to the commitment and engagement of the employees who work for the organization. "Your employee's decisions, attitudes, and actions make or break your organization ability to innovate, deliver superior customer service, and manage cost efficiently".

Gebauer and Lowman (2008) introduced the concepts of employee engagement as the most important operational strategy for today's organizations when they wrote, "the most valuable source of high performance and competitive advantage is a workforce that consistently performs at its best. But employees do their best only if they're engaged in their work" (p. vii). Cameron et al. (2003) share a perspective that in today's environment "empowered employees are also viewed as an essential feature of decentralized systems that build control around results, rather than inputs, written rules, and processes" (p. 347).

The evolution of medicine and the demands of an aging society have lead to heightened expectations in the performance of the health delivery system; demanding more direct accountability and higher quality of care outcomes. Health care organizations are responding to these new pressures through the adoption of clinical practice guideline, introduction of integrated delivery methods, implementation of new treatment modalities, and development of health care information infrastructure. These efforts are transforming the organizational structure and operational methods/practices of health care organizations. They are also requiring employees to function in collaborative partnerships, generating new and unique ideas to find solutions for complex problems and issues, and being recognized for the professionalism they provide in achieving the common purpose of the organization (Freshman, Rubino, & Chassiakos, 2010).

Health care organizations confronted with an environment of continuous change must construct an organizational culture that will produce highly engaged and committed employees. Without engaged employees, health care organizations will not be able to cross the widening chasm, which will be created by health care reform. The demands by society for a health care system that provides equal access for all citizens, at the highest attainable level of quality, and within reasonable costs will require excessive levels of employee participation in both the design and delivery of health care services.

EMPLOYEE MOTIVATION

Employee engagement is directly related to the level of motivation that an individual engenders when performing their assigned tasks, enhancing a product or service, or working more collaboratively with colleagues. For employee to be fully engaged there must be three influencing factors at play – the appropriate work environment, retention of the skills to perform the required tasks, and the motivation to perform at an optimal level (Johnson, 2009). The literature reveals that motivation is influenced by two conditions – extrinsic motivational elements or intrinsic motivational elements.

Most health care organizations are proficient in implementing extrinsic motivators such as compensation, recognition, and job promotion. These extrinsic rewards were excellent means of motivation when employees were closely supervised and the standard of conduct were rigidly dictated – offering little flexibility and personal adaptation. However, intrinsic motivators are less likely implemented, such as worker-directed performance, personal enrichment programming, and self-management processes. Health care organizations will need engaged and empowered workers who are energized through the constant intervention of intrinsic motivators to function in the health care systems of the future.

Thomas (2009) describes four intrinsic rewards that drive employee engagement. These four intrinsic rewards relate to the concept of *self-management* required by today's health care workforce. Self-management produces "the sense of meaningfulness, the sense of choice, the sense of competence, and the sense of progress," which is motivated from the individualized spirit of the employee (Thomas, 2009, p. 193). Thomas' model suggests that employees must be committed to the mission, vision, and values of an organization, which is needed to create an environment of meaningfulness. "Meaningfulness is about the passion you have for a task purpose" (Thomas, 2009, p. 51).

Health care workers need to be connected to the organization and feel passionate about their role within that organization. The intrinsic reward of choice is reflected by "being able to do what makes sense to you to accomplish the purpose" (Thomas, 2009, p. 54). Choice provides the freedom to perform those activities that will achieve the stated objectives of the health care organization while utilizing the employee's unique talents and experiences. The third intrinsic reward is compliance, which is acquiring the skills necessary to produce at peak performance. Thomas described compliance as performing activities most competently and in such a way "that performing well is making an important difference in achieving something you care about" (p. 56). The final intrinsic reward is progress or the reinforcement of achieving desired results. Thomas describes progress as "having a meaningful purpose can be enough for you to begin a task with enthusiasm, but you need to keep experiencing a sense of progress toward that purpose in order to sustain that enthusiasm" (p. 57). Health care organizations must create operations processes that emulate the four intrinsic rewards of self-management, which results in a perpetual culture of enthusiastic employee engagement.

Kimball and Nink's (2006) research drew some interesting findings based on intrinsic motivators – engaged workers have a stronger commitment to the organization and have higher levels of productivity. The authors also found that matching the job demands with the strengths of the employee have higher levels of performance, are more innovative, and strive to become highly effective. These findings were confirmed by an earlier study by Baard, Deci, and Ryan (2004) who found that the intrinsic motivator of satisfaction at work was related to greater levels of performance. Thus, intrinsic motivators lead to engaged employees and, as a secondary result, higher levels of productivity and profitability, which are in much demand by health care organizations in these economic times.

Cameron et al. (2003) reviewed the constructs of employee empowerment linking it to participatory management, drawing an association with employees defining the work of the organization and creating an environment that "breaks through bureaucratic tendons that constrain the capacity of organizations to innovate and change" (p. 347). Cameron et al. identify the transformative form of empowerment because the process involves "altering and building relationships that share and create power" (p. 350). Cameron et al.'s concept of shared power is a critical component to employee empowerment. The authors suggest that a manager who retains "formal authority uses it in a way that generates power by sharing it with others" creates a collaborative connection and generate new capacity of organizational performance (p. 350). Based upon Cameron's works, health care organizations must develop management arrangements through the sharing of decision making responsibility with groups of employees to create an environment of innovation and empowerment.

CREATING EMPLOYEE ENGAGEMENT

Thomas (2009) defined worker engagement as individuals who are "engaged in the new work to the extent that they are actively self-managing at that work" (p. 11). Thomas suggests that worker reach a level of engagement when they are committed to the organization's mission, having the ability to use their intelligence to make choices about their role and responsibilities, and provided with information about how their performance accomplishes the purposes of the organization.

Gebauer and Lowman defined employee engagement as "a deep and broad connection that employees have with a company that results in a willingness to go above and beyond what's expected of them to help their company succeed" (p. 9). These authors suggest that for engagement to be successful, the connection of the employer and employee must occur at three levels – (1) employees' ability to understand their role and responsibilities within the organization; (2) employees' personal passion and energy for their work; and (3) employees' capability and proficiency to perform their role and tasks. Gebauer and Lowman's (2009) definition is constructed on the premise that "the employee understands what to do to help her company succeed, she feels emotionally connected to the organization and its leaders, and she is willing to put that knowledge and emotion into action to improve performance, her own and the organization" (p. 10).

Another view of employee engagement is presented by Cummings and Worley (2005). They use the term employee involvement to describe the concept of engaged employees. These authors described "engagement as seeking to increase members' input into decisions that affect organization performance and employee well-being" (p. 306). They conclude with a definition of employee involvement as including four elements that promote meaningful involvement in the workplace: power, information, knowledge and skills, and reward. Cummings and Worley (2005) suggest that power means providing employees with the authority, responsibility, and accountability to make work-related decisions. They believe that employees can contribute to the success of the organization only if they have the required skills and knowledge to perform the work and make good decisions. The authors state that information needs to flow freely to those who have decisional responsibility. Finally, the authors shared that intrinsic and extrinsic rewards when linked to performance outcomes enhance employee engagement (Cummings & Worley, 2005).

These researchers have not only provided a definition of employee engagement but also provided insight into the elements that promote and sustain an environment of engagement. For health care organizations to prosper, professional staff and management team members must be engaged in their work and the performance of the organization. Developing enthusiastic and aspired employees is a critical task in achieving both individual and organization success. The primary purpose of health care managers is to create a culture where employees are fully involved and energized by the work they do within the organization. Engaged employees care about the future of the organization and are willing to invest in the future success of the organization through their individual and collective actions (Seijts & Crim, 2006).

INDIVIDUAL AND ORGANIZATIONAL ENGAGEMENT

Individual employee engagement is a prerequisite to the development of organizational engagement. Linking the individual employee to each other and the organization is supported by the level of social connectivity that exists within the organization. Creating a strong family atmosphere in the workplace and energetic collegial connections will lead to a dynamic social life. Sandelands (1995) suggests that social life within an organization is developed through the use of language and interactions between the organization's participants. Social life creates powerful relationships and organizational capacity (Sandelands, 1995).

Health care organizations should develop programming that enhances the feeling of *valuing the individual* and strengthen the collegial relationships among the employees. Many organizations promote that employees are *their most important asset/resource*. However, promotional statements are often developed with little direct connection to the employee development functions implemented within the organization. Personal engagement is constructed on the collective feeling of employees being valued. The social life in and of organizations is created through the interrelationship of individuals (Sandelands, 1995). Thus, health care organizations need to focus on both valuing the individual and communal relationships among its employees.

Some health care organizations use the term family when describing the relationship among and between employees. Glynn and Wrobel (2007) discuss how organizations that reflected family relationships both increased social capital and enabled strategic adaptation. The identification and implementation of familial relationships as an operational ideology of a firm create an endogenous resource to achieve the objectives of the firm. Organizations that create a culture founded upon familial relationships develop an internal capacity for continuous positive identity. Glynn and Wrobel (2007) describe organizations that create "positive identity" as those organizations that can provide an "attractive, legitimate, or desirable [service] that serves as a touchstone for customer, employee, or public identification and that legitimates its products and services" (p. 308). They continue to suggest that positive identity provides "a more positive view of the way in which family functions in service of business goals" (p. 309). The notion of family in organizational life is embedded in the structure, culture, and operational methods employed by health care organizations. The authors claim that, "family relationships are arguably the most enduring of all relationships" (p. 307).

Putnam (2000) introduced the concept of "social capital" that connects individuals in a common purpose within networks of relationships. Creating social capital develops an intrinsic resource that allows management to achieve the organization's mission or purpose of being. Glynn and Wrobel (2007) conclude with the suggestion that health care managers could use familial relationship to enhance the implementation of strategy, promote trust, and achieve institutional purpose. The authors propose that organizations could create "positive synergy between the institution of family and the institution of the firm" (p. 322).

Kahn (1990) recognized that individuals who are valued and engaged offer greater creativity, authenticity, ethical behavior, and speak with a personal voice to the workplace. Kahn's works discussed the concepts of engagement and its effect on organizational effectiveness. Kahn's research was an in-depth approach to determine psychological experiences of work and how work shaped the processes of people's engagement or disengagement in task performance. The concept of engagement, or as Cummings and Worley (2005) suggest, "*employee involvement*, provides an expanded definition of the role employees play in organizational success. The term *employee involvement* places emphasis on how employees can contribute more to running the organization so it can be more flexible, productive, and competitive" (p. 12).

Kahn proposed a definition of engagement that centers on a "person's *preferred self* in task behaviors that promote connections to work and to others" (1990, p. 700). People's personal engagements and/or disengagements have an influencing effect on their involvement and commitment at work (Kahn, 1990). Cummings and Worley (2005) corroborate Kahn's work by confirming that much of the employee involvement leads to higher productivity: "Studies have found a consistent relationship between *employee involvement* practices and such measures as productivity, financial performance, customer satisfaction, labor hours and waste rates" (p. 308). Health care organizations that have implemented some form of employee involvement programming has seen increased levels of employee participation, which generated positive outcomes such as enhanced productivity and improved financial performance.

A seminal work by Dutton and Ragins (2007) describes the dynamics of positive relationships at work. The authors review connections at work, emphasizing the importance of the different levels in the human connection within organizations. They suggest that sustainable organizational performance and effective individual development are directly dependent on workplace relationships. They believe that employees of today are more tied to personal relationships than to the organization itself. The authors propose that organizational performance is related to the positive relationships that exist within an organization: "Workplaces and work itself are increasingly interdependent, making connection the norm and relationships the means by which work occurs" (p. 6).

Other authors such as Blatt and Ashford (2006) discussed how meaning-making assists in sustaining goal-directed activity in organizations with workers who have a high degree of independence such as health care professionals. These authors found that professionals operate more independently desiring freedom from direct organizational influence and requiring less managerial supervision. Blatt and Ashford suggest that independent professionals use meaning-making practices to resolve specific kinds of on-the-job tensions and to provide a sense of flexibility that allows them to perform and find meaningfulness at work. Blatt and Ashford believe that the ability to set aside distractions and environmental conflicts "allows independent workers to focus mental energies toward sustaining goal-directed activity" (p. 42). The health care system is a hallmark industry whose workers have a high degree of job independence and goal-directed activity. Because of the professionalism and technical training of the health care worker, these individuals will be well positioned to respond to a changing system of care delivery as long as the organizational culture perpetuates employee involvement, managerial flexibility, and meaningfulness at work.

DEVELOPING HIGH-PERFORMING TEAMS

The delivery of health care services is provided by high-performing teams connected through collaborative efforts to meet the needs of each individual patient. Connectivity is a concept studied by Losada and Heaphy (2004), who noted that team flourishing is related to the interactions of team members. The collaborative nature of team members may be related to team functioning. In fact, Losada and Heaphy conducted a study on connectivity, which revealed that, "the connectivity of the team is strongly linked to its performance" (p. 748). The relationships among health care team members and their interlocked behaviors generate and represent the level of the team's connectivity in the way patient care is delivered. The authors found that high-performing teams have a high level of connectivity, emulating liberating and enriching organizational performance (Losada & Heaphy, 2004).

Dutton and Glynn (2008) contend that organizations can enhance performance through flourishing by leveraging the processes of positive meaning making, positive emoting, and positive interrelating. The authors suggest that one means of enhancing the concept of flourishing is through leadership (p. 15). Dutton and Glynn describe the positive state generated by the optimal functioning of organizations and they constructed a framework that seeks to explain "behavior in and of organizations" (p. 1). According to the authors, there are three core features of positive organizational scholarship: flourishing, development of strengths, and the generative dynamics of organizing. The main premise of Dutton and Glynn's work is that flourishing and strength-building creates an opportunity for optimal functioning of health care teams and related organizations.

Positive meaning-making is described as "processes in which people imbue stimuli with significance, implications, and consequences that imply something is good, desirable or beneficial in some way" (Dutton & Glynn, 2008, p. 10). In a working paper by Blatt and Ashford (2006), the authors noted that individuals with more enjoyment and greater satisfaction at work were more effective and productive, including more resilient in times of hardship or organizational change. Among their conclusions is that employees who operated more independently and had a greater capacity to enjoy and to make work more meaningful had a positive impact on the total organization. Dutton and Glynn (2008) contend that the collective positive meaning of individuals within an organization can foster flourishing through heighten levels of cooperation.

Positive emoting refers to the feelings of positive emotions – "joy, contentment, gratitude and excitement" – by individuals or groups (Dutton & Glynn, 2008, p. 13). Dutton and Glynn (2008) propose that positive emoting creates resources that promote flourishing. When [health care] employees are led by managers who evoke positive emotions and who express positive effect, the result is heightened group performance (Anderson, Keltner, & John, 2003; Anderson & Thompson, 2004; Dutton & Glynn, 2008).

Positive interrelating is defined as patterns of interrelationships between individuals. It "captures modes of interacting where the parties engaged experience their connection as mutual, thrusting, respectful and mutually beneficial" (Dutton & Glynn, 2008, p. 14). Dutton and Glynn suggest that positive interrelating contributes to flourishing, "which enables the favorable resource flow and exchanges that build economic, financial, reputational, human and social capital" (p. 14) (see also Lounsbury & Glynn, 2001). Today more than any time in the historical past, health care organizations require favorable resource flow to develop social capital and economic wealth. The concepts of positive meaning-making, emoting, and interrelating are leadership techniques emulated through participative management theory that has a profound effect on the operating culture of an organization.

Many health care employees speak about their work as a *calling*. Wrzesniewski (2003) suggested that individuals who perceive work as a calling have more enjoyment and greater satisfaction, which may enhance productivity. *Calling*-orientated work generates a deeper meaning, creating fulfillment that "the work contributes to the greater good and makes the world a better place" (p. 301). A 1997 study by Wrzesniewski, McCauley, Rozin, and Schwartz found that individuals who have a calling have a "stronger and more rewarding relationship to their work, which is associated with spending more time at work, and gaining more enjoyment and satisfaction from work" (p. 302).

Positivism's link to human performance may be a key to organizational success. Dahlsgaard, Peterson, and Seligman (2002) have developed 24 positive traits, grouped into six core virtues that capture positive human strengths: wisdom and knowledge, courage, love, justice, temperance, and transcendence. The literature has linked these positive human strengths, found in the six core virtues, to the phenomenon of flourishing, which, in turn, has been correlated to enhanced organizational performance. The authors suggest that health care organizations that engage individuals who emulate positive traits will generate positive organizational cultures, thereby in turn creating positive subjective experiences (Cameron et al., 2003). Cameron et al. (2003) conclude that the activation of these human traits is affected by organizational policy, rules, norms, and the prevailing reward and recognition programming. The affect of policy, rules, and rewards in turn creates a self-generating influence, shaping organizational culture that manifests employee engagement.

HUMAN CAPITAL: AN INDISPENSABLE ASSET

Luthans and Youssef (2004) have discussed the indispensable asset of human resources by describing people as "an investment that needs to be effectively managed so that they can yield the high return of sustainable completive advantage" (p. 143). The importance of human capital to organizational success should not be overlooked. For example, some researchers, such as Jim Collins (2001), have proposed a twist to general management theory, "People are your most important assets turns out to be wrong. People aren't your most important asset; the right people are" (p. 13). A health care organization must create a human capital pool constructed of the "right people." A full-time equivalent is no longer relevant or is reducing the workforce by a specific percentage to decrease operating costs. What is germane is having the precise number of competently trained employees performing the proper functions that meets the specific needs of each patient.

Luthans and Youssef's (2004) empirical research describes organizational human and social capital as "positive psychological capital." The authors suggest that for a health care organization to remain competitive they must develop methods for employees to "become socialized into the organization, become part of its culture, understanding the dynamic structure, and learn how it operates as a whole" (p. 146). Luthans and Youssef's research has culminated in a framework for managing human, social, and psychological capital.

First, Luthans and Youssef (2004) present the technique of *Human Capital Management,* which is composed of careful human resources selection, supplemented by training and development activities. Selection of talented employees is recognized by the Gallup organization as a "strengths-based approach that involves selecting employees based on their talents, and placing them where they get to do what they do best every day" (p. 148). The objective is to create tacit knowledge across the health care organization – knowledge that is organizational specific and is constructed "over time as members become socialized into the organization and become part of it culture" (p. 146).

Grant (2006) suggests that the concept of strategic placement could be highly correlated with competency modeling. Competency modeling "requires the identification of skills, content knowledge, attitudes, and values associated with superior performers," which is used to "link to technical and professional abilities and overall job performance" or in this case, matching the employees skills to the specific needs of the health care organization (Grant, 2006, p. 144). Selection, training, and development of the *right* employees with the proper disposition, attitudes, and values are critical components in creating an engaged workforce.

Second, Luthans and Youssef (2004) propose the technique of *Social Capital Management,* which consists of thorough open communication, cross-functional work teams, and work–life balance programming. "Social capital is recognized to include interpersonal, inter-group, and inter-organizational relationships, networks and connections, as well as the underlying group and community resources, social structure, and cultural dynamics" (p. 149). These relationships are created through social networks that facilitate the sharing and exchange of ideas, the formation of norms and common held behaviors, and collaborative trust, which guides the organization to achieve its purpose. Luthans and Youssef (2004) emphasize that "employees' trust in their leaders is related to their performance, organizational citizenship behaviors, turnover intentions, organizational commitment, and job satisfaction" (p. 150).

Third, Luthans and Youssef (2004, pp. 153–154) present the technique of *Positive Psychological Capital,* which they define as a positive orientation of human resource strengths and psychological capacities that can improve workplace performance. Positive psychological capital includes positive performance-related components: self-efficacy/confidence, hope, optimism, and resiliency. These relational components of positive psychological capital are described as follows:

> *Self-efficacy* (self-confident): individuals who "choose challenging tasks and endeavors, extend motivation and effort to successfully accomplish their goals, and persevere when faced with obstacles."
> *Hope*: individuals who "accomplish their goals by their sense of agency, which provides them with an internalized determination and willpower to invest the energy necessary to achieve their goals."
> *Optimism*: individuals who "exhibit positive explanatory style that practices positive events to internal, permanent, and pervasive causes, and negative events to external, temporary, and situation-specific ones."
> *Resiliency*: individuals who "bounce back from adversity, uncertainty, failure, or even positive but seemingly overwhelming changes such as increased responsibility."

We can learn much from Luthans and Youssef's (2004) research. It is imperative that a health care organization creates positive psychological capital. The creation of positive psychological capital requires the proper selection and ongoing training of employees (human capital management), the development of open communication and formation of work–life balance programs (social capital management) and an operational culture that emulates hope, optimism, and self-confidence (positive psychological capital). If human capital is an indispensable asset, then the health care organization needs to align its economic resources to support positive psychological capital programming. Luthans and Youssef shared that when "employees gain trust that their managers truly perceive them as the most important asset, [and] a positive spiral is likely to develop, paving the road for a measurable return on the psychological capital and resulting competitive advantage" (2004, p. 157).

A CULTURE OF EMPLOYEE ENGAGEMENT

Employee engagement is supported through a organizational culture that transitions power, shares information, provides aligned intrinsic and extrinsic rewards, values the individual, allows employees to operate with greater flexibility, links individual roles to organizational performance, develops methods for employees to become socialized into the organization, creates human resources selection and development programming, and embeds family concepts within organization life.

The data analyzed for this chapter indicate that employees who are engaged are more enthusiastic and aspired to achieve both individual and organizational success. Empirical studies revealed that a greater level of engagement leads to higher productivity and improved performance (Cummings & Worley, 2005). These studies also suggest that employees perform at higher levels of achievement and secure more meaningfulness at work (Blatt & Ashford, 2006). Finally, employees who gain trust in management and perceive themselves as important assets to the organization create a positive spiral and as a result create a competitive advantage for the organization (Luthans & Youssef, 2004).

In the future, health care organization will require greater levels of productivity and innovation to compete in a rapidly changing environment. The unique nature of the health care sector places human capital at the fulcrum of the patient experience. Health care is distinctive because its services can only be provided through the use of human capital. So the practice of increasing employee involvement in decision making that affects the organization and the employee's well-being is a prescription for organizational success. Creating a culture of employee engagement has practical value to health care organizations who choose to enhance organizational performance or to position their organization to respond to an industry in transition. Briefly described in the following text are actionable tasks that can assist a health care organization in implementing a *culture of employee engagement*.

The operating practices to establish an employee engagement culture are five – defining the employee's role in fulfilling the organizations purpose, selecting employees with capability and passion, supporting and valuing the employee, creating sustainable reward systems, and developing feedback and reinforcement mechanisms.

Employee's Role

Health care organizations should define the role and responsibility of each employee in fulfilling the mission, vision, and values of the organization. All management practices (i.e., individual performance standards, management's expectations, and individual and team performance review processes) should be clearly communicated to each employee and across the organization. The work environment should be socially connected, including the active implementation of employee interrelationship practices. Adaptability and flexibility need to be the hallmarks of the organization's human capital practices.

Employee Selection

Health care organizations should interview, select, and retain individuals who have the tactic knowledge, operational experience, innate talents, and passion for the assigned tasks and job responsibilities. The health care organization must assure that the prescribed values and norms of the organization are personally endorsed by leadership and will be "modeled" by the each individual employee. Employees need to be collaborative in nature and interested in establishing relationships through sharing and exchanging of ideas and work processes to achieve the organization's purpose.

Employee Valuing

Health care organizations should develop a respectful and trusting relationship with its employees. Management should have a sincere interest in employee well-being. The creation of a strong family atmosphere is encouraged, as represented by characteristics of teamwork, respect, flexibility, and an unrelenting commitment to the pursuit of excellence. Health care organization should establish a work environment that is constructed on open and honest communication, self-managed work arrangements, and participatory decision making. Organizations should create an atmosphere of enjoyment, recognition, fulfillment, and well-being.

Employee Rewards

Health care organizations should create an integrated recognition and rewards program, which represents the organization's values and supports the strategic intent of the organization. The rewards program should reflect elements of a competitive compensation and benefit practice, an employee recognition agenda, and work–life balance programming. All compensation practices should be meaningful and designed to incentivize goal achievement across the organization.

Employee Reinforcement

Health care organizations should establish processes to gain employee input into the goals and objectives of the organization. Systems should be created for management to share organizational expectations openly and report measurable progress across the organization. Communication of the organizations purpose, priorities, and strategic direction should be routinely shared with the workforce. Finally, organizational success should be shared equally with management and employees.

REFERENCES

American Hospital Association. (2008). *The economic crisis: Impact on hospitals*. Chicago: American Hospital Association.

Anderson, C., John, O. P., & Keltner, D. K. (2003). Emotional convergence between people over time. *Journal of Personality and Social Psychology*, *84*(5), 1054–1068.

Anderson, C., & Thompson, L. (2004). Affect from the top down: How powerful individuals' positive affect shaper negotiations. *Organizational Behavior and Human Decision Processes*, *95*(2), 125–139.

Baard, P. P., Deci, E. L., & Ryan, R. M. (2004). Intrinsic need satisfaction: A motivational basis of performance and well-being in two work settings. *Journal of Applied Social Psychology*, *66*, 950–967.

Blatt, R., & Ashford, S. (Eds). (2006). *Making meaning and taking action in knowledge and creative work: Insights from independent workers*. Working Paper. University of Michigan, MI, USA.

Cameron, K. S., Dutton, J. E., & Quinn, R. E. (2003). *Positive organizational scholarship*. San Francisco: Berrett-Koehler.

Collins, J. (2001). *Good to great*. New York: Harper Collins Publishing.

Cummings, T. G., & Worley, C. G. (2005). *Organization development and change*. Mason, OH: South-Western.

Dahlsgaard, K., Peterson, C., & Seligman, M. E. P. (2002). *Virtues converge across culture and history*. Unpublished manuscript. University of Pennsylvania.

Dutton, J. E., & Glynn, M. A. (2008). Positive organizational scholarship. In: C. Cooper & J. Barling (Eds), *Handbook of organizational behavior* (pp. 1–28). Thousand Oaks, CA: Sage Publications.

Dutton, J. E., & Ragins, B. R. (2007). *Exploring positive relationships at work: Building a theoretical and research foundation*. New York: Lawrence Erlbaum Associates.

Freshman, B., Rubino, L., & Chassiakos, Y. R. (2010). *Collaboration across the disciplines in health care*. Sudbury, MA: Jones & Bartlett Learning.

Gebauer, J., & Lowman, D. (2008). *Closing the engagement gap: How great companies unlock employee potential for superior results*. New York: Penguin Group.

Glynn, M. A., & Wrobel, K. (2007). My family, my firm: How familial relationships function as endogenous organizational resources. In: J. E. Dutton & B. R. Ragins (Eds), *Exploring positive relationships at work* (pp. 307–323). New York: Lawrence Erlbaum Associates.

Grant, R. M. (2006). *Contemporary strategy analysis*. Malden, MA: Blackwell.

Ivanitskaya, L. V., Glazer, S., & Erofeev, D. A. (2009). Group dynamics. In: J. A. Johnson (Ed.), *Health organizations: Theory, behaviors, and development*. Sudbury, MA: Jones & Bartlett Learning.

Johnson, J. A. (2009). *Health organizations: Theory, behavior, and development*. Sudbury, MA: Jones & Bartlett Learning.

Kahn, W. A. (1990). Psychological conditions of personal engagement and disengagement at work. *Academy of Management Journal*, *33*(4), 692–724.

Kimball, L. S., & Nink, C. E. (2006). How to improve employee motivation, commitment, productivity, well-being and safety. *Corrections Today*, *68*, 66–74.

Losada, M., & Heaphy, E. (2004). The role of positivity and connectivity in the performance of business teams. *American Behavioral Scientist*, *47*(6), 740–765.

Lounsbury, M., & Glynn, M. A. (2001). Cultural entrepreneurship: Stories, legitimacy and the acquisition of resources. *Strategic Management Journal*, *22*, 545–565.

Luthans, F., & Youssef, C. M. (2004). Human, social, and now positive psychological capital management: Investing in people for competitive advantage. *Organizational Dynamics*, *33*(2), 143–160.

Putnam, R. (2000). *Bowling alone: The collapse and revival of American community*. New York: Simon & Schuster.

Sandelands, L. (1995). The idea of social life. *Philosophy of the Social Sciences*, *25*(2), 147.

Seijts, G. H., & Crim, D. (2006). The ten C's of employee engagement. *Ivey Business Journal*, *6*, 37–42.

Thomas, K. W. (2009). *Intrinsic motivation at work: What really drives employee engagement*. San Francisco: Berrett-Koehler.

Wrzesniewski, A., McCauley, C., Rozin, R. P., & Schwartz, B. (1997). Jobs, careers, and callings: People's relations to their work. *Journal of Research in Personality*, *31*, 21–33.

Wrzesniewski, A. (2003). Finding positive meaning in work. In: J. E. Dutton, K. S. Cameron & R. E. Quinn (Eds), *Positive organizational scholarship: Foundations of a new discipline*. San Francisco: Berrett-Koehler.

THE RELATIONSHIP BETWEEN THE SURVEY-GUIDED ASSESSMENT OF CULTURE WITHIN SPECIFIC NURSING WORK GROUPS AND READINESS FOR CHANGE

Corinne Haviley

ABSTRACT

Change within health care systems is constant as it relates to the external and internal demands that require continual adaptation by providers. This chapter provides a summary of the history and research contributions related to the study of culture and change through the lens of the nursing profession. The review focuses upon nursing research publications and the knowledge gained, ranging from the earliest to current studies. There has been a substantial increase in research interest regarding the relationship between nursing culture and ability to change; however, there is a considerable gap that remains in understanding subgroups such as individual nursing units or departments, consistent use of tools to measure culture, and interventions that have made a difference over time. From a practical perspective, this discussion provides insight into the importance

Organization Development in Healthcare: Conversations on Research and Strategies
Advances in Health Care Management, Volume 10, 97–116

ISSN: 1474-8231/doi:10.1108/S1474-8231(2011)0000010012

of recognizing the importance of assessing culture and integrating cultural feedback into operational improvement plans.

Keywords: Organization culture; Change management; Nursing care models; Appreciative inquiry; Performance improvement; Planned change

Little is known about how ready nursing staff are to change in hospital settings, yet the internal and external demands within health care continue to require repeated adjustments. Nurses need to respond to internal environmental shifting such as continually changing patient conditions and acuity level (Casida & Pinto-Zipp, 2008), life and death issues, the introduction of new technology, medications and procedures types, differing staffing models and nurse to patient ratios, work force shortages (Ingersoll et al., 2002), and appropriate care delivery processes to avoid errors and patient harm. External changes are requiring nurses to rethink how care is provided as evidenced by a reduction in payment from Medicare and Medicaid Services who will no longer reimburse hospitals for "never events." Effective from October 2008, never events will be classified as nonreimbursable as they have been deemed avoidable conditions or problems developed or occurring within a hospital such as the development of advancing pressure ulcers, falls with serious reportable injury, suicide etc. (Centers for Medicare and Medicaid Services, 2009). Disaster preparedness, cost reduction burdens, changing legal requirements, for example, new Health Insurance Portability and Accountability Acts (HIPPA), and increasing liability continue to place demands upon the nursing process. Regulatory standards also significantly influence the need for change as seen through The Joint Commission Standards on Hospital Accreditation, requiring organizations to engage in and demonstrate success with process improvement activities in response to error reduction and promoting quality care (The Joint Commission, 2009).

The purpose of this chapter is to present a summary of the history and research contributions related to the study of culture and change through the lens of nursing. The review focuses upon nursing research publications and knowledge gained, ranging from the earliest through current studies.

The review focuses upon following five subtopics:

1. The relationship between organizational culture and change as seen through the implementation of new models of care delivery systems, physical structures, and response to regulatory requirements

2. The association between leadership, culture, and change
3. Noted limitations and challenges regarding the above studies
4. Other factors affecting culture in nursing and the organizational call for change
5. The need for future investigation regarding the assessment of culture and the integration of cultural feedback into operational improvement plans

Prior to discussing this literature review it may be helpful to define the context of the environment where the reported research studies have been carried out. Hospital, long-term care facilities, and nursing home environments are divided into designated nursing units where nurses, support staff such assistive personnel including secretaries and unlicensed caregivers are assigned to deliver nursing care to select patient populations. These units have a predetermined number of beds housing patients with either broad based or specific problems/diagnoses. Staff may self-select to work on these units or be assigned depending upon the hospital or health care facility. These units may be referred to as subgroups or work groups in the literature.

THE STUDY OF CULTURE AND ITS RELATIONSHIP TO NEW MODEL IMPLEMENTATION, PHYSICAL STRUCTURES AND REGULATORY REQUIREMENTS

The early study of culture in nursing focused upon understanding the relationship between organizational culture and change as seen through the implementation of new models of care delivery systems. These newly developed models were the result of health care organizational redesign in the late 1980s, which has continued into the 2000s, in response to the demand for improving service efficiency, while maintaining quality care (Ingersoll et al., 2002). Many of the initiatives were intended to reduce the number of steps required in care delivery (Jones & Redman, 2000; Watson & Kimberly, 1997). Other redesigns were intended to decentralize services and reduce the number of employee interactions and service duplication. There was little understanding regarding the impact of these process changes and the effects upon interrelationships (Ingersoll et al., 2002; Cassidy, 1992).

Qualitative approaches were used early in the nursing research history; however, there was an evolution toward trialing different quantitative measurement tools developed both within the organization development and nursing fields. The study samples were small and confined to one organization at the outset of cultural research in nursing; however, they expanded over time to include multiple subcultures and hospital systems, thereby adding to breadth to the body of knowledge. The learning from this research targeted management understanding, recognition of the meaning of culture, and suggestions for potentially managing change and behavior. This section provides a historical overview of the culture studies within the nursing profession.

Coeling and Wilcox (1988) were the first authors to publish on the subject matter of organizational culture research specific to nursing. They used a qualitative approach to identify cultural behaviors of 35 staff nurses, managers, and unit secretaries from two different specialty nursing units in one organization. Utilizing participant observer and interview techniques, they sought to identify agreed upon rules for the work groups including working together, telling others what to do, following established standards, organization and use of time, psychosocial perspective taking, and change. Implications for nursing management were identified suggesting to (1) tailor hiring personnel so that they would "fit in" or "buy into" a group's norms and values, (2) orient new employees by identifying group norms to assist with adjustment, (3) use knowledge gained from nursing unit's display of culture to adapt teaching methodology, and (4) consider cultural differences among work groups when facilitating change.

These same authors conducted a second qualitative organizational culture study comparing two nursing unit work group cultures within one hospital (Coeling & Wilcox, 1990). They further wanted to determine which patient care delivery system was appropriate for a specific work group. Their sample included 18 participants (staff nurses, licensed practical nurses, clerical specialists, and a nurse aide) from one nursing unit and 15 participants from a second unit (including staff nurses, licensed practical nurses, clerical specialist, a manager, and assistant manager). This study organized data collection around cultural rules that included four dimensions: individualism/collectivism, physical/psychological focus, power relationships, and uncertainty avoidance. Their findings helped to target proposed interventions addressing the select nursing unit's culture reflected in the cultural rules. Additionally, they gained understanding related to the nursing barriers to adopting new patient care systems and on project implementations strategies specific to the inpatient nursing units. They further suggested consideration of professional and societal values when choosing patient care systems for select nursing units and that models should be identified based upon the subgroup culture. The authors recognized, however, that they were unable to measure the degree in work group differences and that there was a need for quantitative research to further uncover how the cultural rules might vary in different work groups.

Thomas, Ward, Chorba, and Kumiega (1990) published the first quantitative study related to measuring and interpreting organization nursing subcultures across several hospitals including two subgroups. The comparison groups consisted of a total of 76 participants including staff nurses working multiple shifts and management. Through the use of the Organizational Culture Inventory tool (OCI), they compared the staff perception of what should be the ideal versus their actual cultural profile. They viewed culture as cognitive consistent with what people are thinking. They further believed that culture may be molded and shaped. The authors contended that some cultures are strong and move in a positive direction. Other cultures tended to be strong but move in an opposing or negative direction. Gaps between the positive and negative cultures may signal a need for change related to communication, organizational structures that promote undesired norms and values and beliefs that may be dissimilar at different levels within the organization. The authors used the results from this study to speculate what might have contributed to the participants' responses and how management might use the results to better understand behavior and identification of change to enhance efficiency.

In 1992, Grau and Wellin published a qualitative research to examine the organizational cultures of two nursing homes in response to external regulatory controls. The investigators collected data over a six-month period utilizing participant observation and informal interviewing techniques in formal settings including all staff from both institutions (administrative personnel, recreational therapists, registered and licensed practical nurses, social workers, and randomly selected nursing aides, totaling 93 participants). The facilities chosen for the study were located in the same metropolitan area with similar operating characteristics such as size, ownership, reputation, and fee for services. Multiple facility dissimilarities were identified such as surrounding geographic areas, socioeconomic, religious, and ethnic background of the residents. The authors drew correlations between the nursing homes interpretation of the regulatory standards and identified differences between nursing home practices and characteristics including centralized decision making, division of labor, relationships between staff and residents, complaints, patient safety with a focus on fall risk and restraint use, and treatment of difficult residents. The authors concluded that nursing homes are service organizations that possess complex behaviors that have not been researched in the past, but the results were important for those who work in them and for those who establish the regulations governing the institutions.

Coeling and Simms (1993a, 1993b) published the second quantitative study in nursing, assessing organizational culture that was also the first multicentered trial using nursing personnel from multiple nursing units. There were reportedly 607 nursing personnel from 33 different nursing units located within a metropolitan health care center, a community hospital, and an international health care resource center that participated in the study. The definition of nursing personnel was not provided. Utilizing a structured approach to culture assessment, the authors developed the Nursing Unit Cultural Assessment tool (NUCAT) and a five-step cultural innovation or change process including assessing culture, identifying cultural elements of the innovation or change, determining potential forces that drive or restrain an innovation, strengthening the driving forces, and decreasing the resistance. The authors identified values characteristic of a unit that may allow for easier adaptation to the proposed new model of care. They cautioned that culture is not only a powerful but a subtle force and that resistance may be unnoticed. They further presented strategies such as listening and observing that may be of benefit when attempting the introduction of new practice patterns on a specific nursing unit and advise that transforming change occurs slowly.

Rizzo, Gilman, and Mersmann (1994) built upon Coeling and Simms's (1993a, 1993b) previously cited work. These authors proposed to facilitate the redesign of a care delivery model by measuring nursing unit specific culture and work characteristics on multiple nursing departmental staff from multiple nursing units. The researchers used the NUCAT tool in combination with the Work Characteristics Instrument (WCI), which measures staff perception of the exciting, interesting, and frustrating aspects of their existing work environment. They reported on how they used Coeling and Simms's five-step cultural innovation process within the study. The authors used specific data to identify potential behaviors that promote change such as accountability and problematic behaviors that inhibit change such as telling others what to do. They provided one example related to the promotion of work excitement and the correlation with the need for being part of the team leading to team development strategies. The authors indicated that they shared the findings with staff; however, they did not indicate how the feedback affected adaptation to the change process.

Fleeger (1993) surveyed nurses working in three hospitals in Oregon assessing the strength, nursing unit ideologies, and the extent of cultural homogeneity. The sample size was not included in the publication. Through the use of the Harrison instrument that assessed staff perception of culture in terms of four categories including power, role, achievement, and support, and a Qualitative Cultural Assessment Inventory tool, the author reported significant cultural differences between one of the hospitals in comparison to the other two. Membership in the two hospitals demonstrating harmony shared the same goals, which was the motivating force related to the delivery of optimum patient care for both managers and staff. In the hospital demonstrating cultural dissonance, the goals and motivators differed and there was conflict between units. These authors developed a cultural blue print with detailed action items to promote consonance; however, there was no discussion regarding the implementation or effectives of the strategies.

In 1998, Luk, Chen, Yau, Tsang, and Leung published a study evaluating the culture related to 130 staff of various "grades" and departments that had recently moved into a newly constructed hospital located in China. The move required staff to adapt to a new environment of care. The staff was reported as a blend of transferees from the hospital that was replaced and other new staff hired into the organization. The Harrison questionnaire was used in this study. The authors surveyed employees three months post move into the new facility. Results indicated that role orientation and achievement orientation were the dominant themes displayed by the staff. The advantage to role orientation was that it was often equated to a structured and orderly environment that may provide stability; however, it was also associated with those who have difficulty changing. Additionally, achievement orientation was closely associated with the organization. Achieving goals were reported as highly characteristic of the hospital's Christian origin in the sense that there was emphasis on the employee committing to the organization so that overall goals can be achieved. The limitation identified related to this orientation was the difficulty in sustaining over time, which can lead to potential exhaustion. Neither of these orientations was reflective of the preferred orientation by the hospital. The authors indicated that they intended to use this study as a baseline for highlighting opportunities for improvement and future growth and adaptation.

In 2000, Manley studied organization culture and the effects of a nurse consultant delivery of education and skill development in one intensive care nursing unit in a British hospital. The sample was described as insiders and outsiders on a post; however, role delineation and sample size were not available. Using a qualitative approach, the researcher interviewed staff and functioned as a participant observer after the clinical nurse consultant had been introduced into the environment. The findings indicated that there was a cultural change in response to the consultant work seen through the feedback from staff reflecting upon the past in terms of value clarification, direction, and unit vision. Leaning and supervision were believed to enhance gap reduction between desired values and actual practice. The author linked the leadership of the nurse consultant as transformational to quality nursing outcomes.

Wilson, McCormack, and Ives (2005) investigated the workplace culture of a special care nursery unit after implementing an emancipatory practice development. The sample included all 27 nursing staff defined as casual and permanently employed nurses and midwives. The researchers used a qualitative approach including participant observer and interview techniques along with a staff satisfaction questionnaire, which was acknowledged as developed by Traynor and Wade. The survey findings indicated that there was a reported close relationship between teamwork, learning in practice, inevitably of change, and family centered care, which formed the unit core beliefs. A deeper and more comprehensive view through observation and interview demonstrated that there were contrasts such as between teamwork and individualism. They identified that the team was actually working in a tense and anxious atmosphere that might have been missed had they relied on survey tools alone. Opportunities became available for staff to reevaluate their own assumptions about their roles.

Another quantitative study focusing upon correlating organizational culture and change studied the before and after culture assessment related to the implementation of a patient-focused care model on two nursing units (Jones, DeBaca, & Yarbrough, 1997). The study sample included 260 pre-implementation participants (defined as unit caregivers including pharmacy and admitting) and 278 post-implementation participants. The authors identified that the Competing Values Framework tool was valuable in establishing a baseline and an ongoing assessment enabling the researchers to use the information to manage attitudes and beliefs that were considered to impact upon the current and potentially future model implementation. The baseline data was crucial in identifying that dysfunctional cultures needed interventions. They further identified that staff members in different job categories did not perceive the organizational culture consistently and that there were changes in the strength of beliefs over time.

These differences in caregivers were identified as important needs to be addressed during the change process and that the findings had implications for future roll out plans in other areas of the organization.

In contrast, Goodridge and Hack (1996) found in a sample of 176 nursing personnel (comprised of registered and license practical nurses and nursing assistants from multiple nursing units) that there was a too wide variation in responses using the NUCAT tool, which did not lead to a meaningful analysis. They further found that there was no difference in response ratings regarding the stratified job categories of registered nurses and unlicensed staff. This finding was not anticipated. They were, however, able to identify preferred behaviors by all staff and those behaviors that staff would like to change, which were proposed to be used as a starting point for intervention.

In a more recent study, Seago (2000) conducted a quantitative organizational culture research study that targeted 525 nursing personnel (consisting of 448 registered nurses and 77 unlicensed personnel) across five large academic hospitals. This author found differences among the ratings between job categories. Although the findings were not unit specific they identified that unlicensed personnel scored higher on the OCI tool on thinking and behavior types such as dependence and opposition as compared to the registered nurses. These findings lead the authors to suggest strategies to help the unlicensed staff feel rewarded as they may be resistive to authority. They further suggested paying attention to the categories that are rated similarly by both groups such as affiliative, self-actualization, achievement categories and so on, as they may strive toward positive relationships, acceptance, and cooperation. Regardless of position, gender, or education, these authors introduced results indicating that people of "color" compared to white staff scored higher on indicators suggesting the subgroup had a tendency toward trying to please, avoiding conflict, and being accepted.

There has been only one study published in the nursing literature incorporating the concept of readiness for change and organizational culture. Ingersoll et al. (2002) studied two large academic hospitals in the Midwest six months prior and six months after a model redesign implementation. The sample reported was 684 nursing, administrative, and support staff. The staff represented all work shifts. The authors evaluated the effects of the redesign using the Sociotechnical System Theory, while investigating change on employee perceptions, the work environment, and group relationships. Tools utilized in this study included the OCI tool to measure organizational culture, whereas organizational commitment was measured by the Commitment/Energy Subscale, which had a focus upon commitment to the organizational goals. Further, job satisfaction was measured by a previously used survey tool employed by the organization. Organizational readiness was evaluated by the Innovativeness and Cooperation Subscale for the Sociotechnical Systems Assessment Scale, which measured rewards for innovation, propensity for risk taking, and extent to which the organization leaders and members maintain a futuristic rather than historical orientation. Work group performance and social relationships were measured by the Perceived Group

Attractiveness and Cohesiveness Scale. This scale reportedly measured productivity, efficiency, and feelings of belonging, morale, liking and desire to work with the group. Team collaboration was measured by the modified Collaborative Practice Scale. Results indicated that there was no change in the organizational culture pre- and post-implementation of the redesign and that there was an equal distribution between the ratings in perception of culture as constructive, passive defensive, and aggressive defensive. Organizational readiness, job satisfaction, and organization commitment declined from pre- to post-implementation, which was speculated to be associated with a decrease in staffing and managers throughout the organization that was unrelated to the study. Staff perceptions regarding collaboration, desirability, and cohesiveness increased over the time period, which was expected as the model was believed to enhance these perceptions. There were subcultures that had different perceptions, which was believed a significant finding for organizations that expect to implement initiatives across large work groups without reframing for individual areas. Finally, value was identified in the ability to identify changes over time.

THE ASSOCIATION BETWEEN LEADERSHIP, CULTURE, AND CHANGE

There have been several studies in the literature examining the relationship between leadership, organizational culture, and correlation to change management.

McDaniel and Stumpf (1993) studied 194 staff nurses and 56 managers within seven acute care hospitals to assess the organizational culture to provide recommendations for strategies to enhance service and ultimately improve patient outcomes. Using the OCI tool and the Multifactor Leadership Questionnaire, the authors identified that culture assessment is relevant to work redesign and empowerment issues inherent within nursing staff. They compared the current participant survey ratings to previously cited ideal ratings and noted where disparity existed. Specifically, they noted nursing service items including job knowledge, leadership, retention, recommending the organization as a good place to work, and "fitting in" were positively related to culture. The authors suggested that assessment of administration is critical to enhance service.

According to Webb, Price, and Coeling (1996), differences in the individual values of 213 nurses and 21 managers employed by three urban hospitals compared to group values demonstrated the potential for conflict. These authors studied separate work groups on two separate units who adopted different models of care, specifically primary versus total patient care. The NUCAT tool was used to describe discrete values of the work groups and managers. Staff nurses working on the primary care unit expressed a preference for more accountability and autonomy as compared to the alternate unit. Both groups of nurses valued communication and authority at a higher level as compared to what was perceived as reality. There was a difference between the nurses working on the two units' ratings of autonomy and authority as compared to the managers rating. This discordance provided an opportunity to reexamine leadership styles and the impact of style upon staff. The authors further identified that the managers were educated at a higher level and had more years of experience as compared to the staff. Experience, education preparation, and personal values were all deemed important in reaching unit-based outcomes. It was, therefore, concluded that the variability of the values were important for management at the unit level.

Bond and Fiedler (1998) investigated the rankings of how well all staff members had reshaped organizational norms and attitudes, while implementing a new resident centered model of care in a long-term care facility. The reported sample size equaled 121 staff members and managers. The staff members' job types were not described. Using a qualitative approach, they identified that there was disparity between administration's perceptions as compared to staff and families leading to questions regarding the ability of administration to judge important changes in the culture of an organization.

A qualitative survey was conducted targeting 25 nurses working within a hospital-based operating theater in Italy (Yamaguchi, 2004). The author used interview techniques to learn more about the interpretation of culture from an external perspective (e.g., thoughts about the economic and political systems), internal environment (e.g., job responsibilities and teams), and role behaviors and practices. The author noted that the nursing staff were recognized as less educated then doctors and took direction from physicians who were the dominant force within the department and not from hospital leadership. The nurses functioned as an assistant to the physicians. It was reported that the nurses felt angry, fearful, and not having power due to the physicians. As a result staff developed strong internal alliances and their team was described as open and constructive. The nurses were reported as defensive against change and conflict. They were not in favor of a potential proposal to bring in surgical technicians to be included in their work force as it had implications for job stability. The author recognized that her findings were informative related to the organization under study only, which offered a way of thinking about the internal social systems and potential ways to make improvements.

Seren and Baykal (2007) carried out a quantitative study examining organizational change and culture on 570 physician and nurse participants within eight private and public hospitals located in Istanbul, Turkey. The researchers examined organizational culture and the relationship with change through the use of multiple tools. The researcher self-developed an information tool and used the Culture Score, which was subdivided culture into four categories including power, role, competition, and cooperation. The authors also used the Attitude Toward Change Scale in the study, which was subdivided into four scales including institutional policy in change, change outcomes, resistance to change, and management style in change. The results demonstrated that the power culture was more prevalent in the public hospitals and that senior management was viewed as autocratic. They further identified that collaboration culture was predominant in the private hospitals and that leadership was viewed as democratic. The authors suggested that organization culture be defined prior to change initiation and that a democratic management style be adapted. They additionally recommended encouraging employees to become involved and listen to their opinions.

A descriptive and correlational study was conducted by Casida and Pinto-Zipp (2008) exploring the relationship between nurse manager leadership types and organizational culture on high-performing inpatient nursing units from four hospitals. The sample included 37 nurse managers and 278 staff nurses. High-performing units were defined by those that had a high rating inpatient satisfaction scores. The authors used the multifactorial Leadership Questionnaire, which measured three leadership dimensions including transformational, transactional, and nontransactional Leissez-faire styles, and the Denison's Organizational Culture Survey, which measured four culture traits including adaptability, mission, involvement, and consistency. The results indicated a strong correlation between organizational culture traits and leadership style. They generalized that a transformation leadership style likely molded a high-performing nursing unit as seen through elevated levels of cultural traits including mission, adaptability, involvement, and consistency. They further identified value in the transactional leader that molded culture traits such as consistency and involvement, which are important to unit operations. Lastly, they identified that the Leissez-faire style did not have a positive influence on culture due to the lack of manager relationship with nursing staff.

LIMITATIONS AND CHALLENGES REGARDING THE ABOVE NURSING STUDIES

The reported culture studies summarized in this chapter have demonstrated variability in terminology use, design, sample, instrumentation, and unit analysis consistent with findings from other authors that have conducted reviews on nursing culture research studies (Scott-Findlay & Estabrooks, 2006; Gershon, Stone, Bakken, & Larson, 2004). The difficulty with the variability lies in the inability to generalize the application of the study findings. If studies are not well defined, then there is the danger of misinterpretation, misrepresentation of information and a risk of inappropriate or suboptimal implementation.

The definitions of culture varied among the studies in this review. There were over 17 different definitions used in the studies and some authors did not provide a definition. This finding is not surprising as there is no universally accepted definition (Schein, 1990). Schein further indicated that defining organizational culture is difficult because it is an ambiguous concept.

Scott-Findlay and Estabrooks (2006) additionally cautioned that terminology ambiguity such as using climate and culture interchangeably is not productive in terms of adding to knowledge and may cause confusion. This ambiguity was noted in several studies including Grau and Wellin (1992) and Ingersoll et al. (2002).

There were multiple different survey instruments used in this review of nursing studies. Gershon et al. (2004) defined five major dimensions of quantitative culture instruments used in health care, which provided a framework and cross reference for identifying the scope of the tools. These dimensions include "leadership characteristics, group behaviors and relationships, communication, quality of work life and health care worker outcomes" (p. 37) and are helpful in understanding the similarities and differences between survey tools. None of the instruments in this review possessed all of the same dimensions that Gerhson identified. Instrument characteristics and dimensions are paramount in determining applicability and comparison of data. Disparity between instruments can create the potential for confusion. It should be duly noted that the development of instrumentation underscores the complexity in the measurement of culture.

Scott-Findlay and Estabrooks (2006) identified the importance of defining the unit analysis in culture studies differentiating between subgroups such as specialty nursing units, department, and organizations. Unit distinction is important when data is aggregated so that it can be differentiated at the subgroup(s) or organizational level. The studies reported in this paper had a wide variation in identified subgroups and several were unclear. These details were identified within the content of the study overviews.

In this review, it has been noted that the samples were neither reliably reported nor clearly defined consistent with Gershon's findings (2004) in an earlier review of culture studies published in the nursing field. There are a variety of health care positions that have distinct job functions that many interrelate, whereas some may not have relationships. When the sample is not clear then the results become difficult to interpret.

Another challenge regarding this review was the lack of reported follow up related to the information gained and how it was applied to operations. These studies did not discuss how the information or data had been used to make improvement or enhance change.

OTHER FACTORS AFFECTING CULTURE AND THE ORGANIZATIONAL CALL FOR CHANGE

The momentum has continued through the study of culture and its relationship to other factors or characteristics that are complex variables influencing nursing practice and outcomes, which may impact upon change. The following studies underscore the expanded interest in culture.

Klakovich (1996) found that there is a relationship between nurses' perception of empowerment and culture. Stumpf (2001) further identified that hospital shared governance structure versus a traditional model had a positive correlation with a constructive culture, which had linkages to nurse retention and work satisfaction. Lin et al. (2005) provided evidence that individuals' perception of their organization affects their effort to improve upon the implementation of models of care particularly in chronic care. Manojlovich and Ketefian (2002) found that culture is a significant predictor of nursing professionalism.

Recently, organizational culture has been studied as it relates to error reduction. Stock, McFadden, and Gowen (2007) found error reduction to be positively correlated to group culture that demonstrates an emphasis on human development, participation, and commitment to others.

According to Gifford, Zammuto, and Goodman (2002), there is a positive relationship between unit specific organizational "human based" culture in specialty labor and delivery units with organizational commitment, job involvement, empowerment, and job satisfaction. Further, the authors contend that culture has an inverse relationship with nursing intent to turnover. Tzeng, Ketefian, and Redman (2002) studied the cause and effect relationship between nurses' assessment of organizational culture, staff and patient satisfaction in which a positive correlation was noted. Gregory, Way, LeFort, Barrett, and Parfrey (2007) developed a model linking nurses' intent to stay with job satisfaction, trust, and organizational culture. Another study conducted in multiple health care organizations located in Belgium identified a correlation between nurses cultural fit and turnover rate (Vandenberghe, 1999). Research conducted by Kangas, Kee, and McKee-Waddle (1999) targeting nurses across three hospitals, demonstrated that a supportive environment was most important to nursing satisfaction.

Undesirable affects have been investigated by Seago (1996a, 1996b) related to the relationship of culture and workplace stress and hostility to outcomes such as absenteeism and nursing turnover, which had cost implications for hospital operations. The author demonstrated that job stress, absenteeism, and turnover in nurses working in hospitals correlated with higher lack of control, decision making, and autonomy. This same investigator reported a separate descriptive study in 1996 surveying nurse managers and administrators defining the most frequently reported characteristics of troubled nursing units, which were found as heavy workload, staff that had difficulty changing, stressful environment, poor staff attitudes and high levels of anger and a reputation for being emotionally destructive to new employees. The author developed multiple strategies to target these negative behaviors to improve upon the environment.

THE NEED FOR FUTURE INVESTIGATION AND EXPLORATION REGARDING THE ASSESSMENT OF CULTURE AND THE INTEGRATION OF CULTURAL FEEDBACK INTO OPERATIONAL IMPROVEMENT PLANS

From what has been learned in the above literature review related to the study of culture and its relationship to change in the nursing profession, there is much yet to be learned from the surveying process of nurses. This review indicates that there is strong evidence that the nursing profession finds value in studying culture; however, none of the reported studies to date have investigated intercessions to strengthen culture or facilitate change.

There is a need to begin filling that void through the examination of targeted interventions and their impact culture and organizational performance.

This can be accomplished through a variety of approaches including qualitative and quantitative research. According to Cooke and Rousseau (1988), qualitative methods such as action research allow for subgroups to describe in depth information when little information is apparent. Quantitative methods such as surveys have the advantage to facilitate systematic comparisons between studies, limitation in hypotheses testing, and theory building (Lim, 1995) and may have more practical application for analyzing data-driven change within or perhaps between organizations (Cooke & Rousseau, 1988).

Presenting the information gained from survey feedback to nursing staff and leadership begins the process of first cultural and then subsequently change management, which is lacking in nursing history. Knowledge gained from the survey process and results benefits organizations by bringing structure to the assessment, reduction of uncertainty, and resistance to change. Further surveys allow for members to generate their own ideal culture that can be compared to actual profiles. Parameters for change are inherent in the process providing unique organization or unit direction for improvement. The power behind the assessment is further seen in the people who will ultimately implement the changes (Cooke & Rousseau, 1988). According to Sorensen and Yaeger (2004), "perceptions and descriptions of an organization are a function of the nature of the inquiry or questions asked and the organization profiles resulting from these questions have the dramatic potential for the development of shared positive energy and a common bond for moving the organization forward" (pp. 272–273).

Behavioral patterns stem from the underlying values and assumptions that are within an organization. Studying culture is a way of looking backwards and understanding what has lead up to and what has been influential in the past. As environments change and new demands evolve, the learning and adaptation from the past may not work in the present or future. What may complicate responsiveness to changing environments is not being able to identify core values because they have been covered by defensiveness to avoid fear or threats (Beer & Spector, 2003). Cummings and Worley (2005) suggested that organizational leaders need to assist employees by understanding how to create readiness for change. Based upon different cognitions, each individual reacts differently to messages related to change (Armenakis & Harris, 2002). People are believed to react differently influenced by previous experiences, personality, organizational culture, mental processing, and personal habits. Hence, general change techniques may not be effective for all employees (Cummings & Worley, 2005). Change readiness can be seen as an intellectual antecedent to behaviors that demonstrate resistance or support for adaptation to change (Armenakis, Harris, & Mossholder, 1993). Readiness is reflected in the extent that individual(s) are cognitively and emotionally prepared to embrace and accept change (Holt, Armenakis, Field, & Harris, 2007). Creating readiness for change includes the influence on individual's beliefs and attitudes (Armenakis et al., 1993).

Armenakis and Harris (2002) proposed a five-step readiness model focusing on communication of the change message. These components include self-efficacy – level of confidence that the change can succeed; principal support – key leaders are in support of the change; discrepancy – a gap analysis has identified the ideal versus the current state; appropriateness – corrective action to remedy the difference between the ideal and current has occurred; and personal valence - clarifies the benefits of change.

Moran and Brightman (2000) further explained from their research that the more intense or deep the change represents to an organization, then the greater the importance on facilitating opportunities for people to examine their beliefs and values. Change needs to come from both the top and the bottom of the organization. They further have outlined the following change management cycle: "1) understand the current situation; 2) determine the desired state and develop a change plan; 3) enlist others and develop a critical mass and 4) track and stabilize results" (p. 69). Smith (2003) contends that the key steps for change include creating a need for change, communicating the change message, while ensuring participation in the process, and provide a base for the achievement of change.

In summary, there has been a substantial increase in research interest related to the relationship between nursing culture and ability to change. The organizational research conducted to date does not support a solid understanding of the observable cultural experience and its impact upon the ability to change over time within the nursing profession (Scott-Findlay & Estabrooks, 2006). It is important to develop a uniform definition of culture, apply consistent instrumentation that is reliable and valid, target measurements that are specific and transferable (Gershon, Stone, Bakken, & Larson, 2004), and begin the process of setting standards related to industry adoption of a systematic approach to changing culture.

Health care organizations can benefit from gaining an understanding of existing departmental or unit's based culture styles and determine what components of the culture can be released to increase capacity for change leading to improved organizational performance. It is not known today if any defined interventions such as process improvement, appreciative inquiry, or problem solving produce quantifiable results related to change in culture and performance measures. And it is not well understood how the cascading effect resulting from the evolutionary discovery of unit-based culture over time and its effects upon the ability to change. Hence, there is opportunity to apply existing tools and use the information gained to provide feedback to shape the change process. Longitudinal studies are needed to demonstrate the significance of the impact of culture and work groups, measure the effectiveness of the interventions to facilitate change, and begin to establish leadership practices in change management with the nursing profession.

REFERENCES

Armenakis, A., & Harris, G. (2002). Crafting a change message to create transformational readiness. *Journal of Organizational Change Management*, *15*, 169–183.

Armenakis, A., Harris, S., & Mossholder, K. (1993). Creating readiness for organizational change. *Human Relations*, *46*, 681–703.

Beer, M., & Spector, B. (2003). Organizational diagnosis: Its role in organizational learning. *Journal of Counseling and Development*, *71*, 642–650.

Bond, G., & Fiedler, F. (1998). The visibility of organizational culture in a long-term care facility. *Journal of Nursing Administration*, *28*, 7–9.

Casida, J., & Pinto-Zipp, G. (2008). Leadership-organizational culture relationship in nursing units of acute care hospitals. *Nursing Economics*, *26*, 7–15.

Cassidy, J. (1992). Patient focused delivery promises to reshape hospitals. *Hospital Progress*, *73*, 20–28.

Centers for Medicare and Medicaid Services. (2009). Available at http://www.cms.hhs.gov

Coeling, H., & Simms, L. (1993a). Facilitating innovation at the nursing unit level through cultural assessment: Part 1: How to keep management ideas from falling on deaf ears. *Journal of Nursing Administration*, *23*, 46–53.

Coeling, H., & Simms, L. (1993b). Facilitating innovation at the nursing unit level through cultural assessment: Part 2: Adapting managerial ideas to the unit work group. *Journal of Nursing Administration*, *23*, 13–20.

Coeling, H., & Wilcox, J. (1988). Understanding organizational culture: A key to management decision-making. *Journal of Nursing Administration*, *18*, 16–24.

Coeling, H., & Wilcox, J. (1990). Using organizational culture to facilitate the change process. *ANNA Journal*, *17*, 231–236.

Cooke, R., & Rousseau, D. (1988). Behavioral norms and expectations: A quantitative approach to the assessment of organizational culture. *Group and Organization Studies*, *13*, 245–273.

Cummings, T., & Worley, C. (2005). *Organization development and change*. Madison, WI: Thomson South-Western.

Fleeger, M. (1993). Assessing organizational culture: A planning strategy. *Nursing Management, 24*, 39–44.

Gershon, R., Stone, P., Bakken, S., & Larson, E. (2004). Measurement of organizational culture and climate in healthcare. *Journal of Nursing Administration, 34*, 33–40.

Gifford, B., Zammuto, R., & Goodman, E. (2002). The relationship between hospital unit culture and nurses' quality of work life. *Journal of Healthcare Management, 47*, 13–25.

Goodridge, D., & Hack, B. (1996). Assessing the congruence of nursing models with organizational culture: A quality improvement perspective. *Journal of Nursing Care Quality, 10*, 41–48.

Grau, L., & Wellin, E. (1992). The organizational cultures of nursing homes: Influences on responses to external regulatory controls. *Qualitative Health Research, 2*, 42–60.

Gregory, D., Way, C., LeFort, S., Barrett, B., & Parfrey, P. (2007). Predictors of registered nurses' organizational commitment and intent to stay. *Health Care Manager Review, 32*, 119–127.

Holt, D., Armenakis, A., Field, H., & Harris, S. (2007). Readiness for organizational change: The systematic development of a scale. *Journal of Applied Behavioral Science, 43*, 232–255.

Ingersoll, G., Wagner, L., Merk, S., Kirsch, J., Hepworth, M., & Williams, M. (2002). Patient focused redesign and employee perception of work environment. *Nursing Economics, 20*, 163–187.

Jones, K., DeBaca, V., & Yarbrough, M. (1997). Organizational culture assessment before and after implementing patient-focused care. *Nursing Economics, 15*, 73–80.

Jones, K., & Redman, R. (2000). Organizational culture and work redesign: Experiences in three organizations. *Journal of Nursing Administration, 30*, 604–610.

Kangas, S., Kee, C., & McKee-Waddle, R. (1999). Organizational factors, nurses' job satisfaction and patient satisfaction with nursing care. *Journal of Nursing Administration, 29*, 32–42.

Klakovich, M. (1996). Registered nurse empowerment: Model testing and implications for nurse administrators. *Journal of Nursing Administration, 26*, 29–35.

Lim, B. (1995). Examining the organizational culture and organization performance link. *Leadership and Organization Development Journal, 16*, 16–21.

Lin, M., Marsteller, J., Shortell, S., Mendel, P., Pearson, M., Rosen, M., & Wu, S. (2005). Motivation to change chronic illness care: Results from national evaluation of quality improvement collaboratives. *Health Care Manage Review, 30*, 139–156.

Luk, A., Chen, R., Yau, F., Tsang, E., & Leung, C. (1998). Assessment of the organizational culture in a new hospital. *Hong Kong Nursing Journal, 34*, 13–22.

Manley, K. (2000). Organizational culture and consultant nurse outcomes: Part 2: Nurse outcomes. *Nursing Standard, 14*, 34–39.

Manojlovich, M., & Ketefian, S. (2002). The effects of organizational culture on nursing professionalism: Implications for health resource planning. *Canadian Journal of Nursing Research, 33*, 15–34.

McDaniel, C., & Stumpf, L. (1993). The organizational culture: Implications for nursing service. *Journal of Nursing Administration, 23*, 54–60.

Moran, J., & Brightman, B. (2000). Leading organizational change. *Journal of Workplace Learning, 12*, 66–74.

Rizzo, J., Gilman, M., & Mersmann, C. (1994). Facilitating care delivery redesign using measures of unit culture and work characteristics. *Journal of Nursing Administration, 24*, 32–37.

Schein, E. (1990). Organizational culture. *American Psychologist*, *45*, 109–119.

Scott-Findlay, S., & Estabrooks, C. (2006). Mapping the organizational culture research in nursing: A literature review. *Journal of Advanced Nursing*, *30*, 31–38.

Seago, J. (1996a). Culture of troubled work groups. *Journal of Nursing Administration*, *26*, 41–46.

Seago, J. (1996b). Work group culture, stress and hostility: Correlations with organizational outcomes. *Journal of Nursing Administration*, *26*, 39–47.

Seago, J. (2000). Registered nurses, unlicensed assistive personnel and organizational culture in hospitals. *Journal of Nursing Administration*, *30*, 278–286.

Seren, S., & Baykal, U. (2007). Relationships between change and organizational culture in hospitals. *Journal of Nursing Scholarship*, *39*, 191–197.

Smith, M. (2003). Changing an organization's culture: Correlates of success and failure. *Leadership and Organization Development Journal*, *24*, 249–261.

Sorensen, P., & Yaeger, T. (2004). Feedback from the positive question – The integration of appreciative inquiry with survey feedback: From corporate to global cultures. In: D. Copperrider & M. Avital (Eds), *Constructive discourse and human organization advances in appreciative inquiry* (pp. 263–281). JAI Press.

Stock, G., McFadden, K., & Gowen, C. (2007). Organizational culture, critical success factors, and the reduction of hospital errors. *International Journal Production Economics*, *106*, 368–392.

Stumpf, L. (2001). A comparison of governance types and patient satisfaction outcomes. *Journal of Nursing Administration*, *31*, 196–202.

The Joint Commission. (2009). Available at www.jointcommission.org

Thomas, C., Ward, M., Chorba, C., & Kumiega, A. (1990). Measuring and interpreting organizational culture. *Journal of Nursing Administration*, *20*, 17–24.

Tzeng, H., Ketefian, S., & Redman, R. (2002). Relationship of nurses' assessment of organizational culture, job satisfaction and patient satisfaction with nursing care. *International Journal of Nursing Studies*, *39*, 79–84.

Vandenberghe, C. (1999). Organizational culture, person-culture fit and turnover: A replication in the health care industry. *Journal of Organizational Behavior*, *20*, 175–184.

Watson, S., & Kimberly, J. (1997). Reengineering hospitals: Evidence from the field. *Hospitals and Health Services Administration*, *42*, 143–163.

Webb, S., Price, S., & Coeling, H. (1996). Valuing authority/responsibility relationships: The essence of professional practice. *Journal of Nursing Administration*, *26*, 28–33.

Wilson, V., McCormack, B., & Ives, G. (2005). Understanding the workplace culture of a special care nursery. *Journal of Advanced Nursing*, *50*, 27–38.

Yamaguchi, S. (2004). Nursing culture of an operating theater in Italy. *Nursing and Health Sciences*, *6*, 261–269.

ACHIEVING ORGANIZATIONAL CHANGE IN HEALTH CARE THROUGH PEOPLE AND CULTURE: A COMMENTARY

Jim Goes

Organizational change has been a consistent and growing theme in health care management, and research on the topic reflects this interest. Amid continuously rising health care costs, major regulatory and policy reform, and technological evolution, health care executives continue to search for effective models and methods of leading and directing change to position their organizations in an increasingly unstable industry and sector. As industry leaders look for answers, researchers have shown a growing interest in understanding how health care organizations are evolving to fit the needs of the new marketplace.

As recently as a decade ago, research on most organizational change issues in health care was narrow and limited. Our review of organizational change research in the first volume of *Advances in Health Care Management* (Goes, Friedman, Seifert, & Buffa, 2000) concluded that research on change was fragmented, unsystematic, and somewhat disconnected from the practical issues faced by health care leaders. We developed a framework to classify existing research and articulated future research needs along three dimensions: the *level* at which change is taking place (e.g., organizational or industry), the *type* of change underway (incremental or radical), and the

Organization Development in Healthcare: Conversations on Research and Strategies
Advances in Health Care Management, Volume 10, 117–121

ISSN: 1474-8231/doi:10.1108/S1474-8231(2011)0000010013

mode or nature of change (whether change was driven by outside factors or internally generated). Of the eight focus areas of organizational change research that our model specified, we found nearly all were both conceptually and empirically underdeveloped, and we concluded there was a substantial need for more research in the field.

A decade later, there is evidence that health care researchers have responded to this need. A brief of the literature identified over 200 referred journal articles published in the last 10 years that directly or indirectly addressed organizational change issues. The chapters by Halm and Haviley in this volume are both helpful examples of the new scholarship in this field. Both chapters illustrate the importance of widening our view of the organizational change problem to include the individual and group levels of analysis. Much of the earlier research on organizational change in health care tended to focus at the organizational and industry levels, with attention to macro forces driving change (e.g., certificate of need regulations, or competition between hospitals and systems). However, efforts at organizational restructuring and transformation enjoyed limited success, in part because of cultural resistance and limited motivation to change among health professionals (Friedman & Goes, 2001). In short, the grand plans for restructuring and repositioning that were in vogue a decade ago ran aground at least partly because of insufficient attention to the critical role played by processes and people inside the organization. The timely chapters by Halm and Haviley speak directly to the human and group dynamics that can facilitate or prevent effective organizational change initiatives.

Halm begins by exploring the need for hospitals and systems to respond to a changing environment, including simultaneous expectations for expanded coverage of underserved populations and cost containment that are driving hospitals toward "radical adjustment and organized transformation." Yet, are these two dynamics the same? Regulatory changes, both at the state level and through the recently passed "Patient Protection and Affordable Care Act" at the national level, are externally driven mandates to which health care organizations must react and ultimately adapt. However, this sort of adaptation to external change drivers contrasts with the usual notion of organizational transformation as a consciously designed and planned, leader driven change effort, often years in the making (Levy & Merry, 1986). This illustrates both the need for consistent use of terminology like "transformation," which is a widely used and abused term, and also the need for clarity in understanding the impetus of an organizational change. Externally driven changes are most likely to be resisted, because they do not originate from within the organization.

Perhaps the challenge facing hospital and system leaders is to frame external mandates as opportunities for transformation, craft a change model and plan that meets external mandates, while transforming the organization to meet future strategic challenges, and even uses the real threat of financial or human resource cuts as a lever to heighten awareness and stimulate momentum for change within the organization.

Transforming organizations is achieved through structures, processes, and people, and Halm's primary focus for the rest of the paper is on the individual – how to *engage* employees in the important work of transforming the organization at the same time they are engaged in their professional work and social groups. As one system CEO explained it to me some years ago: "how can I get physicians to think not just of the impact of their decisions on their patients, or their profession, but also on the organizations as a whole?" Halm views culture as the means to achieve engagement: "The primary purpose of health care managers is to create a culture where employees are fully involved and energized by the work they do within the organization." If only it were that easy. The notion of employee engagement, defined as "seeking to increase members' input into decisions that affect organization performance and employee wellbeing" (Cummings & Worley, 2005, p. 306), is very attractive – but although engagement may be a new label, it is not a new idea. We have been discussing it for years with terms like motivation, empowerment, alignment, etc. How does labeling it as "engagement" enable us to advance understanding about this important element of organizational change?

Indeed, Halm goes on to discuss theory and research around engagement by focusing on established and well researched ideas like creating meaning in work, intelligent job design, creating effective work teams, and related concepts. These ideas are collapsed into updated classifications of human, social, and psychological capital. This discussion was interesting, but of limited practical value, as it appeared to be more of a review of the latest terminology and concepts than a road map for health care leaders about how to achieve engagement. Moreover, how is the idea of engagement qualitatively different from other established ideas about leading individuals to change – ideas that are both well established in the field, and apparently have delivered mixed success in transforming health care?

Health care organizations are often unruly venues where professional, ethnic, and organizational cultures mix and churn, and designing and executing a cultural change is a long and arduous process. Halm's chapter rightly brings our attention to the critical need of professionals in these organizations to embrace a change initiative in order for it to succeed, and therefore, the need for leaders to educate, persuade, and cajole these individuals out of their professional, departmental, and social silos and into an understanding of both the imperative for change and the threat of failure. One need look no further than the many hospital closures and system failures over the last decade to appreciate that success matters in organizational change, be it externally driven or internally designed.

Leaders who wish to create a culture of employee engagement should recognize that cultures are changed only with great effort, particularly in the presence of strong professional cultures and established practices. Therefore, the process of cultural change may not be entirely or even mostly driven from the top. Halm's work points to some possible levers for leaders seeking to increase employee engagement, but engagement by itself may not lead to either cultural change or organizational transformation. Such transformation seems more likely when strategies, structures, processes, and people are all aligned around the same vision and imperative. This requires leadership recognition that transformation must work at multiple levels of analysis (organizational, group, and individual) and must have influential champions at each of these levels.

Culture is the point of departure for the chapter by Haviley. The chapter attempts to provide "a summary of the history and research contributions related to the study of culture and change through the lens of nursing." That's a tall order for one paper, but Haviley does provide an extensive review of literature on efforts to change culture in nursing units, and how culture change was measured. This is a good contribution, and the discussion provides useful guidance to researchers interested in culture as a mechanism of organizational change, particularly at the operational level of a nursing unit. However, the author correctly concludes that existing research is inadequate, and does not support confident conclusions about the value of cultural change initiatives in nursing.

Like Halm's focus on the importance of engaging individuals as elements of change efforts, Haviley's focus on the cultural level adds a useful piece toward understanding the need for multiple levels of action in achieving organizational change. The approaches and evidence Haviley cites are more reasonably actionable by change designers, although the chapter could provide more practical guidance, synthesized from the literature, about how to design and execute successful cultural change initiatives. Moreover, given the strong culture of the nursing profession, it is not clear how far results from cultural change efforts in nursing will generalize to other departments and cultures within hospitals and systems.

Taken together, the two chapters nicely illustrate that effective organizational change in health care requires leadership focus and initiative at the top, buy-in at the group or culture level, and enthusiasm at the level of individual employees. Yet there is a real need for more research that incorporates these multiple levels of analysis, and investigates how they interact. For example, to what extent are efforts to increase employee engagement stifled by the power or cultural norms of particular groups in the institution? How do departmental efforts at cultural change around a specific operational problem fit with cultural change efforts elsewhere in the organization, or the transformational vision at the top? More research is needed to understand how to design change efforts at multiple levels to interact and reinforce rather than work against each other.

Finally, for health care researchers, both chapters illustrate the importance of precision in terminology, conceptualization, and measurement to advance scholarship on organizational change. Developing consistent definitions and models of concepts like transformation, engagement, or culture, and arriving at standard ways of measuring these phenomena will establish a strong foundation for future research and evidence-based results to guide health care leaders in designing organizational change strategies that work.

REFERENCES

Cummings, L., & Worley, C. (2005). *Organizational development and change*. Mason, OH: South-Western.

Goes, J., Friedman, L., Seifert, N., & Buffa, J. (2000). A turbulent field: Theory, research, and practice on organizational change in health care. In: J. Blair, M. Fottler, & G. Savage (Eds), *Advances in healthcare management* (1st ed., Vol. 1, pp. 143–180). Bingley, UK: Emerald.

Friedman, L., & Goes, J. (2001). Why integrated health networks have failed. *Frontiers of Health Services Management*, *17*(Summer), 3–28.

Levy, A., & Merry, U. (1986). *Organizational transformation: Approaches, strategies, and theories*. Santa Barbara, CA: Praeger.

PART III
LEADERSHIP

THE FOUR C'S OF LEADERSHIP DEVELOPMENT

Cynthia Roberts and Carolyn Roper

ABSTRACT

One of the top domestic issues of concern to Americans is access to high-quality and affordable health care, and there is a growing concern about how institutions struggling to survive within this trillion-dollar industry will increase their effectiveness in the future. This chapter outlines a process of leadership development using an action learning approach in one Midwestern health care system over a period of three years. The process addresses both the development of the individual leader as well as the collective leadership capacity in an effort to sustain organizational learning and effectiveness over time. A model is presented that covers four phases or **Four C's** *of development, which includes movement from individual* ***Competency*** *development, to the development of social capital through the enhancement of* ***Connections*** *and* ***Creation of shared understanding****, ultimately expanding* ***Capacity for change*** *within the organization. We also address other factors that must be taken into consideration that will either enhance or impede the concentric movement such as culture, sponsor support, and alignment of systems and structures.*

Keywords: Leadership development; action learning; concentric collaboration

Organization Development in Healthcare: Conversations on Research and Strategies
Advances in Health Care Management, Volume 10, 125–149

ISSN: 1474-8231/doi:10.1108/S1474-8231(2011)0000010014

INTRODUCTION: HEALTH CARE AND LEADERSHIP

One of the top domestic issues of concern to Americans is access to high-quality and affordable health care (Institute, 2007). In addition, there is a growing concern about how institutions struggling to survive within this trillion-dollar industry will increase their effectiveness in the future.

From an internal perspective, the typical health care organization is fairly fragmented and comprised of many distinct groups of professionals who are typically socialized according to their respective disciplines rather than to the organization as a whole. Multiple missions within any one health care organization including quality care, research, teaching, community service and outreach, financial success, and in some cases reinforcement of religious values can also serve to either create synergy or add to the chaos. The task environment is also dynamic, complex, and at times ambiguous as professionals are expected to practice according to standard protocols but yet maintain the flexibility to improvise when the situation calls for it (Ranga & Rousseau, 2006). A fourth issue is the forecasted shortage of qualified professionals as a large percentage of experienced physicians, nurses, and other practitioners move toward retirement within the next few years (Institute, 2007).

The external stakeholders such as the government, insurance companies, and employers also exert pressure as they call for higher standards of quality while reducing costs (Ranga & Rousseau, 2006). Patients with enhanced access to information exert demands based on their own Internet research or the latest pharmaceutical marketing campaign for more convenient, lower cost alternatives (Institute, 2007). Mergers, acquisitions, and reorganizations, phenomena once found only in the traditional business sector, have become commonplace in the health care industry as well (Embertson, 2006).

The challenges discussed above are similar for Health Systems, a regional system serving a community within the Midwestern United States. The LEAD Institute (Leadership Education and Development), established in late 2006, was a leadership development program designed by the executive team of Health Systems and our nearby university to develop leadership capability in all members of the management team for increased personal and organization effectiveness. According to the Director of Organizational Development, we were chosen as consultants because of our local presence, academic background, and willingness to engage and commit for an extended duration. Previously, leadership programming was developed without any systematic planning, and consisted of either sending one or two managers offsite or bringing in-house a well-known professional speaker to present a seminar or two. There was little consistency in content between programs, no alignment with organizational mission or values, and no system in place to promote accountability of the participants upon program completion. Therefore, no real change was effected in the organization. With the university partnership, the Health Systems initiative would incorporate best practices in leadership development.

LEADERSHIP DEVELOPMENT IN REVIEW

Throughout recent history, there have been several notions of leadership put forth from individual traits and effectiveness of one singular agent (Kirkpatrick & Locke, 1991; Goleman, 1998; Judge, Bono, Ilies, & Gerhardt, 2002) to a focus on the process and relationship between leaders and followers (Bass, 1985; Burns, 1978) to the consideration of leadership as a function of the entire collective (Barker, 2001; Dachler & Hosking, 1995; Drath, 2001; Manz & Sims Jr, 1991; Marion & Uhl-Bien, 2001; Rost, 1991). As the notion of leadership broadens from the singular "hero" to the work of the collective, the facilitation of leadership development becomes increasingly complex. Day (2001) and Day & Harrison (2007) offers a useful distinction between the notion of individual leader and the collective, emergent process of leadership and suggests that organizations intending to build effective leadership capacity need to develop both individual human capital as well as collective social capital.

Leader development according to Van Velsor and McCauley (2004, p. 2) is defined as "the expansion of a person's capacity to be effective in leadership roles and processes ... those that facilitate setting direction, creating alignment, maintaining commitment in groups of people who share common work." Individuals must become cognizant of their own values, and develop greater self-awareness and an ability to continuously learn, think, and act creatively and strategically (Day, 2001; Kouzes & Posner, 2002; Van Velsor, 2004).

Leadership development, on the other hand, addresses the collective and encompasses "the expansion of the organization's capacity to enact the basic leadership tasks needed for collective work" (Van Velsor, 2004, p. 18). Leadership as capacity is developed through building interpersonal skills, social awareness, mutual respect, and trust. Effective leadership development not only enhances individual effectiveness, but also serves to build relationships, coordinate actions, and extend and strengthen the social network. Development must occur over time in an iterative manner, be grounded in experience, and foster reflection not only individually but also collectively (Conger, 2004; McCall, 2004; Connaughton, Lawrence, & Ruben, 2003; Daudelin, 1996; Torbert, 1994; Mintzberg, 2004).

A common approach to leader development (Leatt & Porter, 2003; Van Velsor & McCauley, 2004) employs a process that starts with an assessment of an individual leader's current strengths and weaknesses to identify gaps between his or her present state and the ideal. Once the person is aware of the gaps, he or she can then work to close them in some manner through various experiences, training, coaching, or mentoring. A key component in this process is the provision of some type of "challenge" that forces the person to stretch and work outside of his or her comfort zone. Challenges that create disequilibrium and discomfort for the individual must be balanced, however, with other activities such as coaching or mentoring that support, encourage, and maintain positive self-images. This approach is common in many organizations, remains focused primarily on the individual, and does little to build collective capacity.

While formal education, particularly when linked with individual reflection, clearly has a role in competency development, Leatt and Porter (2003) suggest an approach to leadership development in health care that employs a comprehensive, interdisciplinary process. This process should strengthen teams, promote appropriate ethics and values, be grounded in a framework of quality improvement, and can work to address larger organizational initiatives.

LEADERSHIP DEVELOPMENT THROUGH ACTION LEARNING

Action learning, due to its collaborative nature, is well suited to facilitate leadership development as it unfolds as a reflexive and relational process (Raelin, 2006; Coghlan, 2004). It can provide the platform for leadership development through collaborative work-based "learning-in-action." Dialogue, learning teams, and action projects create opportunities for members to reflect upon their experience together, challenge their assumptions, and shift from using a singular perspective as the leader to one that is much more collective or, in Raelin's words (2003), "leaderful." Central to the process is its cyclical nature, an engagement with real issues, a process of inquiry that attempts to uncover all aspects of a particular issue in question, exploration of potential resolutions through action and reflection, and promotion of a group dynamic that encourages critical reflection and learning (Revans, 1998). According to Revans (1980, p. 309), "*... action learning is about real people tackling real problems in real time, observing the impartial discipline of* *the business setting and looking after a lot of people ...*" The use of external experts is minimal, and participants take control of their own learning. This process can be particularly valuable in the health care setting as a means to bridge professional silos and promote interdisciplinary collaboration and a sense of collective agency.

THE LEAD INSTITUTE

The LEAD program was an attempt to systematize leadership development in a manner that could impact the organization on a larger scale, create a shared understanding of leadership at all levels, and work to support the organization's mission and values. The program, originally intended for middle managers as a succession planning tool, was extended to include front-line supervisors, team leaders, coordinators, and others who have shown an interest. To date, 150 employees have participated in the program in three separate cohorts representing all areas of the system: patient care, diagnostics, administrative support, ancillary services, and off-site satellite facilities.

The first phase or LEAD I focused primarily on individual leader development and skill building, but secondarily also began the process of connecting those from different professional disciplines. LEAD II facilitated collaboration between each participant and the development of collective leadership. The third phase, LEAD III, was driven by the members themselves to meet emerging needs going forward. The underlying philosophy incorporated many of the tenets of action learning (Raelin, 2006): collaboration, multiple cycles of learning, a focus on action and application, an opportunity for reflection at individual and group levels, creation of social capital, empowerment of participants to drive each discussion and suggest concepts for future programming, and the beginnings of an impact on organizational operations. Table 1 contains a detailed review of the actual topics. A brief overview of content and format is also discussed below.

The following issues were considered in an effort to facilitate leader development, individual learning, and skill building:

- *Content delivery*: content areas were developed and presented based on several conversations with members of Health Systems administration. Topics were later added based on what emerged from dialogue within each seminar. Content included leadership theory, personality, effective communication, conflict management, time and meeting management, coaching, performance management, group dynamics, appreciative inquiry, and

Table 1. LEAD Programming.

LEAD I: Leader Development

Goal: Individual skill development, network development

Topics, learning objectives, and activities:

- True colors (personality profiles)
  - Develop a greater understanding of personality differences and strategies for working through differences effectively
  - Use the assessment as a mechanism for strengthening your own team and relationships with peers
- Leadership theory
  - Discuss differences between managing and leading
  - Develop awareness of personal leadership style
  - Compare the differences between leadership and followership
  - Create an action plan for utilizing some of the concepts of effective leadership
- Effective communication
  - Develop and practice skills for making requests, suggestions, proposals, or demands
  - Utilize effective listening techniques
  - Practice delivering negative messages as positively as possible
  - Practice using assertive communication for action
  - Develop strategies for using email communications effectively
- Coaching for success
  - Understand the nature and mindset of coaching
  - Develop a strategy for creating a climate that fosters coaching and the learning organization
  - Utilize strategies that seek out the strengths in others and support their growth
  - Work through an actual situation using a coaching process
- Delegation and empowerment
  - Understand the importance and purpose of delegating
- Time and meeting management
  - Develop a strategy for utilizing time more effectively
  - Develop an awareness of group process and stages of team development
  - Practice behaviors that facilitate effective meetings and productive behavior
- Review, reflection, action planning

LEAD II: Leadership Applications

Goal: Relationship development, collaborative problem solving, application of concepts, practice

Topics, learning objectives, and activities:

- Servant leadership
  - Review key concepts and identify opportunities that can enhance the growth of individuals in the organization, and increase teamwork and personal involvement
- Appreciative inquiry
  - Understand the key principles behind appreciative inquiry
  - Experience the process of appreciative inquiry
  - Practice an appreciative process with your team back on the job

Table 1. (*Continued*)

- Change management I and II
  - Understand the process of change from personal as well as organizational perspectives
  - Utilize strategies for working through a change process in your own department
- Review, reflection, action planning

LEAD III: Leadership in Action

Goal: To enact leadership by leading an organizational initiative – propose and implement a project

Possible projects to work on:

- Development of new manager mentoring program
- Building trust/culture change
- Exploration of opportunities for further network development; working past the "silos"; shadowing and learning about each other's jobs
- Dealing with staffing shortages, call schedule
- "Meeting free day"
- Email policies and guidelines

Some skill development, possible topics include conflict management, strategic planning, financial management

---

change management. Printed resources were also developed and provided to each participant for future reference.

- *Personal assessment and reflection*: several opportunities for self-assessment and reflection were built into the process through post-program surveys, journal writing, and group dialogue.
- *Application and action*: each session ended with a challenge to the participants to return to their respective departments, apply one of the concepts, and then return ready to share observations and reflections of the outcome. This in turn created an additional cycle of learning.

Leadership development, group learning, and enhanced social capital were facilitated by incorporating the following activities:

- *Group inquiry and dialogue*: each session was structured to include a large portion of time for group conversation, providing the relational space for sharing relevant issues and resolving problems.
- *Development of the social network*: members were encouraged to sit at tables with others who were less familiar. The intent was to create mutual understanding and expand each member's awareness of issues outside of one's own department or discipline.

- *Practice collaborative leadership*: as programming progressed, the control of the process shifted from being consultant-driven to one that was co-directed by the group and consultants. The content for LEAD II was derived based on the issues that arose in LEAD I. The content as well as format for LEAD III was driven primarily by the participants, as actionable projects.

Outcomes of the LEAD program

The LEAD program, at its inception, was intended to assist current managers and team leaders in developing skills to make them more effective leaders. Content provided was also intended to help raise awareness and create alignment with organizational values. By the end of the first year, however, we had become more embedded within the organization and the program evolved into a process that also supported the development of collective leadership capacity.

Several opportunities for garnering feedback were developed throughout the LEAD process and have provided data related to outcomes of the program. We utilized individual surveys, one-on-one dialogues with select participants, personal observations and journaling, as well as periodic meetings with key personnel. Yammarino, Dansereau, and Kennedy (2001) suggest that leadership in general can be analyzed at four different levels using four different "lenses": the person, the relationships between leader and follower, the group, and the collective organization as a whole. Leadership development programs, therefore, could likewise be assessed for effectiveness at each of those levels and, in fact, effective programs should impact multiple levels (Day, 2001; Leatt & Porter, 2003). Because leadership development is such a multifaceted phenomenon, however, determining effectiveness becomes increasingly complex. In the following sections, we have used the lenses suggested by Yammarino and colleagues (2001), altering them slightly to highlight outcomes from the LEAD program according to the individual, group, and organization.

Within the individual framework, we have included both knowledge acquisition as well as the development of relational skills. The group perspective reviews changes in departmental dynamics and processes. The organizational perspective includes overall changes in processes as well as the development of networks and social capital. The development of social capital can be seen to be especially important to health care organizations that have historically operated in a fragmented manner, within discipline-based silos. Although we have addressed each level below, a summary of key outcomes can be found in Table 2.

The Individual Leader: Knowledge Acquisition and Relational Skills Development

Prior to beginning our engagement, we worked in concert with Health Systems to develop core areas of focus for competency development important from

Table 2. Outcomes of the LEAD Program.

Individual Leader Development
Improved self-confidence and comfort as leader
Competency development
- Reconceptualization of leadership
- Appreciation of diversity (personality styles, generational differences)
- Comprehension of change processes
- Better communication/listening skills
- More involvement, delegation, and empowerment of staff
- Use of coaching mindset

Group-Level Outcomes
Intradepartmental relationships
- More focus on team-building
- Dealing effectively with dysfunction
- More collaborative problem solving
- Implementation of new career ladder
- Changed layout of department
- Developed new process for third shift staffing
- Revised training process for new equipment

Organization-Level Outcomes
Network development – collective leadership
- Creation of connections beyond department
- More transparency and information sharing between levels
- Systems-thinking perspective/more collaboration between departments
- Projects for LEAD III (mentoring, staffing strategies, trust, etc.)
- Desire to expand LEAD program to others

Process changes
- New meeting management procedure
- Revitalization of organizational communication venue
- Development of training for new 360 review system

Unintended Outcomes
- Increased awareness, frustration with those not modeling content presented
- Desire for more collaboration with executive team

the perspective of the client. Since we were using an action learning approach, individuals were able to learn what was relevant to them, reflect upon that learning, and use that information back within their own setting. Our findings suggested that all cohorts experienced several of the same "learning points" that included a reconceptualization of the notion of leadership, better understanding and appreciation of style differences, and a more complete understanding of the process of change management. In addition, less experienced team leaders from later cohorts reported that they had gained more self-confidence and comfort within their roles as leaders, crucial for their further development (Lord & Hall, 2005).

The participants also reported that they had improved their relational skills, noting better communication skills, increased involvement and empowerment of their staff, more delegation, and a shift in practice to employing more positive forms of performance management such as coaching and mentoring. In addition to self-reports of learning and behavior change, we had the opportunity to have the junior team leaders in the second and third cohorts share observations of changes that they had noticed in their own managers who were a part of the earlier cohort. Their reports also corroborated the self-reports of more communication, involvement, and delegation.

Although participants of the program noted the acquisition of knowledge as well as the development of relational skills, the perceived impact of the LEAD program could have been strengthened by the inclusion of a recurring 360 assessment process. Participants could have been assessed at the very beginning, and then each year thereafter to track changes in behavior over time, particularly as seen by others. At the time of this project, a 360 process had just been implemented. Although many of the topics mirrored concepts introduced in the LEAD program, the adoption system-wide created challenges in consistency and validity that still needed to be addressed.

The Group: Intradepartmental Dynamics and Processes

Group dialogue, focus groups, interviews, and progress reports on team projects can all be considered valid methods for assessing impact of leadership development at the group level (Martineau, 2004). This project employed the use of observation, multiple rounds of surveying, and individual dialogues to gather data. A concern about relationships within the individual departments or units frequently emerged. Team-building, dealing with dysfunctional group dynamics, employee performance, coaching, and delegation were all discussed. One manager implemented a department-wide career ladder and noted that this had helped retain entry-level employees. Another reported that she had changed the layout of her unit to promote more dialogue and collaboration between caregivers and support personnel. Several participants reported that they have seen better teamwork within their department. Others noted more collaborative problem solving and a willingness to share leadership. A few members of the second and third cohorts reported that they had actually seen changes in their own managers to be more inclusive and collaborative.

Time and relative length of experience within a leadership role also affected the focus of the participants – those who had been in a management position for some time appeared to focus on more global organizational issues while those who were relatively new had concerns that were much more locally driven. For example, the participants in the less senior, second cohort were much more interested in how the programming would help in the immediate context of their team, and conversations centered on personal struggles in making the transition to a leadership role as well as more departmentally oriented operational issues. The groups covered issues such as staffing and training, relationship building through better communication, addressing generational issues, improving morale, and facilitating more involvement of their team members. One group actually left a session and returned with a new plan for handling staffing on the third shift. Another team leader worked with her group to craft a strategy for training nurses from across the organization how to use a new piece of equipment.

The more senior cohort addressed some of the same challenges, but then went further to engage issues dealing with organizational policies and procedures. Some of the topics explored included the implementation of a new 360 evaluation process, exploration of a new process for scheduling and conducting meetings across the organization, changes in organizational culture, and consideration of a system-wide mentoring program for new managers. This group also expressed more frustration with the organization in general, especially when their managers behaved in a manner that did not align with concepts presented in the LEAD program.

The Organization: Culture and Process Changes

There are many strategies for assessing the impact of leadership development programs at the organizational level, which can include culture change, examination of evidence of process changes, assessment for changes in productivity, absenteeism, satisfaction, turnover, degree of innovation, return on investment, or an assessment of customer satisfaction (Martineau, 2004). Organizational impact, however, is much more difficult to directly correlate with programming, and although there is strong evidence that leadership development programs can be effective at enhancing individual competency, there is a paucity of evidence that connects leadership development to improved organizational effectiveness (Collins & Holton III, 2004). The difficulty may lie in the existence and interplay of several internal elements such as mission, strategy, culture, structure, as well as the external environment (Waclawski, 2002). The fragmented nature of health care as well as constantly changing clinical protocols, technology, and reimbursement schemes further compound the issue. As we worked through the series, it became clear that several different programs were ongoing simultaneously – the inception of a "Beyond Blame" program that shifted problem-solving practice from a punitive process to a learning process, the introduction of a new system for flowcharting, the establishment of a new 360 performance management system, and a major change in senior executive staff, which resulted in reorganization of reporting structures as well as project priorities. Since isolating the effects of a LEAD program intervention would be extremely challenging, this project did not employ the use of metrics for assessing changes in culture, productivity, turnover, satisfaction, or return on investment.

Raelin (2006) argues that although a leadership development approach utilizing action learning may employ conventional forms of outcomes assessment, measurement may take unconventional forms such as narrative since individuals and teams create their own reality through ongoing reflection and inquiry. Since this has been, and continues to be, an ongoing process rather than a finite intervention with a known endpoint, it has been difficult to pinpoint the effects directly attributable to the engagement. Stories and self-reports are key to providing insight into this process (Wenger, 2000; Bradbury & Reason, 2001).

In our case, the most noticeable changes in the organization were reported at the process and procedural levels. A routine Friday meeting (called TGIF) was taken over and revitalized through the efforts of the first cohort. This forum has provided another venue for managers to assemble and share information with others outside of their area. Changes were also made to the format of other meetings to encourage efficiency and effectiveness, and a system-wide training program was developed for the newly implemented 360 evaluation process. Since there were several different individual reports and observations of increased delegation and involvement, this may suggest there has been some incremental change toward more empowerment overall.

The Organization: Networks and Leadership Development

The LEAD process facilitated the growth of the individual "leader" as it supported the development of connections necessary for the practice of collective "leadership," both of which are necessary for effectiveness (Day,

2001; Day & Harrison, 2007; Raelin, 2003). Bartol and Zhang (2007) suggest thinking of leadership development outcomes in terms of the creation of multiple linkages or networks. Networks foster more effective leadership processes in three very important ways: task accomplishment and problem solving (task), career advancement and mentoring (career), and friendship and emotional support (support). In our experience, the creation of connections was seen as one of the major outcomes of the LEAD program as the value of having the opportunity for dialogue and collaboration repeatedly emerged through this project. The importance of connectivity, particularly in a historically fragmented organization such as a hospital, should not be underestimated.

The members of the first cohort, consisting of managers who were fairly experienced, appeared to be a much more connected group from the very beginning. Since they had considerable experience working together on other projects, they were quick to rely on each other as resources for problem resolution as well as emotional support. The members of this cohort have also taken responsibility for other organizational projects such as a new manager-mentoring program, working through holiday coverage issues, building trust between each other, and working more closely with upper administration. They have collectively tried to grapple with and make sense of recent changes in organizational structure and key personnel, the enactment of empowerment within the context of a formal hierarchal structure, and organizational strategies for leveraging their time more effectively (meetings, emails, schedules, etc.). As several of the managers have noted, they are starting to work from a systems-thinking perspective by involving others from outside of the unit when appropriate.

Unintended Outcomes of the LEAD Program

The LEAD program has also resulted in some unintended consequences. Although the CEO endorsed the creation of leadership at all levels, the growth of the "leaderful" organization has been met with some resistance by other members of the executive team. On several occasions, participants expressed frustration with a lack of congruence between the tenets of leaderful practice and the behavior of a few members of the executive team. Ford and Harding (2007), in their musing "*could leadership courses develop leaders who do the opposite of what the organization requires,*" offer several different outcomes that can result from leadership development programs. Participants may not change at all, or they may experience an awakening of a different way of being and gain a greater awareness of "iniquities and inequities" within the organization. The desire to change the state of the organization may result in rebellion, cynicism, or even departure, or it may actually effect a more emancipatory workplace. According to Raelin (2003), those in power must be comfortable with sharing it rather than keeping it for themselves, and it may take a leap of faith for them to let go a bit.

In our case, the emancipatory concepts discussed may have awakened the need for more information sharing, empowerment, and collaboration between the executive team and the managers, beyond what the executive team was willing to do. Although most levels of the organization have gone or will go through the LEAD program sometime in the future, the uppermost level did not fully engage in the process. In retrospect, it would have been helpful to involve the entire team earlier in the process rather than later.

A MODEL OF LEADERSHIP DEVELOPMENT: THE FOUR C'S

The process of leadership development has emerged in this organization in a manner that includes both growth of individual leaders as well as the development of collective leadership capacity, and as we have worked through this process, the image of dropping a pebble into a pond comes to mind. The pebble breaks the surface of the water, causing a series of ripples to form and move outward in ever-enlarging concentric circles. We suggest that the process of leader/leadership development can be conceptualized similarly. As each "pebble" or concept is dropped into the "pond," the ripples of knowledge, learning, connection, and influence move from the individual leader (center) outward to his or her immediate team, then expands to reach other departments, and finally causes ripples that extend throughout the entire organization.

This model of leadership development involves a process called "concentric collaboration," which bridges the growth and development of the individual leader with proponents of the notion of the development of leadership capacity as considered part of a collective process. The model, presented in Fig. 1, integrates not only the growth and learning of the individual leader but also the development of social capital by enhancing connections and creating shared meaning, ultimately increasing the capacity to catalyze organizational change (Roberts, 2009).

The expanding concentric circles represent the phases of leadership development, which moves from a leader-centric individual focus to one that considers and enacts leadership and change as a collective process. The model attempts to provide movement not only outward but upward as well

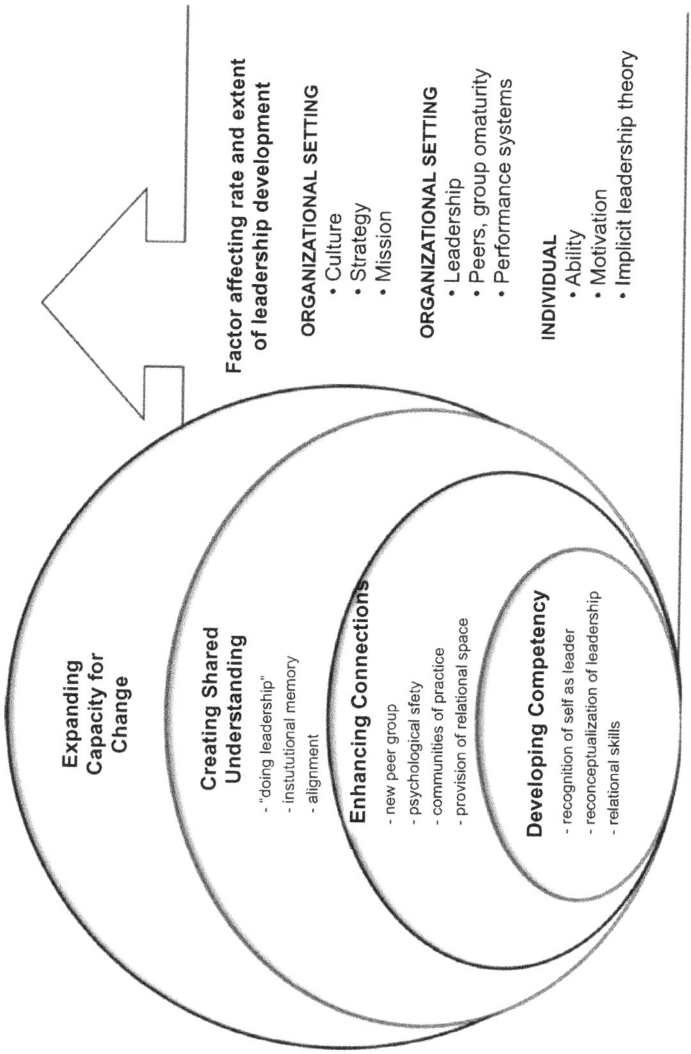

Fig. 1. Model of Leadership Development.

(hence the offset in the circles to try and illustrate a three-dimensional movement). The process, facilitated through the use of multiple cycles of action learning and inquiry, addresses Day's call (2001, 2007) for an approach that develops human as well as social capital. The four phases or ***Four C's*** elucidated below include the movement from the individual **Competency** development, the development of social capital through the enhancement of **Connections** and **Creation of shared understanding**, and finally expanding **Capacity for change** within the organization. After discussing the four phases below, we also address other factors that must be taken into consideration that will either enhance or impede the concentric movement such as culture, sponsor support, and alignment of systems and structures.

Developing Individual Competency

In order for effective leadership to emerge, one must begin with the development of the individual first. This phase is addressed in most traditional leader development programs and focuses on building individual knowledge and skills (Day, 2001). Implicit notions of leadership and an internal focus are gradually replaced by more collective concepts (Lord & Hall, 2005; Rooke & Torbert, 2005). In the earliest sessions of the LEAD program, one discovers new ways of thinking about leadership, develops appreciation for differences, and assimilates more effective relational and managerial skills. Development of a more collaborative style allows for the individual to engage others in problem solving, learning, and information sharing, which sets the stage for increasing connections and network development.

Enhancing Connections

The collaborative nature of action learning provides relevance, encourages reflection, and helps to develop interdisciplinary relationships or networks that continue even after the programming is finished (Raelin, 2006; Raelin & Coghlan, 2006; Torbert, 1994). The expansion of interdisciplinary networks can result in increased social capital, which is essential to individual, group, and organizational effectiveness (Bartol & Zhang, 2007; Nahapiet & Ghoshal, 1998; King, 2004; O'Connor & Quinn, 2004). In essence, social capital is considered to be the value and resources embedded within networks that enable collective action (Nahapiet & Ghoshal, 1998; O'Connor & Quinn, 2004). The development of social capital not only involves the creation of new connections and the enhancement of relational dynamics such as respect, trust, shared norms, values, and expectations, but also allows for a cognitive recognition of a collective identity through shared language and meaning making (Nahapiet & Ghoshal, 1998). This portion of the model, therefore, addresses the creation of social capital in two ways – by enhancing connections and relationships, and creating shared meaning.

One of the distinctive aspects of the LEAD program that has evolved over time is its focus on building relationships and collaborative learning. Uhl-Bien (2006) suggests that contemporary notions of leadership have less to do with the individual or position and more to do with the influence exerted from relational dynamics. The value of the collective experience has been supported in the literature (Raelin, 2001; Senge, 2004), and in this context, the value of the collaborative process may be fourfold:

- Assistance in the transition to "leader" through the establishment of a new peer group that transcends practice boundaries or organizational "silos."
- Provision of psychological safety – Edmondson (1999) notes the importance of psychological safety to team learning. The supportive environment provided by the LEAD program may provide a degree of psychological safety for some members to take risks and share their dilemmas, ultimately enhancing the learning of all.
- Development of a stronger network through creation of communities of practice or learning communities that can assist in problem solving, professional skill development, and the transfer of best practices (Senge, 2004; Wenger, 2000). Several members have noted that they have learned a great deal from their colleagues and have recognized that they have more in common than originally perceived, grappling with many of the same issues such as problematic employees, budgetary constraints, and organizational policies. A community of practice that joins together participants from different professional disciplines may also help alleviate some of the isolation and fragmentation issues found in health care organizations as noted by Ranga and Rousseau (2006).
- Creation of relational space – Bradbury, Lichtenstein, Carroll, Senge, and Powley (2007) assert that the creation of relational space precedes the development of collaborative work between different organizational entities. As members develop trust, peer-to-peer learning becomes possible. Over time, the connections can result in collaborative efforts and action across the organization.

Creating Shared Understanding

The process of action learning and the resulting community of practice facilitates the creation of shared understanding of what effective leadership is, clarifies issues within the organization, and enhances the institutional memory (Raelin, 2006). It assists with the dissemination of knowledge throughout the organization, and facilitates the emergence of a singular notion of "who we are."It is in essence "doing leadership" (Rost, 1991; Uhl-Bien, 2006). Shared understanding may also serve to reinforce new behaviors and sustain them over time. Senge (2004) notes that the collective dialogue deepens relationships, creates alignment, and enables new realities.

Expanding Capacity for Change

Effective leadership development processes should enhance organizational capability for meeting complex challenges that are larger than any one set of individuals (Raelin, 2003). O'Connor and Quinn (2004) maintain that expanded leadership capacity, which allows for multiple responses to any given situation, is essential to health and survival. This increased capacity becomes evident through organizational changes and improvements in performance such as efficiency and productivity gains, process improvements, innovation and adaptation, or improved employee relations (Yukl & Lepsinger, 2005). We have begun to see preliminary evidence of this in our setting as well. As the LEAD program has progressed, several initiatives have begun to emerge.

Factors Affecting Leadership Development Initiatives

Continuing with the metaphor of expanding ripples and concentric collaboration, one must also keep in mind factors that will either enhance or impede the height of each "wave" and the rate of its progression. Holton (2005), in his comprehensive model of the evaluation of human resource development initiatives, suggests that there are multiple factors that influence what an individual learns in the first place, then how that learning is enacted in the workplace, and finally how individual performance impacts organizational performance. Each stage is briefly addressed below:

- *Factors affecting individual learning* – Individuals enter any developmental engagement with a wide variety of traits and motivational factors that will either enhance or inhibit their receptiveness to the experience (Holton, 2005). With respect to leadership specifically, one also must struggle with adopting a new understanding of effective leadership as a function of the collective that may directly contradict his or her implicit construction of this phenomenon of leader as singular hero (Ford & Harding, 2007). Learning is less likely to occur if concepts presented are too far removed from the status quo or if there is no perceived connection of the learning experience with organizational strategy or mission (Montesino, 2002).

- *Factors affecting individual performance* – Transformation of behavior is dependent upon personal motivation to do so as well as other organizational factors such as culture or climate, opportunity to use new behaviors, support of leadership and peers, and performance systems that align with intended outcomes. Those learning new ways of leadership will be fearful to try out new behaviors if their own leaders are not in alignment with concepts or supportive of the change. Participants expecting a more emancipatory culture may become frustrated or disengaged if expectations are not met by their superiors. Human performance systems must also encourage, support, and reward new behaviors so that they can be sustained over time.
- *Factors affecting organizational performance* – Waclawski (2002), drawing from the work of multiple researchers such as Burke, Schein, Gersick, Tichy, Mohrman, Tushman, and Romanelli, suggests that mission, strategy, culture, structure, and leadership all serve as levers for successful organizational change. Clearly if there is a lack of alignment, it will be difficult to effect change at the personal level as mentioned above, let alone at the organizational level.

The model set forth in this section can be used to illustrate leadership development within any level of the organization. Individuals who occupy positions higher in the organizational hierarchy and are more seasoned have a larger perspective to consider and likewise will have a network that has a larger span of influence as well as effect. It is within this level that the strength of interdisciplinary connections have most relevance. Those individuals who are relatively new and hold positions with less authority can still effect change within a more local or regional scope through creation of connections and shared meaning making within their own group. Before one can leverage the network, however, it is important to note that personal transformation and reconceptualization must also occur in which one's focus shifts from reliance on self as leader and sole actor to a focus outward toward building relationships with others to enact leadership as a group phenomenon. It also stands to reason that the degree of alignment between leadership development programming and other individual as well as organizational factors would directly influence the rate and degree of impact.

LEADERSHIP DEVELOPMENT: IMPLICATIONS FOR PRACTITIONERS

In order for organizations to engage in leadership development activities, the facilitator of that process as well as key representatives from the organization should collaborate to consider not only how the process is structured, but also how the organization will support and sustain the changes that result. This section provides recommendations below for two crucial aspects of the process:

Leadership Development Processes

1. Effective leadership development fosters the development of intrapersonal as well as interpersonal skills, provides the relational space to create connection and shared meaning across boundaries (Day & Harrison, 2007; Bradbury et. al., 2007), and can serve as the catalyst for organizational change.
2. An ongoing iterative process that engages all participants such as action learning can facilitate effective leadership development. This process allows for participants to collaboratively work on real problems and develop knowledge from the respective experiences of their colleagues (Raelin, 2006).
3. The process should encompass all areas and levels of the organization to create shared meaning of what is as well as what could be, foster organizational memory, and catalyze organizational change. Working across disciplines can help to transcend organizational boundaries inherent in the health care system.
4. Facilitators need to make participants at all levels and most importantly those within upper executive levels aware that this process may unfold rather organically as issues emerge from the conversations of the group. In addition, conflict may arise between those who wish to maintain their current authority and power and those who wish to see a more collective approach that shares information and functions more democratically (Raelin, 2003; Marsick & O'Neil, 1999).

Organizational Structures and Supports

As with any change effort in which results are to be sustained over time, serial programming or action learning initiatives alone may be ineffective.

Additional organizational structures must be in place, which recognize and reinforce individual learnings as well as support new ways of "being together."

1. Most importantly, members of the uppermost levels of administration need to be active participants in the process in some fashion, at minimum serving as role models who demonstrate a willingness to share more information and decision-making capability (Raelin, 2006). Participants will not change if their managers do not understand, practice, or reward new behaviors. In fact, it may be risky for participants to try new behaviors if they will not be welcomed by their superiors (Marsick & O'Neil, 1999).
2. Human resource management systems must function more collaboratively to provide feedback consistent with new ways of working together. If there are new expectations for behavior based on leadership development initiatives, then those behaviors should be explicitly stated and mirrored in performance management systems.
3. The organization must continue to foster ongoing relationships and network integrity by providing further opportunities for interaction across disciplines. King (2003) suggests that talk is crucial for fostering organizational ways of knowing. Although the organization featured in this process is still within the early phases of the process, there has been some discussion about how to maintain the viability of relationships through the possible use of retreats, interdisciplinary task forces, and peer mentoring.
4. Leadership development takes time. Those engaging in this process must be willing to commit the time and resources it takes to make real change. It does not happen upon the completion of a series of workshops. The workshops should be considered a starting point of an ongoing cyclical process that encourages new ways of being and interacting together. Individuals develop as leaders throughout their entire lives. The development of leadership capacity or the "leaderful organization" is also a journey as connections are made, colleagues enter and leave the organization, and new challenges emerge from the field.

CONCLUSION

The current American health care system, fraught with chaos and complexity, is now more than ever in need of effective leadership that transcends occupational and hierarchal boundaries. As the notion of leadership has evolved from one that narrowly considered one actor as "hero" to the notion of collective capacity within an organization, the work around how it develops has also expanded from taking a few classes or reading a few books to a process that fosters individual learning, creates new connections and knowledge networks, and serves as a stimulus for organizational transformation. Effective leadership development must incorporate the development of the individual leader as well as leadership as a collective capability. Action learning is well suited to develop leadership because it can provide a way to develop individual intra- and interpersonal competency, and can create connections and opportunities for collaboration as it strengthens social networks, facilitates shared meaning, and catalyzes organizational change. One must be aware, however, that this process takes time and necessitates additional supportive structures that nurture and reinforce leadership capacity at all levels.

This study was conducted in collaboration with colleagues from one health system. Although there is a growing body of work that supports a comprehensive approach to leadership development that includes both individual as well as collective processes (Raelin, 2003, 2006; Day, 2001; Day & Harrison, 2007; Leatt & Porter, 2003), it is difficult to find many actual accounts of the process. Work shared from within other organizations even when embedded in context can add to our understanding of what effective leadership development entails. Broadening the perspective from leader to leadership provides the opportunity for multiple entry points for further research. Although much is known about leader and leadership development, a comprehensive approach may be somewhat new to the literature, and other researchers are encouraged to share their stories.

REFERENCES

Barker, R. (2001). The nature of leadership. *Human Relations, 54*(4), 469–494.

Bartol, K. M., & Zhang, X. (2007). Networks and leadership development: Building linkages for capacity acquisition and capital accrual. *Human Resource Management Review, 17*(4), 388–401.

Bass, B. M. (1985). Leadership: Good, better, best. *Organizational Dynamics, 13*(3), 26–40.

Bradbury, H., Lichtenstein, B., Carroll, J., Senge, P., & Powley, E. (2007). *Relational space: Creating a context for innovation in collaborative consortia.* Working Paper. University of Massachusetts. Accessed from: http://www.umb.edu/management/faculty_research/fac_papers/

Bradbury, H., & Reason, P. (2001). Broadening the bandwidth of validity: Issues and choice-points for improving the quality of action research. In: P. Reason & H. Bradbury (Eds), *Handbook of action research* (pp. 447–455). London: Sage.

Burns, J. M. (1978). *Leadership.* New York, NY: Harper and Row.

Coghlan, D. (2004). Action research in the academy: Why and whither? Reflections on the changing nature of research. *Irish Journal of Management*, *25*(2), 1–10.

Collins, D. B., & Holton III, E. (2004). The effectiveness of managerial leadership development programs: A meta-analysis of studies from 1982–2001. *Human Resource Development Quarterly*, *15*(2), 217–248.

Conger, J. (2004). Developing leadership capability: What's inside the black box? *Academy of Management Executive*, *18*(3), 136–139.

Connaughton, S., Lawrence, F., & Ruben, B. (2003). Leadership development as a systematic and multidisciplinary enterprise. *Journal of Education for Business*, *79*(1), 6.

Dachler, H. P., & Hosking, D. M. (1995). The primacy of relations in socially constructing organizational realities. In: D. M. Hosking, H. P. Dachler & K. J. Gergen (Eds), *Management and organization: Relational perspectives* (pp. 1–29). Brookfield, VT: Avebury/Ashgate Publishing.

Daudelin, M. W. (1996). Learning from experience through reflection. *Organizational Dynamics*, *24*(3), 36–48.

Day, D. V. (2001). Leadership development: A review in context. *The Leadership Quarterly*, *11*(4), 581–613.

Day, D. V., & Harrison, M. M. (2007). A multilevel, identity-based approach to leadership development. *Human Resource Management Review*, *17*(4), 360–373.

Drath, W. (2001). *The deep blue sea: Rethinking the source of leadership*. San Francisco, CA: Jossey-Bass.

Edmondson, A. (1999). Psychological safety and learning behavior in work teams. *Administrative Science Quarterly*, *44*, 350–383.

Embertson, M. K. (2006). The importance of middle managers in healthcare organizations. *Journal of Healthcare Management*, *51*(4), 223–232.

Ford, J., & Harding, N. (2007). Move over management: We are all leaders now. *Management Learning*, *38*(5), 475–493.

Goleman, D. (1998). What makes a leader? *Harvard Business Review*, *76*(6), 93–102.

Holton III., E. F. (2005). Holton's evaluation model: New evidence and construct elaborations. *Advances in Developing Human Resources*, *7*(1), 37–54.

Institute, P. C. H. R. (2007). *Top eight health industry issues in 2008*. Pricewaterhouse Coopers, LLP.

Judge, T. A., Bono, J. E., Ilies, R., & Gerhardt, M. W. (2002). Personality and leadership: A qualitative and quantitative review. *Journal of Applied Psychology*, *87*(4), 765–780.

King, I. W. (2003). Making space: Valuing our talk in organizations. *Journal of Management Studies*, *40*(5), 1205–1223.

King, N. K. (2004). Social capital and nonprofit leaders. *Non-Profit Management and Leadership*, *14*(4), 471–486.

Kirkpatrick, S. A., & Locke, E. A. (1991). Leadership: Do traits matter? *Academy of Management Executive*, *5*(2), 48–60.

Kouzes, J., & Posner, B. (2002). *The leadership challenge*. San Francisco, CA: Jossey-Bass.

Leatt, P., & Porter, J. (2003). Where are the healthcare leaders? The need for investment in leadership development. *HealthcarePapers*, *4*(1), 14–31.

Lord, R. G., & Hall, R. J. (2005). Identity, deep structure and the development of leadership skill. *The Leadership Quarterly*, *16*(4), 591–615.

Manz, C. C., & Sims, H. P., Jr. (1991). SuperLeadership: Beyond the myth of heroic leadership. *Organizational Dynamics*, *19*(4), 18–35.

Marion, R., & Uhl-Bien, M. (2001). Leadership in complex organizations. *The Leadership Quarterly*, *12*(4), 389–418.

Marsick, V. J., & O'Neil, J. (1999). The many faces of action learning. *Management Learning*, *30*(2), 159–176.

Martineau, J. (2004). Evaluating the impact of leader development. In: C. McCauley & E. Van Velsor (Eds), *The center for creative leadership handbook of leadership development* (pp. 234–267). San Francisco, CA: Jossey-Bass.

McCall, M. W. (2004). Leadership development through experience. *Academy of Management Executive*, *18*(3), 127–130.

Mintzberg, H. (2004). *Managers not MBA's: A hard look at the soft practice of managing and management development*. San Francisco: Berrett Kohler.

Montesino, M. (2002). Strategic alignment of training, transfer-enhancing behaviors, and training usage: A posttraining study. *Human Resource Development Quarterly*, *13*(1), 89–108.

Nahapiet, J., & Ghoshal, S. (1998). Social capital, intellectual capital, and the organizational advantage. *Academy of Management Review*, *23*(2), 242–266.

O'Connor, P., & Quinn, L. (2004). Organizational capacity for leadership. In: E. Van Velsor & C. McCauley (Eds), *The center for creative leadership handbook of leadership development* (pp. 417–437). San Francisco, CA: Jossey-Bass.

Raelin, J. (2003). *Creating leaderful organizations: How to bring out leadership in everyone*. San Francisco, CA: Berrett-Kohler Publishers.

Raelin, J. (2006). Does action learning promote collaborative leadership? *Academy of Management Learning & Education*, *5*(2), 152–168.

Raelin, J. A. (2001). Public reflection as the basis of learning. *Management Learning*, *32*(1), 11–30.

Raelin, J. A., & Coghlan, D. (2006). Developing managers as learners and researchers: Using action learning and action research. *Journal of Management Education*, *30*(5), 670–689.

Ranga, R., & Rousseau, D. (2006). The challenges are organizational not just clinical. *Journal of Organizational Behavior*, *27*(7), 811–827.

Revans, R. (1980). *Action learning: New techniques for managers*. London: Blond and Briggs.

Revans, R. (1998). *ABC of action learning: Empowering managers to act to learn from action*. London: Lemos and Crane.

Roberts, C. (2009). *Leadership at all levels: An action learning approach in healthcare*. Ph.D. dissertation, Benedictine University, IL.

Rooke, D., & Torbert, W. R. (2005). 7 transformations of leadership. *Harvard Business Review*, *83*(4), 66–76.

Rost, J. (1991). *Leadership for the twenty-first century*. Westport, CT: Greenwood Publishing.

Senge, P. (2004). Creating communities. *Executive Excellence*, *21*(9), 4–5.

Torbert, W. R. (1994). Managerial learning, organizational learning: A potentially powerful redundancy. *Management Learning*, *25*(1), 57–70.

Uhl-Bien, M. (2006). Relational leadership theory: Exploring the social processes of leadership and organizing. *The Leadership Quarterly*, *17*(6), 654–676.

Van Velsor, E., & McCauley, C. (2004). Our view of leadership development. In: E. Van Velsor & C. McCauley (Eds), *The center for creative leadership handbook of leadership development* (pp. 1–22). San Francisco, CA: Jossey-Bass.

Waclawski, J. (2002). Large-scale organizational change and performance: An empirical examination. *Human Resource Development Quarterly*, *13*(3), 289–305.

Wenger, E. (2000). Communities of practice: The organizational frontier. *Harvard Business Review*, *78*(1), 139–145.
Yammarino, F. J., Dansereau, F., & Kennedy, C. J. (2001). A multiple-level multidimensional approach to leadership: Viewing leadership through an elephant's eye. *Organizational Dynamics*, *29*(3), 149.
Yukl, G., & Lepsinger, R. (2005). Why integrating the leading and managing roles is essential for organizational effectiveness. *Organizational Dynamics*, *34*(4), 361–375.

LEADERSHIP AND ORGANIZATION DEVELOPMENT IN HEALTH CARE: LESSONS FROM THE CLEVELAND CLINIC

Margaret M. Hopkins, Deborah A. O'Neil, Kathleen FitzSimons, Philip L. Bailin and James K. Stoller

ABSTRACT

Leaders in health care today are faced with a wide array of complex issues. This chapter describes an innovative physician leadership development program at the Cleveland Clinic intended to enhance the leadership capacities of individuals and the organization. Propositions regarding the program's impact on organizational innovation, organizational commitment, social capital, and the human element of physician practice are offered for future examination.

Keywords: Leadership development; physician leadership; health care

Organization Development in Healthcare: Conversations on Research and Strategies
Advances in Health Care Management, Volume 10, 151–165

ISSN: 1474-8231/doi:10.1108/S1474-8231(2011)0000010015

CHALLENGES OF LEADING TODAY

Effective leadership today is both an art and a science. Increased competition, new technologies, changing organizational structures, a diverse workforce, and the constant pace of change all contribute to the complexities of leading. In addition to facing these universal problems, leading in the field of health care, the largest service industry in the world, has its own unique set of challenges (Schwartz & Pogge, 2000). Increased regulatory scrutiny and pressure to streamline operations, to reduce costs, and to improve the quality of patient care are critical concerns that confront leaders in health care organizations. Reimbursements for physician and hospital services are regulated by a multitude of outside entities. Hospitals must juggle the competing demands of various internal and external constituencies in order to find the best ways to serve patients and the communities in their service areas.

The demand for quality health care will increase, particularly because the number of people in older age groups with greater-than-average health care needs will grow faster than the total population between 2004 and 2014 (www.bls.gov/oco/cg/cgs035.htm). Thus, employment in health care will continue to grow in that same timeframe at a decidedly faster rate than in other industries.

Concerns have been raised about filling the leadership needs of health care organizations in the future (Mecklenburg, 2001; Schneller, 1997). One primary reason for a potential leadership void is the pending retirement of the baby boom generation. Health care organizations have only recently begun to invest in developing their leaders. A 1995 survey of 122 CEOs of health care institutions discovered that 31% of these organizations offered in-house leadership programs (Scott, Tangalos, Blomberg, & Bender, 1997). In 2002 the health care industry spent only 1.25% of their payroll on training and development while the top corporations spent 4% of payroll on these activities (Melum, 2002).

This chapter describes an innovative physician leadership development program designed to address these leadership challenges at the Cleveland Clinic (CC). This program had its origins almost two decades ago. We first establish the context by describing the culture of physician training and the challenges of leadership development in the health care industry. Leadership development as a critical component of organization development is discussed next, followed by descriptions of leadership development program components and the identification of best practices. A brief history of the CC physician leadership program is then presented with a focus on its current objectives and elements. Finally, propositions concerning the program's impact on individuals and on the organization are offered for future examination and research.

CHALLENGES PRESENTED BY PHYSICIAN EDUCATION AND THE HEALTH CARE INDUSTRY

Lengthy and rigorous training requirements prepare individuals to be physicians. The traditional medical school model for physician education grooms physicians to practice four primary roles: teacher, healer, guardian of the public good, and leader (Kosa, 1970). Medical schools have been reported to nurture and reward commanding and pacesetting styles of leadership (Thilo, 2005). The pacesetting leader is one who establishes challenging goals and achieves results, and the commanding leader is particularly effective in times of emergency or crisis (Goleman, Boyatzis, & McKee, 2002).

An overreliance on certain styles of leadership contributes to ineffectiveness in the leader's response to a variety of situations or circumstances. Prior research has supported the importance of a broad set of skills and a balance of behaviors for successful leaders (Hooijberg, 1996; Humphrey, 2002; Kim & Yukl, 1995; Luthans, 1988). For example, while the commanding style of leading is appropriate in an emergency, it is not useful when trying to inspire or motivate others or to develop relationships that build teamwork and collaboration. Pacesetting leaders tend to establish very high standards both for themselves and for others who sometimes find them impossible to meet. Both the commanding and the pacesetting leaders can fail to understand or appreciate other's perspectives and be inclined to lead with a lone ranger outlook.

Physician leaders are critical to modern medicine for a variety of reasons, particularly due to the coordinated care model of health care delivery and the wide-ranging and complex issues in health care today. Physicians are required to enact multiple functions – administrator, clinician, researcher, teacher, and leader, to name a few (Schwartz & Pogge, 2000). Yet physicians are trained to be "independent thinkers, skeptical scientists and self-reliant professionals" (Henochowicz & Hetherington, 2006, p. 183). The medical culture embraces autonomy, analytical thinking, and fast decision making and is generally averse to unneeded ambiguity (McAlearney, Fisher, Heiser, Robbins, & Kelleher, 2005).

The professional norms and standards in the preparation of physicians and the subsequent practice of medicine contribute to the lagging attention to leadership development. The traditional standpoint of medical leadership portrays physician leaders as strong, decisive, directive, and hierarchically oriented. In contrast, however, a contemporary perspective of leadership has shifted to valuing emotional intelligence, interpersonal relationships, and a participatory approach to successful leadership. Individuals trained as autonomous and independent agents need to develop competencies in teamwork and collaboration. The current business models and approaches to leadership are new to health care organizations and to the education of physicians in particular, but old models die hard. For example, in a study of women health care professionals' perceptions of effective leadership and successful career advancement, when the authors asked what characterized people who successfully advanced in their careers in the health care context, a self-focused trend emerged. Participants noted characteristics such as ambitious, hardworking, interpersonally competent, politically savvy, and confident (Hopkins, O'Neil, & Bilimoria, 2006).

Finally, six challenges to leadership development in health care institutions were recently identified in a qualitative study by McAlearney (2006). First, the health care industry is lagging behind other industries in leadership development. Second, it is difficult for health care institutions to develop leaders who are representative of the diverse group of patients and the community at large. Third, there are chasms among the professional groups within health care. Fourth, time constraints are always present. Fifth, there are challenges in the organization's technical capabilities to deliver a leadership development program. And sixth, financial considerations given lean budgets may relegate leadership development to the background of organizational priorities.

EFFECTIVE LEADERSHIP DEVELOPMENT: PROGRAMS AND EVALUATION

Leadership development has its origins in the modern perspective of leadership that emphasizes relationships (Day, 2001). Leadership development has been defined as "expanding the collective capacity of organizational members to engage effectively in leadership roles and processes" (Day, 2001, p. 582; McCauley, Moxley, & Van Velsor, 1998). Capacity building of an organization's human capital is the fundamental intention of leadership development. Developing the individual, socializing company values and vision, supporting strategic leadership initiatives, and action learning comprise four objectives of leadership development proposed by Conger and Benjamin (1999).

In order for leadership development to be effective, programs must focus on two levels of learning and development simultaneously – the individual level and the organizational level (Conger & Benjamin, 1999; Melum, 2002; Vicere & Graham, 2002). The individual level of learning and development concentrates on competency building and increased content knowledge. Leadership development is intended to increase one's human capital, i.e., individual skills, and social capital, i.e., networks of relationships. Interpersonal competencies in the areas of social awareness and relationship management are primary developmental targets (Day, 2001).

Additionally, leadership development ultimately should enhance a person's contributions to their organization. Therefore, links between the content of a leadership development program and the organizational strategic objectives must be evident (Abernathy, 1999). It is important to establish the relevance of leadership development to organizational outcomes because effective leadership development occurs in the context of ongoing work experiences that relate to the strategic direction of the organization (Dotlich & Noel, 1998). Providing individuals with a variety of developmental activities that are linked directly to their work is central to any value-added leadership development program. McCall posited that the primary source of learning to lead is through experience, giving the right experiences to individuals who will learn the most from them (2004).

Leadership development can be considered a particular form of organization development. The intent is to work with individual members to improve their skills and knowledge in the service of building the overall capability and effectiveness of the organization as a whole (Cummings & Worley, 2005). Leadership programs that link individual and organization development objectives together will likely result in greater overall sustained benefits to both individuals and their organizations.

General Electric, Motorola, and 3M are organizations noted for their exemplary leadership development programs. In all three examples, leadership development aligns with organizational vision and strategic direction. Driving sustainable change at the individual and the organizational level, in individual behavior, and in business performance is the ultimate objective of these leadership development programs (Alldredge, Johnson, Stoltzfus, & Vicere, 2003).

The very nature of development is an ongoing process, not a static one. Thus, programs designed and implemented to develop leaders must understand the constancy of leadership development and its realization beyond a formal classroom experience. Successful leadership development practices toward this end include coaching, mentoring, 360-degree feedback, developmental job assignments, and action learning projects. Van Velsor (1984) described three phases with relevant factors in each phase for any leadership development program: the preprogram phase attending to top leadership advocacy and aligning the program's need with organizational goals; the implementation of the program, incorporating such design factors as feedback mechanisms and peer interactions; and postprogram elements, for instance, debriefing and follow-up training.

The classical evaluation of leadership development comprises four stages: reaction, learning, behavior, and results (Kirkpatrick, 1977). An unsigned evaluation form from program participants is an example of measuring the reaction stage. The assessment of learning through leadership development programs can be achieved through experimental and control groups or pretests and post-tests. Behavior changes are effectively measured through preprogram and postprogram instruments. Results typically relate to return on investment or climate and job satisfaction surveys (Hannum, 2004). Ultimately, some level of increased individual learning and performance, and organizational impact, is proposed as effective evaluations of leadership development programs (Holton, 1996).

In summary, leadership education is a necessity. Critical success factors for leadership development incorporate an ongoing system of development embedded in the organization. Senior organizational leadership must be the champions of the leadership development system. Individual leadership competency development and challenging developmental opportunities connected to the individual's work context and rooted in organizational priorities are integral to effective leadership development.

LEADING IN HEALTH CARE AT THE CLEVELAND CLINIC

The Cleveland Clinic (CC) is a world-class health care institution. The CC is a "not-for-profit, multi-specialty academic medical center that integrates clinical and hospital care with research and education. The Clinic was founded in 1921 ... with a vision of providing outstanding patient care based upon the principles of cooperation, compassion and innovation" (www.clevelandclinic.org/aboutus). Today, the CC is one of the largest and most respected hospitals in the United States. The annual ranking of America's Best Hospitals by U.S. News and World Report ranks Cleveland Clinic number four in the country in their 2009–2010 survey (Comerow, 2009).

Prior to 1990, the CC supported staff physicians in attending external courses regarding management practices and leadership development. These courses were conducted by such groups as the American College of Physician Executives and the Harvard School of Public Health. While this approach increased individual participants' knowledge, skills, and abilities, there were limitations in the overall relevance of the programs to the CC and an impression that return to the organization as a whole could be enhanced.

An Executive Program in Practice Management was developed at the CC in 1990 to "foster collaboration between emerging physician leaders and administrators" (Stoller, Berkowitz, & Bailin, 2007). Staff physicians and administrators were nominated to participate in the program that addressed a broad range of health-related business topics including accounting, finance, marketing, management information systems, human resource management, and organizational behavior. A distinguishing component of the program was that teams of physicians and administrators created formal business plans to address self-generated topics for improvement.

The Practice Management Program was reorganized in 2003 and entitled Leading in Health Care. Contemporary leadership subjects such as emotional intelligence, situational leadership, and conflict management as well as medicolegal issues were included in the new curriculum. A 360-degree assessment of emotional intelligence and a series of one-on-one coaching meetings with an executive coach were novel additions to the program. The majority of the traditional management aspects of the program were maintained including the development of business plans. The final in-class session of the program was dedicated to presentations of the team-based business plans to senior leadership of the CC.

Physicians are nominated to participate in the Leading in Health Care program by their department and division chairs. The program directors, two physicians well-versed in modern leadership and management practices, select the annual cohort group based on the nominations as well as considerations of diversity in specialty, age, gender, race, and practice location. A maximum of 36 physicians participate annually over the course of nine sessions offered once a month from September to May. It is important to note that the CC considers participants' time in the program as Clinic business time, which signals a significant investment and commitment to growing leaders at the institution. Senior leadership at the Clinic endorses and champions this physician leadership program.

The main objectives of the program are as follows:

> to present a useful series of participatory sessions in which issues of health care policy, regulation, business and finance, and leadership are presented in the context of CC; to enhance your knowledge and skills regarding these issues, and to facilitate your development as physician-leaders; to foster ideas and projects regarding improving CC based on these skills and learnings; and to create a learning community for all of us (Stoller & Bailin, 2006).

The benefits of the Leading in Health Care program are numerous. First, the context of the program and its subject matter are specialized and applied to the CC. Second, an "environment is created that encourages networking among a diverse group of physicians" (Stoller et al., 2007). Third, a multidisciplinary group of colleagues learns to collaborate and develop synergies to advance the CC. Fourth, a learning laboratory for innovative ideas generates business plans developed by teams of physicians to specifically address institutional change. Fifth, leadership competencies are developed by individual participants. Sixth, a concentration on the human dimension of physician practice underscores the entire program.

The Leading in Health Care program is home-grown and taps into the expertise of both CC staff and external professionals to deliver the program. The content of the program is specifically crafted to meet the growing physician leadership needs at the CC. The subject matter draws on best practices from the disciplines of management and organizational behavior as well as from the health care arena.

THE IMPACT OF LEADERSHIP DEVELOPMENT ON ORGANIZATION DEVELOPMENT IN HEALTH CARE

In this section we offer propositions based on the specific features of the physician leadership program at the CC. These propositions highlight the positive impact of the program on the individual participants and the organization as a whole. While these propositions are conveyed relative to our experience with the Cleveland Clinic Leading in Health Care program, we believe that they may be applicable to leadership development programs with similar components in other populations.

Individual physicians from a variety of specialties and locations within the CC have an opportunity to meet, work, and socialize together over the course of the nine-month Leading in Health Care program. The business plan activity described previously specifically requires physicians to learn to work effectively in teams, a unique aspect often lacking in their prior training and development as physicians. As noted earlier, teamwork and collaboration are necessary leadership competencies in today's complex working environments where hierarchical roles are less effective and working across established lines of authority is essential to achieve results. Ultimately, the primary beneficiary of the cross-disciplinary collaboration among physicians is the patient. The integrated systems of care that are now necessary "demand that physician executives transcend their operating units and actively participate in a broader delivery system" (Schneller, Greenwald, Richardson, & Ott, 1997, p. 90).

The leadership development program provides multiple occasions for interactions among the physicians, thereby contributing to their developing relationships across disciplines. This in turn enhances their social capital. Their source of social capital is within their social connections (Coleman, 1988). Social capital offers additional resources to the physicians based on the relationships they develop with other physicians in the program. Medicine is a siloed industry where individuals interact within their disciplines but typically not across disciplines. By intentional design, this program seeks to break down those silos and encourage cross-disciplinary learning and teamwork. The opportunities for cross-collaboration and organizational learning increase exponentially as a critical mass of physician leaders builds within the organization.

Proposition 1. Working in multidisciplinary teams in a physician leadership development program expands the participants' social and professional networks, thus enhancing social capital within the organization.

Business plans developed by the teams of physicians provide a relevant activity grounded in their work experience, an occasion for action learning (Conger & Benjamin, 1999). The business plan activity is also directly associated with the organization's strategic direction. Work-related relevance and alignment with the organization's objectives are two key elements of effective leadership development (Dotlich & Noel, 1998).

In addition, the business plan component of the program encourages creativity and innovative thinking among the physicians. In effect, the physicians are encouraged to be intrapreneurs (Pinchot, 1985). The creation of business plans allows the physicians in the leadership development program not only to apply their learnings directly to their real-world context, but also to think outside the box and significantly impact the future of the organization.

Since the inception of the business plan activity in the leadership development program at the CC, 61% of the plans have been implemented. Some examples of innovations that have been implemented as a result of the Leading in Health Care business plans include a dedicated women's health program, an expansion of sports medicine to secondary school athletic programs, the introduction of a system-wide electronic medical record, and a Web-based program for patients to access their personal health information and to schedule appointments (Stoller et al, 2007).

Proposition 2. The more a health care organization fosters ventures aligned with the organization's strategic objectives in a physician leadership development program and adopts and implements those new ideas, the more likely an environment of innovation will be realized throughout the organization.

The physicians at CC are highly accomplished in their respective fields and characteristically have been trained in highly respected institutions. The medical model of education is focused on developing physicians who are highly competent in their areas of specialization. The model emphasizes the acquisition of knowledge relevant for technical, functional competence to a greater degree than the development of knowledge relevant to understanding and managing the emotions of self and others (with the exception of mental health training).

One of the nine Leading in Health Care sessions is devoted to the topic of emotional intelligence as it relates to leadership and leadership development. Emotional intelligence, defined as understanding and managing one's own emotions and those of others, has been reported to make a greater contribution to leadership and overall performance than IQ (Dulewicz, Young, & Dulewicz, 2005; Goleman, 1998; Goleman et al., 2002). All physician participants in the CC program complete a 360-degree assessment of their emotional intelligence competencies.

Following best practices in leadership development, an executive coach is provided to assist each participant in the interpretation of the emotional intelligence competencies' feedback report and in the development of new behaviors to improve their leadership emotional intelligence (Day, 2001). The process of coaching gives participants an opportunity to reflect on their behaviors and actions and to increase their self-awareness. Coaching helps the physicians integrate their learnings and ultimately prepare a personal development plan for the future. Through a series of conversations with their coach, the physicians undertake a mindful and intentional change process (Boyatzis & McKee, 2005) to enhance their emotionally intelligent leadership.

The development of emotional intelligence competencies in addition to the technical functional expertise already possessed by these physicians leads to an increased understanding and appreciation of the relational nature of leadership in health care.

> **Proposition 3.** The more that physician leadership development programs integrate emotional intelligence and coaching into their programs of study, the more likely it is for the human elements of physician leadership to be developed and enhanced.

The organization–employee relationship and attachments have been investigated through psychological contracts or social exchanges, to name a few (Blau, 1964; Kotter, 1973). One might expect that an institution's investment in their physicians as leaders would result in strengthening participants' commitment to the institution. Organizational commitment is a belief in and acceptance of an organization's values, a willingness to work hard on behalf of the organization, and a desire to continue organizational membership (Porter, Steers, Mowday, & Boulian, 1974). Committed employees may be more inclined to perform extraordinary behaviors such as creativity or innovativeness (Katz & Kahn, 1978). It has been reported that when there is an overinvestment by the employer or a mutual investment in the employee–organization relationship, i.e., open-ended inducements by organizations such as training and open-ended contributions from employees willing to trust that these investments will yield results in the long term, then affective commitment will be higher on the part of the employees (Tsui, Pearce, Porter, & Tripoli, 1997).

Given that attendance in the Leading in Health Care program is on Clinic time, not the individual physician's time, the cost to the CC is significant in physician time away from patients and other Clinic business. This substantial investment in their physicians demonstrates the value held by senior leaders of the Clinic for developing physician leaders throughout the organization.

> **Proposition 4.** A health care organization's investment in physician leadership development will result in an increased level of engagement and organizational commitment on the part of the program's participants.

CONCLUSION

There are two distinguishing features of the Leading in Health Care program at the Cleveland Clinic. First, the program provides opportunities for innovative ideas to be created and fulfilled. The organization values innovation and encourages research, leading to novel health care discoveries. However, the leadership development program promotes advancements developed collectively by small groups of physicians from various disciplines who design a plan for change that has the capability to impact the entire organization. The business plan proposals are aligned with the strategic objectives of the CC, an essential step for effective leadership development outcomes.

The second unique aspect of this leadership development program is the concentration on the human dimensions of the practice of medicine. Recently, the importance of emotional intelligence for physician leaders has been noted (Henochowicz & Hetherington, 2006). Since 2003, emotional intelligence has been integrated into the Leading in Health Care program's curriculum through a day-long module as well as 360-degree assessments of the physicians' emotional intelligence competencies. In addition to these leadership development components, executive coaches work with the participants to enhance their competency development based on the 360-degree feedback. The physicians also experience the efficacy of coaching as an important method for leading and developing others in their organization. Coaching has been identified as one of several principal roles for physician leaders (Coile, 1999; Henochowicz & Hetherington, 2006).

Gains from the Leading in Health Care program at the Clinic are realized at the individual and organizational levels, a fundamental aspect of successful leadership and organization development. Individual competency development is supported through assessment and executive coaching. Knowledge of effective business practices relevant to hospitals and health care is shared through the program's class sessions, assignments, and supplementary readings. Team skills are encouraged through sessions on teamwork and team-building activities, and through the business plan activity.

At the organizational level, a pipeline of leaders is being developed through the CC's investment in their leadership. The Leading in Health Care program is an effective succession planning tool as it supports an organizational culture of leadership development. An environment of innovation is encouraged through the business plan activity. Organizational change is driven by the wealth of business plans generated as well as by the individual behavioral changes realized through competency development and knowledge acquisition. Leading edge business and leadership practices are incorporated throughout the Clinic not only as a result of the curriculum but also due to the diverse group of physicians who participate in the program. Attention paid to the human dimension of the physician's practice elevates the relationships among all health care service providers within the Clinic and ultimately should improve the quality of patient care across the organization.

In line with the four objectives of leadership development proposed by Conger and Benjamin (1999), the Leading in Health Care program at the Cleveland Clinic is intended to develop the individual, socialize the values and vision of the organization, and create opportunities for strategic leadership initiatives and action learning across the organization. This program relies on an innovative, strategic approach to creating synergies between individuals and across the organization as it develops physician leaders at one of the top hospitals in the United States.

REFERENCES

Abernathy, D. J. (1999). Thinking outside the evaluation box. *Training and Development*, *53*(2), 19–23.

Alldredge, M., Johnson, C., Stoltzfus, J., & Vicere, A. (2003). Leadership development at 3M: New process, new techniques, new growth. *Human Resource Planning*, *26*(3), 45–55.

Blau, P. M. (1964). *Exchange and power in social life*. New Brunswick, NJ: Transactional Publishers.

Boyatzis, R., & McKee, A. (2005). *Resonant leadership*. Boston: Harvard Business School Press.

Coile, R. (1999). Physician executives in the 21st century: New realities, roles, and responsibilities. *The Physician Executive*, *25*(5), 8–13.

Coleman, J. (1988). Social capital in the creation of human capital. *American Journal of Sociology*, *94*(Suppl.), S95–S120.

Comerow, A. (2009). http://health.usnews.com/articles/health/best-hospitals/2009/07/15/americas-best-hospitals-the-2009-2010-honor-roll.html

Conger, J. A., & Benjamin, B. (1999). *Building leaders: How successful companies develop the next generation*. San Francisco: Jossey-Bass.

Cummings, T. G., & Worley, C. G. (2005). *Organization development and change* (8th ed.). Mason, OH: Thomson-South-Western.

Day, D. V. (2001). Leadership development: A review in context. *Leadership Quarterly*, *11*(4), 581–613.

Dotlich, D. L., & Noel, J. L. (1998). *Action learning: How the world's top companies are recreating their leaders and themselves*. San Francisco: Jossey-Bass.

Dulewicz, C., Young, M., & Dulewicz, V. (2005). The relevance of emotional intelligence for leadership performance. *Journal of General Management*, *30*(3), 71–86.

Goleman, D. (1998). *Working with emotional intelligence*. New York: Bantam Books.

Goleman, D., Boyatzis, R., & McKee, A. (2002). *Primal leadership: Realizing the power of emotional intelligence*. Boston: Harvard Business School Press.

Hannum, K. (2004). Choosing the right method for evaluation. *Leadership in Action, 23*(6), 15–20.

Henochowicz, S., & Hetherington, D. (2006). Leadership coaching in health care. *Leadership and Organization Development Journal, 27*(3), 183–189.

Holton, E. (1996). The flawed four-level evaluation model. *Human Resource Development Quarterly, 7*(1), 5–21.

Hooijberg, R. (1996). A multidirectional approach toward leadership: An extension of the concept of behavioral complexity. *Human Relations, 49*, 917–946.

Hopkins, M. M., O'Neil, D. A., & Bilimoria, D. (2006). Effective leadership and successful career advancement: Perspectives from women in health care. *Equal Opportunities International, 25*(4), 251–271.

Humphrey, R. H. (2002). The many faces of emotional leadership. *Leadership Quarterly, 13*, 493–504.

Katz, D., & Kahn, R. L. (1978). *The social psychology of organizations* (2nd ed.). New York: Wiley.

Kim, H., & Yukl, G. (1995). Relationships of managerial effectiveness and advancement to self-reported and subordinate-reported leadership behaviors from the multiple-linkage model. *Leadership Quarterly, 6*, 361–377.

Kirkpatrick, D. L. (1977). Evaluating training programs: Evidence vs. proof. *Training and Development Journal, 31*(11), 9–12.

Kosa, J. (1970). Entrepreneurship and charisma in the medical profession. *Social Science and Medicine, 4*, 25–40.

Kotter, J. P. (1973). The psychological contract: Managing the joining-up process. *California Management Review, 15*(3), 91–99.

Luthans, F. (1988). Successful vs. effective real managers. *Academy of Management Executive, 2*, 127–132.

McAlearney, A. S. (2006). Leadership development in health care: A qualitative study. *Journal of Organizational Behavior, 27*(7), 967–982.

McAlearney, A. S., Fisher, D., Heiser, K., Robbins, D., & Kelleher, K. (2005). Developing effective physician leaders: Changing cultures and transforming organizations. *Hospital Topics, 83*(2), 11–18.

McCall, M. W. (2004). Leadership development through experience. *Academy of Management Executive, 18*(3), 127–130.

McCauley, C. D., Moxley, R. S., & Van Velsor, E. (Eds). (1998). *The Center for Creative Leadership handbook of leadership development*. San Francisco: Jossey-Bass.

Mecklenburg, G. (2001). Career performance: How are we doing? *Journal of Healthcare Management, 46*(1), 8–13.

Melum, M. (2002). Developing high-performance leaders. *Quality Management in Healthcare, 11*(1), 55–68.

Pinchot, G. (1985). *Intrapreneuring: Why you don't have to leave the corporation to become an entrepreneur*. New York: Harper & Row.

Porter, L. W., Steers, R. M., Mowday, R. T., & Boulian, P. V. (1974). Organizational commitment, job satisfaction and turnover among psychiatric technicians. *Journal of Applied Psychology, 59*(5), 603–609.

Schneller, E. S. (1997). Accountability for healthcare: A white paper on leadership and management for the U.S. healthcare system. *Health Care Management Review, 22*, 38–48.

Schneller, E. S., Greenwald, H. P., Richardson, M. L., & Ott, J. (1997). The physician executive role in the adaptation of American medicine. *Healthcare Management Review, 22*(2), 90–96.

Schwartz, R. W., & Pogge, C. (2000). Physician leadership: Essential skills in a changing environment. *The American Journal of Surgery, 180*, 187–192.

Scott, H. M., Tangalos, E. G., Blomberg, R. A., & Bender, C. E. (1997). Survey of physician leadership and management education. *Mayo Clinic Proceedings, 72*, 659–662.

Stoller, J. K., & Bailin, P. L. (2006). Leading in Health Care IV (PowerPoint presentation).

Stoller, J. K., Berkowitz, E., & Bailin, P. L. (2007, January/February). Physician management and leadership education at the Cleveland Clinic Foundation: Program impact and experience over 14 years. *Journal of Medical Practice Management, 22*(4), 237–242.

Thilo, J. (2005). Leadership in the ASC: Opportunity and responsibility. *Ambulatory Surgery, 12*, 11–14.

Tsui, A. S., Pearce, J. L., Porter, L. W., & Tripoli, A. M. (1997). Alternative approaches to the employee-organization relationship: Does investment in employees pay off? *Academy of Management Journal, 40*(5), 1089–1121.

Van Velsor, E. (1984). Can development programs make a difference? *Issues and Observations, Center for Creative Leadership, 4*(4), 1–5.

Vicere, A. A., & Graham, K. R. (2002). Crafting competitiveness: Toward a new paradigm for executive development. *Human Resource Planning, 13*(4), 281–295.

www.bls.gov/oco/cg/cgs035.htm

www.clevelandclinic.org/aboutus

THE EVOLVING LEADERSHIP DEVELOPMENT AGENDA IN HEALTH CARE: A COMMENTARY

Andrew N. Garman and Christy Lemak

Health care in the United States is on the verge of substantial change. Health reform legislation, and the goals it seeks to pursue, are likely to drive transformational change across many corners of the health care system. Preparing for and navigating these changes will, in turn, require health care leaders to learn new approaches to many of the core parts of their jobs (Clark, Savitz, & Pingree, 2010; Shortell & Casalino, 2010). The sheer magnitude of change and uncertainty also seems a likely driver of the uptick in CEO retirement, which rose almost to an annual rate of 18% in 2009, the highest rate increase since the American College of Health care Executives began tracking the statistic in 1981 (American College of Healthcare Executives, 2010). Taken together, these trends suggest the need for leadership development and succession planning has never been greater.

The two articles in this section describe admirable efforts to move the leadership development agenda forward in important ways. But they also illustrate how much farther we need to go.

In "The Four C's of Leadership Development," the authors describe an approach that more directly addresses this need for an increasingly interdisciplinary approach to leadership development. Partnerships between academia and practice can form thriving learning communities, as has been the case here. The program's philosophies and approach to its development

Organization Development in Healthcare: Conversations on Research and Strategies
Advances in Health Care Management, Volume 10, 167–169

ISSN: 1474-8231/doi:10.1108/S1474-8231(2011)0000010016

were well described, and the authors' willingness to share the unanticipated consequences of the program was a welcome addition to a literature that tends to emphasize successes over objectivity. A key concern we had with the LEAD program is one the authors themselves noted – i.e., the importance of a perceived connection between the learning experience and the organizational strategy or mission. If such ties were there, they were not explicit in the article. This could have been due to the program evolving from a focus originally on succession planning, or it could have been symptomatic of the lack of full senior leadership buy-in, as the authors noted. In either case, and regardless of the positive experiences of participants, any program not explicitly associated with an organization's mission and vision will be particularly vulnerable when times get tight.

In "Leadership and Organization Development in Health Care: Lessons from the Cleveland Clinic," authors describe the physician leadership development approach taken by one of the most respected health care provider systems in the world. As the authors note, the Cleveland Clinic has a long and admirable track record of valuing and emphasizing the development of management and leadership skills within their physicians. And their record of implementing business plans developed during the capstone of their physician leadership development program provides a good indication of their success.

But at least as described in this article, the model focuses development within the silo of medicine. Given the considerable recent focus on the importance of interdisciplinary continuing education (Institute of Medicine, 2010), we question whether discipline-specific leadership programs will be sufficient to take organizations where they need to go next.

Taken together, these articles illustrate numerous components that are currently considered state-of-the-art in leadership development, including the work-based/action-learning approach (Raelin, 2006) and an emphasis on relationships ("leadership" vs. "leader" development – Day, 2001). In both cases, however, evaluative data are conspicuously absent. In our experience, this oversight is hardly unique to these two cases; indeed, evaluation continues to be one of the most glaring examples of how leadership development in health care continues to lag behind other sectors. While these case examples provide important lessons to the field about what works and what can be done to improve the effectiveness of leader and leadership development in health care, their ongoing support should not be taken for granted. Leadership development programs lacking explicit ties to mission and vision, or disciplined evaluation, or both are less likely to support an organization's efforts to improve efficiency – indeed, they are more likely to become its casualties.

REFERENCES

American College of Healthcare Executives (2010). Hospital CEO turnover. Retrieved from: http://www.ache.org/PUBS/research/CEO_TurnoverStats10.pdf

Clark, D. D., Savitz, L. A., & Pingree, S. B. (2010). Cost cutting in health systems without compromising quality care. *Frontiers of Health Services Management*, *27*(2), 19–30.

Day, D. V. (2001). Leadership development: A review in context. *Leadership Quarterly*, *11*, 581–613.

Institute of Medicine. (2010). *Redesigning continuing education in the health professions*. Washington, DC: The National Academies Press.

Raelin, J. (2006). Does action learning promote collaborative leadership? *Academy of Management Learning & Education*, *5*, 152–168.

Shortell, S. M., & Casalino, L. P. (2010). Implementing qualifications criteria and technical assistance for accountable care organizations. *JAMA*, *303*, 1747–1748.

PART IV
RELATIONSHIPS AND TEAMS

ADDRESSING DYSFUNCTIONAL RELATIONS AMONG HEALTH CARE TEAMS: IMPROVING TEAM COOPERATION THROUGH APPLIED ORGANIZATIONAL THEORIES

Sujin K. Horwitz, Irwin B. Horwitz and Neal R. Barshes

ABSTRACT

Previous research has demonstrated that communication failure and interpersonal conflicts are significant impediments among health care teams to assess complex information and engage in the meaningful collaboration necessary for optimizing patient care. Despite the prolific research on the role of effective teamwork in accomplishing complex tasks, such findings have been traditionally applied to business organizations and not medical contexts. This chapter, therefore, reviews and applies four theories from the fields of organizational behavior (OB) and organization development (OD) as potential means for improving team interaction in health care contexts. This study is unique in its approach as

Organization Development in Healthcare: Conversations on Research and Strategies
Advances in Health Care Management, Volume 10, 173–197

ISSN: 1474-8231/doi:10.1108/S1474-8231(2011)0000010017

it addresses the long-standing problems that exist in team communication and cooperation in health care teams by applying well-established theories from the organizational literature. The utilization and application of the theoretical constructs discussed in this work offer valuable means by which the efficacy of team work can be greatly improved in health care organizations.

Keywords: Health care teams; Ideological currency; Transformational leadership; Learning organization; High reliability organization theory

INTRODUCTION

The impact of medical errors has been quantified to be a significant source of mortality in the United States, with the Institute of Medicine having estimated that between 40,000 and 100,000 patients unnecessarily die annually from errors in medical treatment as opposed to their condition itself (The Institute of Medicine, 1999). While there are numerous sources of error that take place in the complex administration of health care, investigators are increasingly finding that the majority result from mismanagement and poor communication among caregivers in providing and delivering patient care. For example, evidence from recent reviews of clinical operations have demonstrated that common medical practices are rife with failures in communication (Chang, Waid, Martinec, Zheng, & Swanstrom., 2008; Yule, Flin, Paterson-Brown, & Maran, 2006) and ineffective team coordination is frequently the causes of medical errors (Gawande, Studdert, Zinner, & Brennan, 2003). Other studies of medical treatment have also identified that a common lack of cooperation among health care teams often promote mistakes during patient care processes, such as the induction of anesthesia, trauma resuscitation, administration of drugs, and management of patients in intensive care units (Donchin et al., 1995; Michaelson & Levi, 1997; Santora, Trooskin, Blank, Clarke, & Schinco, 1996).

Previous research on medical protocol has demonstrated that too often, approaches to patient treatment are dominated by a strict hierarchical approach and thus myopically adhere to outdated techniques in patient care. The importance of seeking opinions from those lower in status than attending physicians are often negated and consequently impedes open communication and team-based collaboration. The role of effective teamwork in accomplishing complex tasks and promoting a culture that emphasizes the safety of patients in the caregiving process is quickly becoming seen as essential (Mathieu, Maynard, Rapp, & Gilson, 2008), and other investigations have begun to demonstrate that replacing the traditionally strict hierarchical approach with operational practices promoting team-based care significantly optimizes patient treatment and profoundly reduces medical errors (Nemeth, 2008).

Unfortunately, such findings have been met with considerable resistance when put into actual practice by some health care practitioners; while much of this resistance stems from changing medical practices and traditions that span decades, another particularly difficult hurdle has been overcoming the reluctance to utilize many of the findings within the body of literature on team work that has emerged from studies of business processes and not medical contexts. However, there has been a growing recognition that utilizing organic team cooperation as opposed to relying on rigid hierarchical management is an essential conduit to reducing medical errors and improving overall patient care. This chapter thus demonstrates how integrating theories from the fields of organization development (OD) and organizational behavior (OB) could in tandem reduce communication error and improve conflict resolution among health care teams and thus improve the quality and safety of patient care.

DEFINITION OF HEALTH CARE TEAMS

Health care teams are often subject to multiple interpretations and thus operationally defining what constitutes a team in health care settings is needed prior to presenting our thesis. Although the review of both the management and health care literature revealed multiple definitions of "team," while reflecting the ubiquity and diversity of team studies in both fields (Guzzo & Shea, 1992; Hackman & Oldham, 1980; Nemeth, 2008; Salas, Dickinson, Converse, & Tannenbaum, 1992; Sundstrom, DeMeuse, & Futrell, 1990), commonalities can be found in defining essential characteristics of teams in the context of health care. One such commonality is the requirement for individuals to engage in cooperative and interdependent actions to achieve the common goal of improving the quality of patient care. It is this requirement for interactions and mutual goal alignment that differentiates a "team" from simply an informal group of individuals (Stout, Salas, & Fowlkes, 1997). Teams can also be either temporary with a finite time line or a permanent feature of organizations. This definition also fits the temporal dimension of health care teams as some teams are formed to carry out specific patient care with a finite time span (e.g., surgical team and operating-room team), while others are an on-going apparatus of the clinical system (e.g., neonatal intensive care team and hospice care). Furthermore, team members in health care settings have highly specialized knowledge and skills that are complementary and thus often necessitate the coordination of such specialized skills to achieve team goals. In this study, consistent with the widely used definition of Salas et al. (1992), a team in health care is defined as a distinguishable set of two or more individuals who interact interdependently with highly specialized yet complementary skills in order to accomplish a common goal of patient care.

THE GENERAL STRUCTURE OF HEALTH CARE TEAMS

In reviewing health care team structures and delineating dysfunctional team interactions, Donabedian's structure–process–outcome model (1980) was adopted as the analytical framework because of the model's explicit linkage between structure and process of care to subsequent patient outcomes, which is a paramount concern in health care research. Despite its limitation of the linear progression of care processes, Donabedian's model has proved valuable in examining clinical process of care and thus widely used for assessing patient outcomes for the past three decades. As in the input–process–output approach to analyzing teamwork in businesses and organizations (McGrath, 1984; Hackman, 1987), Donabedian's model explicitly links three components – structure, process, and outcomes – in assessing health care activities and ensuing outcomes. In the structure–process–outcome model, Donabedian (1980) conceptualized the structure as the setting where patient care is provided, which encompasses organizational structures, material resources, and human resources. The process part is defined as treatment and procedures that are done for a patient and includes both technical and interpersonal process for patient care. Finally, outcomes are the assessment of the effectiveness of patient care. The analysis of health care teams in this study was built upon the Donabedian's approach and further expanded the model to delineate health care team structures and show how hierarchical structures within care providers can lead to intragroup and intergroup conflicts, thereby ultimately compromising patient outcomes.

As shown in Fig. 1, the core members of primary medical teams who direct patient care include faculty members, attending physicians, medical residents, fellows, and nurses. Although team membership may change over time (as with resident and/or faculty rotations), the membership of primary medical teams are formally defined. Most commonly, a hierarchical structure is utilized, with faculty members and/or attending physicians at the top, senior residents in the middle, and junior residents and nurses at the bottom (Sexton, Thomas, & Helmreich, 2000). While the authority structure may be hierarchical, the transfer of information in medical decision-making groups is, however, frequently done in a network-fashion and includes not only core members of the medical team but also those who comprise the informal and/or secondary caregiving network. Such groups of caregivers who participate in patient care include consulting physicians, radiologists, therapists, dieticians, and even patient family members. In some cases, members of these secondary groups may have a dependable, structured meeting schedule, while others meet informally on an ad hoc basis. Aside from these meetings, many other informal interactions can also take place in

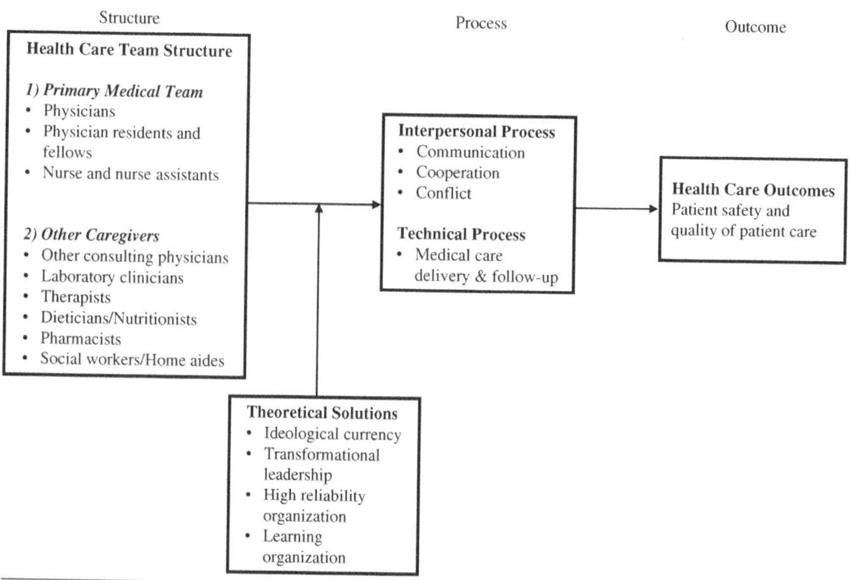

* Note: Adapted from Donabedian's Structure-Process-Outcome Model (1980).

Fig. 1. Application of OB/OD Theoretical Solutions to Health Care Teams. *Source*: Adapted from Donabedian's Structure–Process–Outcome Model (1980).

an unstructured and informal fashion, resulting in poor communication, an inadequate coordination of activities, and duplication of efforts. The transfer of information between these individuals often becomes haphazard and informal (Friedman & Berger, 2004). Importantly, while these individuals are not formally included in the decision-making process, their influence is often a key source of relevant clinical information upon which medical decisions are based and treatment administered and monitored.

SOURCES OF TEAM CONFLICT IN THE DELIVERY OF PATIENT CARE

Because of the hierarchical structure that characterizes health care providers, the relationship between caregivers is often complex and strained. While the areas of conflict between medical personnel are numerous, the following section identifies and analyzes the two most common sources of communication problems and conflict in health care teams that inhibit effective team cooperation and ultimately lead to medical errors and suboptimal treatment outcomes: (1) conflict between physicians and nurses and (2) conflict between/among physicians themselves.

Dysfunctional Physician–Nurse Interactions

The roles of physicians and nurses in the delivery of health care are intimately interrelated and complementary. Yet, despite the frequency of interaction between these two groups, communication between them is often dysfunctional. Nurses are often dissatisfied with their interactions with physicians, complaining that physicians do not invite or consider their input (Manias & Street, 2001; Thomas, Sexton, & Helmreich, 2003). This relationship has been found to underlie the most commonly ascribed reason for the perceived difference in hierarchy between physicians and nurses (Manias & Street, 2001; Sutcliffe, Lewton, & Rosenthal, 2004). The nurses' perceptions may be well-founded as one study quantified that verbal communication between physicians and nurses took place in only 2% of patient care activities initiated by physicians (Donchin et al., 1995). Communication between nurses and physicians often occurs exclusively through written orders despite the fact that there may be a long delay between the time orders are written and when they are actually executed (Sutcliffe et al., 2004).

It has been reported that some physicians engage in overt intimidation and other confrontational behavior with nurses that may serve as a significant deterrent to nurse-initiated communications and exacerbate the already tenuous relationship (Duldt, 1981; Sutcliffe et al., 2004). In a recent survey by the Institute for Safe Medication Practices (2003), 7% of nurses reported that they had been involved in a medication error within the past year in which physician intimidation had been a factor. More than half of the respondents reported having "often" or "sometimes" experienced a refusal or reluctance to answer questions or return pages, experiencing condescending tone/language, or impatience with questions. Fifty-seven percent of respondents had also experienced "strong" verbal abuse at some time (Institute for Safe Medication Practices, 2003; Morrissey, 2004). Another study examined the perceptions of disruptive feedback from 1,509 physicians and nurses through a questionnaire and demonstrated that the majority of respondents had witnessed antagonistic behavior in patient-care settings, and 22% said they observed such behavior on a weekly basis. Further, 13% noted that they had seen preventable adverse events resulting from this dysfunctional conduct with many of the written comments describing relationships characterized by anger and coercion, and even in some instances, the refusal of physicians to respond to the requests of nurses to evaluate patients (Rosenstein & O'Daniel, 2005).

While the recent aforementioned studies demonstrate the extreme to which physician–nurse interactions can be strained, tensions between the parties have been recognized for nearly four decades and is described as the "Doctor–Nurse game" (Stein, 1967). In this taxonomy, the inability to reconciliate the hierarchical status and divergences in opinion over optimal courses of treatment is held to fuel emerging conflicts between nurses and physicians. The most important assumption established in the paradigm's framework is that open conflict is mutually disadvantageous, and hence, to be avoided at all costs. Because of this constraint, nurses must not be perceived as questioning physicians' authority and, thus, present their recommendations through passive and subtle verbal and nonverbal cues. Both parties realize maximum gain when the parties achieve a Pareto-optimal equilibrium: nurses are able to direct physician attention to an option they feel is most beneficial, and physicians are able to include alternative interpretations of the information without compromising their perceived hierarchical status. In a variation of the Doctor–Nurse game referred to as "staging," nurses begin with a specific solution in mind that requires physician approval (Manias & Street, 2001). Rather than explicitly requesting an order for the solution, nurses attempt to get physicians to choose the solution through the selective presentation of information and information withholding.

A significant downside of such informational gate-keeping is the circumvention of doctors' full expertise in decision-making processes, which becomes inherently compromised due to information being intentionally omitted. While there is growing evidence that nurses are becoming increasingly recognized as equals in the delivery of health care and consequently voice their opinions more frequently than in the past, some physicians still tend to hold disregard for their input and continue to engage in abrasive behaviors (Van Eaton, Horvath, Lober, & Pellegrini, 2004). When such attitudes become manifested in condescending communication, further deterioration of the relationship between the two parties often occurs, thereby creating greater impediments to information flow (Larson, Christensen, Franz, & Abbott, 1998). It has been further demonstrated that when the relationship deterioration between parties becomes particularly profound, it not only interferes with the transfer of information between the parties, but the receivers are more apt to overly discount the information from the transmitting parties, thereby increasing the probability that decision quality will suffer (Schulz-Hardt, Frey, Luthgens, & Moscovici, 2000). Additionally, the proclivity for conflict between physicians and nurses may be intensified by the degree to which their tasks are interdependent and resources are shared. Research has demonstrated that when resources are finite and their allocation is split between parties to which they are of high value, goals are not aligned, and activity is interdependent (as is often the case between physicians and nurses in medical care teams), then the probability of conflict increases as a function of this interaction (Schulz-Hardt et al., 2000). Therefore, on both the interpersonal and situational levels, the impetus for physician–nurse conflict to arise and become institutionalized in health care settings is significant.

Conflict between/among Physicians

Poor communication between primary medical decision makers often leads to a duplication of efforts (Friedman & Berger, 2004). In spite of their clearly defined structures, health care teams are often not coordinated, and the role of each member is particularly unclear when several providers are involved in the care of a patient (McCue & Beach, 1994; Sutcliffe et al., 2004). In academic medical centers, interactions between resident trainees and attending physicians are particularly constrained by imbalances in authority, power, and demographic differences (McCue & Beach, 1994). For example, a study of internal medicine residents observed that the willingness of residents to disagree with attending physicians was dependent on the future career plans of the residents (Farber, Weiner, Boyer, & Robinson, 1990).

It has long been recognized that there is an inadequate transfer of information between physicians in the context of consultation (Kunkle, 1964). Several of the same barriers that inhibit the communication between physicians and other parties also affect interactions between physicians themselves, with time limitations being a complicating moderator. Difficulty in determining which clinicians are involved in patient care and in maintaining communication with these clinicians also may inhibit optimal care (McKnight, Stetson, Bakken, Curran, & Cimino, 2002). Poor communication between physicians has been blamed as causing disruptions in the continuity of care, delayed diagnoses, unnecessary testing, and iatrogenic complications (Epstein, 1995). On account of their superior knowledge in a specialized field, consultants may abuse the consultant–patient relationship by undermining trust in the primary physician, dictating a particular therapeutic option, and withholding responsibility or credit from a primary physician (Emanuel & Richter, 1994). The medical record may become the primary mode of communication in lieu of more direct and effective means. This means of communication does not facilitate the exchange of information and ideas as readily as verbal communications, and "chart wars" can result in delays in the delivery of medical care or other management problems (McCue & Beach, 1994; Sutcliffe et al., 2004).

The "sign-out" of patients to a cross-covering clinician represents another common scenario in which poor information transfer may lead to near-misses or direct errors (Drazen, 2004; Mukherjee, 2004). As explained by Van Eaton et al. (2004), the transfer of information between physicians is now more critical than ever before, as work hour limitations have prevented any one physician from being both knowledgeable of all the relevant information concerning a patient and available to act on this information when needed. During the transformation to the 80-hour workweek, what used to be perceived by doctors as "my patient" has increasingly been referred to as "our patient." Consequently, while there may be several physicians who are familiar with some of the patient's history, laboratory and imaging results, medications, plan of care, and preferences for outcomes, there may be no one individual who is intimately familiar with a combination of all this information. Moreover, in such cases where a low percentage of information has been previously shared prior to collective discussion, the information that individuals choose to share upon team consultation may be prone to bias through limiting it to that which supports the preexisting opinion of the team and thereby omitting information that may cause dissention (Epstein, 1995).

Similarly, communication among physicians in the operating room appears to be susceptible to many of the same problems described. In one observational study, communication failures (defined as verbal or nonverbal exchanges that had poor timing, conveyed inaccurate or missing information, specific information not addressed to key individuals, or a problem was identified but was not acted upon) occurred in about 30% of exchanges (Lingard et al., 2004). While the majority of these failures had no visible immediate consequences, a significant number resulted in inefficiency, tension, delays, wasting of resources, or procedural errors, ultimately compromising patient care.

APPLICATION OF THEORETICAL SOLUTIONS TO HEALTH CARE TEAMS TO PROMOTE PATIENT SAFETY CULTURE

In the preceding sections, we demonstrated how the lack of cooperation and communication among various care providers can create significant problems in patient care. As discussed, health care professionals are often confronted with situations where severe time constraints are imposed and the slightest mistake in judgment leads to fatal patient outcomes. Although health care professionals' unique duties and temporal stress from various medical shifts are quite different from those of traditional work teams and groups in nonclinical settings, we believe that some of the established communication and conflict resolution practices that have been found to augment a more cooperative and integrated workplace can be applicable and useful in medical settings. While there are numerous such theories and models that can be delineated, four in particular are selected that we feel produce the best synergy for improving communication and reducing conflict under the special circumstances engendered when providing health care. These theories collectively embody what has culminated as a "Patient Safety Culture" among health care professionals (Scott, Mannion, Davies, & Marshall, 2003; Davies, Nutley, & Mannion, 2000) in which a process of patient-centered goal alignment becomes the paramount means by which the actions and relationships between individuals in the organization are moderated. Importantly, the very root of a patient safety culture stems from the primary shared beliefs of health care professionals; the well-being of patients under their professional care. Needless to say, the ability to create a patient-driven safety culture is highly dependent on the shared values and beliefs of care providers at all levels and their ability to communicate between groups in order to create a dynamic clinical environment capable of adapting to new situations and challenges in patient care (Clark, 2003; Hart & Hazelgrove, 2001). Research has indeed operationalized "patient safety culture" as one in which the beliefs in safety are shared, while organizational learning occurs within a "no blame/no shame" approach to accident analysis and thus trust and honesty are encouraged to promote safety measures (Kirk, Parker, Claridge, Esmail, & Marshall, 2007). For example, research indicates that nearly 90% of near-misses (reporting of errors that were caught before they happened) are either unreported or overlooked and the lack of near-misses reporting is frequently related to the reluctance of employees to report such errors with fear of retribution and punitive cultures within their clinical settings. Consequently, a significant amount of information that could potentially be used for error prevention analysis is lost. In a patient safety culture, in which no negative repercussions would affect the person reporting the near-miss, such information could be extremely valuable for preventing actual errors in the future, identifying valuable interventions, and thus ensuring the safety of patients.

In the ensuing section, we examine four theories taken from OD and OB literature and describe how they can create a patient safety culture that reduces conflict, improves communication, and ensures the quality of patient care when used interactively. The four theoretical solutions examined are (1) ideological currency as a complementary element of the psychological contract; (2) transformational leadership; (3) high reliability organization theory (HROT); and (4) organizational learning. These four solutions are further analyzed with respect to their pragmatic applications within clinical environments, how their implementation could lead to significant improvements in team cooperation in health care contexts, as well as caveat to their use by noting potential limitations inherent to each method.

Ideological Currency and Transformational Leadership

Ideological Currency in the Psychological Contract

Psychological contract theory postulates that in the course of employment, individuals and organizations enter into psychological exchange agreements that act like written contracts that define their mutual obligations (Rousseau, 1990, 1995). Although there are varying definitions of the term "psychological contract," the term generally denotes "multifaceted obligations" as a central theme encompassing dynamic relationships and expectations between employers and employees (Kotter, 1973; Rousseau, 1995; Schein, 1978). Psychological contracts are further subdivided into economic/transactional (work for money) and socioemotional/relational (commitment for filling belief) components (Rousseau, 1995, 2004). Employees who perceive emotional contract fulfillment experience feelings of loyalty and exert extra effort to facilitate an organizational success; conversely, those perceiving breach experience feelings of mistrust in proportion to the amount of breach and may experience cynicism and withhold effort accordingly (Bunderson, 2001; Robinson, 1996). Although in theory, psychological contract is dichotomized, in practice, the distinctions between the economic and noneconomic components that comprise such contracts are often blurred. Furthermore, there seems to be another emerging concept that explains the dynamic nature of employer–employee relationships. Ideological currency, defined as the amount by which the organization promotes the philosophical values and beliefs held by the individual employees, is considered to be integral to strengthening the socioemotional/relational component of the employer–employee relationship (Thompson & Bunderson, 2003).

Organizations that emphasize value-driven missions often rely heavily on ideological currency as a means of promoting employees' affective commitment and moral attachment (Bunderson, 2001). Ideological currency is, thus, particularly applicable in health care settings where professionals are intrinsically driven by causes and purposes in work and commitment to their profession (O'Donohue & Nelson, 2007). That is, health care professionals are intrinsically motivated, work with the commitment to promote their values, and often measure their success in lives saved and suffering reduced (O'Donohue & Nelson, 2007). In this regard, ideological currency becomes more important for satisfying employees than economic currency. As Bunderson (2001) elaborated, ideology, as a complementary element of the psychological contract, helps to explain why some health care professionals remain committed to the cause of their organization despite breaches in the transactional and economic portions of their psychological contract.

Because ideological currency is believed to affect intrinsic motivation, it is an especially strong means of achieving cohesiveness and cooperation among organizational members when common values are shared. Aligning the core values among all employee segments is an important nexus for getting individuals and groups that traditionally have patterns of conflict to subordinate their self-interests, improve communication, and engage in team collaboration for what is seen by all as the greater good, providing quality patient care. Recent research indicates that intrinsically valued goals facilitate both employee morale and patient satisfaction in health care organizations (Tjosvold, 1988).

However, achieving perceptions of psychological contract fulfillment is often challenging, especially for the relational aspects based on ideological currency. While value-laden organizational mission statements, such as "providing the best patient care" and "helping our patients with compassion" are ubiquitous among health care centers, the ingrained personnel practices long manifested in many of the same institutions, as described earlier, are often incongruent with the employees' intrinsic values, hence breaching the ideological facets of the psychological contract and resulting in cognitive dissonance, organizational cynicism, and increased conflict (Johnson & O'Leary-Kelly, 2003). This is particularly pervasive among health care teams, as scholars have noted that while the hierarchical authoritarianism is effective at forcing individuals to comply with orders, it is quite poor in garnering even little organizational commitment (Cavanagh & Tross, 1996). Research has revealed, not surprisingly, that only when individuals see such values intentionally pursued and put into practice do they become committed to subordinating their own self-interest to achieve purely altruistic, patient-centered goals.

Transformational Leadership

A significant body of evidence suggests that an effective way to attain value-based goal congruence and thus maintain the validity of ideological currency is through the use of transformational leadership techniques by organizational leaders (Bass, 1990; Burns, 1978). Prior to elaborating their application in health care team settings, distinctions between transactional and transformation leadership should clearly be delineated. Transactional leadership holds that leaders influence follower behavior by meeting the extrinsic needs of followers through fairly perceived exchange parity; in contrast, transformational leadership maintains that leaders are most effective when they align the intrinsic beliefs and attitudes of the followers with the higher order values of their organization's goals. Importantly, these two forms of leadership are not mutually exclusive but often work in tandem to fulfill the transactional and relational components comprising the psychological contract (Bass, Avolio, Jung, & Berson, 2003). For example, a recent leadership study of surgical residents at a major US teaching hospital found that both transformational and transactional leadership loaded on the same dimension, while a second factor emerged for passive-avoidant leadership qualities (Horwitz et al., 2007). While transactional leadership techniques often utilize bonuses, raises, or other perquisites for performing specific duties or meeting specified performance criteria, research findings strongly indicate that utilizing transformational leadership methods best elicits team cohesion and cooperation particularly when high-value intrinsic outcomes (such as saving lives in medical organizations) are at stake. Ultimately, in the transformational leadership approach, leaders aim to align the beliefs of their followers with that of the organizations, and do so by acting as an example of the values they promote. Indeed, a substantial body of research exists to link transformational leadership to positive organizational outcomes. Falbe and Yukl (1992), for example, found that the influence tactics of inspirational appeals and consultation, which are considered strong transformational leadership qualities, more often solicit commitment from employees compared to motivations stemming from transactional rewards, which were actually found to be met with resistance.

Transformational leadership strongly advocates focusing on employee development and autonomy. Transformational leaders, while not immune to expressing anger and dissatisfaction, overwhelmingly prefer to respect followers and oversee their development with concern for their personal feelings and needs. Followers are more likely to respond to the initiatives of leaders who share and promote the same ideas they believe in as individuals. According to House and Mitchell (1974), this is especially true when work conditions are stressful, frustrating, or highly demanding as in health care settings. By receiving personal support and respect from their leaders, organizational members are more inclined to align their beliefs with the organizational goals. Equally important, the results from several studies have found that transformational leadership significantly improves communication between individuals and departments (Jung & Sosik, 2002; Yammarino, Spangler, & Bass, 1993). The findings of other investigations have critically demonstrated that transformational leadership style can be learned, and medical residency programs are thus beginning to incorporate transformational leadership training as part of their physician and surgical training curriculums (Itani, Liscum, & Brunicardi, 2004; Kuhnert, 1994).

One important caveat to using transformational leadership strategies in health care teams is that in many cases, expertise must take precedence over consultation in specific situations. For example, physicians with nine years of graduate medical education and years of medical experience have more specialized knowledge than a nurse fresh out of school with little clinical experience. In such cases, especially where decisions must be made quickly or are highly technical regarding patient treatment, a consultative approach may be inferior to a directive one; however, the directive approach, while necessary, may undermine some degree of the transformational relationship the physician tries to develop with the nurse taking orders. This is particularly true if coercive power and threat of punishment for noncompliance is invoked when a disagreement occurs in medical teams. To offset potentially negative effects, a balance must be struck between situations where consultation is welcome and appreciation shown and when hierarchical rank must be invoked. Still, even when rank is necessary to elicit compliance given instances of disagreements with members with less seniority and/or less expertise, doing so within the context of justifying such action for the intrinsic purpose of patient benefit as opposed to simply displaying arrogant disregard, may offset much of the negative effect of pulling rank and thus maintain the transformational leadership legitimacy, continue to strengthen a collaborative relationship in the future, and most importantly, maintain the validity of the psychological contract.

It should also be recognized that while the reduction of destructive conflict is a paramount goal, not all conflicts are destructive, and in some cases lead to operational improvements. In part, whether conflict is constructive or destructive depends on whether it results from relational-based or task-driven origins. Studies of working groups in organizational settings have suggested that while relationship conflict does impair group performance, conflict regarding the group's task may actually enhance performance to a certain extent (Jehn, 1995). In particular, when tasks are of a nonroutine nature, open conflict can enhance the depth of problem evaluation and assessment of options. Consistent with the above notion, it has been empirically shown that too little dissent, or the extreme need to arrive at a consensus, can lead to overlooking potential options and thus result in poor decisions (Payne, 1982). The well-known concept of Groupthink is said to arise when the value of maintaining group cohesiveness through unanimous consensus and often opting for a suboptimal decision choice because of member reluctance to thoroughly argue through all possible options to a problem, choosing instead to myopically support the leader on solutions and concurrently minimize dissention among group members (Janis, 1972; Janis & Mann, 1977). Therefore, it is critical that transformational leaders emphasize to followers that the voicing of diverse opinions is a necessary part of the process by which shared values can best be attained, while being especially cognizant to maintain the focus of conflict on task-related issues.

High Reliability Organization Theory and Organizational Learning

High Reliability Organization Theory

Several health care scholars have argued that a systems-based paradigm can be effectively adopted to examine the impact of team cooperation on conflict reduction and patient care (Reason, 1997). Largely borrowed from Bertalanffy's General Systems Theory (GST) (1969), O'Connor (1980) originally proposed a systems model of interdependent teamwork that focused on dynamic relationships among variables. Similarly, in investigating teamwork in organizations, Sundstrom et al. (1990) formulated an "ecological" model that was mainly based on the notion of the interconnected variables to examine work group dynamics in organizations. Consistent with many of the concepts in GST, teams in health care settings are often highly interdependent because patient care requires multiple inputs from various care providers and their relationships are often intricately and reciprocally related. For instance, the output of one group (a primary physician's initial diagnosis necessitating imaging tests) frequently serves as the input for a second group (imaging tests requested by the primary physician), and the output of the second group (imaging test results) might reciprocally be the input for the very first group. This reciprocal interdependence necessitates that health care teams work collaboratively to optimize patient outcomes. Therefore, when optimizing the functioning of diverse yet interdependent cross-disciplinary health care teams, cross-collaboration with members of the other teams is essential to solving difficult problems and determining appropriate interventions.

Extensive research has characterized the administration of health care as highly complex, requiring close interdependent relationships between departments and individuals. Because many situations arising from inadequate treatment or error are potentially life-threatening, hospitals and health care environments have also been characterized as "high-hazard" environments by organizational scholars (Gaba, 2000). Any miscommunication between caregivers in patient care coordination can cause a ripple effect, in which the effects from small mistakes can become exacerbated during the course of treatment. As explained in Perrow's hierarchy of failure (1984, p. 70), the smallest incident can lead to the entire system failure. A failure at the most elementary level of a highly interconnected system may not have an immediate effect on the system as a whole; however, as this failure spreads to the higher levels of the system hierarchy, the impact gets exacerbated, triggers subsequent component failure, and ultimately causes a system failure. Such a systems driven theory, called high reliability organization theory (HROT) was first articulated by researchers from Berkeley, who initially began this line of research through examining errors arising from the complex coordination of military operations on aircraft carriers (Rochlin, La Porte, & Roberts, 1987).

Subsequently applied to teams in health care settings, HROT postulates that for the quality of patient care to be fully optimized, it is necessary to develop an organizational culture in which a commitment to safety is viewed as a collective top priority and a collaborative team effort. Central elements for achieving the high reliability organization have been identified as setting specific safety goals and measuring their success, developing redundant checks and balances to ensure errors are caught early or not perpetuated, encouraging trial-and-error learning, and incorporating simulations to enhance response dependability (Gaba, 2000). HROT is in essence a means by which an organization "learns", either through methods such as root cause analysis, or near-miss analysis, and the lessons of such are transmitted to and debriefed among other organizational members and teams. While such knowledge is informally shared in organizations, in HROT systems, "organizational learning" is maintained as a regular practice in which all relevant employees are expected to take part.

Of critical importance, HROT is highly compatible with a patient safety culture and shares much of the same philosophy. For example, while HROT holds that both individual- and group-level interventions generate mutual support and trust between individuals, teams, and departments to cultivate cordial and open interpersonal communications, while promoting decentralized decision making (Ruchlin, Dubbs, & Callahan, 2004), advocates of building a patient safety culture see such collaboration stemming from underlying intrinsic goal alignment and belief. Both views agree that conflict reduction, improved communication, and collaboration are fundamental to reducing medical errors and improving patient care. The primary difference is essentially one of formalization. Patient safety culture, while certainly developed with intent, is generally informally created. Built upon the foundation of mutual goals and intrinsic beliefs, it flows from the deeply held personal beliefs of those in the organization, acts as a philosophy that permeates the health care workforce and guides their interpersonal interactions around the well-being of the patient. In HROT, the well-being of patients is likewise the most important organizational goal, but behavior and interactions are much more directed by rules and training. The development of a high reliability organization emphasizes the development of behavioral skills (e.g., communication and team-building) and system familiarity (Billings & Reynard, 1984; Gaba, 2000). Therefore, while patient safety culture guides overall intrinsic motivations and beliefs, HROT directs how such shared beliefs can best be operationalized, externalized, and learned in a dynamic system. Several health care scholars call for the concepts of organizational learning to be a viable means to incorporating HROT into clinical settings to improve patient safety and the ensuing section elucidates the key points of organizational learning that are fundamental to such integration in health care organizations.

Organizational Learning

While the original conceptualization of organizational learning was published over 40 years ago, formal frameworks of the concept were not fully explored until a couple of decades later, and even today many variations of the concept exist (Argyris & Schon, 1978; Argyris, 1990; Cyert & March, 1963). However, common to most conceptualizations is the idea that learning organizations constantly undergo a process of transformation, in which such change leads to adaptations, hence facilitating more efficient operations and goal attainment (Senge, 1994). A central precept of organizational learning is that full employee participation is necessary for such transformation to take place, as described by Watkins and Marsick, "Learning organizations are characterized by total employee involvement in a process of collaboratively conducted, collectively accountable change directed towards shared values or principles" (Watkins & Marsick, 1992, p. 118).

Learning organizations constantly develop and revise structures and systems to become more adaptable and responsive to change (Kanter, 1989; Senge, 1990). Another salient facet of learning organizations is that the process for developing responsive systems is inherently viewed as an integrative process that bridges learning between the individual and collective levels, as reflected in Watkins and Marsick's description. It is the internal integration of individuals within a shared culture that ultimately facilitates organization-wide learning (Dodgson, 1993). Finally, learning organizations engage in double-loop learning in which errors are detected and corrected by not only modifying actions and behaviors but also evaluating underlying assumptions and norms in order to produce significant and long-term impact on their system (Argyris & Schon, 1978; Argyris, 2002). Incorporating these tenets of organizational learning into promoting patient safety is, thus, an effective means by which to compliment the goal of optimizing patient care by reducing medical errors and creating a high reliability system.

Furthermore, it is of the utmost importance that health care organizations fully support the collective learning process to facilitate employee engagement in knowledge generation and sharing in order to adequately address complex errors in health care environments. That is, the mechanism to establish and sustain a high reliability organization for ensuring the culture of patient safety is the system-wide adoption of organizational learning, which contends blame be excised and replaced by a commitment to examine and learn from errors without threat of reprisal when such errors were not the results of unacceptable negligence. Indeed, research has uncovered that learning in complex and high-risk environments is often impeded by poor information transfer and inadequate feedback resulting in poor analysis and suboptimal performance (Sterman, 1994). Organizational learning is, therefore, a conduit for collaborative process to promote a highly reliable patent safety culture and to build a learning organization where team members feel safe to share information, seek feedback for clarification, ask questions to support decision making, challenge assumptions, and admit mistakes without threat of coercion. In a culture where underlying assumptions are challenged, routine rules and procedures are questioned, and open discussions of errors and mistakes are encouraged, a greater understanding of systematic events leading to errors and suboptimal patient care can be achieved. Through the promulgation of such information sharing in a safe and noncoercive organizational learning environment within the framework of HROT, improvements in health care provider communication and cooperation can bring about positive changes in decision making, operational policy, and ultimately patient safety and care.

CONCLUSION

The Integration of Theoretical Solutions for Improving Patient Care

The thesis that improved communication and reduction of conflict in organizations improves decision-making quality and operational effectiveness is not new. Other disciplines such as aviation and maritime management have demonstrated cited the most common root-causes of accidents involve failed communication and lack of team cooperation rather than purely technical failure (Helmreich, 1997). However, in the realm of health care, investigations on patient treatment and safety have only recently discovered that the problem is pervasive and consequences often severe. In spite of decades where the dysfunctional relationships between doctors and nurses, physicians with each other, and caregivers were well known, little progress has been made to remedy the situation. In some cases, such conflict has been simply seen as inherently embedded, or grudgingly accepted as "traditional" (Chassin & Becher, 2002). The high stakes inherent to treating patients in environments characterized by inadequate communication and pervasive conflict undermine the ability to optimize treatment. Consequently, the culture that has emerged has resulted in a system that unnecessarily comprises patient safety and care.

This work offers potential solutions to these vexing problems through applying cross-disciplinary approaches in which organizational theories are applied to health care situations. In doing so, the importance of developing a patient safety culture through employing the four well-established OD and OB theories has been presented. Our choice regarding the four theoretical solutions was to focus on a value-oriented approach beginning with the assumption that the utmost intrinsic value to health care workers is their patients' welfare. The conceptualization of using these shared values to create a patient safety culture is both reasonable and possible. At the same time, such a patient-driven culture does not simply evolve from good intentions and common values of health care professionals particularly in long-standing institutions ingrained with interpersonal problems. Rather, the value-driven solutions suggested in this work are both complementary and integrative with an emphasis of creating synergy between caregivers. For example, once a patient safety culture is established, the psychological contracts and ideological currency that support the patient safety culture flow more freely in such an environment. Applying the transformational leadership techniques works to take the emphasis off extrinsic values which often lie at the heart of bickering and dysfunction in health care teams, and instead promote shared goals and beliefs that reinforce this value-driven approach. Through integrating high reliability organizational theory combined with organizational learning, improved communication and operational mechanisms for error reduction and patient safety will be established.

Common to the efficacy of all the theories examined in this work is the notion that health care teams must be prepared to first identify and then address problems within their organizational cultures that impede effective communication and breed conflict. The theories elucidated in this work are not meant to be construed as the only viable blueprints to improving the efficacy of teamwork where problems exist. Moreover, differences in organizational structures and composition of organizational stakeholders may affect the way in which any of these theories could be most effectively applied. Indeed, the preceding discussions of the proposed theoretical solutions should not be qualified as an exhaustive approach to facilitating team cooperation in all health care teams. Generating prolific discussions on other means of utilizing the works from organizational theory to improve teamwork should be considered in determining specific and tailored solutions once organizational specific problems are identified in health care institutions. In spite of the limitation of focusing largely on the value-driven approaches, the prudent utilization and application of the theoretical constructs discussed in this work potentially offers valuable means by which teamwork can be improved and conflict reduced in health care organizations and should thus be considered in the formation and modification of operational policies in clinical settings for error reduction and improved patient care.

REFERENCES

Argyris, C., & Schon, D. (1978). *Organizational learning: A theory of action perspective.* Reading, MA: Addison-Wesley.

Argyris, C. (1990). *Overcoming organizational defenses: Facilitating organizational learning.* New York: Prentice-Hall.

Argyris, C. (2002). Double-loop learning, teaching, and research. *Academy of Management Learning & Education*, *1*(2), 206–218.

Bass, B. M. (1990). From transactional to transformational leadership: Learning to share the vision. *Organizational Dynamics*, *18*(3), 19–31.

Bass, B. M., Avolio, B. J., Jung, D. I., & Berson, Y. (2003). Predicting unit performance by assessing transformational and transactional leadership. *Journal of Applied Psychology*, *88*(2), 207–218.

Bertalanffy, L. V. (1969). *General system theory: Foundations, development, applications.* New York: George Braziller.

Billings, C. E., & Reynard, W. D. (1984). Human factors in aircraft incidents: Results of a 7 year study. *Aviation Space and Environmental Medicine*, *55*, 960–965.

Bunderson, J. S. (2001). How work ideologies shape the psychological contracts of professional employees: Examining doctors' responses to perceived breach. *Journal of Organizational Behavior*, *22*(7), 717–741.

Burns, J. M. (1978). *Leadership.* New York: Harper and Row.

Cavanagh, S. J., & Tross, G. (1996). Utilizing research findings in nursing: Policy and practice considerations. *Journal of Advanced Nursing*, *24*(5), 1083–1088.

Chang, E., Waid, E., Martinec, D. V., Zheng, B., & Swanstrom, L. L. (2008). Verbal communication improves laparoscopic team performance. *Surgical Innovation*, *15*(2), 143–147.

Chassin, M. R., & Becher, E. C. (2002). The wrong patient. *Annals of Internal Medicine*, *136*(11), 826–833.

Clark, S. (2003). The contemporary workforce: Implications for organizational safety culture. *Personnel Review*, *32*, 40–57.

Cyert, R. M., & March, J. G. (1963). *A behavioral theory of the firm*. New York: Prentice Hall.

Davies, H. T. O., Nutley, S. M., & Mannion, R. (2000). Organizational culture and quality of health care. *Quality Health Care*, *9*(2), 111–119.

Dodgson, M. (1993). Organizational learning: A review of some literatures. *Organization Studies*, *14*(3), 375–394.

Donabedian, A. (1980). *The definition of quality and approaches to its assessment*. Ann Arbor, MI: Health Administration Press.

Donchin, Y., Gopher, D., Olin, M., Badihi, Y., Biesky, M., Sprung, C. L., Pizov, R., & Coter, S. (1995). A look into the nature and causes of human errors in the intensive care unit. *Critical Care Medicine*, *23*(2), 294–300.

Drazen, J. M. (2004). Awake and informed. *New England Journal of Medicine*, *351*(18), 1884–2001.

Duldt, B. W. (1981). Anger: An alienating communication hazard for nurses. *Nursing Outlook*, *29*(11), 640–644.

Emanuel, L. L., & Richter, J. (1994). The consultant and the patient-physician relationship: A trilateral deliberative model. *Archives of Internal Medicine*, *154*(16), 1785–1790.

Epstein, R. M. (1995). Communication between primary care physicians and consultants. *Archives of Family Medicine*, *4*(5), 403–409.

Falbe, C. M., & Yukl, G. (1992). Consequences for managers of using single influence tactics and combinations of tactics. *The Academy of Management Journal*, *3*(3), 638–652.

Farber, N. J., Weiner, J. L., Boyer, E. G., & Robinson, E. J. (1990). How internal medicine residents resolve conflicts with attending physicians. *Academic Medicine*, *65*(11), 713–715.

Friedman, D. M., & Berger, D. L. (2004). Improving team structure and communication: A key to hospital efficiency. *Archives of Surgery*, *139*(11), 1194–1198.

Gaba, D. M. (2000). Structural and organizational issues in patient safety: A comparison of health care to other high-hazard industries. *California Management Review*, *43*, 83–102.

Gawande, A. A., Studdert, D. M., Zinner, M. J., & Brennan, T. A. (2003). Analysis of errors reported by surgeons at three teaching hospitals. *Surgery*, *133*(6), 614–621.

Guzzo, R. A., & Shea, G. P. (1992). Group performance and intergroup relations in organizations. In: M. D. Dunnette & L. M. Huough (Eds), *Handbook of industrial and organizational psychology* (pp. 269–313). Palo Alto, CA: Consulting Psychologists Press.

Hackman, J. R. (1987). The design of work teams. In: J. W. Lorsch (Ed.), *Handbook of organizational behavior* (pp. 315–342). Englewood Cliffs, NJ: Prentice-Hall.

Hackman, J. R., & Oldham, G. R. (1980). *Work redesign*. Reading, MA: Addison-Wesley.

Hart, E., & Hazelgrove, J. (2001). Understanding the organizational context for adverse events in health care services: the role of cultural censorship. *Quality Health Care*, *10*, 257–262.

Helmreich, R. L. (1997). Managing human error in aviation. *Scientific American*, *276*(5), 62–67.

Horwitz, I. B., Horwitz, S. K., Daram, P., Brandt, M. L., Brunicardi, F. C., & Awad, S. S. (2007). Transformational, transactional, and passive-avoidant leadership characteristics of a surgical resident cohort: Analysis using the Multifactor Leadership Questionnaire and implications for improving surgical education curriculums. *Journal of Surgical Research*, *148*(1), 46–59.

House, R. J., & Mitchell, T. R. (1974). Path-goal theory of leadership. *Journal of Contemporary Business*, *3*, 81–97.

Institute for Safe Medication Practices. (2003, February 6). The reports are in … or are they? Awareness of medication error reporting programs needs a boost. Available at http://www.ismp.org/Newsletters/acutecare/articles/20030206.asp. Retrieved on March 24, 2009.

Institute of Medicine. (1999). *To err is human: Building a safer health system*. Washington, DC: National Academy Press.

Itani, K. M., Liscum, K., & Brunicardi, F. C. (2004). Physician leadership is a new mandate in surgical training. *American Journal of Surgery*, *187*(3), 328–331.

Janis, I. L. (1972). *Victims of groupthink: A psychological study of foreign policy decisions and fiascoes*. Boston: Houghton Mifflin.

Janis, I. L., & Mann, L. L. (1977). *Decision making: A psychological analysis of conflict, choice, and commitment*. New York: Free Press.

Jehn, K. A. (1995). A multimethod examination of the benefits and detriments of intragroup conflict. *Administrative Science Quarterly*, *40*, 256–282.

Johnson, J. L., & O'Leary-Kelly, A. (2003). The effects of psychological contract breach and organizational cynicism: Not all social exchange violations are created equal. *Journal of Organizational Behavior*, *24*(5), 627–647.

Jung, I. D., & Sosik, J. J. (2002). Transformational leadership in work groups: The role of empowerment, cohesiveness and collective-efficacy on perceived group performance. *Small Group Research*, *33*(3), 313–336.

Kanter, R. (1989). *When giants learn to dance*. London, England: Simon and Schuster.

Kirk, S., Parker, D., Claridge, T., Esmail, A., & Marshall, M. (2007). Patent safety culture in primary care: Developing a theoretical framework for practical use. *Quality and Safety in Health Care*, *16*, 313–320.

Kotter, J. P. (1973). The psychological contract. *California Management Review*, *15*(3), 91–99.

Kuhnert, K. (1994). Transforming leadership: Developing people through delegation. In: B.M. Bass & B. J. Avolio (Eds), *Improving organizational effectiveness through transformational leadership*. Newbury Park, CA: Sage.

Kunkle, E. C. (1964). Communication breakdown in referral of the patient. *The Journal of the American Medical Association*, *187*, 663–679.

Larson, J. R., Christensen, C., Franz, T. M., & Abbott, A. S. (1998). Diagnosing groups: The pooling, management, and impact of shared and unshared case information in team-based medical decision making. *Journal of Personality and Social Psychology*, *75*(1), 93–108.

Lingard, L., Espin, S., Whyte, S., Regehr, G., Baker, G. R., Reznick, R., Bohnen, J., Orser, B., Doran, D., & Grober, E. (2004). Communication failures in the operating room: An observational classification of recurrent types and effects. *Quality and Safety in Health Care*, *13*(5), 330–334.

Manias, E., & Street, A. (2001). The interplay of knowledge and decision making between nurses and doctors in critical care. *International Journal of Nursing Studies*, *38*(2), 129–140.

Mathieu, J., Maynard, T. M., Rapp, T., & Gilson, L. (2008). Team Effectiveness 1997–2007: A review of recent advancements and a glimpse into the future. *Journal of Management*, *34*(3), 410–476.

McCue, J. D., & Beach, K. J. (1994). Communication barriers between attending physicians and residents. *Journal of General Internal Medicine*, *9*(3), 158–161.

McGrath, J. E. (1984). *Groups: Interaction and performance*. Englewood Cliffs, NJ: Prentice Hall.

McKnight, L., Stetson, P. D., Bakken, S., Curran, C., & Cimino, J. J. (2002). Perceived information needs and communication difficulties of inpatient physicians and nurses. *The Journal of American Medical Informatics Association*, *9*(6), s64–s69.

Michaelson, M., & Levi, L. (1997). Videotaping in the admitting area: A most useful tool for quality improvement of the trauma care. *European Journal of Emergency Medicine*, *4*(2), 94–96.

Morrissey, J. (2004). Dr. intimidation: Surly prescribers increase risk of errors. *Modern Health care*, *34*(18), 10–11.

Mukherjee, S. (2004). A precarious exchange. *The New England Journal of Medicine*, *351*(18), 1822–1824.

Nemeth, C. P. (2008). *Improving health care team communication: Building on lessons from aviation and aerospace*. Burlington, VT: Ashgate Publishing.

O'Connor, G. G. (1980). Small groups: A general system model. *Small Group Behavior*, *11*(2), 145–174.

O'Donohue, W., & Nelson, L. (2007). Let's be professional about this: Ideology and the psychological contracts of registered nurses. *Journal of Nursing Management*, *15*, 547–555.

Payne, J. W. (1982). Contingent behavior decisions. *Psychology Bulletin*, *92*, 382–402.

Perrow, C. (1984). *Normal accidents: Living with high-risk technologies*. New York: Basic Books.

Reason, J. (1997). *Managing the risks of organizational accidents*. Burlington, VT: Ashgate Publishing.

Robinson, S. L. (1996). Trust and breach of the psychological contract. *Administrative Science Quarterly*, *41*(4), 574–599.

Rochlin, G. L., La Porte, T. R., & Roberts, K. H. (1987). The self-designing high reliability organization: Aircraft carrier flight operations at sea. *Naval War College Review*, *42*, 76–90.

Rosenstein, A. H., & O'Daniel, M. (2005). Disruptive behavior and clinical outcomes: Perceptions of nurses and physicians. *American Journal of Nursing*, *105*(1), 54–64.

Rousseau, D. M. (1990). New hire perspectives of their own and their employer's obligations: A study of psychological contracts. *Journal of Organizational Behavior*, *11*(5), 389–400.

Rousseau, D. M. (1995). *Psychological contracts in organizations: Understanding written and unwritten agreements*. Newbury Park, CA: Sage.

Rousseau, D. M. (2004). Psychological contracts in the workplace: Understanding the ties that motivate. *Academy of Management Executive*, *18*(1), 120–127.

Ruchlin, H. S., Dubbs, N. L., & Callahan, M. A. (2004). The role of leadership in instilling a culture of safety: Lessons from the literature. *Journal of Health care Management*, *49*(1), 47–60.

Salas, E., Dickinson, T. L., Converse, S. A., & Tannenbaum, S. I. (1992). Toward an understanding of team performance and training. In: R. W. Swezey & E. Salas (Eds), *Teams: Their training and performance* (pp. 3–29). Norwood, NJ: Ablex.

Santora, T. A., Trooskin, S. Z., Blank, C. A., Clarke, J. R., & Schinco, M. A. (1996). Video assessment of trauma response: Adherence to ATLS protocols. *The American Journal of Emergency Medicine*, *14*(6), 564–569.

Schein, E. H. (1978). *Career dynamics: Matching individuals and organizational needs*. Reading, MA: Addison-Wesley.

Schulz-Hardt, S., Frey, D., Luthgens, C., & Moscovici, S. (2000). Biased information search in group decision making. *Journal of Personality and Social Psychology*, *78*(4), 6556–6569.

Scott, J., Mannion, R., Davies, H. T. O., & Marshall, M. N. (2003). Does organizational culture influence health care performance? *Journal of Health Services Research and Policy*, *8*, 105–117.

Senge, P. (1990). The leader's new work: Building learning organizations. *Sloan Management Review*, *32*(1), 723.

Senge, P. M. (1994). *The fifth discipline: The art & practice of the learning organization*. New York: Doubleday.

Sexton, J. B., Thomas, E. J., & Helmreich, R. L. (2000). Error, stress, and teamwork in medicine and aviation: Cross sectional surveys. *British Medical Journal*, *320*, 745–749Available at http://www.bmj.com/cgi/content/full/320/7237/745. Retrieved on March 13, 2009.

Stein, L. I. (1967). The doctor-nurse game. *Archives of General Psychiatry*, *16*, 699–703.

Sterman, J. D. (1994). Learning in and about complex systems. *System Dynamics Review*, *10*, 291–330.

Stout, R. J., Salas, E., & Fowlkes, J. E. (1997). Enhancing teamwork in complex environments through team training. *Group Dynamics: Theory, Research, and Practice*, *1*(2), 169–182.

Sundstrom, E. S., DeMeuse, K. P., & Futrell, D. (1990). Work teams: Application and effectiveness. *American Psychologists*, *45*, 120–133.

Sutcliffe, K. M., Lewton, E., & Rosenthal, M. M. (2004). Communication failures: An insidious contributor to medical mishaps. *Academic Medicine*, *79*(2), 186–194.

Thomas, E. J., Sexton, J. B., & Helmreich, R. L. (2003). Discrepant attitudes about teamwork among critical care nurses and physicians. *Critical Care Medicine*, *31*(3), 956–959.

Thompson, J. A., & Bunderson, S. I. (2003). Violations of principle: Ideological currency in the psychological contract. *The Academy of Management review*, *28*(4), 571–586.

Tjosvold, D. (1988). Cooperative and competitive dynamics within and between organizational units. *Human Relations*, *41*(6), 425–436.

Van Eaton, E. G., Horvath, K. D., Lober, W. B., & Pellegrini, C. A. (2004). Organizing the transfer of patient care information: The development of a computerized resident sign-out system. *Surgery*, *136*(1), 5–15.

Watkins, K., & Marsick, V. (1992). Building the learning organization: A new role for human resource developers. *Studies in Continuing Education*, *14*(2), 115–129.

Yammarino, F. J., Spangler, W. D., & Bass, B. M. (1993). Transformational leadership and performance: A longitudinal investigation. *Leadership Quarterly*, *4*, 81–102.

Yule, S., Flin, R., Paterson-Brown, S., & Maran, N. (2006). Non-technical skills for surgeons: A review of the literature. *Surgery*, *139*, 140–149.

CHARACTERISTICS OF POSITIVE WORKING RELATIONSHIPS BETWEEN NURSING AND SUPPORT SERVICE EMPLOYEES

Debra E. Orr

ABSTRACT

Developing greater synergies will become increasingly necessary as the pressure on the health care industry continues to increase. This research looks at the required characteristics to create positive working relationships with clinical staff in a health care organization from the perspective of nonclinical staff. Ten different U.S. hospitals participated in this qualitative study with over 200 individual participants. A recipe for successful relationship building from a nonclinical perspective is included.

Productivity is a problem. Disengaged employees are the subject of discussion from serious research in universities and consulting firms to comic strips, such as Dilbert, to the circulation of pictures on the Internet depicting highway stripers painting over or around objects in their path, rather than taking the 20 seconds required and the minimal effort necessary to remove them.[1] According to the Gallup Employee Engagement Index, in 2004 disengaged employees cost U.S. businesses over $300 billion a year (Crabtree, 2004).

Organization Development in Healthcare: Conversations on Research and Strategies
Advances in Health Care Management, Volume 10, 199–213

ISSN: 1474-8231/doi:10.1108/S1474-8231(2011)0000010018

Kahn (1990) is the first to discuss how fully and variably individuals are psychologically present in their work lives. And, to be more specific, how much discretionary effort is given to work, above and beyond the necessary rationality to function in the everyday world (Orr & Matthews, 2008).

Engagement and productivity are, however, profoundly affected by negative relationships (Cox, 1991; Manderino & Berkley, 1997). The nature and functionality of those negative workplace relationships have the capacity to affect organizational outcomes, turnover and ongoing productivity (Mowday, Porter, & Steers, 1982). This is especially true in workplace relationships that offer a distinct power structure, with a clear superior and subordinate relationship, such as those in traditionally structured organizations with professional employees and support service workers, such as hospitals. Professional employees, or knowledge workers, are defined as "people who do much of their work with their hands, but whose pay is determined by the knowledge between their ears, acquired in formal education rather than through apprenticeship" (New Workforce, 2001, p. 9). Conversely, support service employees are defined by the tasks that they do, rather than the decisions that they make and have less formal education. The hegemony inherent in traditional organizational structures, specifically those that employ both professional employees and support service workers can create dysfunctional working relationships.

The negative emotions, such as personal distrust, distress, and anger, generated by dysfunctional working relationships can cause behavior to be prioritized differently (Nussbaum, 2001; Damasio, 1999; Pinker, 1997), thus harming organizations. Pinker says of emotions and their relationship to behavior:

> Once triggered by a propitious moment, an emotion triggers the cascade of subgoals and sub-subgoals that we call thinking and acting. Because the goals and means are woven into a multiply nested control structure of subgoals within subgoals within subgoals, no sharp line divides thinking from feeling, nor does thinking inevitably precede feeling or vice versa. (p. 373)

Pinker (1997) adds an additional and central note about the relationship of emotions to organizations. Emotions tell us how to prioritize. They define what to do next and why to do it. "... we have to commit ... to one goal at a time and the goals have to be matched with the best moments to achieve them ... emotions are the mechanisms that set the brains highest level goals" (p. 373). Therefore, how we feel will impact what we do and the way we do it. This is true of human beings within the context of organizations, as well as within the construct of individual cognition.

This writing highlights the roadblocks that distinct power structures create in the establishment of positive working relationships and explores the characteristics that contribute to the creation of productive working relationships between professional and support service employees with the hopes that these positive characteristics, once identified, can be enacted as a means to increasing productivity and engagement in the workplace. Wisely using human resources already available includes ensuring that current employees are engaged and collaborating with one another.

Recently, over 7,000 nurses participated in the Nursing Satisfaction with Support Services Survey (NS3). This survey, sponsored jointly by the American Organization of Nursing Executives (AONE), Aramark Health care, and the Studer Group, asks nurses how well they are being supported in their care-giving role by various support service departments. (For more information on the NS3 survey, please see the AONE website at http://www.aone.org/aone/about/SpecialEvents/NS3/NS3.html) Although the NS3 seeks to identify those elements that drive satisfaction on behalf of nurses, the question as to what factors create a collaborative working relationship from the perspective of support service employees was previously unstudied. This study seeks to discover which characteristics create positive working relationships between nursing and support service workers, from the perspective of support service workers. Identifying those factors that help create positive working relationships for support service workers will advance how care can be delivered efficiently and effectively.

THE LITERATURE

It is clear that the notion of what it means to be involved in one's work has evolved over time, from a static conception of an isolated, individual perception of meaningfulness (Lodahl & Kejner, 1965) to behavioral aspects that can be demonstrated and thus measured (Blau & Boal, 1987) to current work on the notion of engagement as expending discretionary effort (Orr & Matthews, 2008). What is becoming more sharply in focus is that the web of relationships that support collaboration are complicated by leadership structures and notions of status and authority (Rosenstein, 2002).

Traditional organizations, such as hospitals, are precise in terms of superior–subordinate relationships with those with the most specialized skill sets and more formal education, such as physicians, located at the top of the hierarchy, and therefore, are invested with greater power and control; and those with less specialized skill sets and less formal education, such as support service workers, located toward the bottom of the hierarchy, and therefore, are invested with less power and control. Traditional organizations are also organized around function-related areas. Knowledge workers have command of a specific task related to the work of the organization. Knowledge workers often delegate pieces of the specialized task to support staff. It is in this process of communication and delegation where dysfunctional, power-based and hegemonic behaviors tend to occur. Nonfunctional behaviors that negatively impact workplace relationships include, according to Rosenstein's 2002 research, yelling, raising the voice, disrespect, condescension, berating colleagues or customers, and the use of abusive language. Further, those near the top of organizational hierarchies are often less aware of how profoundly such nonfunctional behavior impacts those near the bottom of organizational hierarchies (Rosenstein, 2002).

Relationships are key in creating workplace engagement (Woodruff, 2006; Sejits & Crom, 2006; Buchannan, 2004). Engagement is defined various ways in the literature. Ranging from "a positive, fulfilling, work-related state of mind that is characterized by vigor, dedication and absorption" (Schaufeli & Bakker, 2004; Schaufeli, Salanova, González-Romá, & Bakker, 2002) to the amount of emotional and intellectual commitment to the organization (Shaw, 2005).

METHODOLOGY

This study uses a grounded theory/qualitative approach. The methodology for this study was chosen because of its active nature, its application to actual organizational situations, the emergent nature of the topic, and the need for the research to reflect the nuances inherent in a problem of complexity. Grounded theories are likely to offer insight, enhance understanding, and provide a meaningful guide to action (Strauss & Corbin, 1990). Experiencing the conditions necessary for collaboration from the perspective of a group lower in the organizational hierarchy requires a sense of trust on the part of the participant group and the ability to recognize and hear the data embedded in multifaceted experiences.

Ten hospitals from various geographic regions across the U.S. participated in the study. The hospitals represented rural, urban, suburban locales, large and small institutions, those with outsourced support service employees as well as those that were self-operating. Among the participants is a specialty children's hospital.

Two hundred and ninety-eight support service employees participated in the 65 focus groups. Participants in the study were assured of their anonymity. Aside from their workplace role as a support service employee, no demographic information was gathered about the participants. For purposes of this research, support service departments in the hospital environment were confined to: environmental services (housekeeping), food and nutrition services, patient transportation, security, biomedical (clinical) engineering, facilities management, security, laundry and linen services. Many other areas, from human resources to information services to switchboard operators, were potential support services employees. This study, however, chose to select those departments, which provide direct support to nursing units, thus offering the greatest potential for increase in communication and potentially patient care benefits.

During regular working hours, each hospital gathered small groups of support service employees together into focus groups of no more than 10 employees. To assure a wide variety of input, focus groups were held during all shifts at each hospital.

The focus group process was consistent from group to group. After introductions, the researcher explained the purpose of the study and offered informed consent consistent with the University Internal Review Board approval that was obtained for this research. Then, the researcher asked the questions of the focus group, taking notes as the participants discussed their feedback. All participants received a $20.00 gift card to a major coffee retailer immediately after participating. Immediately following each focus group, the researcher transcribed the notes and began a process of coding the text and creating any memos that would illuminate meaning. Over 2,200 individual comments were transcribed from participant responses. Over 180 distinct, open codes were created from those comments. Textual data was coded, analyzed; and the relationships between the discrete parts connected to create a model that is presented in this chapter.

The questions in the research used an appreciative approach. Participants were asked about:

A time when the work they do made a difference.
The impact that their specific job has on the core of the business.
What others in the organization currently do to support their work.
What others in the organization could do differently to support their work.
To think of a great nurse that they have worked with. Describe him/her.
How do they know what the nurses they work with expect of them?

RESULTS

Overall, the model (see Fig. 1) demonstrates the relationships between the most prominently developed themes revealed by the data.

The primary elements of the model are:

- Mindset and
- Modeling of behavior

Secondary to mindset and modeling of behavior are the ideas of:

- Learning,
- Communication, and
- Relationship.

This model demonstrates how the most prominent themes relate to one another. The characteristics of mindset and modeling of collaborative behaviors are the overriding ideas that drive collaboration most strongly, particularly from a leadership perspective. The characteristics of communication, learning, and relationship also drive collaborative behavior, but in more specific and personal ways. A discussion of these characteristics continues.

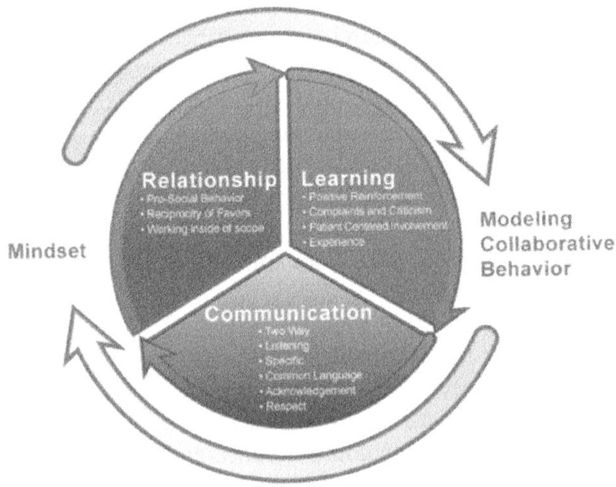

Fig. 1. Model of Collaborative Working Relationships.

MINDSET AND MODELING OF COLLABORATIVE BEHAVIORS

The research reveals that the attitudes present in leaders as they approach support service employees, entitled mindset, effects how leaders demonstrate collaborative behaviors, is entitled modeling. The internalized attitudes that leaders hold toward those with less education, lower socioeconomic status, and less power in organizations become apparent in their actions. The way that leaders think and act becomes a self-reinforcing process. Support service employees articulated the mindset that they experience with many stories. A few are below:

- *"People call and express a need. They'll say things like, "I need a phone, like, now." I'll tell them they need to enter it into the work order system and they'll say they don't have time to do that. I'll remind them to have the unit secretary do it, and they'll say they still don't have time to do it. With all the back and forth it could've been done by now. I'll walk them through the process, but they don't want to do it. I don't know if the younger nurses have had too much just given to them. Their attitude is not as cooperative. We're supposed to be a team. One person is not better than another. The dishwasher is as important as the nurse-manager or the cardiologist. It all filters down – these attitudes."*
- *"Understanding what we do is important. There is a caste system here. But everybody has a job to do and that gets forgotten."*
- *"Steve – he's a SWOT nurse. He's flexible. He always has his stuff together. He takes the leads off the patients. Some people ask why we can't do it, but we're not supposed to. He understands his responsibilities and does them. It's like we're friends. He's laid back. At night when we work it's like more of a friendship. He doesn't have that snooty thing going that he's better than you. Some of them are like that, not Steve."*
- *"Don't throw urine in the trash. Be clear in your requests in patient areas. For a temperature change etc. If it's important enough for a phone call, it's important enough for specifics. There are 2 million square feet in this hospital we have to manage and maintain-we have other responsibilities. Their attitude is that our time is less important than their time. There is a lack of understanding of the big picture."*

The various ways in which hospital leadership *models* collaborative behaviors is affected by a preexisting mindset discussed above. How we act is determined by what we feel. The relationships between what is occurring in the mind and how that occurrence is born out in demonstrated behavior is critical to the model.

- *"Nursing leadership is important. They pave the way for us to come through with their staff."*
- *"If we are like this to each other, then how are the patients being treated?"*
- *"Tony. He's always keyed in, even to little things like ceiling tiles. He looks at us as a partner. He enforces the way things should be ... we're secondary to vomit and stuff. That means nurses do the initial clean up and we do the secondary sanitizing. He makes them do that. Our people, we tell them, you have to work with these people every day, so just do it. But he makes the nurses do it."*
- *"Older nurses engage in more camaraderie with us. Newer people don't say hello, no laughing or joking. It's almost like they don't like their job."*
- *"A nurse manager I know. She's understanding about time frames. She's not abrupt or domineering with a tradesman. She'll make arrangements to ensure that our job is performed in a timely manner with no obstructions from the clinical side."*

In a smaller, more intimate and direct ways, the ability to collaborate well is determined by the manner in which we communicate, the way we learn about one another's expectations, and the nature of the relationship.

COMMUNICATION

In the development of positive working relationships between support service workers and nursing, the nature of communication is impacted by six specific factors:

1. Two-way communication,
2. Listening,
3. Specific communication,
4. Common nomenclature,
5. Acknowledgement, and
6. Respect.

Two-way communication is indicated by support service workers and nurses as having the ability to have conversations where the support service worker is able to ask questions, clarify issues, or determine intent.

The factor of listening describes the need of support service workers to be heard by nursing around issues pertaining to the work at hand, as well as personal communication.

Specific communication refers to the type of communication required by support service workers to maximize their efficiency and speed. Support service workers are referring to times, dates, plans, and the nature of equipment problems.

The factor of common language means that equipment and procedural names are used in common across the organization. An item that one nurse may call a "donut" another may call a "comfort ring." These differences can be quite confusing when referring to technical supplies or when encountered by persons whose first language is not English.

The factor of acknowledgement refers to the presence of support service workers and their need to discuss a patient with nursing to transport them, enter their room, or complete some job-related need. Support service workers are often ignored when trying to seek information or permissions required to accomplish their tasks.

Lastly, and most importantly, respect is key to successful communication with support service workers. Repeatedly, support service workers expressed that they were willing to go the extra mile, work above and beyond their required scope for those nurses who treated them respectfully. Support service workers often feel that they are people devoid of identity. Making eye contact, treating others with basic human dignity, and learning the names of the people one works with everyday is a significant step toward a more collaborative environment.

- *"One day a nurse called and said that the patient was allergic to dust and asked me to clean her room again. I said no, and asked her if there was an empty room on the floor. She said yes, so I went in there and cleaned it from top to bottom for dust. Then we moved the patient to the empty room. It prevented her from being exposed to more dust while I cleaned."*
- *Sometimes there are signs that say, "Do Not Enter Room without Talking to My Nurse." We have to enter, so I try to talk to the nurse, but she won't talk to me. She'll just walk away.*
- *"Sometimes we'll come up to the nurse's station and we'll have to ask 3 or 4 times. They won't listen and they ignore you. Am I invisible? I'm here."*
- *"Communicate better – directly – face to face. Messages go through 3 – 4 – or 5 people and it gets garbled. A typical thing that happens, the nurse calls down for a bed to be brought up. We bring it up. When we get there with it, they don't know where it's supposed to go and end up sending it back."*

- *"Two days ago, in Labor and Delivery called me about the leads of a fetal monitor malfunctioning. The nurse called me because the monitor was showing drops in heart rate from 120 to 60 beats per minute. I asked the nurse if she checked the monitor by using an intercranial lead. She tried it and discovered that it wasn't the monitor that was malfunctioning, the baby was actually in distress. They took the mother to the OR and she had an emergency c-section. The baby might not have made it otherwise."*
- *"Some units meet me with a smile and tell me what's going to happen that day – we've got four patients going home and I know what to expect all day. Other units it's not like that. I don't know why there is a difference. Maybe it's individuals."*
- *"Certain nurses explain things good to you. Others just assume you know what they want and where stuff is that they want worked on."*

RELATIONSHIPS

Relationships are impacted by three factors: prosocial behavior, reciprocity of favors, and working inside scope.

1. By prosocial behavior, support service workers mean those behaviors done for altruistic reasons and most often characterized by a focus on the patient or patient's family. Nurses that were focused on the patient, the patient's family and their needs were viewed as excellent partners in the eyes of support service workers.
2. The factor of reciprocity of favors denotes that support service workers were far more likely to do tasks for nurses or others that were technically outside of their scope of work if the nurse occasionally did things for the support service worker that were outside the scope of his/her work. Practically speaking, what this amounts to is that if a support service worker needs a pillow case while making a bed, the nurse might hand it to him or her. On a personal level, it might be as simple as asking the support service worker if they would like a piece of birthday cake that is in the lounge.
3. The final factor associated with the development of relationships is the idea of working within scope. Support service workers often feel that nursing is unaware of exactly what the support service worker is supposed to do and consequently, the support service worker is in a frequent position of having to tell a figure of authority (nursing) that he or she is not supposed to do the requested task. This is uncomfortable for

the support services worker and contributes to bad feelings about the support service worker from nursing staff. This particular factor is especially relevant in the health care setting, as an organization that depends on a strong hierarchical structure. Defining the scope of work for both the support service worker and for nursing will contribute to the development of a positive working relationship by clarifying the roles of each in a complex process.

- *"You've got to talk to them and ask them. We'll help out with anything as long as it's not ridiculous. They don't understand why we have to go and make beds on other units."*
- *"There's a list of things we're not supposed to touch when we're doing a room. Nursing doesn't seem to know about this list. What we do and what CNA's do is so close. Like in L & D-there's a basin after the baby is born. If there is more than 2 ounces of fluid in the basin we aren't supposed to touch it. The CNA is. But she won't. I have to tell her to do it. She says it's my responsibility. I know it's hers. Some people just end up doing it. But I don't have the time all the time. For a nurse who's really nice and sweet all the time, I'd do it. But then other people get confused and say well, you did it for so and so."*
- *"Once this lady vomited and an aide tried to get me to clean it by ordering me to do it. I said, 'you clean, I disinfect.' Then a day or so later, there was a trauma and there was blood all over the floor and Art was going to clean it up. I told him no. That I'll take care of it. He said, 'it's my responsibility'. I said, 'I know, but I'll do it for you'. The aide couldn't understand the difference. If you respect us, we'll go out of our way for you. If everyone was like Art, there would never be a problem."*
- *"It's not always clear who does what."*

LEARNING

Many support service workers also expressed that different nurses often wanted very different things from them and it took time and familiarity to learn what these needs were. This familiarity includes experience over time like the positive reinforcement they receive, the manner in which complaints or criticisms are delivered, and the opportunity to assist nurses in patient-centered ways. Relative to experience-as-a-teacher, many support service workers expressed that they were well-trained technically, but felt that they did not really know what nurses wanted from them until they had worked with them for a period of time. This time of experiential learning is critical to meeting expectations.

1. Positive reinforcement was also a motivator for learning and meeting expectations. Support service workers want to meet the expectations of nurses whom they admire and when an admired colleague offers positive reinforcement it is both motivating and a learning experience.
2. Support service workers also learn a great deal from complaints and/or criticisms, not all feedback has to be positive for it to be educative or valuable. What does seem to be important is that the reasons for the negative feedback are made known (why was what was done or not done a problem) and that it is done respectfully (in private and not belittling). It is often most helpful if the complaint and/or criticism be given to the employee directly so that he or she can ask questions about what was done or to explain his or her actions and an opportunity to repair the personal relationship is there.
3. Finally, the closer that support service workers are invited to work with nurses on patient-centered concerns the more they learn about how to better meet expectations in the future.
   - *"It's different on different units in the hospital. Respect us. The way they speak to us. We want to work together. We can help each other."*
   - *"Learn to talk to people properly. In environmental service, we're people too. If we weren't here, they wouldn't get the job done. A beautiful house that's dirty is no good."*
   - *"If we don't meet their expectations, they'll have an attitude on. If there are no complaints we just assume we're meeting their expectations. Otherwise communication is lacking."*
   - *"Melanie the nurse-One of my staff was stuck by a needle in OB. She helped me to call Workman's Comp. I didn't know how to do it all, my manager was out that day. She helped me fill out all the papers and make all the appointments. I didn't know why we had to do it all. She was a great help to me. I feel safe and comfortable asking her anything, even if I feel stupid."*
   - *"I've helped to clean a patient for the nurse."*
   - *"Shelly – Friendly, gorgeous in the morning ... she says 'good morning, glad to see you' She acknowledges that you're there. She says, 'thank you for coming in to work' she makes your day. She'll ask you nicely to do something, she'll pat your shoulder, but we move fast in an emergency."*

DISCUSSION

Many issues cloud the relationships between nurses and support service employees. For example, there are significant issues of the power structure, education, culture, language, nomenclature, expectations, and socioeconomic status that impact the development of a collaborative work approach.

This study reinforces what has been known about the nature of interaction in organizational relationships. In his 1950 work, *The Human Group*, Homan (1950) discussed the reinforcing nature of activity, interaction, and sentiment: how our actions impact the nature of our interaction with others, thereby creating a feeling. This feeling will drive the next action that is taken. This study builds on Homan's ideas in two ways:

1. It identifies the contributory nature of mindset of the participants in a human system. That is to say, the way in which individuals think about one another impacts the way they choose to interact. This mindset and the subsequent modeling of it by leadership, acts as a precursor to the activity phase of Homan's model.
2. This study identifies how positive and negative cycles can be created out of our initial thinking about others. There is a choice present at the beginning of an interaction that makes our pathway within the context of the relationship much more difficult to alter in the future.

IMPLICATIONS FOR ORGANIZATION DEVELOPMENT PROFESSIONALS

This research has direct implications for organization development (OD) professionals who need to create greater collaboration in their organizations.

Help members of your organization to become conscious of their own mindset and the mindsets of the professional staff concerning support service workers. Discover your biases and work against those biases.

Remember that your actions will reflect your mindset and if you are trying to develop greater collaboration your internal thinking needs to reflect that.

1. Ensure that good communication is used and pay specific attention to two-way communication, listening, specific communication, common nomenclature, acknowledgement, and respect.

2. Most support service employees want to meet expectations of those with whom they are working. They simply need to learn what those expectations are. Reinforce learning with positive comments, focus on patient needs and try to keep turnover low among support services staff to foster greater experience levels.
3. Encourage relationships that have an easy give and take to them, while respecting the scope that each group (support service workers and nursing) must take responsibility for.

CONCLUSIONS

The mindset brought to a system impacts the system. Mindset is reflected back to the organization through the actions that animate it. It can be a positive or a negative feedback loop. The manner in which work, and those who do work, are approached, brings assumptions about human dignity, the value of human work and the balance of needs between nursing and support service workers to the forefront of the issue of collaboration and engagement. Organizations that are dependent on support service workers for collaborative working relationships would be wise to examine the assumptions that are being expressed in the workplace, specifically around the notion of mindset. The assumptions brought to the workplace, which are animated by staff through their communication processes, are key to how the communication is accomplished. The most productive collaborative working relationships appear to be focused on client needs, allow for discussion, include specifics around needs and are full of active listening. These factors appear to help develop connections between support service workers and professional staff, which lead to greater collaboration. This can only set the stage for greater productivity generated by more positive relationships.

NOTE

1. Several infamous photos have circulated via e-mail depicting an animal killed on the roadway, striped over or painted around by a road crew painting the sides of a highway.

REFERENCES

Blau, G., & Boal, K. (1987). Conceptualizing how job involvement and organizational commitment affect turnover and absenteeism. *Academy of Management Review*, *12*, 288–300.

Buchannan, L. (2004). The things they do for love. *Harvard Business Review, 82*(12), 19–20.

Cox, H. (1991). Verbal abuse nationwide, part II: Impact and modifications. *Nurse Manager, 22*(3), 66–69.

Crabtree, S. (2004). Getting personal in the workforce: Are negative relationships squelching productivity in your company? *Gallup Management Journal*. Available at http://govleaders.org/gallup_article_getting_personal.htm. Retrieved on April 29, 2008.

Damasio, A. (1999). *The feeling of what happens: Body and emotion in the making of consciousness*. New York: Harcourt.

Homan, F. (1950). *The human group*. New York: Harcourt, Brace & World.

Kahn, W. (1990). Psychological conditions of personal engagement and disengagement at work. *Academy of Management Journal, 33*, 692–724.

Lodahl, T. M., & Kejner, M. (1965). The definition and measurement of job involvement. *Journal of Applied Psychology, 49*, 24–33.

Manderino, M., & Berkley, N. (1997). Verbal abuse of staff nurses by physicians. *Journal of Professional Nursing, 13*(1), 48–55.

Mowday, R., Porter, L., & Steers, L. (1982). *Employee-organization linkages: The psychology of commitment, absenteeism and turnover*. New York: Academic Press.

New Workforce. (2001). A survey of the near future – Knowledge workers are the new capitalists. *Economist, 361*(November 3, Special section), 8–11.

Nussbaum, M. (2001). *Upheavals of thought: The intelligence of emotions*. Cambridge, MA: Cambridge University Press.

Orr, D., & Matthews, H. (2008). Employee engagement and OD strategies. *OD Practitioner, 40*(2), 18–23.

Pinker, S. (1997). *How the mind works*. New York: Norton & Company.

Rosenstein, A. (2002). Nurse-physician relationships: The impact on nurse satisfaction and retention. *American Journal of Nursing, 106*(2), 26–34.

Schaufeli, W. B., & Bakker, A. B. (2004). Job demands, job resources, and their relationship with burnout and engagement: A multi-sample study. *Journal of Organizational Behavior, 25*, 293–315.

Schaufeli, W. B., Salanova, M., González-Romá, V., & Bakker, A. B. (2002). The measurement of engagement and burnout: A two sample confirmatory factor analytic approach. *Journal of Happiness Studies, 3*, 71–92.

Sejits, G., & Crom, D. (2006). What engages employees most: Or the ten C's of employee engagement. *Ivey Business Journal Online, 70*(4). Available at http://www.ivey.uwo.ca/ResearchAndDevelopment/UI/ViewAbstracts.aspx

Shaw, K. (2005). An engagement strategy process for communicators. *Strategic Communication Management, 9*(3), 26–29.

Strauss, A. L., & Corbin, J. M. (1990). *Basics of qualitative research: Grounded theory procedures and techniques*. Newbury Park, CA: Sage.

Woodruff, C. (2006). Employee Engagement – The real secret of winning a crucial edge over your rivals. *British Journal of Administrative Management December 2005/January 2006* (50), 28–29.

THE IMPACT OF SUPERVISOR–SUBORDINATE RELATIONSHIPS ON NURSES' ABILITY TO SOLVE WORKPLACE PROBLEMS: IMPLICATIONS FOR THEIR COMMITMENT TO THE ORGANIZATION

Yvonne Brunetto, Rodney Farr-Wharton and Kate Shacklock

ABSTRACT

This chapter uses the structural and relational dimension of social capital theory (SCT) as a lens for examining the impact of the supervisor–subordinate relationship on nurses' perceptions of the usefulness of their workplace networks, sociability, and affective commitment. A survey was used to collect data from 1,064 Australian nurses.

The findings suggest that nurses rely on very small workplace networks (typically only one other person) with which they have strong ties. Further, in over half of the cases, the supervisor (the Nurse Unit Manager (NUM))

Organization Development in Healthcare: Conversations on Research and Strategies
Advances in Health Care Management, Volume 10, 215–237

ISSN: 1474-8231/doi:10.1108/S1474-8231(2011)0000010019

holds the centric position. Moreover, for those nurses who did not include the NUM in their workplace network, their position appears even worse. For example, the usual reason given by nurses for not including the NUM was that the NUM was unavailable. This is a concern for health care management because the past two decades have delivered many changes to the nursing profession, including a reduction in the number of nursing positions and subsequent higher workloads. The consequences suggest that without effective workplace networks, nurses are working under conditions where solving problems is more difficult.

Keywords: Workplace social networks; supervisor-subordinate relationship; sociability; affective commitment

INTRODUCTION

Past research suggests that the quality and quantity of workplace relationships affect outcomes such as job usefulness and commitment for all employees (Adler & Kwon, 2002; Lin, 2001) and nurses in particular (Brunetto & Farr-Wharton, 2006, 2007). However, there has been less research examining who (if anyone) comprises the workplace networks of nurses. This study examines who nurses access for advice, information, and support when addressing work-based problems, and how important the supervisor is in their workplace networks. Further, the chapter examines the impact of the supervisor–subordinate relationship on nurses' perceptions of the usefulness of their workplace networks and the implications for their levels of affective commitment (commitment to the organization).

This research is important for both researchers and managers because Australia is similar to other OECD countries in facing a shortage of nurses (Buchan & Calman, 2004; OECD, 2006) equivalent to approximately 3% of practicing registered nurses (AIHW, 2004; Productivity Commission, 2005). Similar to other OECD countries, the main factors affecting supply include the aging population, inadequate numbers attracted to the professions, and high turnover (Buchan & Calman, 2004; Buerhaus, Staiger, & Auerbach, 2000; Schofield & Beard, 2005). While one of the reasons suggested as explaining high turnover of nurses is poor management practices, particularly in relation to perceived low levels of support from supervisors (Cheung, Bessell, & Ellis, 2004), there have been few studies examining whether nurses have well-developed workplace networks that they can use to help solve problems in the workplace. Similarly, few studies have examined who nurses access when faced with a workplace problem, how useful they perceive that support to be, and the implications for commitment to their organization.

It is management's responsibility to ensure that employees have embedded workplace networks so they can solve problems in the workplace efficiently and effectively. In addition, part of the supervisor's responsibility is to provide support and assistance for employees in solving work-based problems (Lin, 2001), and effective supervision is one human resource activity that has been identified as important in affecting organizational effectiveness (Gollan, 2005; Ostroff & Bowen, 2000; Ostroff, Kinicki, & Clark, 2002). When supervisors fail to embed a culture of supporting employees to solve problems, employees are likely to be left without an effective workplace network. Without such networks, employees probably experience frustration in negotiating everyday workplace problems. Perhaps this is why nurses reporting dissatisfaction with management policies and practices have a 65% higher probability of leaving than those reporting satisfaction (Gray & Phillips, 1994; Secombe & Smith, 1997). In this study, affective commitment is examined because past research has identified it as a predictor of labor turnover and job performance (Pitt, Leyland, Foreman, & Bromfield, 1995) as well as organizational effectiveness (Meyer & Herscovitch, 2001).

This chapter uses social capital theory (SCT) as a framework for examining the quality and quantity of work-based social networks available for use by nurses facing an everyday management or clinical problem in the workplace. In particular, SCT is useful to examine the role and importance of supervisors (called Nurse Unit Managers (NUMs) in the Australian context) within those networks. The basis of SCT is that the quality of network relationships affects members' access to a range of resources and information (Lin, 2001). The quality of the ties used to bond members together is in turn dependent on whether there are established rules and norms about mutual trust, reciprocity, and obligation behaviors (Adler & Kwon, 2002). These norms are the basis on which relationships are built because they determine what are acceptable behavior and actions in the workplace. Over time, management generally, and supervisors in particular, have the task of establishing the codes of behavior that they want via their rewarding practices.

On the one hand, this means that if collegial behavior is not promoted, supported, and rewarded in the workplace, then such behavior is likely to be lacking in an organization. On the other hand, in workplaces that encourage the development of networks for solving problems, it is more likely that the invisible bonds among members will grow stronger over time as their level of mutual trust increases, thereby facilitating the reciprocal flow of information, resources, favors, and/or other privileges (Kessels & Poell, 2004). Consequently, SCT argues that individuals and groups are more productive if they have effective workplace relationships that can be used to assist them to get the required information to solve workplace problems.

The findings from this study will provide new knowledge about the impact of the quality and quantity of workplace social networks on nurses, especially in terms of their access to support from management (particularly from the NUM) and the implications for their perceived commitment to the organization. This study uses survey data from 1,064 nurses (analyzed using path analysis) to address the primary research questions:

1. *What are the quality, quantity, and perceived usefulness of nurses' workplace social networks for solving workplace problems and how important are supervisors within these networks?*
2. *What is the relationship between nurses' perceived usefulness of their workplace social networks and affective commitment?*

This chapter has three parts. The first part provides a targeted review of the literature from which the secondary research questions (SRQs) emerge. The second part describes the sample and methods to test the research questions. The third part reports the results and uses the discussion section to identify pattern-matching with relevant past research, outlining implications for hospital managers and the health care management field, followed by the concluding remarks.

BACKGROUND

Social Capital Theory

There are three dimensions of SCT that can be used for examining the quality of social capital in a workplace. They are the structural, relational, and cognitive dimensions (Nahapiet & Ghoshal, 1998). The structural dimension provides an avenue for examining SC by analyzing the structures embedded within organizations that promote ties between workplace social network members. This involves examining the quantity and quality of interpersonal linkages (or ties) between workplace social network members (Nahapiet & Ghoshal, 1998). The relational dimension provides an avenue for examining the rules and norms about reciprocity and obligation behaviors within organizations (Kessels & Poell, 2004). The cognitive dimension provides an avenue for examining SC by analyzing the array of understandings that develop among individuals depending on their shared meaning of language, codes, and culture (Nahapiet & Ghoshal, 1998). This chapter uses both the relational and structural dimensions of SCT to address the research questions, as discussed next. The cognitive dimension is not used because it would make the chapter overly lengthy.

Testing the Structural Dimension

As stated, social capital results from the formation of effective social networks. Workplace social networks develop as invisible bonds (ties) among colleagues, based on a repetition of interactions. One way of examining the quality and quantity of nurses' informal ties is by analyzing their network content (Hoang & Anroncic, 2003). Network content refers to the quality and quantity of relationships in place to either promote or thwart employees' attempts to exchange information and resources as needed. This information is captured by identifying how many people nurses contacted when faced with a workplace problem. The following SRQ guided the data collection process:

SRQ1. What is the network content of nurses and how useful are their networks for solving work-based problems?

The information derived from this analysis will provide a preliminary understanding about the quantity of colleagues available to nurses to solve work-based problems and nurses' perceptions about the usefulness of such networks.

Another way of analyzing the role and impact of social networks is to examine who holds the central network position. Burt (1992) has suggested that some members who are positioned centrally within a network may be more important than others because of their power and subsequent access to information. These "centric" positions tend to be characterized by the absence of linkages between other members of the network, and the centric position then becomes a "broker," managing all information flow within the network. The centric position would provide maximum benefit in terms of access to information and the control of that information. It may be that supervisors occupy this centric position in relation to nurses' networks. In Burt's view, this means that the supervisors play a pivotal role in either facilitating or thwarting their nurses' ability to solve workplace problems efficiently and effectively. To capture this information, the next SRQ was used to guide data collection:

SRQ2. How important is the supervisor for nurses when faced with solving a workplace problem?

Examining the tie strength among members offers an alternative for analyzing the role and impact of workplace social network. Social network theory argues that social capital forms because of the relationship that develops between each pair of actors and the strength of the quality of this dyadic relationship will subsequently affect what information and resources are shared (Burt, 1992). Hansen (1999) argues that the concept of tie strength is dependent on the frequency and closeness of the interactions between two parties. Similarly, Granovetter (1973) argues that the strength of a tie is a combination of four properties, namely, the amount of time, the emotional intensity, the intimacy, and the reciprocal services that characterize the tie. That is, strong ties are characterized by lots of interactions and high emotional intensity, intimacy, and reciprocal services; plus, members trust one another and therefore can expect to exchange lots of information, resources, and favors (Granovetter, 1973). To examine what ties nurses have, the following research question was proposed:

SRQ3. Who belongs to nurses' workplace social networks and are the ties mainly weak or strong?

If effective workplace relationships are embedded within the work context of nurses, then it is expected that nurses will have strong ties with both their supervisors and their colleagues.

Testing the Relational Dimension

The relational dimension of SCT is used to explore the impact of the supervisor–subordinate relationship on nurses' perceptions of the usefulness of their workplace networks, and subsequently, their levels of affective commitment. The theory argues that when managers use management strategies aimed at building social capital, they would also promote information-sharing in formal and informal meetings and would be available to their nurses as support when problem-solving. As a consequence, nurses would report high levels of usefulness of their workplace social networks because their access to information, support, and resources would result in them solving problems efficiently and effectively. Hence, the relationship with their supervisor is crucial to nurses' ability to solve workplace problems.

The Supervisor–Subordinate Relationship

The supervisor–subordinate relationship is operationalized in this chapter by examining the quality of leader–member exchange (LMX), which describes how supervisors develop different working relationships with their subordinates, depending on the quality of their workplace relationship. When supervisors like and trust their subordinates, the theory argues that a high-quality LMX relationship develops, characterized by a high level of mutual support, trust, and respect. Such employees are deemed the "in-group" and receive easy access to information, support, and participation in decision-making, thereby making it easier for them to undertake tasks and solve work-related problems (Gerstner & Day, 1997; Mueller & Lee, 2002). Additionally, the in-group tend to be liked by their supervisors, irrespective of their performance (Graen & Uhl-Bien, 1995) and consequently, supervisors are more likely to assist them to solve workplace problems. According to Wayne, Shore, and Linden (1997), supervisors also benefit because subordinates are more likely to show initiative in the workplace. In contrast to the in-group, the "out-group" tends to suffer from poor levels of information-sharing and involvement in decision-making and, in turn, is more likely to have difficulty getting support and assistance when solving workplace problems.

Using the relational dimension of SCT, the ideal situation is that all employees experience high-quality LMX because this will provide the most effective support and information for nurses to solve problems. High-quality LMX is evident by high levels of satisfaction with the supervisor–subordinate relationship, probably resulting from increased access to relevant information and resources as well as an empowering relationship because supervisors allocate increased levels of organizational resources (time) toward such subordinates (Sparrowe & Linden, 1997). Supervisors would also promote information-sharing as the norm among colleagues. In addition, when high-quality LMX relationships are present, supervisors provide employees with meaningful feedback (consequently increasing their access to relevant information) and delegate decision-making and power (Wayne et al., 1997; Yrie, Hartman, & Galle, 2003). Hence, using the theoretical frame provided by relational dimension of SCT, it seems likely that the quality of supervisor–subordinate relationship could affect nurses' perceptions of the usefulness of their workplace networks. To examine the impact of the supervisor–subordinate relationship on nurses' perceptions of the usefulness of their workplace networks, the following hypothesis is proposed:

Hypothesis 1. There is a positive significant relationship between LMX and nurses' perceptions of the usefulness of their workplace networks.

Sociability

Sociability refers to the social skill required to facilitate effective social interactions (Ferris, Witt, & Hochwarter, 2001; Lizardo, 2006). Each individual enters an organization with different levels of social skills, influencing how well employees build effective workplace networks (Nie, 2001). In particular, it can affect how effective employees are at influencing colleagues to assist and support them in the workplace (Ferris et al., 2001). Also, in social interactions, the ability to read and understand different social situations, knowledge of social roles, norms, and interpersonal problem-solving skills is aided by sociability (Riggio & Reichard, 2008).

Management can enhance sociability by providing organizational mechanisms, such as formal and informal meetings and presentations, which facilitate the development of connections among employees. Such mechanisms can promote the development of ties and increase the flow of information that may assist problem-solving for employees (Brunetto & Farr-Wharton, 2004; Levin & Cross, 2004). Hence, it is important to examine the impact of sociability on nurses' perceptions of the usefulness of workplace networks, and therefore the following hypothesis is proposed:

Hypothesis 2. There is a positive significant relationship between sociability and nurses' perceptions of the usefulness of their workplace networks.

Affective Commitment

Past research has identified a significant positive relationship between the quality of supervisor–subordinate relationships and employees' affective commitment (Gerstner & Day, 1997). Further, when employees experience high-quality LMX, they are more likely to want to stay in the organization (Pitt et al., 1995). Allen and Meyer (1990) describe affective commitment as the emotional attachment to, and identification with, an organization. As stated, those employees with high levels of affective commitment are likely to be loyal and attached to the organization, thereby reducing their likelihood of leaving – that is, turnover is low (Meyer & Allen, 1997; Pitt et al., 1995).

Previous research has identified a positive significant relationship between LMX and levels of affective commitment for nurses (Brunetto & Farr-Wharton, 2004, 2006, 2007), yet there is minimal research linking nurses' perceptions of the usefulness of their workplace networks with their levels of affective commitment. Moreover, there is a void linking LMX, nurses' perceptions of the usefulness of their workplace networks, and propensity for sociability with their levels of affective commitment. Therefore, two hypotheses are proposed:

Hypothesis 3. There is a significant positive relationship between nurses' perceptions of the usefulness of their workplace networks and their levels of affective commitment.

Hypothesis 4. There is a significant positive relationship between nurses' levels of satisfaction with LMX, the usefulness of their workplace networks, propensity for sociability, and their levels of affective commitment.

METHODS

A survey-based, self-report strategy (Ghauri & Grønhaug, 2002) was used to obtain data from nurses about their workplace networks, their supervisor–subordinate relationships, their sociability, and levels of affective commitment. In total, quantitative data was collected from 900 private sector and 164 public sector nurses from four states of Australia (see Table 1 for demographics).

Measures Used

All except one measure used in this study has been validated in previous management research. The measures included in the questionnaire are outlined as follows (see further detail in Table 2):

a) The LMX validated test-bank survey traditionally measures the satisfaction with the relationship with their supervisor (Mueller & Lee, 2002). In this study, a seven-item unidimensional scale (LMX-7) developed by Graen and Uhl-Bien (1995) was used. According to Gerstner and Day (1997), the unidimensional scale updated by Graen and Uhl-Bien (1995) is the most commonly used tool for measuring

Table 1. Demographics of Survey Respondents.

Variable	Private-Sector Nurses	Public-Sector Nurses	Total
Gender			
Male	33 (4%)	20 (12%)	53 (5%)
Female	867 (96%)	144 (87%)	1011 (95%)
Total	900 (100%)	164 (100%)	1064 (100%)
Age			
Less than 30 years	74 (8.2%)	36 (22%)	110 (10.3%)
30–45 years	339 (37.6%)	73 (44.5%)	412 (38.7%)
Over 45 years	487 (54%)	55 (33.5%)	542 (50.9%)
Total	900 (100%)	164 (100%)	1064 (100%)

LMX quality and has the best psychometric properties of all the instruments reviewed.

b) This study operationalized nurses' perceptions of usefulness of workplace networks by composing a new instrument comprising three questions (see Table 2).

c) The study operationalized nurses' sociability by using the "propensity to connect with others" scale developed and validated by Totterdell, Holman, and Hukin (2008), comprising four subscales: "propensity to make friends," "propensity to make acquaintances," "propensity to join others," and "propensity to belong to groups." Examples of items used are in Table 2.

d) Allen and Meyer's (1990) commitment instrument was used to measure the dependent variable – affective commitment (commitment to the organization). Researchers have reported Cronbach's alphas ranging between .74 and .90 for this measure (see Allen & Meyer, 1996).

Sample

Sampling choices were made based on typicality to ensure that the sample was representative of public and private sector hospitals; urban and regional hospitals; large (metropolitan), medium, and small hospitals; and hospitals located in at least four states of Australia. To obtain data from nurses, 4,800 anonymous surveys were randomly distributed to nurses working in the wards of nine hospitals (two public and seven private sector hospitals) specifically chosen to meet the criteria listed above (see Table 3). The survey was accompanied with a letter explaining the purpose of the survey, an invitation to voluntarily participate, and a return envelope to ensure

Table 2. Measures Used in this Research.

Leader–Member Exchange (LMX) (the quality of supervisor–subordinate relationship) (Graen and Uhl-Bien, 1995)						
My supervisor is satisfied with my work	SD	DA	SE	SL	AG	SA
My supervisor understands my work problems and needs	SD	DA	SE	SL	AG	SA
My supervisor knows how good I am at my job	SD	DA	SE	SL	AG	SA
My supervisor is willing to use her/his power to help me solve work problems	SD	DA	SE	SL	AG	SA
I have a good working relationship with my supervisor	SD	DA	SE	SL	AG	SA
My supervisor is willing to help me at work when I really need it	SD	DA	SE	SL	AG	SA
I have enough confidence in my supervisor that I would defend and justify his/her decision if he/she were not present to do so	SD	DA	SE	SL	AG	SA
Sociability – "Propensity to connect with others" scale (Totterdell et al., 2008): *Examples of statements:*						
I have many friends (both at work and generally)	SD	DA	SE	SL	AG	SA
I have many acquaintances (both at work and generally)	SD	DA	SE	SL	AG	SA
Becoming part of a tight knit group is something I do naturally	SD	DA	SE	SL	AG	SA
I find it easy to bring individuals together	SD	DA	SE	SL	AG	SA
Usefulness of social networks (new instrument)						
My network was useful in helping me solve workplace clinical problems	SD	DA	SE	SL	AG	SA
My nurse colleagues are useful in helping me solve workplace clinical problems	SD	DA	SE	SL	AG	SA
My NUM is useful in helping me solve workplace clinical problems	SD	DA	SE	SL	AG	SA
Affective commitment (Allen & Meyer, 1990) (commitment to the hospital): *Examples of statements:*						
I would be very happy to spend the rest of my career with this hospital	SD	DA	SE	SL	AG	SA
This hospital has a great deal of personal meaning for me	SD	DA	SE	SL	AG	SA
I do not feel emotionally attached to this hospital (reverse score)	SD	DA	SE	SL	AG	SA
I feel a strong sense of belonging to this hospital	SD	DA	SE	SL	AG	SA
I feel strong ties with this hospital	SD	DA	SE	SL	AG	SA
Control – location	SD	DA	SE	SL	AG	SA
Where are you located (a) Queensland, (b) NSW, (c) Victoria, or (d) Western Australia?						

SD = Strongly Disagree; DA = Disagree; SE = Slightly Disagree; SL = Slightly Agree; AG = Agree; SA = Strongly Agree.

Table 3. Details about Each Hospital from which Nurses were Surveyed.

	Urban/ Regional	Dealing with Acute Cases	Teaching Hospital	Classed as Large >500 beds, Medium 300>x<500 beds, Smaller <300 beds
Private hospital 1	Urban	Yes	Yes	Large (578 beds)
Private hospital 2	Urban	Yes	No	Medium (317 beds)
Private hospital 3	Urban	Yes	No	Small (219 beds)
Private hospital 4	Urban	Yes	No	Medium (416 beds)
Private hospital 5	Regional	Yes	No	Small (206 beds)
Private hospital 6	Regional	Yes	No	Small (260 beds)
Private hospital 7	Urban	Yes	No	Small (239 beds)
Public hospital 1	Urban	Yes	Yes	Large (760 beds)
Public hospital 2	Regional	Yes	No	Small (160 beds)

confidentiality. In total, the response was 1,064 completed useable surveys, inferring a response rate of approximately 23%.

Data Analysis

Path analysis was used to test the impact of supervision practices on first, nurses' perceptions of the usefulness of their workplace networks, sociability, and in turn, their affective commitment. In particular, path analysis using an ordinary least square (OLS) approach was used to test the hypotheses. The advantage of path analysis is that it permits more than one equation to predict the dependent variable (affective commitment) and therefore it includes the indirect impact of LMX into the bigger equation. OLS is an explanation of variance and the overall R^2 measure identifies the overall "goodness-of-fit" for the proposed model (Ahn, 2002). Another advantage of using path analysis with an OLS approach is that it estimates parameters within an independent system, which could avoid the problem of multicollinearity (Grapentine, 2000). For these reasons, OLS was used for analysis of the data.

RESULTS

The sample was predominantly female (95%) and the majority (50.9%) was aged over 45 years (see Table 1). In terms of rank, 52 were either in a position of a NUM or higher, 156 were clinicians, 697 were registered nurses, 132 were enrolled nurses, and 27 were "other." In terms of length of time in their position, 152 respondents had been in their position less than 1 year, 317 between 1 and 5 years, 203 between 5 and 10 years, 93 between 10 and 15 years, and 299 for more than 15 years.

Factor Analysis

The correlation matrix identified many correlations exceeding .3, indicating the matrix was suitable for factoring. The Bartlett's test for sphericity was significant (χ^2 value = 12,805.52, $p < .001$, df = 276) and the KMO measure of sampling adequacy was .887 – well above the .6 requirement. When Principal Axis Factoring was undertaken to extract the variables, four factors had eigenvalues greater than 1 and 61.48% of the variance could be explained using these four factors. The factor transformation matrix suggests a relatively high correlation between factors. As stated, the advantage of using an OLS approach can avoid the problem of multicollinearity.

Correlation Coefficients

Table 4 details the correlation coefficients for each variable and the Cronbach's alpha scores, measuring reliability. All variables were significantly related to one another, except for the control variable – location.

Table 4. Means, Standard Deviation, Correlations, and Cronbach's Alpha Reliability.

Variable	*M*	SD	1	2	3	4	5
1. Location (control)			1				
2. LMX	4.35	.8	−.014	1	(.93)		
3. Usefulness of networks	4.09	.69	.010	.3**	1	(.71)	
4. Sociability	5.03	.71	−.039	.107**	.18**	1	(.81)
5. Affective commitment	4	1	−.045	.35**	.31**	.18**	1 (.87)

N = 1,064.

Numbers in parentheses on the diagonal are the Cronbach's alpha coefficients of the composite scales.

* Correlation is significant at the 0.05 level (2-tailed).

** Correlation is significant at the 0.01 level (2-tailed).

ADDRESSING THE SECONDARY RESEARCH QUESTIONS

To address the SRQ1 nurses were asked to respond to the following question:

> Q42. Who do you normally approach with a frustrating work-based problem? Examples may include how to use a particular piece of equipment or how to perform a clinical procedure. You may use more than one person/position regularly. Please place a (1) next to the position/person you approach the most and a (2) next to the position/person you approach the next most, and so on. Place an N (for never) next to those positions/persons you never approach.

Position/person	Q42
Nurse unit manager	
Clinical nurse	
After-hours coordinator	
Clinical educator/facilitator	
Nurse educator	
Nurse preceptor	
Other nurse (same ward)	
Other nurse (different ward)	
Other medical professional	
Nurse friend (not at same Hospital)	
Nonnurse friend	
Family	
Other	

Table 5 indicates the network content of nurses and the perceived usefulness of their workplace networks. The overwhelming majority of respondents (73%) had only one contact and approximately 9% had no contacts that they could approach with a work-based problem. These findings suggest that the vast majority of nurses had very poor network content – that is, minimal workplace networks. However, nurses did appear to be satisfied with their small workplace networks (mean = 4.96, SD = .92), suggesting they considered their networks to be fairly useful to very useful in solving workplace problems.

To address the SRQ2 nurses rated the position/person choices of Q42 (detailed above). Table 6 indicates that over 55% of the 1,064 nurses

Table 5. Number of Contacts used for Work-Based Problems.

Number of Contacts	Frequency	Percentage
0	94	8.8
1	776	72.9
2	103	9.6
3–5	59	5.5
6–10	19	1.7
11+	12	1.1

Table 6. Who Nurses Access When They have a Workplace Problem.

Member Status	Percentage
NUM	53.3
Senior clinical nurse	15.1
Other nurse same ward	14.6
After-hours coordinator and clinical educators (not on ward and not in all hospitals)	7.5
Other nurse, different ward	0.02
Other medical professionals	0.03
Nurse friend not at this hospital	0.03
Family	0.03
Nobody	8.8
Other	.5

approached their NUM and approximately 30% approached either a clinical nurse and/or other nurses in the same ward.

When those nurses who did not list their NUM were asked why, the findings suggest that the NUM was considered "too busy," was not in the ward, or was unapproachable for the nurses (see Table 7). This finding is supported by the findings about nurses' usefulness of their social networks in solving workplace problems (see Table 8).

To address the SRQ3 nurses were asked how well they knew the people they approached. Table 9 suggests that the majority (45%) knew their workplace network "very well" and another 30% knew their network members "fairly well." These findings suggest that nurses' workplace networks comprise strong ties dyads, which are ideal for information sharing.

Table 7. The Reasons Why Nurses did not Approach their NUM.

Response	Percentage
NUM was too busy	25.80
NUM was not in ward	26.88
NUM was unapproachable	20.43
Easier to ask another nurse	10.75
Work it out myself	7.52
Fear of being viewed incompetent by NUM	7.52
Feel I have more knowledge in the ward	1.07

Table 8. Nurses' Usefulness of Workplace Networks.

Statements	Means (out of 6) and Standard Deviation
My network was useful in helping me solve workplace clinical problems	4.96 (0.9)
My nurse colleagues are useful in helping me solve workplace clinical problems	5.22 (0.77)
My NUM is useful in helping me solve workplace clinical problems	4.5 (1.34)

1 = Strongly Disagree; 2 = Disagree; 3 = Slightly Disagree; 4 = Slightly Agree; 5 = Agree; 6 = Strongly Agree.

Table 9. How Well did You Know the Top 5 Persons used to Help Address Problems?

Frequency of Contacts	Percentage
No one	1.1
Slightly	10.7
Fairly well	30.4
Very well	45.8
Closely	11.1

This next section addresses the results for the hypotheses. In response to the Hypothesis 1, a linear regression analysis was undertaken with LMX as the independent variable and nurses' perceptions of the usefulness of their workplace network as the dependent variable. The findings support the hypothesis ($F = 130.699$, $p < .001$, $R^2 = 11\%$, $\beta = .3$, $p < .001$).

In response to the Hypothesis 2, a linear analysis was undertaken with sociability as the independent variable and nurses' perceptions of the usefulness of their workplace network as the dependent variable. The findings support the hypothesis:

1. Propensity to make friends as the independent variable and nurses' perceptions of the usefulness of their workplace network as the dependent variable ($F = 41.45$, $p < .001$, $R^2 = 4.4\%$, $\beta = .2$, $p < .001$);
2. Propensity to make acquaintances as the independent variable and nurses' perceptions of the usefulness of their workplace network as the dependent variable ($F = 15.52$, $p < .001$, $R^2 = 1.7\%$, $\beta = .1$, $p < .001$);
3. Propensity to join others as the independent variable and nurses' perceptions of the usefulness of their workplace network as the dependent variable ($F = 29.959$, $p < .001$, $R^2 = 3.2\%$, $\beta = .1$, $p < .001$);
4. Propensity to join others as the independent variable and nurses' perceptions of the usefulness of their workplace network as the dependent variable ($F = 10.410$, $p < .001$, $R^2 = 1.1\%$, $\beta = .1$, $p < .001$).
5. Combined sociability as the independent variable and nurses' perceptions of the usefulness of their workplace network as the dependent variable ($F = 10.410$, $p < .001$, $R^2 = 11.1\%$, $\beta = .18$, $p < .001$).

In response to the Hypothesis 3, a linear regression analysis was undertaken with nurses' perceptions of the usefulness of their workplace network as the independent variable and nurses' levels of affective commitment as the dependent variable. The findings support the hypothesis ($F = 115.448$, $p < .001$, $R^2 = 9.8\%$, $\beta = .3$, $p < .001$).

In response to the Hypothesis 4, path analysis was undertaken with LMX as the predictor, nurses' perceptions of the usefulness of their workplace network as the mediator, sociability as moderator, and nurses' levels of affective commitment as the dependent variable. The findings support the hypothesis ($F = 78.941$, $p < .001$, $R^2 = 20.9\%$, β for LMX $= .3$, $p < .001$; β for nurses' perceptions of the usefulness of their workplace network $= 133$, $p < .001$; β for sociability $= .17$, $p < .001$). Using the OLS procedure, the goodness-of-fit of the model identified that supervision, nurses' perceptions of the usefulness of their workplace networks, and sociability accounted for approximately a fifth of the variance of nurses' levels of affective commitment.

DISCUSSION

This chapter used the structural and relational dimension of SCT as a lens for examining the impact of the supervisor–subordinate relationship on nurses' perceptions of the usefulness of their workplace networks, sociability, and affective commitment. Data collection specifically aimed to identify first the quality, quantity, and perceived usefulness of nurses' workplace social networks for solving workplace problems, and second, how important are supervisors within these networks, to address the research questions. Using the structural dimension of SCT, the ideal conditions for fostering SC, so as to embed effective networks for solving work-based problems, would be for nurses to have a mixture of strong and weak ties with at least three to five workplace members, including the NUM. In contrast, the findings suggest that nurses rely on very small workplace networks (typically only one other person) with which they have strong ties. Further, in over half of the cases, the supervisor (the NUM) holds the centric position. As long as that person is available every time a nurse has a problem, then the nurse should have no problems in solving workplace problems. However, this situation is likely unrealistic. Hence, there appears to be a significant difference in building SC for nurses in Australia between the ideal situation and reality.

Moreover, for those nurses who did not include the NUM in their workplace network, their position appears even worse. For example, the usual reason given by nurses for not including the NUM was that the NUM was unavailable. This is a concern for health care management because the past two decades have delivered many changes to the nursing profession, including a reduction in the number of nursing positions (Upenieks, 2005) and subsequent higher workloads (Buchanan & Considine, 2002; Newman, Maylor, & Chansarkar, 2002). The consequences suggest that without effective workplace networks, nurses are working under conditions where solving problems is more difficult.

Exacerbating the situation are the role changes that have occurred to nurse supervisors (NUMs), reducing the time available for supporting and assisting their nurses. While there is a strong tradition of professional development and mentoring by NUMs, this may no longer be possible because the work of NUMs has changed, making them now responsible for increased administrative and management tasks (such as performance monitoring) (Brunetto, 2002; Buchan & Calman, 2004; Buchanan & Considine, 2002; Newman et al., 2002). While NUMs are still expected to create empowering social environments (suggesting an investment of both time and resources into developing their subordinates), in practice, they are expected to operate within conditions mandated by "tight budgetary controls and performance measures and targets" that override all other goals (Bolton, 2003, p. 126). With almost half the nurses identifying that they could not access their NUM to solve workplace problems, implications include hospital management generally, and NUMs in particular, as not perceiving one of their responsibilities being the task to build social capital. Even though Australian hospitals have embedded new clinical support positions, such as the "Nurse Educator," these coworkers are not located in the ward and thus may be more difficult to contact for assistance when nurses are time poor. Hence, because NUMs and nurses work in an environment that is time and resources poor, the outcome when they face a workplace problem is probably that the professional development and mentoring of nurses is somewhat compromised.

Several implications for organization development (OD) are revealed by the findings from this study. To increase organization-wide efficiency and viability, the overall aim of OD, health care management must assist NUMs and other management levels to inculcate supportive networks that enable the growth of SC within nurses. As suggested by this study, it appears that currently, those in nurse management (especially NUMs) do not see this as their responsibility. Without the involvement of effective supervision to assist nurses solve work-based problems, the organization will continue to inhibit performance, rather than encourage it. This study found factors that address this issue, suggesting the factors that enable performance include a supervisor–subordinate relationship that is perceived by nurses as accessible and available, that builds social capital and includes mentoring. The consequent outcomes are increased nurse commitment to the organization and thus lower turnover – both crucial to the efficiency and viability of the organization.

The second aim of this chapter was to examine the relationship between the supervisor–subordinate relationship, nurses' perceived usefulness of their workplace networks, sociability, and affective commitment. The study used the relational dimension of SCT as a lens for examining this relationship. Under ideal conditions the theory suggests that workplace networks are developed, nurtured, and rewarded in the wards and that such behavior is role-modeled by senior management and NUMs alike. In contrast, the findings suggest that workplace networks are not promoted in the wards, despite the important role of the quality of the supervisor–subordinate relationship. This relationship predicted approximately 11% of the variance of nurses' perceptions of the usefulness of their workplace networks, implying that what NUMs role model is significant in affecting the perceptions of nurses. Hence, if nurses perceive that no one has extensive workplace networks that they can use for effective problem-solving, then there is no incentive or impetus for them to build their own networks.

The OD implications of these findings include the need for health care management to address the organization-wide perceived usefulness of nurses' relationships with their NUMs, so as to increase the organization's effectiveness and ability to adapt to new challenges. The findings reveal that nurses report the lack of strong workplace networks and supportive relationships with their NUMs, yet these are crucial to the success of an organization. Such situations could be improved, within a systems context, with the help of some action research to measure and diagnose the exact size and nature of the issues. This could be followed with targeted development activities to improve communication between staff on mutual problems, team-building to develop networks, and the like, resulting in action plans to be monitored and evaluated over time. These types of OD activities would demonstrate to nurses that their NUMs (and other health care management) encourage and support workplace networks that they can use for solving workplace problems.

CONCLUSION

Nurses are in short supply in numerous OECD countries and consequently governments have been developing specific policies aimed at importing, recruiting, and retaining them. This study has added new information about the significant role of supervisor–subordinate practices on nurses' perceptions of the usefulness of workplace networks and described implications for their levels of affective commitment, which is a predictor of turnover (Meyer & Allen, 1997; Pitt et al., 1995). The results of this study indicate that the way supervisor–subordinate practices impact on nurses' perceptions of the usefulness of workplace networks is an important contributor to their affective commitment. Even so, more research in different countries is required to examine the generalizability of this finding across nations and cultures.

The findings from this chapter suggest that nurses are only somewhat satisfied with the quality of their supervisor–subordinate relationships and such conditions are unlikely to be ideal for maximizing the flow of resources and information required by nurses to solve workplace problems. Such situations are likely to cause frustration for nurses and therefore are not ideal for promoting high levels of affective commitment, nor their associated lower turnover implications. Moreover, such conditions are not ideal for knowledge retention and quality care within the health care sector and therefore it is likely that hospitals are not operating as efficiently and effectively as they could. This study thus contributes to health care management's ability to begin addressing such issues at the organization-wide level. OD implications include the need to improve supervisor–subordinate relationships, enhancing nurses' ability to cope with organizational problems, plus more appropriate supervision styles to ensure an environment that is supportive of workplace networks, encouraging higher levels of development and accomplishment by nurses. The results of such systems change should see improved organizational outcomes and viability.

REFERENCES

Adler, P., & Kwon, S. (2002). Social capital: Prospects for a new concept. *Academy of Management Review*, *27*(1), 17–40.

Ahn, J. (2002). Beyond single equation regression analysis: Path analysis and multi-stage regression analysis. *American Journal of Pharmaceutical Education*, *66*, 37–42.

AIHW. (2004). *Nursing labour force 2004 (Cat N0 HWL 38)*. Canberra: Australian Institute for Health and Welfare.

Allen, N., & Meyer, J. (1990). The measurement and antecedents of affective, continuance, and normative commitment to the organisation. *Journal of Occupation Psychology*, *61*(1), 1–18.

Allen, N., & Meyer, J. (1996). Affective, continuance, and normative commitment to the organization: An examination of construct validity. *Journal of Vocational Behavior*, *49*(3), 252–276.

Bolton, S. (2003). Multiple roles? Nurses as managers in the NHS. *International Journal of Public Sector Management*, *16*(2), 122–130.

Brunetto, Y. (2002). The impact of growing managerialism amongst professionals in Australia: A comparative study of university academics and hospital nurses. *Research and Practice in Human Resource Management Journal*, *10*(1), 1–25.

Brunetto, Y., & Farr-Wharton, R. (2004). A case study examining the impact of public-sector nurses' perception of workplace autonomy on their job satisfaction: Lessons for management. *International Journal of Organisational Behaviour*, *8*(5), 521–539.

Brunetto, Y., & Farr-Wharton, R. (2006). The importance of effective organisational relationships for nurses: A social capital perspective. *International Journal of Human Resources and Development*, *6*(2/3/4), 232–247.

Brunetto, Y., & Farr-Wharton, R. (2007). Comparing the impact of management practices on public sector nurses' and administrative employees' commitment to the organisation. *Asian Pacific Journal of Health Management*, *2*(1), 17–34.

Buchan, J., & Calman, L. (2004). *The global shortage of registered nurses: An overview of issues and Actions*. Geneva: International Council of Nurses.

Buchanan, J., & Considine, G. (2002). Stop telling us to cope: NSW nurses explain why they are leaving the profession. *A report for the NSW Nurses Association*. Sydney: Australian Centre for Industrial relations Research and Training, University of Sydney Press.

Buerhaus, P. I., Staiger, D. O., & Auerbach, D. I. (2000). Implications of an aging registered nurse workforce. *Journal of the American Medical Association*, *283*(22), 2948–2954.

Burt, R. (1992). *Structural holes: The social structure of competition*. Cambridge, MA: Harvard University Press.

Cheung, J., Bessell, J., & Ellis, M. (2004). The final straw. *Australian Nursing Journal*, *11*(7), 17–18.

Ferris, G., Witt, L., & Hochwarter, W. (2001). Interaction of social skill and general mental ability on job performance and salary. *Journal of Applied Psychology*, *86*(6), 1075–1082.

Gerstner, C., & Day, D. (1997). Meta-analytic review of leader-member exchange theory: Correlates and construct issues. *Journal of Applied Psychology*, *82*, 827–844.

Ghauri, P., & Grønhaug, K. (2002). *Research methods in business studies: A practical guide* (2nd ed.). Harlow, UK: Financial Times Prentice Hall.

Gollan, P. (2005). High involvement management and human resource sustainability: The challenges and opportunities. *Asia Pacific Journal of Human Resources*, *43*(1), 18–33.

Graen, G., & Uhl-Bien, M. (1995). Relationship-based approach to leadership: Development of leader-member exchange (LMX) theory of theory over 25 years: Applying a multi-level multi-domain perspective. *Leadership Quarterly*, *6*(2), 219–247.

Granovetter, M. S. (1973). The strength of weak ties. *The American Journal of Sociology*, *78*(6), 1360–1380.

Grapentine, T. (2000). Path analysis vs. structural equation modeling. *Marketing Research*, *12*(3), 13–20.

Gray, A., & Phillips, V. (1994). Turnover, age and length of service: A comparison of nurses and other staff in the National Health Service. *Journal of Advanced Nursing*, *J19*(4), 819–827.

Hansen, M. (1999). The search-transfer problem: The role of weak ties in sharing knowledge across organization subunits. *Administrative Science Quarterly*, *44*, 82–111.

Hoang, H., & Anroncic, B. (2003). Network-based research in entrepreneurship: A critical review. *Journal of Business Venturing*, *18*(2), 165–187.

Kessels, J., & Poell, R. (2004). Andragogy and social capital theory: The implications for human resource management. *Advances in Developing Human Resources*, *6*(2), 146–158.

Levin, D., & Cross, R. (2004). The strength of weak ties you can trust: The mediating role of trust in effective knowledge transfer. *Management Science*, *50*(11), 1477–1490.

Lin, N. (2001). *Social capital: A theory of social structure and action*. Cambridge, NY: Cambridge University Press.

Lizardo, O. (2006). How cultural tastes shape personal networks. *American Sociology Review*, *71*, 778–807.

Meyer, J., & Allen, N. (1997). *Commitment in the workplace: Theory, research and application*. Thousand Oaks: Sage Publications.

Meyer, J., & Herscovitch, L. (2001). Commitment in the workplace – Toward a general model. *Human Resource Management Review*, *11*(3), 299–326.

Mueller, B., & Lee, J. (2002). Leader-member exchange and organizational communication satisfaction in multiple contexts. *Journal of Business Communication*, *39*(2), 220–244.

Nahapiet, J., & Ghoshal, S. (1998). Social capital, intellect capital and organizational advantage. *Academy of Management Review*, *23*(2), 242–285.

Newman, K., Maylor, U., & Chansarkar, B. (2002). The nurse satisfaction, service quality and nurse retention chain: Implications for management of recruitment and retention. *Journal of Management in Medicine*, *16*(4/5), 271–292.

Nie, N. (2001). Sociability, interpersonal relations and the internet: Reconciling conflicting findings. *American Behavioural Scientist*, *45*, 420–435.

OECD. (2006). *Live longer*. Paris: Organisation for Economic Co-operation and Development.

Ostroff, C., & Bowen, D. (Eds). (2000). *Moving HR to a higher level. HR practices and organizational effectiveness*. San Francisco, CA: Jossey-Bass.

Ostroff, C., Kinicki, A., & Clark, M. (2002). Substantive and operational issues of response bias across levels of analysis: An example of climate-satisfaction relationships. *Journal of Applied Psychology*, *87*, 355–368.

Pitt, M., Leyland, F., Foreman, S. K., & Bromfield, D. (1995). Organisational commitment and service delivery: Evidence from an industrial setting in the UK. *International Journal of Human Resource Management*, *6*(1), 369–389.

Productivity Commission. (2005). *Australia's health workforce*. Canberra: Productivity Commission, Commonwealth of Australia.

Riggio, R., & Reichard, R. (2008). The emotional and social intelligences of effective leadership: An emotional and social skill approach. *Journal of Managerial Psychology*, *23*(2), 169–185.

Schofield, D., & Beard, J. (2005). Baby boomer doctors and nurses: Demographic change and transitions to retirement. *Medical Journal of Australia*, *183*(2), 80–83.

Secombe, I., & Smith, G. (1997). *Taking part: Registered nurses and the labour market in 1997*. Grantham, England: Grantham Book Services.

Sparrowe, R., & Linden, R. (1997). Process and structure in leader-member exchange. *Academy of Management Journal*, *22*(2), 522–552.

Totterdell, P., Holman, D., & Hukin, A. (2008). Social networkers: Measuring and examining individual differences in propensity to connect with others. *Social Networks*, *30*, 283–296.

Upenieks, V. (2005). Recruitment and retention strategies: A magnet hospital prevention model. *Medsurg Nursing*, pp. 21–28.

Wayne, S., Shore, L., & Linden, R. (1997). Perceived organisational support and leader exchange: A social exchange perspective. *Academy of Management Journal*, *40*(1), 82–111.

Yrie, A., Hartman, S., & Galle, W. (2003). Examining communication style and leader-member exchange: Considerations and concerns for managers. *International Journal of Management*, *20*(1), 92–100.

SYSTEMS APPROACH TO ADDRESS INCIVILITY AND DISRUPTIVE BEHAVIORS IN HEALTH CARE ORGANIZATIONS

Elizabeth Holloway and Mitchell Kusy

ABSTRACT

In response to the growing evidence that disruptive behaviors within health care teams constitute a major threat to the quality of care, the Joint Commission on Accreditation of Healthcare Organization (JCAHO; Joint Commission Resources, 2008) has a new leadership standard that addresses disruptive and inappropriate behaviors effective January 1, 2009. For professionals who work in human resources and organization development, these standards represent a clarion call to design and implement evidence-based interventions to create health care communities of respectful engagement that have zero tolerance for disruptive, uncivil, and intimidating behaviors by any professional. In this chapter, we will build an evidence-based argument that sustainable change must include organizational, team, and individual strategies across all professionals in the organization. We will then describe an intervention model – Toxic Organization Change System *– that has emerged from our own research on toxic behaviors in the workplace (Kusy & Holloway, 2009) and*

Organization Development in Healthcare: Conversations on Research and Strategies
Advances in Health Care Management, Volume 10, 239–265

ISSN: 1474-8231/doi:10.1108/S1474-8231(2011)0000010020

provide examples of specific strategies that we have used to prevent and ameliorate toxic cultures.

Keywords: Disruptive behavior; incivility; toxic culture; civility

Since the mid-1990s there has been a growing concern with the incidence of disruptive, uncivil, and toxic behaviors[1] in the workplace. In the last decade, researchers have gone beyond the nature and frequency of toxic behaviors and begun investigating their relation to "bottom-line" factors critical to organizational productivity – absenteeism, retention, motivation, and innovation (Andersson & Pearson, 1999; Felblinger, 2009; Kusy & Holloway, 2009; Pearson, Andersson, & Porath, 2004). Health care organizations have not been immune to these effects and have frequently been identified as cultures that may be more vulnerable to the incidence, intensity, and frequency of uncivil, disruptive behaviors and their concomitant human and financial costs (reference). Since 2005, Rosenstein and his associates (Rosenstein & O'Daniel, 2005a, 2005b, 2006, 2008a, 2008b) have reported on large-scale research projects that have uncovered alarming statistics on the presence of disruptive physician and nurse behaviors that are significantly related to patient care and safety (Rosenstein & O'Daniel, 2005b) productivity (Hutton & Gates, 2008) and staff well-being (Felblinger, 2008). In response to the growing evidence that disruptive behaviors within health care teams constitute a major threat to the quality of care, the Joint Commission on Accreditation of Healthcare Organization (JCAHO; Joint Commission Resources, 2008) has a new leadership standard that addresses disruptive and inappropriate behaviors (LD.03.01.01) effective January 1, 2009:

EP 4: The hospital/organization has a code of conduct that defines acceptable and disruptive and inappropriate behaviors.
EP 5: Leaders create and implement a process for managing disruptive and inappropriate behaviors.

In addition, the standards recommend that interpersonal skills and professionalism be included in the six core competencies that are addressed in the credentialing process (see introduction to MS.4 in JCAHO Standards).

For professionals who work in human resources and organization development, these standards represent a clarion call to design and implement evidence-based interventions to create health care communities of respectful engagement that have zero tolerance for disruptive, uncivil, and intimidating behaviors by any professional. In this chapter, we will build an evidence-based argument that sustainable change must include organizational, team, and individual strategies across all professionals in the organization. We will then describe an intervention model – *Toxic Organization Change System* – that has emerged from our own research on toxic behaviors in the workplace (Kusy & Holloway, 2009) and provide examples of specific strategies that we have used to prevent and ameliorate toxic cultures.

WHAT ARE UNCIVIL, DISRUPTIVE, AND TOXIC BEHAVIORS?

Incivility or rudeness has become increasingly prevalent; Remington and Darden (2002) reported that 79% of 2,013 respondents said that a lack of respect and courtesy in American society is a serious problem and getting worse. Most of us know when a person is being outwardly abusive to us, and depending on the relationship with the person and circumstance of event, we choose our responses. However, there are many times in the workplace when "rudeness" or incivility is more veiled and many of us are left either not knowing if "it happened" or "if it did" just what to say in response. Although there are policy and legal definitions of abuse and harassment in the workplace, the nature of "incivility" is often more nuanced. Current literature in business and health care has used different labels in describing these behaviors. They have included: incivility, rudeness, discourtesy, verbal abuse, disruptive, and toxic. In this chapter, we will use these labels interchangeably except in those instances when we refer to specific research study, in which case we will use the same language as the author.

INCIVILITY IN HEALTH CARE

A place to start in understanding the burgeoning concern with incivility is to recognize the role of civility in our daily social interactions. Civility is expressed interpersonally as regard for another person's dignity and feelings. Civility by its very act reinforces the social norms of mutual respect that are essential to collaboration and communication flow in work teams. Incivility is an interpersonal act. It conveys rudeness and disregard for others that violate the social norms of a specific context (Brown & Levinson, 1987). Workplace incivility, in management and social psychology studies, has been described as "impropriety" (Miller, 2000), "aversive behavior" (Winters & Duck, 2000), and "interpersonal mistreatment" (Cortina, Magley, Williams,

Hunter, & Langhout, 2001; Cortina, Magley, & Linneman, 2002). Pearson et al. (2004) have defined incivility as *low-intensity deviant (rude, discourteous) behavior with ambiguous intent to harm the target in violation of workplace norms for mutual respect* (p. 179). Although diverse norms abound in different organizational settings because of the larger social mores of acceptable behavior, there is a common, often unspoken expectation, for fundamental mutual respect among professionals. In health care, there is a stated understanding that to function effectively and on the behalf of the patient, hospital staff must work in highly coordinated and collaborative team settings with significant cross communication both intra- and inter-professionally. Paradoxically, hospital teams dedicated to treat patients with compassion and care are often not very good exemplars of mutual respect, but rather exhibit some of the most flagrant displays of mutual disrespect and disruptive behaviors (Rosenstein & O'Daniel, 2008a). Findings by Rosenstein and associates research have gained significant attention of health care providers and administrators as the role of a "disruptive" culture has been linked to medical errors (Rosenstein & O'Daniel, 2005b). "*The Joint Commission reports in its root cause analysis of sentinel events that nearly 70% of the errors can be traced back to a problem with communication*" reported in Rosenstein and O'Daniel (2008b, p. 464). A problem with communication has largely been linked to specific types of communication errors linked to disruptive behaviors. Research in the health care industry has identified disruptive behaviors through extensive survey studies of physicians (Rosenstein & O'Daniel, 2008a), nurses (Rosenstein & O'Daniel, 2005a), and allied health care providers (Rosenstein & O'Daniel, 2006). Rosenstein and associates have defined incivility in the language of "disruptive behaviors." Surveys assessing the incidence and severity of these behaviors include such occurrences "as any inappropriate behavior, confrontation, or conflict, ranging from verbal abuse to physical or sexual harassment" (Rosenstein & O'Daniel, 2008b, p. 1564). Survey respondents are asked to report on items such as yelling or raising voice, disrespectful interaction, abusive language, berating in front of peers, condescension, insults, abusive anger, berating in front of patients, berating in private, physical abuse (listed in order of frequency of occurrence in Rosenstein & O'Daniel, 2006). Neff (2000) and Porto and Lauve (2006) have expanded the definition of disruptive behaviors to include "anything a clinician does that interferes with the orderly conduct of hospital business, from patient care to committee work" (p. 2). Their descriptions of disruptive behaviors include items that are more difficult to assess and report such as:

- Comments that undermine a caregiver's self-confidence in caring for patients.

- Intimidating behavior that has the effect of suppressing input by other members of the health care team.
- Comments that undermine a patient's trust in other caregivers or the hospital.
- Criticizing other caregivers in front of patients or other staff.

These types of verbal abuse and denigration have been described as a common experience among health care providers with a prevalence of 80–90% (Sofield & Salmond, 2003). Our research corroborates these findings both with regard to prevalence and types of incivility (Kusy & Holloway, 2009). We found that 94% of our respondents reported having dealt with toxic behaviors in the last 5 years and 92% of the individuals they referenced were rated between 7 and 10 (10 being the greatest severity of toxicity and 1 being the least) on a Likert scale regarding severity of toxic behaviors. In our factor analysis of those behaviors considered highly toxic by targets, behaviors fell into three primary categories: shaming, passive hostility, and team sabotage. These behaviors are consistent with the Joint Commission's report (Joint Commission Resources, 2008) and workplace incivility, in general (Pearson et al., 2004).

A TOXIC CULTURE OF INCIVILITY

Instigators of toxic behaviors have been fodder for many popular trade books such as *Snakes in Suits* (Babiak & Hare, 2006) and the *Emotional Vampires* (Bernstein, 2001). Much of these works try to teach the target of toxic behaviors how to avoid, respond, or get the best of the instigator by understanding what drives the behavior. Unfortunately, much of this advice is predicated on the instigator's motivation and ability to receive feedback. Although particularly destructive (and relatively uncommon) personality disorders such as narcissism and sociopathy are more dramatically and singularly expressed, the widespread incidence of incivility has more insidious and pervasive effects on psychological well-being, team effectiveness, and organizational culture (Andersson & Pearson, 1999; Felblinger, 2008; Kusy & Holloway, 2009; Porath & Erez, 2009). Like a virus if left unchecked, effects of incivility spread quickly throughout an organization.

Research findings have found that incivility by one individual on a team invites complementary rudeness and discourteous behaviors by other members. One bad apple *can* spoil the bunch! A climate of disregard for others through small acts of mistreatment and thoughtlessness become the norm (Andersson & Pearson, 1999; Neuman & Baron, 1997). It has been suggested that these more indirect forms of verbal hostility have been found to be the precursors to more violent acts of interpersonal aggression (Neuman & Baron, 1997) particularly when there is direct reciprocation by the target and the instigator is hot-tempered (Andersson & Pearson, 1999). Specific to health care settings, Spratlen (1994) found workplace mistreatment to be directly related to interpersonal violence.

Incivility, as a social psychological phenomenon, cannot be explained simply by looking at the psychological attributes of the instigator, but only by understanding the intersection of organizational culture, differential authority across professional roles, and interpersonal relations. The highly stressful environment of health care organizations is fertile ground for triggering disruptive and uncivil behaviors. Health care incivility has flourished in recent years because of the significant shift from a paternalistic, physician-dominated culture to a team-based approach where *all members* are held accountable to the team (Porto & Lauve, 2006). Other economically driven pressures for production of billable hours, reimbursement constraints, and short supply of some professionals, particularly nurses, have undermined the cohesion of teams. Moreover, increased governmental oversight and greater liability risks have exacerbated the pressure that many physicians and other professionals experience in their efforts to deliver quality care (Felblinger, 2009; Rosenstein & O'Daniel, 2005a). Research has documented that civility is not simply paying homage to small niceties to create a more pleasant environment, but it is a fundamental attribute of creating culture that facilitates positive relationships of mutual respect and collaboration – essential ingredients for delivering quality health services.

EFFECTS OF INCIVILITY IN HEALTH CARE SETTINGS

The spiraling effects of disruptive and discourteous behaviors can rapidly reach a critical mass – a tipping point (Andersson & Pearson, 1999) – where pockets of incivility feed off of one another eventually creating an "uncivil or toxic organization" (Kusy & Holloway, 2009) "Organization" in this context refers to any workplace context, for example, a team, a department, a division, the nurse's station, or the entire organization. Organizational cultures that tolerate incivility and disruptive behaviors will suffer not just the unpleasantness and threat of escalating disruption in interpersonal relations, but also worker absenteeism, attrition of staff, fragmented work teams, and customer dissatisfaction (Pearson & Porath, 2005). In health care settings, these effects translate to miscommunication among team members, higher turnover, poor patient care, serious consequences in patient safety, and increased malpractice suits (Hutton & Gates, 2008; Porto & Lauve, 2006; Rosenstein & O'Daniel, 2005a).

Patient Safety

It is well documented in the literature that physicians have been the major instigators of incivility (Hickson, Pichert, Webb, & Gabbe, 2007; Leape & Fromson, 2006; Porto & Lauve, 2006). Because of their relative economic and positional power in health care systems, their behaviors have been largely tolerated by hospital administrators (Leape & Fromson, 2006). The power held by physicians over other professionals in combination with the threat of injurious criticism can quickly silence team members from offering valuable opinions or pointing out critical errors in treatment plans. The *Silence Kills* (VitalSmarts and the American Association of Critical-Care Nurses, 2005) study found that more than 20% of health care professionals have seen actual harm come to patients as a result of disruptive and disrespectful behaviors (Grenny, 2009; Porto & Lauve, 2006). Shockingly, 25% of health care workers believe that disruptive behaviors are correlated with patient mortality (Rosenstein & O'Daniel, 2005a) and 49% stated that intimidation by another practitioner resulted in misadministration of medication (Institute for Safe Medication Practices, 2005).

Staff Health and Well-Being

The effects of verbal abuse and discourteous behavior on staff members have deleterious effects on individual health, team collaboration, and patient safety. Recent research has documented the adverse effects of organizational incivility on individual self-esteem and emotional wellbeing. Felblinger (2008) postulates that the "shame response" that nurses experience as the target of demeaning comments and verbal attacks can lead to anger, self-blame, and attack of others. These reactions occur most readily in those environments where such toxic behaviors go unchecked by administration or clinical team leaders (Felblinger, 2009). Ultimately, the widespread emotional negativity culminates in a hostile workplace that tolerates and thus facilitates the establishment of incivility as the norm.

Cultural Effects

Discourteous behavior and verbal abuse is not reserved for physicians; nurses have long reported that horizontal abuse is common within nursing ranks and auxiliary professions (references). The JCAHO (2002) reported that over 50% of the nurses surveyed had been the targets of verbal abuse by another nurse. Rosenstein & O'Daniel (2005a) report that 72% of nurse respondents witnessed disruptive behaviors instigated by another nurse. It is not surprising, albeit unfortunate, that abuse is found among those of similar rank and profession when the same groups find themselves abused by groups above them. Lashing out and exhibiting similar behaviors among one's own group compensate the injury of incivility, verbal abuse, and demeaning comments that come from physicians to those beneath them. In our research (Kusy & Holloway, 2009), we found that teams that had a "toxic" leader began to behave in some of the same ways with each other. This phenomenon of "spreading toxicity" has been corroborated in several studies that have examined team behavior in relationship to workplace incivility (Andersson & Pearson, 1999; Mayer, Nishii, Schneider, & Goldstein, 2007; Porath & Erez, 2009).

APPROACHES TO COMBATING DISRUPTIVE AND UNCIVIL BEHAVIORS

The JCAHO promulgation of a mandate to address professional incivility and disruptive behaviors of staff has challenged health care organizations to develop and implement policies and procedures to comply (Leape & Fromson, 2006). Numerous approaches to the problem have been reported in the literature and range from targeted interventions with the instigator of the abuse to more comprehensive designs that address both educational and remedial interventions at both the individual and team levels. All approaches include a clear statement of policy and procedures for intervening with the charged and aggrieved parties. In this section, first, we will identify examples of the different types of programs that have been reported, and then, describe in-depth the program that we have developed based on research and consulting practices.

Vanderbilt School of Medicine (Hickson et al., 2007) is an excellent example of an individually targeted program that has developed a complement to the more typical professional etiquette programs by focuses on identifying, measuring, and addressing *un*professional behavior. Their approach, along with several other programs, reported in the literature focus on the establishment of policies that address the consequences of unprofessional behavior (e.g., Institute for Safe Medical Practices (ISMP), 2005), maintain "zero tolerance for abuse" standard (American Association of Critical-Care Nurses, 2005; Kerfoot, 2007), develop leadership education to model professional behavior (Kahn, 2008) and intervene in disruptive behavior (Grenny, 2009), develop reporting system for unprofessional behavior (Hickson et al., 2007), create a system of targeted interventions that match severity and frequency of instigator's conduct (Hickson et al., 2007; Rosenstein & O'Daniel, 2008a), establish a conflict resolution process (Institute for Safe Medication Practices, 2005) and service recovery programs that assist staff, patients, and other physicians whose work has suffered from the workplace abuse (Felblinger, 2009, 2008; Hickson et al., 2007).

In spite of the growing research on disruptive behaviors and incivility in health care settings and the mandate by the Joint Commission, there has yet to be reported a cohesive, systemic intervention plan based on the existing empirical literature that organization consultants might adopt.

However, there has been recognition that the role of health care organizational cultures is a contributing factor in medical errors and that "the health care industry has begun to realize that human interaction is an important but largely ignored source of error" (Porto & Lauve, 2006, p. 1). Brier's (2009) anecdotal account of her work as CEO at the Maimonides Medical Center in which she describes the challenges, successes, and failures of initiating a system-wide approach to move a hospital with a reputation of a "culture of nastiness" (p. 27) to a "culture of respect" is a wonderful first-hand account of creating change throughout the organization. Our approach, *Toxic Organization Change System* (TOCS; (Kusy & Holloway, 2009) shares this goal and offers an integrated, systems approach to establishing a culture of civility and healing the aftermath of toxicity.

A THREE-LEVEL SYSTEMS APPROACH TO HEALTH CARE INCIVILITY

Our intervention model, TOCS, was developed from our research findings from over 400 leaders on toxic behaviors, leader reactions, and strategies in organizations (Kusy & Holloway, 2009), the extant empirical literature in organizational incivility, and our practice as consultants. Like several of the programs now being initiated in health care settings (Hickson et al., 2007; Leape & Fromson, 2006), the TOCS approach targets the development of policies, standards, review, and education to greatly reduce and monitor uncivil or abusive behaviors. A critical component of TOCS is that the model tackles toxicity at three levels of the organization – the organizational, the team, and the individual – emphasizing the involvement of all or representative stakeholders from all levels. At each level of intervention, there are specific strategies that can be employed to proactively inoculate the organization from inadvertently facilitating toxic behaviors or to deal strategically with such behaviors when they do take hold. Thus, the TOCS model employs interventions that take a *cohesive*, systemic approach to "incivility."

Our own research and numerous studies in organizational settings have found consistently that incivility, if left to run its own course, will lead to a culture of incivility and may escalate to more violent abuse in the workplace (Andersson & Pearson, 1999). This is a significant shift from the earlier and, unfortunately, still popular view of simply dealing with the "individual" with warnings, reprimands, coaching, that often culminates with a laborious and costly termination process. A systems approach requires either an internal or external consultant to assess and map out the organizational conditions and persons that are perpetuating and often rewarding disruptive behaviors. Or proactively to identify what areas of policy, leadership education, performance management, and team building may be vulnerable to the proliferation of toxic behaviors. Our methods are particularly suited to the health care setting because of the attention to hierarchical structures, professional privilege, and team collaboration. Although it is beyond the scope of this paper to go into specific detail on all interventions identified in our book (Kusy & Holloway, 2009), we will highlight those strategies that may be less familiar to organization consultants and fit specifically with the goals of JCOHA. At this point in our discussion, we will turn to a description and discussion of the strategies that we have used in building organizational foundations for respectful engagement in the workplace.

PRINCIPLES OF THE TOCS MODEL

The TOCS model was built on three primary principles that emerged from our research.[2]

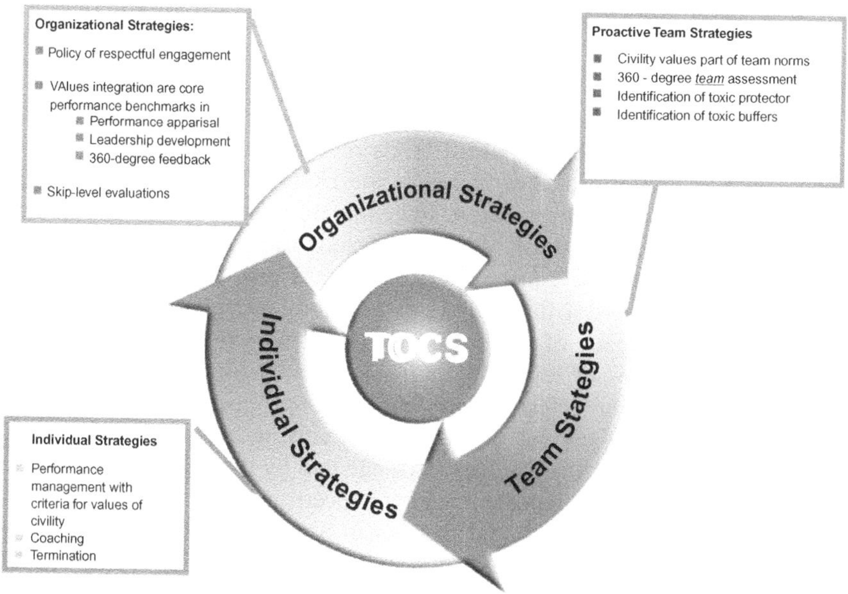

Fig. 1. Toxic Organization Change System: Strategies at Organization, Team and Individual Levels.

1. Interventions that engage a combination of organizational, team, and one-on-one methods have the highest probability of success.
2. If you cannot implement strategies for change at all three levels, start with the organizational first and the team second rather than the one-on-one level.
3. The person in the organization who has sufficient organizational authority to enact clear consequences is the most effectual for implementation of one-on-one strategies with the toxic person.

Fig. 1 depicts the three levels of the organization on which these principles are applied and the associated strategies referred to in the next three sections. Although we have found it preferable to ensure that strong organizational interventions are first established, in some cases it is not feasible to intervene at this level initially. Thus, there are strategies that are specifically directed to the team or individual level.

LARGE-SCALE ORGANIZATIONAL STRATEGIES

With the advent of the Joint Commission mandate, it has become imperative that health care settings establish policy and procedure for handling disruptive behavior at all levels of the organizational structure. The TOCS model approaches this mandate using a "ground-up" strategy that brings together representative stakeholders from the organization to come together and establish concrete, behaviorally specific values that support respectful and courteous behaviors. These values are created, defined, and illustrated with examples in a daylong retreat atmosphere using a "max-mix" process of engagement. The "max-mix" process has a "maximum mixture" of stakeholders from the entire organization, divided into what is commonly referred to as "max-mix" groups. For example, each max-mix group may consist of such individuals as a director, physician, nurse, patient advocate, and others as designated by the planning team. The approach is designed to represent a broad spectrum of the workforce. This process is based on research and theoretical foundations that demonstrate that involvement produces greater commitment, better results, and increased ownership. The large-scale process here is highly respectful of all opinions brought to the table as members of different professions and status levels form each of the small groups. It is important to model throughout this process clear and constructive feedback, nonjudgmental brainstorming, and equal acknowledgement of contributions made by team members. The values become a "living" document that all members of the organization "sign-on to" when hired or at the point in which they are disseminated. These values become the foundation of the development of management practices that reinforce and enforce a zero tolerance approach to disruptive and uncivil behaviors. Critical to success in holding staff to zero tolerance is the integration of these values of civility into performance management systems. The appraisal should give equal weight to behaviors that reflect the values of respectful engagement, such that 50% of one's appraisal relates to the content-specific work and 50% relate to the values-specific work. Depending upon the context of the performance management system the organization adapts, this could mean compensation reflecting this 50–50 split. Although numerous authors in health care have recommended and described the type of Conduct Code that should follow the Joint Commission standards (e.g., Rosenstein & O'Daniel, 2008b), we believe that behavioral criteria around interpersonal relations that reflect the organization's code of conduct be an integral component of performance appraisal. Managers, HR professionals, and other leaders must fully embrace this principle and be prepared to give feedback and enforce established consequences for those workers who do not meet the criteria. Also important is reinforcing those workers who behave in a manner that upholds the values of civility. Unfortunately, rewarding positive behaviors is an often forgotten component of changing workplace behavior because of the overemphasis for monitoring and reprimanding of inappropriate behaviors. Our clients have given us many examples of creative and satisfying strategies that they have used to let their coworkers know that they noticed how an act of consideration or kindness really exemplified a specific value of the organization and team. They have also reported their discouragement and suffering when month after month they see management tolerate disruptive behaviors that abuse coworkers and patients. Felblinger (2008) discusses posttraumatic stress and self-blame in nurses as an aftermath of incivility and bullying. In summary, the critical attributes for making values a living part of day-to-day relations are: (a) develop concrete, behaviorally specific values of respectful engagements with representative stakeholders through a process of dialogue; (b) have members of the organization sign-on to the values; (c) integrate the values into the performance management system; (d) establish criteria related to the values that are given equal weight in performance appraisal; and (e) educate managers, directors and other key leaders on the reinforcement and enforcement of the values both in summative and formative evaluations.

What if the Boss is Toxic?

In our seminars we invariably get the question, "What if it is the boss who is toxic?" And, we have countless stories from our research of the feeling of helplessness and hopelessness that people experience when they are being treated badly by someone who holds a more powerful position. Health care research has consistently reported the disastrous effects on attrition, patient care, and team functioning when a physician or head nurse in power has a documented pattern of abusive behavior (Leape & Fromson, 2006; Rosenstein & O'Daniel, 2005, 2008). Although current programs reported in health care settings have described reporting procedures that guarantee the victim will be protected from retaliation, research has shown that it is very difficult for victims to report such abuse even with these guarantees (Grenny, 2009). Porto and Lauve state, "Since disruptive behavior often produces fear and intimidation, it is unrealistic to expect that voluntary reporting will effectively and reliably identify disruptive behavior. This is aggravated by lack of strong policies and systems to protect those who report or cooperate in the investigation of disruptive behavior" (2006, p. 6). One strategy to mitigate this fear and lack of trust in reporting is the inclusion of "skip-level evaluations as a part of the performance management system, that is, giving feedback to the "boss's' boss." This strategy should be implemented on a regular cycle of performance appraisal and not just done when there is "a problem with the boss." Of course, there has to be consistent use of this process, training in how to engage in it, and sanctions when it is abused. We have found that it is best integrated when the boss's boss coaches the individual having a problem with the boss in how to address the issue directly and with respect. If this fails, we have found that the boss's boss then brings the individual, the boss, and the HR representative into a team meeting to discuss the situation honestly and openly. No one has an upper hand in this process. Not the boss. Not the individual. Rest assured if the system is abused and people use it to "get back at the boss," it will likely fail. The four key elements in its success are that:

It must be a rigidly established policy

1) Everyone in the organization needs to be trained (even briefly) in how to effectively to engage it.
2) No one is exempt from it.
3) The human resources department is the owner of the process and assures that it is handled with integrity and authenticity.

This process offers a simple, yet powerful, mechanism for leaders to routinely hear from those who often know best whether a culture of civility is being upheld at the team levels.

TEAM LEVEL STRATEGIES

A critical finding in both in our research and numerous other authors in the health care (e.g., Brier, 2009) and organizational management fields (e.g., Andersson & Pearson, 1999) is the manner in which toxic behaviors can quickly overtake the climate of a team and begin a downward spiral from petty bickering to serious verbal abuse. It is not only the "toxic" instigator behaving badly, but also many team members who take on similar destructive behaviors to protect themselves and survive. When no action is taken to terminate this escalation, the behaviors become a "normal" part of team functioning. To stop continued deterioration of team productivity and effectiveness, strong interventions must be implemented. In this section, we outline three intervention strategies that we have found to be particularly effective: (a) assessing the team functioning, (b) identifying those individuals or processes that perpetuate the negative climate, and (c) rebuilding a healthy team environment.

Integrating Values into Team Norms

The process of identifying and clarifying values is most successful when team leaders are able to depend on the organizational values that uphold a civil behavior. Assuming that the organization has identified concrete and behaviorally specific values, the leader then engages the team in how these apply to their work environments. These values become a backdrop for translation to the team's unique work setting. When organizational values include explicit descriptions for respect within the organization as well as with clients and customers, the team can build on this foundation to examine and create ways that the team lives these values. Team building around the value of respect becomes a proactive strategy that helps prevent, or at least reduces, the probability that toxic behaviors will be tolerated and enabled.

To translate the organizational values into team-oriented values, we suggest that the leader plan a team development session. Critical to the team-building process are the review of the organizational values and the translation of these values into behavioral norms. The team and each member should make a plan on how to keep the norms reinforced and a part of everyday functioning. We have received many creative ideas from our clients that range from giving emails of appreciation to handing out V.I.P. cards for acts of consideration and care within the team. On the other hand, acts of incivility need to be noted and addressed directly either by the target of the behavior or the team leader. Individuals will have more courage to address the instigator when they know that the team as a whole has signed on to a "zero tolerance" policy for disruptive verbal behaviors.

In circumstances in which the Joint Commission mandate has not yet been implemented and the organization has not promulgated formal procedures for handling disruptive behaviors, leaders can still begin work with their team to design these values. To start the process leaders can engage the team in a values clarification process to identify values around civil engagement and translate these into the associated behavioral norms. The key issue in any of these interventions is (a) follow up with specific consequences for any violations of the behavioral norms and (b) leaders upholding these values in both their own and other's day-to-day operations. Team leaders should require that team values become part of the performance management process – both informally through conversations when team members see values abused or upheld, as well as formally by including them in such systems as annual goals.

Team Feedback Systems

There are few instruments that have been developed to help in the identification and typing of uncivil behaviors (Blau & Andersson, 2005; Martin & Hine, 2005). These instruments have largely been used for research purposes rather than an assessment tool that leads to tailored interventions. Our work with teams has included the Campbell–Hallam Team Development Survey (TDS; (Campbell & Hallam, 1994). The TDS identifies how team members perceive several variables associated with team success. It is a standardized instrument that has been normed on 194 teams with a total of two thousand individuals. The TDS has a 93-item survey for each team member and a 23-item survey for up to eight outside observers who are familiar with the team's work. Essentially, the team receives evaluations from within the team through its team members, and from outside the team through individuals who have opportunities to observe the team as it works. The survey identifies team strengths and weaknesses to stimulate discussion about the most significant team issues. What makes this team assessment instrument so different and useful from many others on the market is its ability to gather feedback about the *team* from those who have opportunities to observe it – hence, its 360-degree *team* assessment format. Team members can see not only how the entire team scored itself, but they have the opportunity to see how observers viewed them on each of the instrument's dimensions. Particularly important in the context of incivility is the opportunity for a facilitator to open up a dialogue about the best and worst of the team. Team members already know who is violating the civility norms, but they probably do not understand completely the impact of these behaviors on overall team functioning. The data gathered using the instrument present a full picture of team operations from within the team and outside it. This instrument does not measure toxicity. However, what it does, and does effectively, is to cull out the critical issues arresting team success that have been associated with workplace incivility.

Toxic Protectors and Toxic Buffers

One of the significant discoveries in our study of toxic personalities was the presence of what we refer to as "toxic protectors" in the organizational system. The protector safeguards the toxic person from harm's way within the organization, with "harm's way" defined as any perceived intrusion on the toxic person's agenda. Sometimes these protectors are peers. Other times they are direct and indirect reports. Even bosses can protect. Protectors are often unaware of their role in encouraging the toxic behaviors. Toxic protectors emerge in different guises and may or may not be intentionally colluding to empower the toxicity. Stories from our interviews and the findings from our survey identified three conditions that invite toxic protectors: special relationships, the need for power, and the need to maintain productivity.

The special relationship protector is someone with either formal or informal power, who forms a relationship with this individual. This protector goes to bat for this individual at team meetings, supports his or her agenda in large public forums, or provides the data that the toxic person needs to advance his or her agenda. The relationship appears almost as a friendship of sorts. And at times it is. But again, the protector benefits in some way from this relationship.

From our research, we discovered that power protectors are typically at a high level in the organization and are used by the toxic person to promote his or her modus operandi. Why do power protectors do this? First, they are often unaware. They engage in this behavior primarily because they receive something in return, usually a benefit of some sort, such as a completed project, expertise in some arena, or even kudos in group meetings.

Our last toxic protector type is a protector who seeks to gain advantage through the toxic person's productivity. This type of protector came up in our leaders' stories of frustration in attempting to terminate a toxic person.

We also found protectors of the victims, who shielded individuals from the toxic behaviors. We refer to these individual as *toxic buffers* because they stand between the toxic person and the team. Often they have formed a special relationship with the toxic person and become that person's "interpreter" to others. In spite of their good intentions, they inadvertently and indirectly protect a toxic individual from being responsible for his or her behavior. The protectors of the toxic person have their most powerful and immediate effect at the team level of the organization because they often prevent people outside the team from recognizing the destructive, insidious effects of the toxic person. With a protector in the system, it is a difficult to recognize that the toxic person is spinning a web of destruction, especially by those at a higher level in the reporting structure. The protector's self-proclaimed role is to protect the toxic person from being discovered by those who may have the authority to do something about the situation. This does not mean that those who report to the toxic person or those in lateral positions do not see the destruction; rather, they are rendered impotent because the protector is more powerful than they are.

Health care with its hierarchical structure often based on professional power and guild mentality is fertile ground for protectors and buffers. Unfortunately, people in these roles only prolong the toxic situation by making it difficult for others who have the authority to take action, for those who are experiencing the abuse to report it without retaliation, and for organizations to recognize where toxicity is festering. Protectors flourish in organizations that do not have a clear and defensible value system that does not tolerate incivility and disruptive behaviors.

It does not matter the reason that the protection system is operational: special relationships, the need for power, or the need to maintain productivity. It is critical to intervene in these systems to promote trust and open communication in teams. Often using the TDS (Campbell & Hallam, 1994) will uncover the role of protector and/or buffer. For example, team leaders are often reluctant to confront highly productive physicians in spite of the destructive impact they may have had on nurse retention (a serious problem in today's shortage of nursing staff!); therefore, they protect by ignoring complaints from team members. We use the TDS to engage all team members to examine the results and have facilitated roundtable discussion with the team and individual interviews with us about their interpretation of the team profile. We have found that this has a powerful effect on *protectors and buffers* as they see in "the numbers" the widespread effect on team collaboration, retention, and motivation. The research corroborates these effects. Pearson and Porath (2009) found:

- 12% of victims of toxic people quit,
- 48% decreased their work effort,
- 47% decreased time at work,
- 38% decreased work quality,
- 68% said their performance declined,
- 80% said they lost time worrying about it,
- 63% lost time avoiding the person, and
- 78% said their commitment to the organization declined.

The TDS results and subsequent team roundtable makes those findings very real and inspires leaders to act courageously and demand respectful collaboration in their teams.

INDIVIDUAL STRATEGIES

There are four specific, individually designed strategies for working with a toxic person: targeted feedback, performance appraisals, coaching, and termination. The most common approach to solving problems of incivility is to give the instigator feedback. A number of health management leadership programs include the delivery of feedback and conflict resolution as one part of their educational training. In some instances, if the person is receptive to feedback and has consistent and frequent follow up evaluations, this strategy might work. The probability of it working will greatly increase if the person delivering the message has the authority to implement consequences for noncompliance and if the organization has strong policies and procedures for incivility. In other words, the organizational and team level values for a dignified and respectful workplace give "clout" to the feedback and consequences for noncompliance.

In the TOCS approach, we encourage team leaders to engage multiple assessors to provide feedback. Felblinger, 2009 has reported that "horizontal violence" of nurses against nurses is second only to physician-perpetrated events. Individuals, who have a history of incivility, often deny or do not recognize the impact of their behaviors and must hear from representative stakeholders to clearly get the message that their behaviors are damaging and intolerable. Hearing from team members who work for the person and those to whom they report, is equally important because some toxic persons are chameleons and display inappropriate behaviors only to those in less powerful positions – that is in the vernacular, "kiss up and kick down."

Many reporting systems of incivility err by focusing solely on reporting problematic incidents of disruptive behavior. This has been a prevalent approach in the response to the Joint Commission's mandate and not surprisingly because traditional tools for reprimanding physician misconduct have been either an ineffectual reprimand or a severe litigious response. An appraisal system that regularly gathers data from the key players will keep the leader better informed and the employee well aware of the quality of his or her own relations within the unit or team. It also normalizes the process of providing feedback with a consistent and systematic process that is used not just when there is a problem, thus building in the opportunity for leaders to hear the strengths and growth of team members and not only the complaints.

In general, the following guidelines apply to performance appraisal processes:

- Collect feedback (by the appraiser) from key stakeholders.
- Set behaviorally specific objectives related to the behavioral change you are seeking from the toxic person.
- Set a time line for periodic review of the toxic individual's progress.
- Include the individual's self-designed professional goals for growth.
- Include behavioral criteria related to respectful engagement.

It's difficult to fire a highly productive and renowned physician. However, termination becomes a more viable option when organizations' policies and procedures around disruptive behavior stipulate that performance appraisal must be done consistently, in writing, and filed. Because instigators generally have a pattern of abuse, having a record of incidences establishes a pattern of misconduct and adds weight to the grounds for termination. With the promulgation of the Joint Commission standards on civility and the well-documented research on the effects of disruptive behavior on patient safety and team effectiveness, health care leaders must be prepared to terminate employment of "star" health care providers, who habitually flaunt their power to intimidate and humiliate others. If the health care organizations have in place performance management practices that include performance appraisal tools that address interpersonal behavior, then firing becomes a more viable option.

In summary, can individual interventions create sustainable change in toxic behaviors? Our response is a qualified yes, under these conditions:

- The interventions are conducted within an organization that has clear consequences for toxic behaviors – whether team leaders, managers, or their top executives exhibit them.
- The performance appraisal system includes behaviorally specific criteria related to civility and respect.
- The manager uses a consistent, systematic feedback plan that includes the views of all relevant stakeholders, such as managers, skip-level managers, team members or leaders, and coworkers.

When these conditions are in place, the opportunity for success increases greatly. The person whose behavior is targeted needs to understand that the organization is serious about its commitment to respectful behavior. Individuals who choose not to conduct themselves in accordance with this value will no longer be welcome. It takes effort, commitment, and courage to implement a plan of this scope and intensity in the organization. At the individual level, it is particularly strenuous because a person who is known to be difficult, manipulative, and verbally abusive must be confronted and handled with fairness and equanimity. In most cases, this will take a skilled professional such as a coach, a human resource professional, or an industrial organizational psychologist to assist leaders in developing and implementing an intervention plan. This plan may seek termination through due process, rehabilitation of the person, or appropriate reassignment. Whatever the final resolution, the changes made will have an effect on all stakeholders: all those who have suffered, questioned, and wondered why nothing was ever done in the past. The effect will include relief, but it also may include a period of guilt, aimlessness, or even loss. These aftereffects need to be recognized and addressed as one part of the TOCS method. In the final section of this chapter, we address strategies for rebuilding teams and healing team members.

RENEWAL OF LEADERS AND TEAMS

Even when a systemic intervention has been successful, there remain people who have lived through the nightmare and survived the ordeal. Leaders and teams who are ready to move forward and renew their commitment to a healthy workplace now need support in rebuilding the culture of the organization. Renewal in this context is about taking the human condition in the workplace and making it into something that inspires, provides hope, and gives meaning to people's lives. It affirms an organization's commitment to creating a respectful, energizing, and dignified place for people to work.

We have a deep conviction that organizational interventions that are in alignment with the values of the organization have the greatest potential to make an impact and create change. It's about creating sustainable change that transforms the leadership of an organization to consider the human and financial value associated with respect. In relation to toxicity, the greatest opportunity for renewal is through leadership and team development. Thus, we have focused our recommendations on programs that target these two venues. The programs target both leaders and teams to create an organizational wide approach to establishing a healthy workplace. Team facilitators and organization development consultants will have a number of team building and leader development programs that align with the examples that we describe briefly in this limited space.

Leadership Development Programs

Leadership development programs that we have targeted for this discussion are: benchmarking, leadership programs, and mentoring. These developmentally focused activities can inhibit the incidence and spread of workplace incivility.

Benchmarking is a process that has been successfully used in many organizations and communities. It is designed to elicit knowledge regarding the best practices around a certain industry or content area. One example of a best practice in the health care industry might be enhanced patient services. An example of benchmarking in a content area might include how social responsibility is enacted across many different industries. Within the context of our discussion on toxicity, benchmarking could be engaged to find the best practices other organizations are using to create concrete, behaviorally specific values related to respectful engagement. With the advent of Joint Commission standards, hospitals can collaborate on best practices for promoting environments of respectful engagement.

Leadership development programs are excellent ways to educate leaders in strategies for preventing toxicity and fostering respectful engagement and many health care organizations have already established such programs. Health care leadership must now incorporate the significant building block of values related to incivility and disruptive behaviors. The programs must go beyond discussing the importance of a healthy, constructive workplace environment and include a training program that (a) integrates behavioral values into performance appraisal systems, (b) teaches strategies that reinforce organizational respectful engagement at the individual and team levels, (c) includes specific education on the nature of incivility and its influence and its systemic effects and bottom-line impact, and (d) insures that all leaders "walk the talk" and exemplify civil and respectful discourse. Recently, we found that many organizations are initiating programs to cope with "difficult people," however, largely related to the more blatant bullying behavior. However, as reviewed earlier in this discussion, researchers have concluded that to enhance the livability of workplace environments, we must also focus on the less apparent and more insidious impact of passive aggression and team sabotage. Our clients have confirmed our belief that the elephant in the room is actually the passive hostility that runs rampant throughout teams, undercutting productivity and well-being.

Mentoring can make a significant contribution to transforming organizational culture. Barrett in his book, *Building a Values-Driven Organization: A Whole System Approach to Cultural Transformation* noted that "the culture of the organization is a reflection of the consciousness of its leaders" (2006, p. 20). Consider the importance of this statement with respect to toxic leaders. An organization that allows a toxic leader to stay in place is making a statement that this type of behavior, sometimes at the highest levels, is tolerable. If instead the leadership creates values that include zero tolerance for toxicity, then a respectful culture can follow. Mentoring as a one-on-one developmental relationship offers a substantial opportunity to seed not only the value of respectful engagement, but to embrace this value in the mentoring relationship itself. In other words, mentoring relationships are built to engage the leader in thoughtful reflection, honest and direct feedback, obtainable and behaviorally specific professional goals, and fair reward structures. Some organizations take mentoring very seriously and have learning programs to prepare mentors. This is a prime opportunity to make respectful engagement one of the criteria. Mentors not only informally teach critical content areas, but they are also preparing prodigies to be socially responsible. Mentoring relationships create the opportunity to expand a person's understanding of self as engaged with others. Being in a mentoring relationship demands awareness of self and others to facilitate the learning environment. Toxicity has no place in such a relationship and can be confronted directly for the purposes of learning rather than punishment. These teaching moments are the embodiment of "in situ" learning for building constructive workplace relationships. These values and skills can now be brought to group processes, customer relations, and policy design of the organization.

Leadership Healing

Many hospitals have put considerable money and effort into the provision of coaching services for the disruptive physician or nurse; we are advocating the use of coaching to help the leader deal with the aftermath of emotional injury caused by the toxic person. Many leaders put hours of effort into trying to change and manage the disruptive behaviors of staff members. Even if they recognize the difficulty in engaging the person and creating behavioral change, they feel that they have no other options available. Finally, even if the person is reassigned or terminated, in spite of the immediate relief, they frequently feel emotionally exhausted, disempowered, and inadequate. If their mental health has severely deteriorated, then a mental health professional may be required. Oftentimes, however, the problem-solving, action-oriented approach of a coach well versed in the systemic and personal impact of workplace toxicity can assist a leader in regaining their confidence and motivation. We believe that it is important for hospitals to recognize the likely effects that dealing with toxic individuals on a day-to-day basis can have on managers and team leaders; we recommend coaching or professional mental health services for those that have been closely involved in these situations.

Team Healing and Building Programs

In some cases, one member of a team might be specifically targeted and require the services of a mental health provider. As discussed earlier, individuals that have been the targets of verbal abuse frequently report depression, psychosomatic illnesses, and stress-related conditions. Team leaders need to address the common occurrence of these health problems in relation to abusive behavior and remove the shame and stigma attached to those that are suffering these after effects. The toxic person's entire team not only suffers from the peripheral effects, but has also become accustomed to expecting and reinforcing a climate of rudeness. Team building should include a period for healing to deal with the emotional aftermath. It is tempting for the team to fall into complaining and bad-mouthing for it is likely that this has been their only form of connecting over the period in which the toxicity was permitted to flourish. Leaders need to focus on building toward the future and a renewal of values that reinforce interactions and collaboration that respect the dignity of all members. Because collaboration is so critical in health care and greatly disintegrates when incivility is the norm, team task exercises to promote cohesion are critical.

In working with teams that are recovering from toxicity, we have found that the best ways to change how the team relates and moves forward to healthier relationships depend on these actions: each individual in the group makes a commitment and reaffirmation to the values of direct communication, individuals should not go behind anyone's back, and individuals should not gossip about the toxic person who has left.

MOVING FORWARD

The Joint Commission has courageously come out with standards to guide health care organizations to establishing healthy work environments for all employees and the patients that they serve. In this chapter, we have presented a significant volume of research findings from management and health care that document the financial and human devastation caused by uncivil, toxic behaviors and support the wisdom of the Joint Commission's mandate. Our model for change, TOCS, addresses the call for action by offering a three-level system of intervention: the large organization, the team, and the individual. Incivility, rudeness, and verbal abuse are rampant in our society and organizations. These behaviors are resistant to change and highly infectious. Incivility will not be stopped simply with educational programs or termination of offenders. It will take systematic, multi-level, and coordinated strategies over a period of time with all stakeholders involved. To realize a community of respectful engagement is everyone's responsibility.

NOTES

1. The descriptors disruptive, uncivil, toxic will be used interchangeably in this document to represent those behaviors that have been used without definitional distinction in the literature.
2. Portions of the following sections have been adapted from Kusy and Holloway (2009).

REFERENCES

American Association of Critical-Care Nurses. (2005). Zero tolerance for abuse position statement. Available at http://www.aacn.org/AACN/pubpolcy.nsf/Files/ZeroposStmt/$file/Zero%20 for%20Abuse%204.12.04.pdf. Retrieved on July 20, 2007.

Andersson, L. M., & Pearson, C. M. (1999). Tit for tat? The spiraling effect of incivility in the workplace. *Academy of Management Review*, *24*(3), 452–471.

Babiak, P., & Hare, R. D. (2006). *Snakes in suits: When psychopaths go to work*. New York: HarperCollins.

Barrett, R. (2006). *Building a values-driven organization: A whole system approach to cultural transformation*. Boston: Elsevier.

Bernstein, A. J. (2001). *Emotional vampires: Dealing with people who drain you dry*. New York: McGraw Hill.

Blau, G., & Andersson, L. (2005). Testing a measure of instigated workplace incivility. *Journal of Occupational & Organizational Psychology*, *78*(4), 595–614.

Brier, P. S. (2009). Teaching respect at Maimonides Medical Center. *Frontiers of Health Services Management*, *25*(4), 25–31.

Brown, P., & Levinson, S. C. (1987). *Politeness: Some universals in language usage*. New York: Cambridge University Press.

Campbell, D., & Hallam, G. (1994). *Campbell–Hallam team development survey*. Arlington, VA: Vangent.

Cortina, L. M., Magley, V. J., & Linneman, H. C. (2002). Individual differences in response to incivility in the workplace. Paper presented at the Annual Meeting of the Academy of Management, Denver, CO.

Cortina, L. M., Magley, V. J., Williams, J. H., Hunter, J., & Langhout, R. D. (2001). Incivility in the workplace: Incidence and impact. *Journal of Occupational Health Psychology*, *6*, 64–80.

Felblinger, D. M. (2008). Incivility and bullying in the workplace and nurses' shame responses. *Journal of Obstetric, Gynecologic, and Neonatal Nursing: JOGNN/NAACOG*, *37*(2), 234.

Felblinger, D. M. (2009). Bullying, incivility, and disruptive behaviors in the healthcare setting: Identification, impact, and intervention. *Frontiers of Health Services Management*, *25*(4), 13–23.

Grenny, J. (2009). Crucial conversations: The most potent force for eliminating disruptive behavior. *Critical Care Nursing Quarterly*, *32*(1), 58–61.

Hickson, M. D., Pichert, J. W., Webb, L. E., & Gabbe, S. G. (2007). A complementary approach to promoting professionalism: Identifying, measuring, and addressing unprofessional behaviors. *Academic Medicine*, *82*(11), 1040–1048.

Hutton, S., & Gates, D. (2008). Workplace incivility and productivity losses among direct care staff. *AAOHN Journal: Official Journal of the American Association of Occupational Health Nurses*, *56*(4), 168–175.

Institute for Safe Medication Practices. (2005). Intimidation: Mapping a plan for cultural change in healthcare. Retrieved on September 8, 2009. Available at http://www.ismp.org/pressroom/pr20040331.pdf

Joint Commission Resources. (2008). Behaviors that undermine a culture of safety. *The Joint Commission Sentinel Event Alert*, *40*, 10–13.

Kahn, M. W. (2008). Etiquette-based medicine. *New England Journal of Medicine*, *358*(19), 1988–1989.

Kerfoot, K. M. (2007). Leadership, civility, and the 'no jerks' rule. *Nursing Economics*, *25*(4), 233–234.

Kusy, M. E., & Holloway, E. L. (2009). *Toxic workplace! Managing toxic personalities and their systems of power*. San Francisco: Jossey-Bass.

Leape, L. L., & Fromson, J. A. (2006). Problem doctors: Is there a system-level solution? *Annals of Internal Medicine*, *144*, 107–115.

Martin, R. J., & Hine, D. W. (2005). Development and validation of the uncivil workplace behavior questionnaire. *Journal of Occupational Health Psychology*, *10*(4), 477–490.

Mayer, D., Nishii, L., Schneider, B., & Goldstein, H. (2007). The precursors and products of justice climates: Group leader antecedents and employee attitudinal consequences. *Personnel Psychology*, *60*, 929–963.

Miller, R. S. (2000). Breaches of propriety. In: R. M. Kowalski (Ed.), *Behaving badly: Aversive behaviors in interpersonal relationships* (pp. 25–42). Washington, DC: American Psychological Association.

Neff, K. E. (2000). Understanding and managing physicians with disruptive behavior. In: S.B. Ransom, W. W. Pinsky & J. E. Tropman (Eds), *Enhancing physician performance: Advanced principles of medical management* (pp. 45–72). Tampa, FL: American College of Healthcare Executives.

Neuman, J. H., & Baron, R. A. (1997). Aggression in the workplace. In: R. A. Giacalone & J. Greenberg (Eds), *Antisocial behavior in organizations* (pp. 37–67). Thousand Oaks, CA: Sage.

Pearson, C. M., Andersson, L. M., & Porath, C. L. (2004). Workplace incivility. In: P. Spector & S. Fox (Eds), *Counterproductive workplace behavior* (pp. 177–200). Washington, DC: American Psychological Association.

Pearson, C. M., & Porath, C. L. (2005). On the nature, consequences and remedies of workplace incivility: No time for "nice"? Think again. *Academy of Management Executive, 19*(1), 7–18.

Pearson, C. M., & Porath, C. L. (2009). *The cost of bad behavior: How incivility is damaging your business and what to do about it.* Hightstown, MJ: McGraw-Hill.

Porath, C. L., & Erez, A. (2009). Overlooked but not untouched: How rudeness reduces onlookers' performance on routine and creative tasks. *Organizational Behavior and Human Decision Processes, 109*, 29–44.

Porto, G., & Lauve, R. (2006). disruptive clinician behavior: A persistent threat to patient safety. *Patient Safety and Quality Healthcare,* (July/August).

Remington, R., & Darden, M. (2002). *Aggravating circumstances: A status report on rudeness in America.* New York: Public Agenda.

Rosenstein, A. H., & O'Daniel, M. (2005a). Disruptive behavior and clinical outcomes: Perceptions of nurses and physicians. *The American Journal of Nursing, 105*(1), 54.

Rosenstein, A. H., & O'Daniel, M. (2005b). Study links disruptive behavior to negative patient outcomes. *OR Manager, 21*(3), 1.

Rosenstein, A. H., & O'Daniel, M. (2006). Impact and implications of disruptive behavior in the perioperative arena. *Journal of the American College of Surgeons, 203*(1), 96–105.

Rosenstein, A. H., & O'Daniel, M. (2008a). Invited article: Managing disruptive physician behavior: Impact on staff relationships and patient care. *Neurology, 70*(17), 1564–1570.

Rosenstein, A. H., & O'Daniel, M. (2008b). A survey of the impact of disruptive behaviors and communication defects on patient safety. *Joint Commission Journal on Quality and Patient Safety/Joint Commission Resources, 34*(8), 464–471.

Sofield, L., & Salmond, S. W. (2003). Workplace violence: A focus on verbal abuse and intent to leave the organization. *Orthopaedic Nursing, 22*, 274–283.

Spratlen, L. P. (1994). Workplace mistreatment: Its relationship to interpersonal violence. *Journal of Psychosocial Nursing, 21*(12), 5–6.

Winters, A. M., & Duck, S. W. (2000). You****!!!. In: R. M. Kowalski (Ed.), *Behaving badly: Aversive behaviors in interpersonal relationships* (pp. 59–77). Washington, DC: American Psychological Association.

CONDITION CRITICAL: INTERVENING IN HEALTH CARE TEAMS AND WORKING RELATIONSHIPS: A COMMENTARY

Victoria A. Parker

It is widely acknowledged that the delivery of health care has been made more complex by a number of factors including technology, information, organizational arrangements, and the increasing burden of chronic illness. This increase in complexity has underscored the need for more effective teamwork and working relationships among health care providers. Although professional education groups such as the Accreditation Council for Graduate Medical Education (ACGME) have mandated competencies such as "work effectively as a member or leader of a health care team or other professional group" since at least 2007, it is clear from both research and anecdotal accounts that there is still room for significant development in this area.

Horwitz, Horwitz, and Barshes provide an important contribution by mapping the different kinds of relational problems that can plague health care teams and connecting them to the significant outcome of patient safety. Team dysfunction does not just cause inefficiency; it can cause real harm and even death – that is a message that should be attention-getting. They, thus, suggest a number of ways in which organizational theory concepts can be applied to bring about improvements in team function. Orr and

Organization Development in Healthcare: Conversations on Research and Strategies
Advances in Health Care Management, Volume 10, 267–268

ISSN: 1474-8231/doi:10.1108/S1474-8231(2011)0000010021

Brunetto et al. each provide a closer look at such patterns in different relational subsystems; Orr exploring relations between nurses and members of support services and Brunetto et al. focusing on the workplace networks of nurses. Orr's paper takes an appreciative inquiry stance in attempting to identify what factors cause nursing–support service relationships to work well, putting the emphasis on functional teamwork. This work also provides a useful reminder that interdisciplinary teamwork in health care is not just about physicians and nurses; there a number of other disciplines and worker groups that make essential contributions to effective teamwork. Brunetto et al.'s work suggests that many nurses may have relatively small networks to support problem solving at work, and that nursing managers are present are important in only about half of such networks. This may indicate a missed opportunity for nursing leaders to cultivate the development of broader workplace networks that would support nurses in problem solving at work. Holloway and Kusy focus on a particular type of problem seen in teams and relationships, that of workplace incivility and hostility, and also convincingly illustrate the ill effects of such behaviors in health care delivery environments that are relationally "toxic." They make the critical point that addressing such behaviors must take place within a systemic approach that addresses the underlying cultural patterns of relations among different disciplines and groups.

In his work on caregiving organizations, Kahn (2003) suggests that teams may become "traumatized" by a history of difficulty in maintaining effective working relationships. Thus, taking a systemic approach to both changing the possibly dysfunctional dynamics of existing teams, and setting up new teams for healthy interrelationships will be essential to improving health care management. These needs present both an opportunity and a challenge for health care managers; one that is essential to address to improve both workforce outcomes such as commitment and patient outcomes such as safety.

REFERENCE

Kahn, W. A. (2003). The revelation of organizational trauma. *Journal of Applied Behavioral Science*, *39*(4), 364–380.

PART V
INFORMATION TECHNOLOGY

IT AND ORGANIZATION: A DELICATE PARTNERSHIP

Stefano Calciolari

ABSTRACT

Information technology (IT) is an important enabler of organization models (OM) and of innovative strategies, as it fosters information integration and streamlines information flows. Two case studies offer evidence about the strategic use of IT innovation (i.e., digital signature) to foster successful OM and partnerships in health care, while results from a survey and some case studies show how institutional reforms can foster the diffusion of mature technologies (i.e., ERP) as an adaptive strategy of health care organizations. Leadership and clear vision lead to consistency between OM and technology and foster the exploitation full benefits associated with innovation.

INTRODUCTION

During the 1990s, in the wave of the international "New Public Management" movement (Hood, 1991), the health care sector underwent several important reforms (Fattore, 1999). Among the most relevant changes were introduction of quasi-markets, decentralization, focus on patients'

Organization Development in Healthcare: Conversations on Research and Strategies
Advances in Health Care Management, Volume 10, 271–286

ISSN: 1474-8231/doi:10.1108/S1474-8231(2011)0000010022

rights (Saltman & Figueras, 1998). The main purpose of these reforms was to pursue both macroeconomic stabilization and microeconomic efficiency.

In particular, in Italy a new accounting system was enforced (Cantù & Carbone, 2003; Donatini et al., 2001) with the aim to introduce enhanced managerial tools that support organizations in their challenge to contrast the virtually rising trend of expenditures. However, the focus on patient rights did not relax the tension between quality and efficiency. As a consequence, health care managers seek to harness information technology (IT) as a competitive tool (Killingsworth, Newkirk, & Seeman, 2006).

The literature suggests that successful technological innovation should be the result of strategic vision and proactive approach to IT (Cocchiara, Davis, & Kinnaird, 2008; Larsson, Löwstedt, & Shani, 2001; Newkirk, Lederer, & Johnson, 2008). However, technological change seems often to drive technological innovation within organizations in an adaptive fashion, rather than belonging to clear, planned strategies (Buccoliero, Calciolari, & Marsilio, 2008a).

In general, IT tends to foster information integration. Information integration is not an easy concept (Waring & Wainwright, 2000), but for our purposes it may be defined as the timely availability of the information needed to carry out the various phases into which processes – clinical, administrative, technical, etc., – are divided either within an organization or among different ones (Calciolari, 2008, p. 43). This is also the case of enterprise resource planning (ERP) systems adopted in administrative departments and digital signature technology used to manage electronic clinical reports or other kinds of formal communications.

In this chapter, we first analyze two case studies of Italian health care organizations that adopted the digital signature technology to support their strategy. The organization model (OM) underneath the organization's strategy is analyzed in relationship with the technological innovation and its enabling potential. Second, a multiple-case study analyzes the different approaches followed by eight Italian health care organizations adopting an ERP system and the consequent economical and organizational impacts. Finally, we draw some conclusions about the success factors leading to consistency between strategy, OM, and technology as a condition to fully exploit the benefits associated with technological innovation.

As far as the adopted methods are concerned, both qualitative and quantitative data were used. The data about the first case study were retrieved on the official Web site dedicated to the project, from press releases available online and from dissemination materials accessed by the author during his meetings at Bruxelles in the period 2006–2008. The analysis of the second case study is mainly based on a one-day interview (initially semistructured and later unstructured, in order to capture some unusual aspects of the change management) in the first half of 2003. The interview was conducted with personnel involved in the development of the Web portal, and the preliminary report was later validated by the organization; data were then updated via e-mail at the end of 2004. The Web portal and press releases currently available online were used to check the occurrence of any relevant change in the last years. Finally, the multiple-case study is the result of a research project that involved the author, as a member of a research team, in the period 2006–2008. The research team conducted semistructured interviews in each enrolled organization and retrieved official documents about both project management and financial information concerning the innovation. Buccoliero, Calciolari, and Marsilio (2008b) reported extensively about the methodology and the results of the study, but in this chapter the author focuses and elaborates on those aspects of the case studies that seem to confirm the importance of a planned, virtuous partnership between strategy, OM, and technological change for the success of technological innovation in health care.

CASE STUDY 1: NETWORKED APPROACH TO SERVICE DELIVERY

In 2006, Health Optimum[1] was awarded as best European project of the year among about 70 examples of IT applications in the health care sector. The local health unit (LHU) #9 of Treviso – in *Regione Veneto* – is currently project leader of the new phase (2007–2009) of the project, involving also the *Gobierno de Aragon* (Spain), the Region Syddanmark (Denmark), and the cities of Uppsala (Sweden) and Timisoara (Romania). The objective of Health Optimum was first to validate and currently to deploy *e-health* services that can support innovative OMs for health care service delivery. The project deals with two specific e-health services: neurosurgical tele-consultation and tele-laboratory service. The last service allows performing blood examinations at the patient's place through portable diagnostic testing (*Point of Care Testing*) – consisting of a palm-size device (*palm-set*) linked to a laptop equipped with a dedicated software application-specifically designed to promote home care assistance. The neurosurgical tele-consultation, meanwhile, is designed to allow peripheral hospitals – without neurosurgery unit – for obtaining formal consultation about emergency patients with head trauma from a neurosurgery center. Both services implement digital signature as a means to enable legal information flows and, thus, to have network relations based on formal evidence.

The strategic intuition behind the project is essentially that information flows represent a crucial resource for any OM and, when logistics is a relevant element of decision-making, they actually become a critical success factor. Here we focus our attention on the neurosurgical tele-consultation and the reference OM is the so-called *hub and spokes* model (Booth, 1996; Nobilio & Ugolini, 2003). This OM interested the Italian policy maker in the last five to six years. It has been considered an important OM, with particular regard to the cardiac surgery and the neurosurgery specialties, as a strategy to foster in each center the minimum caseload required to assure good quality of care. In general, one (or few) hospital(s) play the role of hub(s) treating the most complex cases, while the other hospitals of the system take preferentially care of routine or less complex cases. The matching between the vertical differentiation and the collaborative approach to service provisioning is intended to promote integrated bodies that act collectively as organizational leaders of care provision (Edwards, 2002; Lega, 2005).

In essence, the hub and spokes model is a kind of horizontal network based on cooperative, rather than competitive, relations among health service providers of a geographic area. In Italy, the geographic area is usually represented by the region, which plays a pivotal role in the governance of the national health system after its regionalization (Pessina & Cantù, 2006).

In particular, Regione Veneto (with about 4.8 million inhabitants and about 9.4% of the GDP)[2] formally decided to adopt the OM with regard to specific pathologies: acute myocardial infarction and stroke. However, when a peripheral hospital receives an emergency patient, the clinical staff must decide whether it is a complex case, and thus requiring the patient to be transferred, or if it is possible to treat the patient locally. The decision-making process in such a case may lead to the four different and relevant outcomes showed in Table 1.

As the vertical differentiation results in a lack of standardization of clinical workers' skills (hub vs. spokes), the variation in interpreting the output of the diagnostic process – mainly based on medical imaging for patients with head trauma – can be relevant, especially comparing peripheral hospitals' staff with hub's staff. The logistics and the organizational boundaries are major

Table 1. Possible Outcomes of the Decision-Making Process.

Decision to Transfer a Patient	Actual Need to Transfer a Patient	
	YES	*NO*
YES	–	Type II error
NO	Type I error	–

obstacles for the mechanism of mutual adjustment.[3] Without further mechanisms of coordination there is a risk of excessive either type I error (efficiency orientation: avoid unnecessary costs) or type II error (quality orientation: ensure quality of care), depending on the organization culture and the local environmental pressure.

At the heart of the neurosurgical tele-consultation, there is the idea of providing peripheral hospitals with formal communications (instead of the typical informal ones of the mutual adjustment) among teams; thus, whenever doubts arise, the spoke center can send its diagnostic outputs to the hub hospital and receive a "second opinion" from a highly specialized team of neurosurgeons (Fig. 1). The legal validity of these communications – thanks to the digital signature based on a public key infrastructure – and the efficiency of the transaction makes the coordination mechanism effective at the interorganizational level. As a result, the e-health service is the building block of a counseling network involving neurosurgery centers, peripheral hospitals, and emergency rooms operating in the geographic area.

From the theoretical point of view, the neurosurgical tele-consultation promotes the efficient use or resources by contrasting inappropriate transfers of patients (i.e., type II error), resulting from uncertainty in the decision-making process, without compromising service quality.

Although no natural experiments were conducted on this aspect, the network reported a significant reduction (79%) in the number of patients transferred from peripheral hospitals to spoke centers after the introduction of the technological innovation: from 53% (in 2004) to 11% (in 2005) of the total number of borderline[4] patients received by spoke centers (62 and 57, respectively).[5] At the same time there is no evidence about reduced effectiveness in treating patients affected by head trauma. Therefore, the introduction of a legal tele-reporting system fostered the efficiency of the OM and showed evidence of more rational use of resources without service quality decline.

The OM was clear to the organizations involved in the network and all the nodes agreed on it as a means to enact the regional strategy. On the basis

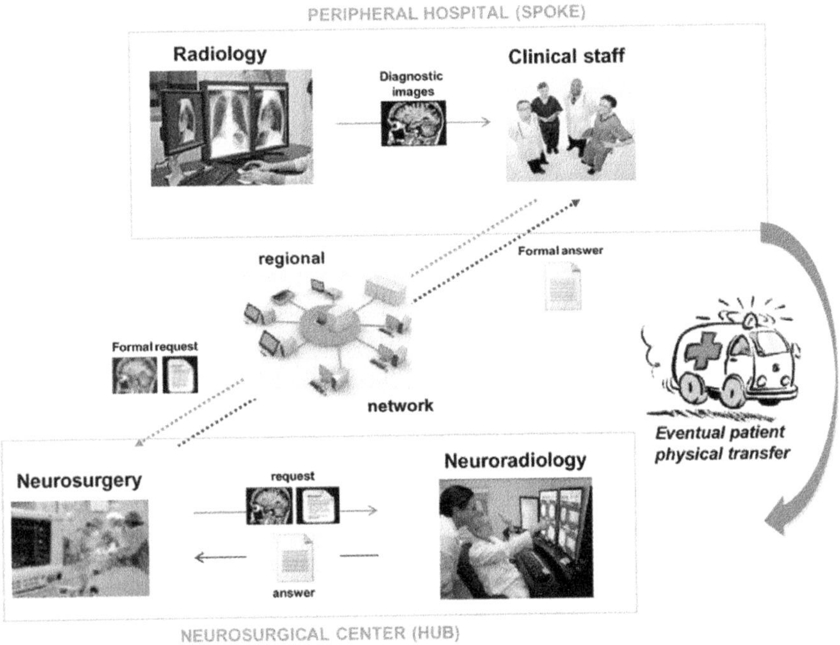

Fig. 1. Information Flows Within Hub and Spoke Hospitals. *Source*: Adapted from http://www.forumpa.it/archivio/4000/4100/4170/4172/HEALTH_OPTIMUM.ppt. Retrieved on April 13th, 2011.

of this clear common vision, the LHU #9 of Treviso could use its leadership, as well-known project leader of international health projects, to gain consensus on the project structure and road map. In addition, the visibility, prestige, and sponsorship of the European project were able to catalyze commitment among members and gain momentum for the change management necessary after the introduction of the new technology. Actually, the legal system requires formal communication flows to ensure that responsibilities are traced back to the individuals/organizations who take medically relevant decisions. Therefore, integration of the digital signature in the information flows enabled organizations to rely on legal certainty of responsibility.

CASE STUDY 2: INTEGRATING SERVICE DELIVERY FOR THE COMMUNITY

Founded in 1865, the hospital "Bambino Gesù" is a private nonprofit pediatric hospital accredited within the regional health system of Lazio. Regione Lazio has about 5.6 million inhabitants (2.7 million residents in the capital city of Rome) and accounts for about 10.9% of the GDP.[6] The hospital was recognized institute for health care and scientific research (IRCCS) with three logistic locations – the main one in the capital city, and two in the province (Palidoro and S. Marinella) – and about 800 beds.

In 2001, the hospital was pursuing an overall strategy oriented to foster an image of excellent service delivery center and, at the same time, a valuable resource for both the local community and the wider health system. The board and the top management selected the emerging channel of the rising information age (Castells, 2000) as a critical success factor of its strategy. Actually, the defined strategy was also intended to answer to the patients' perceived deficiencies of the community health care services and to the general practitioners' (GPs) need to develop better integration between primary and secondary care. The board played an active role initially to share a common vision about innovation, and then to support the top management along the whole road map. In particular, the partnership between the board and the top management boosted the will for an early start of the strategic project. As a consequence, the hospital launched its Web portal (www.ospedalebambinogesu.it) in September 2001.

As a matter of fact, the Web portal was the main building block of a business model where different partners joined in a consortium to sell innovative services (e.g., e-learning, second opinion, and online service booking) to the institutional stakeholders (e.g., LHUs, medical associations, and other hospitals) and patients. The relationships between the consortium and the institutional stakeholders are based on formal contracts to ensure that financial, consulting, and technological partners contribute to the project development with all the necessary complementary resources. The hospital Bambino Gesù has always held the leadership of the initiative with main responsibility on the contents and the portal's editorial management.

As far as services are concerned, the Web portal offered: (a) e-learning, (b) information, (c) online booking system, and (d) second opinion-or specialist tele-consultation. For our purposes, this contribution mainly focuses on the last three services. However, the discussion about the implications for the OM deals with the innovation tout court. The Web portal design distinguishes three categories of users: families, children (with the so-called "baby portal"), physicians, and health care professionals.

The section dedicated to families offers medical suggestions and information about babies' health (ranging from "information pills" to special issue dossier), hospital's services and accessibility, tailored forums, and an online booking system for specialist visits and exams. The second section is an example of how technology can be used to involve patients in building the organization's image: the baby portal welcomes and shows children's outputs (e.g., drawings and fairy tales) belonging to their active involvement in hospital's entertainment activities (thus collecting also material useful to understand how children see the hospital). It also offers interactive games and provides easy-to-understand information about kids' health. The last section is dedicated to physicians and offers evidence-based tools (e.g., medical libraries), epidemiologic and biostatistics database and reports, congresses' proceedings and news, tailored forums, the online booking system for specialist visits and exams (interestingly, 10% of the remote requests are made by GPs for their patients), and the second opinion. The second opinion service is an online application that allows registered health professionals to ask the hospital for a formal tele-consultation about cases whose anamneses are not clear. The service is based on the digital signature technology: the registered user must use a smart card (issued by the hospital) to communicate her/his identity and subscribe the request; the request must follow a standard form, though the online application allows for adding "free-style" notes. The hospital uses the same technology to verify, read, and answer any request. The privacy of the online information flows is protected with secure sockets layer (SSL) encryption technology, and the digital signature provides communication with actual legal value.

From the organizational point of view, the technological innovation required the hospital to develop its OM to cope with the new need for collecting and integrating information coherently with the strategic model and the dynamic environmental pressure (against which the organization's boundaries were now more permeable). Since the planning phase of the project a so-called "virtual department" was created,[7] physicians were involved in defining technical functions of the Web portal and organization processes behind the remote interactions. After the portal's launch, the virtual department persisted in terms of editorial staff – dedicated to publishing communication and archiving activities – and about 50 physicians, who according to their entrepreneurship or the occasional matching of their medical know-how with external requests (from Q&A

services, forums, second opinion, etc.), are involved in publishing online materials or answering to environmental solicitations. The physicians' involvement is organized in permanent groups dealing with recurrent management tasks or, in case of extemporary need, temporary teams supporting the portal development.

Apparently, the introduction of the virtual department represented both a signal of strategic commitment on the innovation and the organizational environment where the vertical integration of skills and knowledge could occur on the basis of active cooperation for the use of fixed resources. The choice of not giving structural relevance to the virtual department (as it did not have an actual budget) was intended as a flexible approach to cope with a rapidly evolving environment.

As a matter of fact, in 2003 the portal accounted for about 1.3 million visitors (with over 70 million accesses and 21,720 registered users, about 10% physicians), over 1,200 monthly online booked visits and diagnostic services (almost 20% of the overall hospital reservations), more than 130 tele-consultations, and provided 90 e-learning courses, with a rising trend compared to the previous year (and projections based on data recorded in September 2004). In the same year, the consortium held contracts and partnerships with – among the others – the Ministry of Health, three regions, three medical associations, twelve LHUs, and five hospitals.

The success of the innovation was surely due to the coherence between organization development and management changes belonging to the new technology, as organization and technology were both explicit elements of the strategy sponsored by the board since the beginning. In addition, there was a timely match between the innovation and the growing demand for more integrated delivery of health services, as both patients were expressing concerns about deficiencies of the community health care services and GPs expressed the need to develop better integration between primary and secondary care.

The Web portal, in a sense, represents a strategic tool to foster, on one hand, patient's empowerment (Dent, 2006; Millenson, 2001; Roth, 1994) and, on the other hand, the actual implementation of an integrated delivery system (IDS) in terms of coordinating health care services along a continuum (Shortell, Gillies, Anderson, Erickson, & Mitchell, 1996, 2000). The coordination, in this case, is limited to formal information exchanges (between community health services and the hospital), but it actually impacts the service delivery: for instance, registered GPs can access reliable information to support their decision-making as gatekeepers of the health system, thus enhancing their responsiveness and the appropriateness of hospitalization. In other words, it is a "virtual" case of *g-design* of IDS (Lega, 2007): a market-based design where the geographical area (i.e., the area served by professionals and organizations who signed a contract or a partnership with the hospital Bambino Gesù) is the criterion around which activities are grouped. As a consequence, the relevance of specialization is subordinated to those integration needs solicited by environmental requests/pressures.

The organization development, in this case, had a marginal role in the initial strategy, as not already defined before the introduction of the technological innovation (as opposed to the previous case study). However, the hospital followed a clear strategy oriented to enhance the information exchanges between the environment and the organization based on the real needs of its stakeholders: patients and their families, GPs, and other peripheral health care providers. In this case, the main role of leadership consisted of gaining consensus around the actual coherence between a service delivery vision and the evolution of demand. The added value of the enabled information exchanges was so relevant that the hospital was able to strengthen its partnership with Hospital Italiano de Buenos Aires (Argentina) by providing it with the second opinion e-service. As a consequence, the success of a local strategy became the premise for fostering the international strategy.

CASE STUDY 3: COMPARING ERP IMPLEMENTATION ACROSS MULTIPLE CASES

As already mentioned, in the second half of the 1990s a wave of reforms introduced several changes in the governance of the health care sector. Organizations and their managerial tools became relevant objects of interest for the policy maker to foster macroeconomic stability through micro-economic efficiency. In particular, long-standing cash accounting was replaced by accrual accounting in all Italian public health care organizations. Accrual accounting was intended to be the first building block of analytical managerial accounting, which has the main purpose of providing information about costs and revenues concerning special management objects (e.g., cost per bed, cost per service, and cost per patient). This information is intended to support both decisions and the control function.

The new accounting method changed fundamental administrative information flows (e.g., payable invoice management) and, as a consequence, accounting departments were called to centralize processes previously managed in peripheral offices. Organizations reacted by redesigning the OM of their administrative offices and, often, changing their accounting information systems.

Since the 1990s, ERP systems have been progressively introduced in many health care structures (Menon, Lee, & Eldenburg, 2000). Results from a survey addressed to chief information officers show that a significant proportion of Italian health care organizations adopted ERP systems (Buccoliero & Calciolari, 2006), as a reaction to the new accounting and management control models introduced by reform. However, decisions of adopting ERP systems were also based on the rhetoric of fostering information integration as a strategy for (a) rationalizing organization processes and resources management (Rosemann, 1999) and (b) supporting managers to deal with the high information intensity of health care (Zviran & Armoni, 1999).

Given the relevance of the investments associated with the introduction of such technological systems, both scholars and practitioners have claimed for evidence about their "value for money." Several authors emphasized the importance of several critical factors contributing to project's success in terms of value for money; in particular (a) strong leadership and top management's support since the planning phase and (b) appropriate training and system users assistance seem to be among the most relevant success factors (Al-Mashari, Al-Mudimigh, & Zairi, 2003; Welti, 1999). Other authors focused on finding evidence about the economic and organizational impacts associated with the introduction of ERP systems (Bancroft, Seip, & Sprengel, 1998; Holland & Light, 1999; Umble, Haft, & Umble, 2003).

One recent multiple-case study, conducted on eight Italian public hospitals and LHUs, found evidence of association between the aforementioned critical factors and the beneficial economic impact of ERP systems after about five years (Buccoliero et al., 2008b). The organizations were all placed in Regione Lombardia (a region with 9.5 million inhabitants and that accounts for about 20.8% of the GDP)[8] and purchased their ERP systems from the same software house, although they followed different implementation approaches. Therefore, technology and institutional setting should not have been variables with relevant explanatory power over the variation in outcomes associated with the eight different projects.

The study assessed the impact associated with the innovation in terms of: (a) cost savings and emerging costs, (b) administrative processes efficiency and integration, and (c) user satisfaction and strategic support. Results concerning the first dimension, which represents the economic perspective of the study, show a dramatic variation across the eight cases, in both absolute – Net Present

Value ranging from –€600,114 to 1,799,137 – and relative terms (Internal Rate of Return ranging from 6% to 47% (Table 2).

As far as the second evaluation dimension is concerned, the study focuses on efficiency indicators of three relevant administrative processes (i.e., reduction in the average time span from payable invoice recording to actual payment, reduction in the average duration of a purchasing process, and increase in the average stock rotation rate). Results show variations among cases that can be explained either with the presence of complementary technologies enabling the automated streamlining of sequential activities (i.e., digitalization of payable invoices in the accounting recordkeeping) or the planned redesign of activities supported by the new system. Finally, results concerning user satisfaction and strategic support show positive impact on all the relevant aspects highlighted in the literature: data reliability, information sharing, enhanced decision-making support with more timely and accurate information, etc.

However, what is most relevant is the fact that the study found a significant correlation between measures of success and (a) the organizational commitment – measured in terms of services and internal organization effort dedicated to organization processes redesign and, in general, to organization development; (b) strategic support and training – measured in terms of training

Table 2. Economic Dimension Results.

Case	Organization Type	Dimensions (b/ca)[a]	Internal Rate of Return (IRR)	Net Present Value (NPV) (€)
A	Hospital	361 (b)	15%	114,322
B	Hospital	1,096 (b)	47%	1,799,137
C	Hospital	719 (b)	*NA*	(600,114)[b]
D	Hospital	922 (b)	34%	250,834
E	Hospital	638 (b)	*NA*	(326,617)
F	Local health unit	208,900 (ca)	6%	17,240
G	Local health unit	497,200 (ca)	9%	84,675
H	Hospital	952 (b)	20%	303,989

Source: Adapted from Buccoliero et al. (2008b, pp. 123, 134).
[a]Hospitals' dimensions are reported in terms of number of beds (b), while numbers of residents in the *catchment area* (ca) are reported for local health units. The distinction belongs to the service delivery model defined by Regione Lombardia, where local health units are responsible of the public health for the residents of a, so-called, catchment area, and hospitals offer hospitalizations and highly specialized services in a quasi-market where local health units and private insurances are purchasers.
[b]Numbers in brackets indicate negative values.

activities and strategic consultancy services associated with the ERP project. Results show that both organizational commitment and strategic support are strongly correlated with organizational benefits,[9] Net Present Value, and managers' satisfaction[10] – with Pearson correlation index ranging from 0.63 to 0.84 – while they are positively but weakly correlated with key users' satisfaction – Pearson correlation index below 0.2 (Buccoliero et al., 2008b, p. 147).

The impact analysis suggests that the attainment of the expected benefits is strongly dependent on non-technological aspects. In particular, devoting efforts to plan and develop an OM and organization rules coherent with the technological innovation represents a critical factor enabling the new technology to fully disclose its potential benefits. The outperforming organizations (B and D) focused the implementation phase to fine-tune the new system with the planned organization design, quoting from an interview with a manager: "During the implementation of the [ERP] system we had the opportunity to set our priorities in the design of the information flows. [...] You could appreciate your participation making some difference. I was always looking for matching the system with people and people with the system." Planning and participation played a key role in projects' outcomes: the institutional reform provided several organizations with the opportunity to take advantage of the new technological developments, but only those who used the opportunity to boost their own planned, coherent strategy were able to fully benefit from the innovation. Therefore, ownership of vision and careful change management demonstrated to be the fundamental breeding ground for successful technological innovation.

CONCLUSIONS

Technological change is an important variable in the health care sector. As far as IT is concerned, its impact has been so relevant in the last decade that the term "e-health" was coined to indicate the revolution generated for both health care organizations and patients (Buccoliero et al., 2008a). However, technological change can result from either an adaptive approach to (environmental or institutional) change or a proactive one based on a clear vision. While there is no conclusive evidence about the superiority of one of the two approaches (in terms off efficiency and effectiveness), the cases and evidence reported suggest that the proactive approach can lead to more homogeneous outcomes in terms of exploitations of innovation benefits.

The Health Optimum project used technology as a tool to reduce transaction costs of decision-making in a networked model of service delivery belonging to a clear regional strategy. The hospital of Bambino Besù designed and implemented a strategy of excellence and care for the local community based on a new communication strategy and the use of Internet and the digital signature as means to foster patient empowerment, peripheral hospitals' and practices' access to highly specialized know-how, and international compassionate partnership.

Finally, the implementation of ERP systems resulted significantly beneficial for those health care organizations that were able to make the technological change an opportunity to revise their OM according to the new requirements of the institutional reform and stimulate managers' participation to the priority setting process and organization fine-tuning.

NOTES

1. Health Optimization through teleMedicine (www.healthoptimum.info).
2. *Source*: www.statistica.regione.veneto.it (data 2007).
3. For a review of the mechanisms of coordination see Mintzberg (1992) and Shortell and Kaluzny (2006).
4. "Borderline" are conventionally called those patients for whom it is dubious the necessity of a neurosurgical consultation.
5. The research design is a *before–after* one and might be affected by the typical history bias (Mohr, 1995). However, the magnitude of the change is in favor of the hypothesis that the innovation has been influential in terms of fostering efficiency.
6. *Source*: www.regione.lazio.it/web2/contents/statistica/(data 2007).
7. In 2002, the hospital accomplished its whole OM redesign based on the departmental model, where departments are responsible for a global budget negotiated with the top management and for products/services results (Lega, 2005, pp. 244–252). In this case, the technological innovation created an opportunity to test a pilot department for the organization development.
8. *Source*: www.statistica.regione.lombardia.it (data 2006).
9. It measures the benefits belonging strictly from organizational changes: for instance, reduction in full-time equivalents previously dedicated to administrative activities.
10. The study uses the term "manager" referring to two figures: chief financial officer and chief information officer. Key users are those people of the organization actively involved in the process of implementing the new system and supporting the personnel's training.

REFERENCES

Al-Mashari, M., Al-Mudimigh, A., & Zairi, M. (2003). Enterprise resource planning: A taxonomy of critical factors. *European Journal of Operational Research*, *146*, 352–364.

Anessi Pessina, E., & Cantù, E. (2006). Whither managerialism in the Italian National Health Service? *International Journal of Health Planning and Management, 21*(4), 327–355.

Bancroft, N., Seip, H., & Sprengel, A. (1998). *Implementing SAP R/3: How to introduce a large system into a large organization.* Greenwich, London: Manning Publication.

Booth, A. (1996). Health service delivery to outback South Australia: A story of organizational change. *International Journal of Health Care Quality Assurance, 9*(2), 15–19.

Buccoliero, L., & Calciolari, S. (2006). Percezioni strategiche dei responsabili di sistemi informativi sull'e-health. In: E. Anessi & E. Cantù (Eds), *Rapporto OASI 2006*. Milano: Egea.

Buccoliero, L., Calciolari, S., & Marsilio, M. (2008a). A methodological and operative *framework* for the evaluation of an *e-health project. International Journal of Health Planning and Management, 23*(1), 3–20.

Buccoliero, L., Calciolari, S., & Marsilio, M. (2008b). *ERP Administrative-accounting systems in healthcare organizations. An approach to evaluation.* Milan: McGraw-Hill.

Calciolari, S. (2008). Integration of information systems in Italian healthcare organizations: State of the art. In: L. Buccoliero, S. Calciolari & M. Marsilio (Eds), *ERP Administrative-accounting systems in healthcare organizations. An approach to evaluation.* Milan: McGraw-Hill.

Cantù, E., & Carbone, C. (2003). La struttura del SSN italiano. In: E. Anessi Pessina & E. Cantù (Eds), *L'aziendalizzazione della sanità in Italia. Rapporto OASI 2003*. Milan: Egea.

Castells, M. (2000). *The rise of the network society: The information age: Economy, society and culture* (2 ed. Vol. 1). Cambridge: Wiley-Blackwell.

Cocchiara, R., Davis, H., & Kinnaird, D. (2008). Data center topologies for mission-critical business systems. *IBM Systems Journal, 47*(4), 695–706.

Dent, M. (2006). Patient choice and medicine in healthcare. Responsibilization, governance and proto-professionalization. *Public Management Review, 8*(3), 449–462.

Donatini, A., Rico, A., D'Ambrosio, M. G., Lo Scalzo, A., Orzella, L., Cicchetti, A., et al. (2001). Health care systems in transition: Italy. *European Observatory on Health Care Systems*. Available at www.euro.who.int/observatory

Edwards, N. (2002). Clinical networks. Advantages include flexibility, strength, speed, and focus on clinical issues. *British Medical Journal, 324*(7329), 63.

Fattore, G. (1999). Cost containment and reforms in the Italian National Health Service. In: E. Mossialos & J. Le Grand (Eds), *Health care and cost containment in the European Union*. Ashgate: Aldershot, UK.

Holland, C. P., & Light, B. (1999). A critical success factors model for ERP implementation. *IEEE Software, 16*(3), 30–36.

Hood, C. (1991). A public management for all seasons? *Public Administration, 69*(1), 3–19.

Killingsworth, B., Newkirk, H. E., & Seeman, E. (2006). An integrative health information systems approach for facilitating strategic planning in hospitals. *Healthcare Management Review, 31*(2), 119–129.

Larsson, P., Löwstedt, J., & Shani, A. B. (2001). IT and the learning organization: Exploring myths of change. *Organizational Development Journal, 19*(1), 73–90.

Lega, F. (2005). *Organizational design and development for health care services. Foundations and perspectives*. Milan: McGraw-Hill.

Lega, F. (2007). Organisational design for health integrated delivery systems: Theory and practice. *Health Policy, 81*(2), 258–279.

Menon, N. M., Lee, B., & Eldenburg, L. (2000). Productivity of information systems in the healthcare industry. *Information Systems Research, 11*(1), 83–92.
Millenson, M. L. (2001). Moral hazard vs. real hazard: Quality of care post-Arrow. *Journal of Health Politics, Policy and Law, 26*(5), 1069–1079.
Mintzberg, H. (1992). *Structures in fives: Designing effective organizations*. Eglewood Cliffs, NJ: Perentice-Hall.
Mohr, L. B. (1995). *Impact analysis for program evaluation* (2nd ed.). Thousand Oaks, CA: Sage.
Newkirk, H. E., Lederer, A. L., & Johnson, A. M. (2008). Rapid business and IT change: Drivers for strategic information systems planning? *European Journal of Information Systems, 17*(3), 198–218.
Nobilio, L., & Ugolini, C. (2003). Selective referrals in a 'hub and spoke' institutional setting: The case of coronary angioplasty procedures. *Health Policy, 63*(1), 95–107.
Rosemann, M. (1999). ERP-software-characteristics and consequences. Paper presented at the European Conference on Information Systems, Copenhagen.
Roth, M. S. (1994). Enhancing consumer involvement in healthcare. The dynamics of control, empowerment, and trust. *Journal of Public Policy and Marketing, 13*(1), 115–132.
Saltman, R. B., & Figueras, J. (1998). Analyzing the evidence on European health care reforms. *Health Affairs, 17*(2), 85–108.
Shortell, S. M., Gillies, R. R., Anderson, D. A., Morgan Erickson, K., & Mitchell, J. B. (1996). *Remaking health care in America: Building organized delivery systems*. San Francisco: Jossey-Bass.
Shortell, S. M., Gillies, R. R., Anderson, D. A., Morgan Erickson, K., & Mitchell, J. B. (2000). *Remaking health care in America. The evolution of organized delivery systems* (2nd ed.). San Francisco: Jossey-Bass.
Shortell, S. M., & Kaluzny, A. M. (2006). *Health care management. Organization design and behavior* (5th ed.). Albany, NY: Thomson.
Umble, E. J., Haft, R. R., & Umble, M. M. (2003). Enterprise resource planning: Implementation procedures and critical success factors. *European Journal of Operational Research, 146*, 241–257.
Waring, T., & Wainwright, D. (2000). Interpreting integration with respect to information systems in organizations: Image, theory and reality. *Journal of Information Technology, 15*(2), 131–147.
Welti, N. (1999). *Successful SAP R/3 implementation: Practical management of ERP projects*. Reading, MA: Addison Wesley.
Zviran, M., & Armoni, A. (1999). Integrating hospital information systems: A bottom-up approach. *International Journal of Healthcare Technology and Management, 1*(1/2), 168–179.

TECHNOLOGICAL IATROGENESIS: THE MANIFESTATION OF INADEQUATE ORGANIZATIONAL PLANNING AND THE INTEGRATION OF HEALTH INFORMATION TECHNOLOGY

Patrick Albert Palmieri, Lori T. Peterson and Luciano Bedoya Corazzo

ABSTRACT

The Institute of Medicine (IOM) views Health Information Technology (HIT) as an essential organizational prerequisite for the delivery of safe, reliable, and cost-effective health services. However, HIT presents the proverbial double-edged sword in generating solutions to improve system performance while facilitating the genesis of novel iatrogenic problems. Incongruent organizational processes give rise to technological iatrogenesis or the unintended consequences to system integrity and the resulting organizational outcomes potentiated by incongruent organizational–technological interfaces. HIT is a disruptive innovation for health services organizations but remains an overlooked organizational development (OD) concern.

Organization Development in Healthcare: Conversations on Research and Strategies
Advances in Health Care Management, Volume 10, 287–312

ISSN: 1474-8231/doi:10.1108/S1474-8231(2011)0000010023

Recognizing the technology–organizational misalignments that result from HIT adoption is important for leaders seeking to eliminate sources of system instability. The Health Information Technology Iatrogenesis Model (HITIM) provides leaders with a conceptual framework from which to consider HIT as an instrument for organizational development. Complexity and Diffusion of Innovation theories support the framework that suggests each HIT adoption functions as a technological change agent. As such, leaders need to provide operational oversight to managers undertaking system change via HIT implementation. Traditional risk management tools, such as Failure Mode Effect Analysis and Root Cause Analysis, provide proactive pre- and post-implementation appraisals to verify system stability and to enhance system reliability. Reconsidering the use of these tools within the context of a new framework offers leaders guidance when adopting HIT to achieve performance improvement and better outcomes.

Keywords: Health information technology; planning; error; iatrogenesis; risk management; failure mode effect analysis; root cause analysis; diffusion of innovation theory; complexity theory; organizational development; patient safety; change management

Each year health care organizations harm about 10% of patients globally (World Health Organization, 2006) and approximately 200,000 patients in the United States due to unsafe and unreliable health systems (Zhan & Miller, 2003). Overall, the health industry "frequently harms [patients] and routinely fails to deliver the appropriate standard of care" (Palmieri, DeLucia, Peterson, Ott, & Green, 2008, p. 34). As safety is "a national problem increasingly difficult to ignore" (Devers, Pham, & Lui, 2004, p. 103), health leaders are forced to identify opportunities for organizational improvement in an attempt to reduce the numbers of poor outcome (Berta & Baker, 2004; Wachter, 2004). The current U.S. agenda to increase organizational effectiveness in health delivery systems is premised on adopting innovative technologies to streamline processes (Thompson, Osberoff, Classen, & Sittig, 2007), improve human performance (Page, 2004), and reduce the overall cost of care (Hillestad et al., 2005).

Expert panels sponsored by the Institute of Medicine (IOM) believe Health Information Technology (HIT) is an essential organizational prerequisite for the delivery of safe, reliable, and cost-effective health services (Aspden, Corrigan, Wolcott, & Erickson, 2004; Aspden, Wolcott, Bootman, & Cronenwett, 2007; IOM, 2001). Despite future prospects, HIT presents the proverbial double-edged sword in generating solutions to limit health errors (Battles & Keyes, 2002) while facilitating the genesis of novel iatrogenic issues (Ammenwerth et al., 2006; Koppel, Wetterneck, Telles, & Karsh, 2008). The introduction of new technology and innovative software is believed to be among the tools necessary to tame the performance complexity experienced by clinicians at the human–system interface (Harrison, Koppel, & Bar-Lev, 2007). However, organizations develop over time with strategic planning to continually improve the effectiveness of organizational processes (Tucker & Edmondson, 2003), which in turn improves work outputs (Bohmer & Edmondson, 2001). Technology contributes a new approach to solve traditional organizational problems, but these problems are seldom eliminated with a silver bullet approach. As such, this paper addresses the exuberant celebration for HIT adoption in health organizations with a cautious, more balanced approach, by considering the potential pitfalls inherent when relying on novel technological products to resolve traditional organizational deficiencies.

In this paper, we begin with a discussion about health organization complexity and expanded HIT adoption to address poorly performing systems. Complexity Theory guides us to consider technology as a disruptive force in organizations, and we label the resulting negative consequences as technological iatrogenesis. Then, we present the Health Information Technology Iatrogenesis Model (HITIM) to illustrate the potential opportunities and threats organizations face with HIT adoption. Next, we discuss HIT project planning and development within the context of the Diffusion of Innovation Theory (DIT) and suggest leaders consider technological iatrogenesis a direct but manageable consequence. As such, we offer traditional risk management tools, such as Failure Mode Effect Analysis and Root Cause Analysis, as proactive pre- and post-implementation evaluations to verify efficacy and maintain system integrity. Finally, we conclude by reviewing the implications for HIT adoption and provide guidance to health leaders undertaking HIT projects. This paper contributes to the health care literature in two ways: (1) identifies the problems reported in the literature when HIT projects are adopted by mature health organizations and (2) it advocates an organizational framework for adopting HIT projects to address system problems. As such, organizational development (OD) strategies can guide leaders in the strategic application of HIT projects within mature health organizations as solutions that stimulate safer and more reliable delivery systems.

HEALTH CARE ORGANIZATIONS AND HEALTH INFORMATION TECHNOLOGY

Complex Adaptive Systems

Health care organizations are complex adaptive systems (CAS; IOM, 2001; Plsek & Greenhalgh, 2001). CAS are defined by their structures, processes, and patterns (Capra, 2005). CAS are multifaceted and demonstrate self-organization as diverse agents interact spontaneously in nonlinear relationships (Anderson, Issel, & McDaniel, 2003). In health care (McDaniel & Driebe, 2001), agents, such as physicians, nurses, and pharmacists, act as information processors (Cilliers, 1998) and co-evolve with their environment (Casti, 1997), both locally, such as within nursing units, and organizationally. These agents act while utilizing a variety of methods to process information (Coleman, 1999) and to solve systemic problems within and across organizational layers (McDaniel & Driebe, 2001). Due to the unpredictable nature of human interactions, these interconnected actions contribute to "generative relationships" (Maxwell, 1996) that change the context for each agent. As such, even seemingly minor or micro-alterations to any process at any organizational level can stimulate unexpected system outcomes, either beneficial or detrimental.

Originating at the clinical micro-system, such as the pharmacy department, agents act to stimulate emergent properties that diffuse over time and throughout the organization. As improvement efforts, such as HIT adoption, modify agent interactions, the organizational outcome includes process realignments and system alterations. The system is adaptive since feedback mechanisms continually function at the agent level, in an attempt to maintain a dynamic homeostasis (Johnson, 2001). Homeostasis is achieved when individual agents contribute critical feedback to the system through decisions, actions, and at times inactions. Ultimately, this feedback mechanism cultivates adaptation in the CAS congruent with the emergence discussed in the DIT (Rogers, Medina, Rivera, & Wiley, 2005). The system, through its agents' work, is continually adjusted and managed at the micro-level in order to maintain system stability despite the macro-level changes introduced by leaders. Therefore, the system is collectively engineered at the micro-level as individual agents are stimulated to respond to decisions made by the leaders.

Emergent Organizational Properties

HIT is a label to describe a variety of computer and electronic applications such as bar code medication systems (BCMS; Poon et al., 2006), electronic health records (EHR; Sidrov, 2006), computerized provider order entry (CPOE; Bates, 2005b), and decision support systems (DSS; Kawamoto, Caitlin, Balas, & Lobach, 2005). HIT adoption projects result in emergent care delivery properties, specifically related to process alterations and agent responses to new working conditions. Emergence is derived from the altered interactions between clinicians, clinical departments, and system components as each new technological innovation is introduced into the system. Under the influence of new technology, the system becomes dynamic and overtly and, at times subvertly, responsive.

Technology promises to reduce costs and improve quality by streamlining processes, facilitating communication, reducing human error, organizing and storing data, and digitizing billing and reimbursement (Aspden et al., 2004, 2007). However, these promises have yet to be fully realized (Ash et al., 2007). One prominent concern is the additional complexity created by new technologies, such as CPOE, with the capability either to reduce adverse drug events and their associated negative consequences (Ford, McAlearney, Phillips, & Menachemi, 2008) or to further deteriorate system performance (Classen, Avery, & Bates, 2007).

For example, research indicates HIT adoption projects for a specific clinical function, such as CPOE, impact every clinical discipline, multiple administrative functions, and numerous clinical processes (Tucker, Nembhard, & Edmondson, 2007), yet CPOE initiatives often address larger superficial tasks assumed to be problems in the pharmacy or on nursing units while ignoring the related underlying complexities associated with system attributes such as policies and procedures. Technology can not only impact specific tasks, such as ordering medications, but also many associated processes and related people (Harrison et al., 2007; Koppel et al., 2008). Inadequate attention to detail manifests as technology vendors market products with little regulatory supervision and limited safety oversight; hence organizational complexities are ignored, negative consequences are understated, and positive attributes are overtly advertised.

Organizational Development

HIT adoption within mature health delivery systems is an overlooked OD concern (Ovretveit, Scott, Rundall, Shortell, & Brommels, 2007; Ramanujam & Goodman, 2003; Shortell, 2004). Beckhard (1969, p. 9) defined organizational development as an effort that is "(1) planned, (2) organization-wide, (3) managed from the top, to (4) increase organization effectiveness and health through (5) planned interventions in the organization's processes" utilizing scientific knowledge. In health organizations, HIT can operate as an agent of change by stimulating predictable system improvements and facilitating unpredictable process technicalities

(Drummond, Ferranti, Lehmann, & Lighter, 2009). For example, the idiosyncratic and potentially severe issues associated with CPOE implementation recently gave rise to novel unexpected outcome reports and adverse event discussions (Campbell, Sittig, Ash, Guappone, & Dykstra, 2007; Weiner, Kfuri, Chan, & Fowles, 2007).

Many organizations continue to approach HIT as a tool to address the obvious symptoms of dysfunction (Loewe & Domininquini, 2006) while leaving problematic remnants in place such as outdated systems or processes that do not fully integrate with the new technology (Harrison et al., 2007). Despite the realization that health care organizations are unsafe and often unreliable in the care delivered (Kohn, Corrigan, & Donaldson, 2000), organizational learning from failures is limited (Edmondson, 2004) and remains a significant challenge (Tucker & Edmondson, 2003). The problems associated with HIT implementation projects have become frequent and serious enough to stimulate publications such as *H.I.T. or Miss: Lessons Learned from Health Information Technology Implementations* to detail factual accounts of seldom discussed mishaps, errors, and adverse events (Leviss, 2010).

TECHNOLOGICAL IATROGENESIS

The ancient directive *Primum non nocere*, or "first do no harm," is the gold standard for every health care professional. For centuries this directive has supported the belief that patient harm caused by a health care professional, whether intentional action, preventable error, or accidental, is a punishable offense; this remains true in modern health care (Palmieri & Peterson, 2008). Iatrogenesis literally means "brought forth by the healer" (*iatros* means healer and *genesis* means brought forth by) and describes unintended consequences of care at the clinical level (Palmieri, Peterson, & Ford, 2007). But leaders and nonclinical professionals are also responsible for iatrogenic occurrences, directly and indirectly, that result from inadequate organizational system (Kohn et al., 2000) and process management (Palmieri et al., 2008).

Health care management and clinical publications often speak of the term iatrogenesis without specific reference to a model, conceptual framework, or philosophical underpinning. In the 1970s, Ivan Illich published *Medical Nemesis*, to describe the etiology of patient harm generated by poorly designed health delivery processes. Illich (1976) explicated the dangers related to the complex and dynamic interactions typically found in health systems. Cultural, social, and clinical iatrogenesis form the fundamental basis for his work. Given the considerable technological advancements in health care, Palmieri, Peterson, and Ford (2007) proposed a fourth iatrogenic type called technological iatrogenesis to address the emergent errors associated with HIT adoption (Aspden et al., 2007). The emergent errors named technological iatrogenesis are defined as *the unintended consequences to system integrity and the resulting system outcomes potentiated by incongruent organizational–technological interfaces.*

Etiology of Technological Iatrogenesis

Technological advancements represent a contemporary form of organizational development in health care (Palmieri, Peterson, Pesta, Flit, & Saettone, 2010). Although technology is an essential component for improvement (Aspden et al., 2007), "for successful implementation, it is secondary to organizational development" (Shortell, 2004, p. 12). Technologies evolve with organizations and transform even the most basic work processes (Harrison et al., 2007). Hence, HIT is a modern instrument for leaders to further potentiate change in health care organizations.

Technological iatrogenesis is a contemporary term to describe the technology-induced failures caused, at least in part, by superimposing new systems within and even upon discrete areas of mature systems (Palmieri et al., 2007). Layering technological "solutions" in organizations is common with technological integration (Harrison et al., 2007) in an attempt to solve particular system problems, yet this layering contributes to unanticipated changes in organizational processes that lead to novel and at times consequential issues (Koppel et al., 2005). In a qualitative study, health care professionals actively engaged in system redesign indicated successful projects involve coordinating changes across multiple organizational levels rather than within specific projects (Wang, Hyun, Harrison, Shortell, & Fraser, 2006).

Technological iatrogenesis is an element that aligns with the other three iatrogenesis types offered by Illich (social, cultural, and clinical). Iatrogenesis associated with system change is not apparent without the visible manifestation of counterproductivity (Illich, 1976), those issues that detract from system reliability. Technological iatrogenesis represents what Marcus, Schuler, Quell, and Humpfner (2002) describe as the visible and paradoxical, or unwanted, side-effects associated with altered organizational inputs that lead to unexpectedly varied outputs. Latent errors are one example of the unwanted side-effects that can lead to an unexpected or varied output such as patient harm. The IOM notes health errors result from system complexity (Aspden et al., 2004) while emphasizing the interdependent variables implicated in the manifestation of adverse events can be formed by technology (Aspden et al., 2007). Therefore, technology is a contemporary health tool that leaders should judiciously regard as a probable solution and a potential threat to system stability.

System stability is at risk as health facilities rapidly attempt to meet the recommendations that the IOM (2001) called for, including the use of electronic prescribing systems, such as CPOE, in all health care organizations by 2010; codified by an executive order and then delayed. This order heightened the urgency for adoption by hospitals, yet there is a noticeable lack of regulatory oversight and substantial variation in system architectures because basic industry standards remain unsettled (Taylor et al., 2005). In addition, many system implementations have experienced costly failures (Ammenwerth et al., 2006). Furthermore, there is ample evidence that electronic prescribing systems contribute to some types of adverse events and other medical errors (Koppel et al., 2005). For example, the period immediately following CPOE implementation resulted in significant increases in reported adverse drug events (Bradley, Steltenkamp, & Hite, 2006), and evidence of other substantial errors has been reported (Bates, 2005a; Bates, Leape, Cullen, & Laird, 1998). Collectively, these accounts depict the phenomena; technological iatrogenesis, stimulated by misaligned processes; disrupted agent interactions; and detached communication networks.

Health Information Technology Iatrogenesis Model

Illich's conceptual framework (1976), with the addition of technological iatrogenesis, explains the role of contemporary organizational attributes in the proliferation of adverse events. The four iatrogenic concerns are illustrated in the HITIM; see Fig. 1. Although we provide the entire model, this paper is principally concerned with the circle identified in Fig. 1 as technology. The point where the system is resilient to error, or the least harm is observed, is identified by Fig. 1a. Alternatively, the system with a propensity for iatrogenesis, or where frequent harm is observed, is illustrated by Fig. 1b. While Fig. 1a illustrates the safer environment, in reality the majority of organizations are represented by Fig. 1b because leaders overlook organizational complexity when addressing seemingly basic problems with HIT solutions. To the extent the various spheres of iatrogenesis do not overlap or

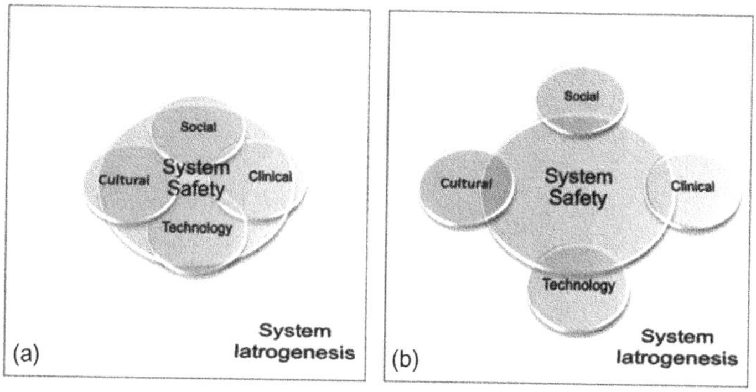

Fig. 1. Health Information Technology Iatrogenesis Model (HITIM). (a) Tendency for Resilient Safety Environment. (b) Propensity for Iatrogenic Safety Environment.

intersect, there is increased opportunity for system failure. For improved patient outcomes, health systems must become more resilient to errors (IOM, 2001; Reason, 2000). In order to progress health delivery systems using innovative technologies, further emphasis on HIT as an organizational development strategy is an essential antecedent and risk assessment a prerequisite for planning and implementation activities.

Previous scholarly work supports the basic model tenets. For example, when evaluating health organization complexity, McDaniel and Driebe (2001) argue neglecting underlying system relationships and the associated interdependent variables are the main causes of technology failures. Furthermore, Palmieri and colleagues (2008, 2010) include health organization complexity such as cultural attributes, social systems, technology innovation, and human resource management as fundamental components to consider when seeking to organize highly reliable processes. Finally, Harrison et al. (2007) offer the Socio-Technical Model to describe the human–user interfaces and the associated organizational attributes that lead to both expected and unexpected outcomes when mature health care systems adopt new technologies.

As we will explain in the coming sections, leaders often contemplate system changes or novel innovations as strategies to improve safety and quality; however, they rarely consider the four iatrogenic typologies that impact the greater organizational culture. Achieving the theoretical point of iatrogenic avoidance, as identified by Fig. 1b, is possible when leaders concentrate on technologies, such as CPOE, as an organizational change agent and a method for system reengineering rather than merely the installation of a technological product to solve specific problems, such as CPOE to help prevent medication errors.

Organizational Incongruence and Misalignment

Active Errors

Health care, with all the scientific advancements, is surprisingly far behind in technical development and system integration compared to other industries (Aspden et al., 2007). As an all-too-frequent artifact of poorly constructed health delivery systems (Helmreich, 2000; Kohn et al., 2000; Reason, 2000), iatrogenesis is a considerable, but controllable, health care reality (Page, 2004; Reason, Carthey, & de Leval, 2001). With continued technological advancement and system improvement, the outcomes that result from common errors (Chiles, 2002) represent "the failure of planned actions to achieve their desired goal, where this occurs without some unforeseeable or chance interventions" (Reason & Hobbs, 2003, p. 39). Reason, Carthey, and de Leval (2001) describe this failure as the "vulnerable system syndrome" and emphasize early identification, evidence-based treatment, and prevention strategies to address process and system failure. Furthermore, vulnerable systems remain suspect and prone to frequent errors (Battles, Kaplan, van der Schaaf, & Shea, 1998; van der Schaaf, 1992) when the iatrogenic typology is not appropriately regarded (Illich, 1976), or is insufficiently addressed by leaders (Reason, 1990).

To facilitate system redesign, errors first need to be accurately described (Benner et al., 2006; Wiegmann & Shappell, 2003) with emphasis on the etiology and the associated system attributes (Palmieri et al., 2008). Broadly stated, there are two products of iatrogenesis – latent and active errors (Reason, 1990, 2000). Active errors are actual breaches, or failures, in system defenses arising from dormant conditions that are energized by some type of stimuli (Reason, 1990; van der Schaaf, Lucas, & Hale, 1991), such as disturbances from system changes.

Manifesting from hidden conditions, active errors in patient care can result from strategic and operational decisions made at the highest organizational levels (Reason, 1998; Reason et al., 2001). Active error materialization provides immediate feedback about the presence of iatrogenic system properties (van der Schaaf, 2002). As such, leaders immediately respond to active errors with simplistic corrective strategies that often implicate a person instead of the system or management (Reason, 1998). In this case, Ramanujam and Rousseau

(2006) argue this challenge is organizational in nature and results from consequential leadership decisions focused on specific clinical problems while often missing the broader system implications. Understanding and recognizing hidden system properties is needed to reduce the likelihood of iatrogenic events (Hoff, Jameson, Hannan, & Flink, 2004), especially those active errors stimulated during HIT adoption.

Latent Errors

Technology implementation, such as CPOE, gives rise to expected benefits that can quickly become overshadowed by new and unanticipated problems (Zahn, Hicks, Blanchette, Keyes, & Cousins, 2006). Primarily, the problems are the production of latent, or unnoticed, errors. Latent conditions, or hidden malfunctions, have been characterized as situations placed into the system, as part of its design, or caused by actions taken by decision makers removed from the direct work (Sasou & Reason, 1999). Reason (1998, p. 10) provides a living comparison: "Latent conditions are to technological organizations what resident pathogens are to the human body." Similar to the pathogen–host analogy, many technology projects expose the existing system to larger-than-anticipated changes and incompatibility manifests progressively with worsening signs and symptoms. The resulting system instability is often exposed as an adverse event (Page, 2004).

As "accidents waiting to happen" (Whittingham, 2004), new technologies are rapidly added to existing system complexity to solve problems (Weiner et al., 2007). With inadequate organizational planning, however, the solution can lead to new problems generated by latent conditions (Reason, 1990). For example, CPOE implementation without workflow analysis can lead to seemingly inert changes to the medication delivery process, at the clinician level, but these can negatively impact system stability. As such, nurses (DeLucia, Ott, & Palmieri, 2010) and pharmacists often develop system workarounds, or improvisations (Palmieri et al., 2008) without management knowledge, in an attempt to reconcile the incongruent work conditions.

System alterations contribute to the occurrence of adverse clinical events that often harm patients (Rasmussen, 1990; Reason, 2000). More importantly, latent errors provide early and perhaps repetitive warnings of imminent accidents of consequence, such as adverse events (Reason, 1998; van der Schaaf, 2002) much like the tremors preceding an earthquake. Thus, in relation to health systems, latent error identification and intercession provide an important adverse event prevention strategy (Cook & O'Connor, 2005; Cook & Woods, 1994; Reason et al., 2001). As indicated by Fig. 1, errors are best identified prospectively as social, cultural, clinical, and technical system characteristics that should be considered in the planning process, prior to system changes.

Change Processes and Organizational Performance

Change processes expected to improve organizational performance often lead to unintended increases in the incidence of latent errors (Rasmussen, 1999; Reason, 1998). Researchers have completed empirical studies that conclude there is a propensity for unplanned changes in nursing performance and workflow following technology implementation (Cheng, Goldstein, Geller, & Levitt, 2003). In particular, CPOE (e.g., Koppel et al., 2005) and BCMA (e.g., Koppel et al., 2008) implementations have caused significant, but unanticipated, workflow changes. For example, nurses are required to engage in additional coordination activities with members of the care team who were not realized during the planning process. These workflow changes reduce the amount of time nurses can spend at the bedside (Rutherford, Lee, & Greiner, 2004), which contributes to time pressure and additional workload and increases cognitive load (DeLucia et al., 2010). These workflow changes often lead to adverse consequences (Kurtzman & Kizer, 2005), which manifest as e-iatrogenic errors (Weiner et al., 2007), the error product of technological iatrogenesis.

The advancement of technological solutions purposed to address health system problems frequently leads to increasingly complex processes. Absent adequate planning and system knowledge, problems can generate cascade iatrogenesis. The term "cascade iatrogenesis" describes a series of multiple issues with increasingly more severe effects (Rothschild, Bates, & Leape, 2000) ultimately leading to system maladjustments. This cascade is caused as a new technology is applied to the system in order to solve a previously recognized problem. The cascading of multiple complications, at different layers, set in action by errors (Reason, 2000; Rothschild et al., 2000) is what leads to HIT-related near and adverse events.

DIFFUSION OF INNOVATION AND TECHNOLOGICAL INTEGRATION

DIT offered by Rogers (2003) provides assistance to leaders intending to adopt HIT as a solution to improve mature systems. While the DIT framework describes various rates of innovation adoption, there are important parallel considerations to determine the "innovation fit" in a CAS. Decisions for HIT implementation ought to be evaluated by leaders while concurrently considering environmental factors, such as those related to the cultural, social, clinical, and technological domains identified in Fig. 1. The relevant characteristics of HIT innovation, relative advantage, complexity, observability, innovation, and adoption are described below.

Relative Advantage

First, leaders should decide if the relative advantage and the impact afforded by the technology are better than the relative norm from the user's perspective, not the top management team (TMT) perspective. This evaluation is the compatibility, or the degree to which the technological innovation is compatible with the experiential knowledge of the organization's collective members (Rogers, 2003). With technology in health care, the specific benefits to reduce system errors and to improve cost containment are not often understood. For example, Rosenstein and O'Daniel (2008) report the disruptions created by technological innovations in hospitals, such as to communication and clinical practices, may overshadow the potential system benefits. As such, prudent leaders should consider the possibilities of disruption early in the planning process.

Complexity

Complexity is the degree to which technological innovation is perceived as difficult or easy to implement and use. Rogers (2003) explains that the more complex an innovation is, the less likely the innovation will be successfully adopted. The degree to which the technological innovation can be tested or used prior to implementation is considered to be "trialability" (Rogers, 2003). By using "trials," an organization can help to decrease innovation adoption uncertainty and increase implementation effectiveness. These trials provide an opportunity for leaders to garner user feedback about implementation and usability issues. With CPOE implementation, the technology has been adopted within entire systems and then studied, with leaders expecting many benefits and little harm. Unfortunately, this strategy has yielded increased mortality (Han et al., 2005) and high rates of adverse medication events (Nebeker, Hoffman, Weir, Bennett, & Hurdle, 2005).

Observability

Rogers (2003) believes observability, the degree to which a technological innovation is viewable to organization members, is perceived as either positive or negative. In reality, observability reflects the extent to which the technological innovation is supported, or perhaps not discouraged, by organizational users. The innovation diffusion rate depends on the extent to which the innovation is tailored to the organization. This tailoring, or best-fit provision, determines the adoption impact and the user commitment to the technology. Rogers (2003) considers innovation complexity to be a key attribute that lessens the need for tailoring to positively influence diffusion. Reports have surfaced about the evolution of stealth errors, such as computerized physician orders not being completed or electronic medical record data disappearing within mature systems, especially those previously considered to be high-reliability systems (Kuehn, 2009).

Innovation

Innovation within organizations, such as hospitals, results in consequences that manifest as system enhancements or detractions and/or result in user adoption or rejection. As such, Rogers (2003) describes three classifications of consequences: desirable or undesirable (related to function or dysfunctional), direct or indirect (immediate or second-order responses), and anticipated or unanticipated consequences (recognized and intended consequences). Since change agents during innovation adoption frequently focus on potential system improvements while discounting possible iatrogenic consequences, it is important to bring these consequences from the background to the foreground. By incorporating heightened awareness and vigilant monitoring in HIT implementation projects, leaders can minimize the manifestation of iatrogenic situations, or at least attempt to mitigate the resulting consequences with early detection.

Adoption

Adoption is important in HIT as both CPOE and EHR have been federally mandated in the United States (Aspden et al., 2007; Bush, 2004). The role of these technologies will expand in the future of hospitals and physician practices. Early indications suggest that the transition will not be easy and will cause tremendous issues in the health system. Presently, the innovators and early adopters are beginning to emerge (Jha et al., 2009). With these implementations, the previously discussed financial costs, poor operational performance, and unanticipated system issues contribute to questions about further adoption. The slow response to innovations adoption and resistance to the diffusion is strong (Ford, Menachemi, & Phillips, 2006). As such, it is unlikely that the adoption will occur by the mandated timeframe, especially where EHR are concerned (Ford, Menachemi, Peterson, & Huerta, 2009; Menachemi, Ford, Beitsch, & Brooks, 2007).

MANAGEMENT STRATEGIES

There are a number of tools leaders can utilize in order to reduce the impact of technological issues in HIT implementation projects. In this section, we briefly address the contributions Root Cause Analysis (RCA) and Failure Mode and Effect Analysis (FMEA) can provide to leaders contemplating HIT projects. These tools assist leaders in understanding organizational weaknesses by dissecting system properties to comprehensively examine the hierarchical processes and to identify the iatrogenic properties that could originate from HIT adoption. The Joint Commission mandates the strategic use of improvement tools such as RCA and FMEA for quality improvement. While FMEA is used as a prospective accident prevention technique, RCA is used as a retrospective accident analysis.

Root Cause Analysis

The RCA is a comprehensive adverse event review. This retrospective approach to evaluate failure causation is described by the Joint Commission as a systematic investigation that elucidates the "process that allowed an error to occur and identifies factors that underlie variability in performance" (Torpy, 2002, p. 178). The RCA can identify the causative etiology for error cascades with a process that identifies basic or casual factors underlying performance variation (Joint Commission Resources, 2007). As the system approach to accident analysis is preferred to human blame, accredited hospitals are required to conduct thorough investigations of each sentinel event, or the most serious iatrogenic occurrence where a patient is harmed or killed. Using a prescribed process for identifying the causal factors that trigger deviation in performance, the RCA permits a cautious survey of the health system to determine the cultural, social, clinical, and technological implications. Often, system abnormalities in areas unrelated to the causative agents are exposed, which can lead to further system intelligence.

Failure Mode and Effect Analysis

While the RCA provides an important mechanism to minimize the probability of repeated events (Battles et al., 1998), the FMEA offers proactive knowledge about potential iatrogenic system properties that may result from new processes or technologies. FMEA is a risk assessment technique, which allows planners to systematically identify system innovation problems throughout the planning process (Stamatis, 2003). Undertaken early in the conceptual design stage and prior to project implementation, FMEA works to highlight potential breaches in processes that can result in system failure (Smetzer & Cohen, 1999). As such, this method is a proactive approach to minimize the probability of adverse effects arising from the iatrogenic system properties (Cohen, Davis, & Senders, 1994; Senders & Senders, 1999).

"Failure mode" describes the place(s) where the system may not perform as anticipated. The area for system concern, or the potential failure(s), leads to an extensive examination and assessment. This "effect analysis" reviews the consequences that might result from each identified but unanticipated failure (DeRosier, Stalhandske, Bagian, & Nudell, 2002). When analyzing a failure, the seriousness of consequence, the probability for failure, and the likelihood system defenses can detect iatrogenesic issues are carefully considered. Leaders need to ask the following questions: (1) what can fail; (2) how can it fail; and (3) what is the cost of failure (Smetzer & Cohen, 1999). For each identified failure mode, system alternatives are considered and change modifications are implemented to minimize the probability for iatrogenic consequences.

With system maturation, signs and symptoms that depict the actual state of system stability begin to surface. Unexpected signs and symptoms often indicate the presence of iatrogenic properties. These iatrogenic attributes signal the probability of future failure and require immediate analysis. Over time, as more system intelligence is gathered, the FMEA can be used to review an aging innovation to determine the degree of system–technology compatibility (DeRosier et al., 2002). The more complex the health care process, the more essential the expert understanding of a system's potential failure modes to minimize iatrogenesis and to ensure the system's expected performance (Palmieri et al., 2008). Diligent FMEA utilization is especially important when layers of process innovations are constructed into a specific system where complexity is increased (Stamatis, 2003).

Both RCA and FMEA activities involve human recovery efforts described by van der Schaff and colleagues (2002, 1991) as an important verification feature where system usability, especially technical factors, is evaluated from the agent's perspective in order to identify latent iatrogenic properties. As is the case with technology implementation projects, mature systems are significantly altered by computerized instruments that impact previously manual processes. FMEA, when utilized early in the planning process, can elucidate latent problems while there is ample time to find solutions and make the appropriate adjustments to the project.

CONCLUSION

Since the inception of the safety movement, leaders seldom seek knowledge from the disciplines of human factors (DeLucia, Ott, & Palmieri, 2009; Leape et al., 1998), safety science (Battles et al., 1998; van der Schaaf, 2002), and organizational development (Alexander, Weiner, Shortell, Baker, & Becker, 2006; Shortell, 2004; Wang et al., 2006) as they work to become a high-risk but low-failure industry (Pidgeon, 1998; Reason, 1998; Roberts, 1990; Roberts, Madsen, Desai, & Van Stralen, 2005). Balancing technological innovation with the role of leadership to develop safety-oriented cultures generates continued tension (Reason, 2000). Designing a functional safety culture and concurrently managing the financial status of a health care organization presents additional challenges for leaders (Joyce, Boaden, & Esmail, 2005). Furthermore, health leaders face increasing pressures for action as they contemplate the penalties soon to be imposed by insurers and the government for not maintaining a safety culture, the culture that exhibits limited iatrogenic properties and is resilient enough to prevent system failures.

Leaders overwhelmed with system problems, innovative technologies, and mounting external pressures engage in "problemistic search" (Cyert & March, 1963, p. 120) as they scan the environment for quick solutions to pressing problems. Frequently, leaders discover the quick solution is to "attribute human unreliability to unwanted variability and strive to eliminate it" (Reason, 2000, p. 770). Consequently, most incident reporting systems used by organizations to identify and remove iatrogenic system properties describe what happened while paying modest attention to the underlying iatrogenic contributors (Battles et al., 1998). Leaders can further appreciate the sources of system error with focus attention on iatrogenesis. The concurrent pressures created by unrecognized cultural, social, clinical, and technological iatrogenic traits contribute to the unreliable processes and the adverse outcomes leaders seek to eliminate (Palmieri & Peterson, 2008). In addressing these organizational issues, leaders can organize reliable systems that achieve high-quality outcomes, an important measure of organizational effectiveness (Ramanujam & Goodman, 2003; Vogus & Welbourne, 2003).

Developing better health care systems through HIT implementation necessitates an organizational approach (Pettigrew, Ferlie, & McKee, 1992) in order to avoid costly disturbances to care delivery. Organizational cultures are created, supported, and sustained when leaders model the expected organizational values (Bennis, 1989). By understanding how culture influences behavior and process, leaders can proactively identify iatrogenic system properties and support organizational change as their response. This system approach to preventing critical failures through organizational development will contribute to improved organizational safety. As HIT innovations diffuse throughout organizations, leaders must be aware of the obstacles to innovation and strive to overcome them (see Box 1). The DIT framework can guide leaders in this regard.

Despite endorsements for developing increased HIT capacity in health organizations (IOM, 2007) and the approach for adoption advocated in this paper, the organizational characteristics and operational strategies necessary for successful adoption remain largely unknown (Jha et al., 2009).

Box 1. Common Obstacles to Successful HIT Adoption Projects.

1) short-term management focus
2) insufficient resources and inadequate time
3) unrealistic payoff and development timeframes
4) misaligned rewards not structured to support innovation adoption and implementation
5) incomplete and disorganized innovation plan
6) mistaken perception that innovation is an inherently risky undertaking (Loewe & Domininquini, 2006)

Although HIT is reported to impact social processes, human factors, workflows, information exchanges, and interpersonal relationships (Chaudhry et al., 2006; Harrison et al., 2007; DeLucia et al., 2009), researchers have only recently designed the first HIT adoption study to understand these phenomena in order to offer leaders evidence-based strategies and practices to facilitate successful HIT adoptions in their facilitates (Kitzmiller, Anderson, & McDaniel, 2010). Health leaders must remain focused on supporting evidence-based practices for both clinical and operational changes in care delivery.

Adopting HIT with attention to planning and development can achieve more cost-effective and reliable systems. However, in the quest for success, vigilant organizational awareness is necessary to identify and prevent costly technological failures. The HITIM provides leaders with assistance in considering all HIT improvements as major organizational changes instead of isolated technological solutions to solve a focused problem. Recognizing the opportunity for incongruent technology–organizational conditions, leaders will teach their organizations to anticipate new system threats. Organizations focused on adopting HIT while understanding the etiology of technological iatrogensis will develop resilient systems with improved quality and safety, and develop the efficiencies required to achieve improved financial outcomes.

ACKNOWLEDGMENTS

We would like to thank David Saettone, from Pacifico Peruano Suiza and Guillermo Garrido Lecca and Michel Flit from PacificoSalud for their support in completing this work. We recognize contributions of Drs. Sharron Docherty and Ruth Anderson from Duke University for their guidance and mentorship in earlier versions of this work. In addition, we would like to acknowledge the sustentative comments we received from the anonymous reviewers at the Academy of Management, specifically for the theoretical guidance and practitioner application feedback. Finally, we are grateful for the Advances in Health Care Management anonymous reviewers' critical assessments and suggestions for improvements.

The final version of this work was funded in part through the support of PacificoSalud. In addition, support was provided by the Center for Health Information, Education and Research at Texas Tech University which we gratefully acknowledge. Finally, the content related to health information technology was funded in part by Duke Health Technology Solutions and the content related to organizational culture and development were funded in part by a Clinical and Translational Science Award (T-32) for the pilot study, Organizational Safety and Culture Survey Reliability and Validity (Palmieri, PI) from the Clinical Research Training Programs of the National Institutes of Health, Road Map for Medical Research at the Duke Translational Medicine Institute (Califf, PI).

REFERENCES

Alexander, J. A., Weiner, B. J., Shortell, S. M., Baker, L. C., & Becker, M. P. (2006). The role of organizational infrastructure in implementation of hospitals' quality improvement. *Hospital Topics*, *84*(1), 11–20.

Ammenwerth, E., Talmon, J., Ash, J. S., Bates, D. W., Beuscart-Zephir, M. C., Duhamel, A., Elkin, P. L., Gardner, R. M., & Geissbuhler, A. (2006). Impact of CPOE on mortality rates: Contradictory findings, important messages. *Methods of Information in Medicine*, *45*(6), 586–593.

Anderson, R. A., Issel, M. L., & McDaniel, R. R. (2003). Nursing homes as complex adaptive systems: Relationship between management practice and resident outcomes. *Nursing Research*, *52*(1), 12–21.

Ash, J. S., Sittig, D. F., Poon, E. G., Guappone, K., Campbell, E., & Dykstra, R. H. (2007). The extent and importance of unintended consequences related to computerized provider order entry. *Journal of the American Medical Informatics Association*, *14*(4), 415–423.

Aspden, P., Corrigan, J. M., Wolcott, J., & Erickson, S. M. (2004). *Patient safety: Achieving a new standard for care*. Washington, DC: National Academy Press.

Aspden, P., Wolcott, J., Bootman, J. L., & Cronenwett, L. R. (Eds). (2007). *Preventing medication errors: Quality chasm series*. Washington, DC: National Academies Press.

Bates, D. W. (2005a). Computerized physician order entry and medication errors: Finding a balance. *Journal of Biomedical Informatics*, *38*(4), 250–261.

Bates, D. W. (2005b). Physicians and ambulatory electronic health records. *Health Affairs*, *24*(5), 1180–1189.

Bates, D. W., Leape, L. L., Cullen, D. J., & Laird, N. (1998). Effect of computerized physician order entry and a team intervention on prevention of serious medical errors. *Journal of the American Medical Association*, *280*, 1311–1316.

Battles, J. B., Kaplan, H. S., van der Schaaf, T. W., & Shea, C. E. (1998). The attributes of medical event reporting systems for transfusion medicine. *Archives of Pathology and Laboratory Medicine*, *122*, 231–238.

Battles, J. B., & Keyes, M. A. (2002). Technology and patient safety: A two-edged sword. *Biomedical Instrument Technology*, *36*(1), 84–88.

Beckhard, R. (1969). *Organization development: Strategies and models*. Reading, MA: Addison Wesley.

Benner, P., Malloch, K., Sheets, V., Bitz, K., Emrich, L., Thomas, M. B., Bowen, K., Scott, K., Patterson, L., Schwed, K., & Farrell, M. (2006). TERCAP: Creating a national database on nursing errors. *Harvard Health Policy Review*, *7*(1), 48–63.

Bennis, W. G. (1989). *On becoming a leader*. Reading, MA: Perseus Publishing.

Berta, W. B., & Baker, R. (2004). Factors that impact the transfer and retention of best practices for reducing error in hospitals. *Health Care Management Review, 29*(2), 90–97.

Bohmer, R. M., & Edmondson, A. C. (2001). Organizational learning in health care. *Health Forum Journal, 44*(2), 32–35.

Bradley, V. M., Steltenkamp, C. L., & Hite, K. B. (2006). Evaluation of reported medication errors before and after implementation of computerized practitioner order entry. *Journal of Healthcare Information Management, 20*(4), 46–53.

Bush, G. W. (2004). *Executive Order 13335 — Incentives for the Use of Health Information Technology and Establishing the Position of the National Health Information Technology Coordinator*. Available at http://a257.g.akamaitech.net/7/257/2422/14mar20010800/edocket.access.gpo.gov/2004/pdf/04-10024.pdf. Retrieved May 16, 2007.

Campbell, E. M., Sittig, D. F., Ash, J. S., Guappone, K. P., & Dykstra, R. H. (2007). In reply to: "e-Iatrogenesis: The most critical consequence of CPOE and other HIT". *Journal of the American Medical Informatics Association, 14*(3), 387–388.

Capra, F. (2005). Complexity and life. *Theory Culture Society, 22*(5), 33–44.

Casti, J. L. (1997). *Would-Be Worlds*. New York: Wiley.

Chaudhry, B., Wang, J., Wu, S., Maglione, M., Mojica, W., Roth, E., Morton, S. C., & Shekelle, P. G. (2006). Systematic review: Impact of health information technology on quality, efficiency, and costs of medical care. *Annals of Internal Medicine, 144*(10), 742–752.

Cheng, C. H., Goldstein, M. K., Geller, E., & Levitt, R. E. (2003). The effects of CPOE on ICU workflow: An observational study. *AMIA Annual Symposium Proceedings*, pp. 150–154.

Chiles, J. R. (2002). *Inviting disaster: Lessons from the edge of technology*. New York: HarperCollins Publishers.

Cilliers, P. (1998). *Complexity and post modernism: Understanding complex systems*. New York: Routledge.

Classen, D. C., Avery, A. J., & Bates, D. W. (2007). Evaluation of certification of computerized provider order entry systems. *Journal of American Medical Informatics Association, 14*(1), 48–55.

Cohen, M. R., Davis, N. M., & Senders, J. (1994). Failure mode and effects analysis: A novel approach to avoiding dangerous medication errors and accidents. *Hospital Pharmacy, 29*, 319–330.

Coleman, H. J. (1999). What enables self-organizing behavior in business. *Emergence, 1*(1), 33–48.

Cook, R. I., & O'Connor, M. F. (2005). Thinking about accidents and systems. In: H. Manasse & K. Thompson (Eds), *Improving medication safety*. Mathesda, MD: American Society for Health-System Pharmacists.

Cook, R. I., & Woods, D. D. (1994). Operating at the sharp end: The complexity of human error. In: M. S. Bogner (Ed.), *Human error in medicine* (pp. 285–310). Hinsdale, NJ: Lawrence Erlbaum.

Cyert, R., & March, J. G. (1963). *A behavorial theory of the firm*. Englewood Cliffs, NJ: Prentice-Hall.

DeLucia, P. R., Ott, T. E., & Palmieri, P. A. (2009). Performance in nursing. In: F. F. Durso (Ed.), *Reviews of human factors and ergonomics* (Vol. 5, pp. 1–40). Santa Monica, CA: Human Factors and Ergonomics Society.

DeLucia, P. R., Ott, T. E., & Palmieri, P. A. (2010). Interruptions and cognitive processes in nursing: Review, analysis, recommendations. *Proceedings of the Annual Meeting of the Human Factors and Ergonomics Society, 53*(11), 743.

DeRosier, J., Stalhandske, E., Bagian, J. P., & Nudell, T. (2002). Using health care failure mode and effect analysis: The VA national center for patient safety's prospective risk analysis system. *The Joint Commission Journal on Quality and Patient Safety*, *28*(5), 248–267.

Devers, K. J., Pham, H. H., & Lui, G. (2004). What is driving hospitals' patient-safety efforts? *Health Affairs*, *23*(3), 103–115.

Drummond, W. H., Ferranti, J. M., Lehmann, C. U., & Lighter, D. E. (2009). Complexity in healthcare information technology systems. In: C. U. Lehmann, G. R. Kim & K.B. Johnson (Eds), *Pediatric Informatics* (pp. 83–117). New York: Springer.

Edmondson, A. C. (2004). Learning from failure in health care: Frequent opportunities, pervasive barriers. *Quality & Safety in Health Care*, *13*(suppl 2), ii3–ii9.

Ford, E. W., McAlearney, A., Phillips, M. T., & Menachemi, N. (2008). Computerized Physician Order Entry (CPOE) adoption in U.S. hospitals: Can the federal mandate be met? *International Journal of Medical Informatics*, *77*(8), 539–545.

Ford, E. W., Menachemi, N., Peterson, L. T., & Huerta, T. R. (2009). Resistance is futile: But it is slowing the pace of EHR adoption nonetheless. *Journal of the American Medical Informatics Association*, *16*(4), 274–281.

Ford, E. W., Menachemi, N., & Phillips, M. T. (2006). Predicting the adoption of electronic health records by physicians: When will health care be paperless? *Journal of the American Medical Informatics Association*, *13*(1), 106–112.

Han, Y. Y., Carcillo, J. A., Venkataraman, S. T., Clark, R. S., Watson, R. S., Nguyen, T. C., Bayir, H., & Orr, R. A. (2005). Unexpected increased mortality after implementation of a commercially sold computerized physician order entry system. *Pediatrics*, *116*(6), 1506–1512.

Harrison, M. I., Koppel, R., & Bar-Lev, S. (2007). Unintended consequences of information technologies in health care: An interactive sociotechnical analysis. *Journal of the American Medical Informatics Association*, *14*(5), 542–549.

Helmreich, R. L. (2000). On error management: Lessons from aviation. *British Medical Journal*, *320*, 781–785.

Hillestad, R., Bigelow, J., Bower, A., Girosi, F., Meili, R., Scoville, R., & Taylor, R. (2005). Can electronic medical record systems transform healthcare? An assessment of potential health benefits, savings, and costs. *Health Affairs*, *24*(5), 1103–1117.

Hoff, T., Jameson, L., Hannan, E., & Flink, E. (2004). A review of the literature examining linkages between organizational factors, medical errors, and patient safety. *Medical Care Research and Review*, *61*(1), 3–37.

Illich, I. (1976). *Medical nemesis: The expropriation of health* (1st ed.). New York: Pantheon Books.

Institute of Medicine (IOM). (2001). *Crossing the quality chasm: A new health system for the 21st century*. Washington, DC: National Academy Press.

Jha, A. K., DesRoches, C. M., Campbell, E. G., Donelan, K., Rao, S. R., Ferris, T. G., Shields, A., Rosenbaum, S., & Blumenthal, D. (2009). Use of electronic health records in U.S. hospitals. *New England Journal of Medicine*, *360*(16), 1628–1638.

Johnson, K. (2001). Barriers that impede the adoption of pediatric information technology. *Archives of Pediatrics & Adolescent Medicine*, *155*(12), 1374–1379.

Joint Commission Resources. (2007). *Front line of defense: The role of nurses in preventing sentinel events* (2nd ed.). Oakbrook Terrace, IL: Joint Commission Resources.

Joyce, P., Boaden, R., & Esmail, A. (2005). Managing risk: A taxonomy of error in health policy. *Health Care Analysis*, *13*(4), 337–346.

Kawamoto, K. H., Caitlin, A., Balas, E. A., & Lobach, D. F. (2005). Improving clinical practice using clinical decision support systems: A systematic review of trials to identify features critical to success. *British Journal of Medicine*, *330*(7494), 765–774.

Kitzmiller, R. R., Anderson, R. A., & McDaniel, R. R. (2010). Making sense of health information technology implementation: A qualitative study protocol. *Implementation Science*, *5*(95).

Kohn, L. T., Corrigan, J. M., & Donaldson, M. S. (Eds). (2000). *To err is human: Building a safer health system*. Washington, DC: National Academy Press.

Koppel, R., Metlay, J. P., Cohen, A., Abaluck, B., Localio, A. R., Kimmel, S. E., & Strom, B.L. (2005). Role of computerized physician order entry systems in facilitating medication errors. *Journal of the American Medical Association*, *293*(10), 1197–1203.

Koppel, R., Wetterneck, T., Telles, J. L., & Karsh, B.-T. (2008). Workarounds to barcode medication administration systems: Their occurrences, causes, and threats to patient safety. *Journal of the American Medical Informatics Association*, *15*(4), 408–423.

Kuehn, B. M. (2009). IT vulnerabilities highlighted by errors, malfunctions at Veterans' Medical Centers. *Journal of American Medical Informatics Association*, *301*(9), 919–920.

Kurtzman, E. T., & Kizer, K. W. (2005). Evaluating the performance and contribution of nurses to achieve an environment of safety. *Nursing Administrative Quarterly*, *29*(1), 14–23.

Leape, L. L., Wood, D. D., Hatlie, M. J., Kizer, K. W., Schroeder, S. A., & Lundberg, G. A. (1998). Promoting patient safety by reducing medical errors. *Journal of the American Medical Association*, *280*(16), 1444–1447.

Leviss, L. (2010). *H.I.T. or miss: Lessons learned from Health Information Technology implementations*. Chicago: AHIMA Press.

Loewe, P., & Domininquini, J. (2006). Overcoming the barriers to effective innovation. *Strategy and Leadership*, *34*(1), 24–31.

Marcus, B., Schuler, H., Quell, P., & Humpfner, G. (2002). Measuring counterproductivity: Development and initial validation of a German self-report questionnaire. *International Journal of Selection and Assessment*, *10*(1), 18–35.

Maxwell, J. (1996). *Qualitative research design: An interpretative approach*. Thousand Oaks, CA: Sage.

McDaniel, R. R., & Driebe, D. J. (2001). Complexity science and health care management. *Advances in Health Care Management*, *2*, 11–36.

Menachemi, N., Ford, E. W., Beitsch, L. M., & Brooks, R. G. (2007). Incomplete EHR adoption: Late uptake of patient safety and cost control functions. *American Journal of Medical Quality*, *22*(5), 319–326.

Nebeker, J. R., Hoffman, J. M., Weir, C. R., Bennett, C. L., & Hurdle, J. F. (2005). High rates of adverse drug events in a highly computerized hospital. *Archives of Internal Medicine*, *165*(10), 1111–1116.

Ovretveit, J., Scott, T., Rundall, T. G., Shortell, S. M., & Brommels, M. (2007). Improving quality through effective implementation of information technology in healthcare. *International Journal of Quality and Health Care*, *19*(5), 259–266.

Page, A. (Ed.) (2004). *Keeping patients safe: Transforming the work environment of nurses*. Washington, DC: National Academies Press.

Palmieri, P. A., DeLucia, P. R., Peterson, L. T., Ott, T. E., & Green, A. (2008). The anatomy and physiology of error in adverse health care events. In: G. T. Savage & E. W. Ford (Eds), *Patient safety and health care management* (Vol. 7, pp. 33–68). Bingley, UK: Emerald Group Publishing Limited.

Palmieri, P. A., & Peterson, L. T. (2008). Technological iatrogenesis: An expansion of the medical nemesis framework to improve modern healthcare organization performance. *Proceedings of the Annual Meeting of the Western Academy of Management*, Oakland, CA, March 26–29.

Palmieri, P. A., Peterson, L. T., & Ford, E. W. (2007). Technological iatrogenesis: New risks force heightened management awareness. *Journal of Health Care Risk Management, 27*(4), 19.

Palmieri, P. A., Peterson, L. T., Pesta, B. J., Flit, M. A., & Saettone, D. M. (2010). Safety culture as a contemporary healthcare construct: Theoretical review, research assessment, and translation to human resource management. In M. D. Fottler, N. Khatri, & G. T. Savage (Eds), *Strategic human resource management in health care*. Advances in Health Care Management (Vol. 9, pp. 97–133). Bingley, UK: Emerald.

Pettigrew, A. M., Ferlie, E., & McKee, L. (1992). *Shaping strategic change: Making change in large organizations*. London: Sage.

Pidgeon, N. (1998). *Safety culture: Key theoretical issues* (Vol. 12). New York: Routledge.

Plsek, P. E., & Greenhalgh, T. (2001). Complexity science: The challenge of complexity in health care. *British Medical Journal, 323*(7313), 625–628.

Poon, E., Cina, J., Churchill, W., Patel, N., Featherstone, E., Rothchild, J., Keohane, C., Whittemore, A., Bates, D., & Gandhi, T. (2006). Medication dispensing errors and potential adverse drug events before and after implementing bar code technology in the pharmacy. *Annals of Internal Medicine, 145*(5), 426–434.

Ramanujam, R., & Goodman, P. S. (2003). Latent errors and adverse organizational consequences: A conceptualization. *Journal of Organizational Behavior, 24*(7), 815–836.

Ramanujam, R., & Rousseau, D. M. (2006). The challenges are organizational not just clinical. *Journal of Organizational Behavior, 27*(7), 811–827.

Rasmussen, J. (1990). The role of error in organizing behavior. *Ergonomics, 33*, 1185–1199.

Rasmussen, J. (1999). The concept of human error: Is it useful for the design of safe systems in health care? In: C. Vincent & B. deMoll (Eds), *Risk and safety in medicine* (pp. 31–47). London: Elsevier.

Reason, J. T. (1990). *Human error*. New York: Cambridge University Press.

Reason, J. T. (1998). *Managing the risks of organizational accidents*. Aldershot: Ashgate.

Reason, J. T. (2000). Human error: Models and management. *British Medical Journal, 320*(7237), 768–770.

Reason, J. T., Carthey, J., & de Leval, M. R. (2001). Diagnosing "vulnerable system syndrome": An essential prerequisite to effective risk management. *Quality & Safety in Health Care, 10*(S2), 21–25.

Reason, J. T., & Hobbs, A. (2003). *Managing maintenance error: A practical guide*. Aldershot: Ashgate.

Roberts, K. H. (1990). Some characteristics of one type of high reliability organization. *Organization Science, 1*(2), 160–176.

Roberts, K. H., Madsen, P., Desai, V., & Van Stralen, D. (2005). A case of the birth and death of a high reliability healthcare organisation. *Quality & Safety in Health Care, 14*, 216–220.

Rogers, E. M. (2003). *Diffusion of innovations* (5th ed.). New York, NY: Free Press.

Rogers, E. M., Medina, U., Rivera, M., & Wiley, C. (2005). Complex adaptive systems and the diffusion of innovations. *The Innovation Journal: The Public Sector Innovation Journal, 10*(3), 579–584.

Rosenstein, A. H., & O'Daniel, M. (2008). A survey of the impact of disruptive behaviors and communication defects on patient safety. *Joint Commission Journal of Quality and Patient Safety*, *34*(8), 464–471.
Rothschild, J. M., Bates, D. W., & Leape, L. L. (2000). Preventable medical injuries in older patients. *Archives of Internal Medicine*, *160*(18), 2717–2728.
Rutherford, P., Lee, B., & Greiner, A. (2004). *Transforming care at the bedside*. Cambridge, MA: Institute for Healthcare Improvement.
Sasou, K., & Reason, J. T. (1999). Team Errors: Definitions and taxonomy. *Reliability Engineering and System Safety*, *65*(1), 1–9.
Senders, J. W., & Senders, S. J. (1999). Introduction to failure mode and effects analysis in medicine. In: M. R. Cohen (Ed.), *Medication errors: Causes, prevention and risk management* (pp. 561–565). Washington, DC: American Pharmaceutical Association.
Shortell, S. M. (2004). Increasing value: A research agenda for addressing the managerial and organizational challenges facing health care delivery in the United States. *Medical Care Research Review*, *61*(Supp 3), 12S–30S.
Sidrov, J. (2006). It ain't necessarily so: The electronic health record and the unlikely prospect of reducing health care costs. *Health Affairs*, *25*(4), 1079–1085.
Smetzer, J. L., & Cohen, M. R. (1999). An application of failure mode and effects analysis. In: M.R. Cohen (Ed.), *Medication errors: Causes, prevention and risk management* (pp. 565–576). Washington, DC: American Pharmaceutical Association.
Stamatis, D. H. (2003). *Failure mode and effect analysis: FMEA from theory to execution* (2nd ed.). Milwaukee, WI: Quality Press.
Taylor, R., Bower, A., Girosi, F., Bigelow, J., Fonkych, K., & Hillestad, R. (2005). Promoting health information technology: Is there a case for more-aggressive government action? *Health Affairs*, *24*(5), 1234–1245.
Thompson, D. I., Osberoff, J., Classen, D., & Sittig, D. F. (2007). A review of methods to estimate the benefits of electronic medical records in hospitals and the need for a national benefits database. *Journal of Healthcare Information Management*, *21*(1), 62–68.
Torpy, J. M. (2002). Raising health care quality: Process, measures, and system failure. *Journal of the American Medical Association*, *287*(2), 177–178.
Tucker, A. L., & Edmondson, A. (2003). Why hospitals don't learn from failures: Organizational and psychological dynamics that inhibit system change. *California Management Review*, *45*(2), 1–18.
Tucker, A. L., Nembhard, I. M., & Edmondson, A. C. (2007). Implementing new practices: An empirical study of organizational learning in hospital intensive care units. *Management Science*, *53*(6), 894–907.
van der Schaaf, T. W. (1992). *Near miss reporting in the chemical process industry*. Eindhoven, Netherlands: Technische Universiteit Eindhoven.
van der Schaaf, T. W. (2002). Medical applications of industrial safety science. *Quality & Safety in Health Care*, *11*(3), 205–206.
van der Schaaf, T. W., Lucas, D. A., & Hale, A. R. (1991). *Near miss reporting as a safety tool*. Oxford: Butterworth-Heinemann.
Vogus, T. J., & Welbourne, T. M. (2003). Structuring for high reliability: HR practices and mindful processes in reliability-seeking organizations. *Journal of Organizational Behavior*, *24*(7), 877–903.

Wachter, R. M. (2004). The end of the beginning: Patient safety five years after "To err is human." *Health Affairs*, W4, 534–545. Available at http://www.healthaffairs.org

Wang, M. C., Hyun, J. K., Harrison, M., Shortell, S. M., & Fraser, I. (2006). Redesigning health systems for quality: Lessons from emerging practices. *Joint Commission Journal of Quality and Patient Safety*, *32*(11), 599–611.

Weiner, J. P., Kfuri, T., Chan, K., & Fowles, J. B. (2007). "e-Iatrogenesis:" The most critical unintended consequence of CPOE and other HIT. *Journal of the American Medical Informatics Association*, *14*(3), 387–388.

Whittingham, R. B. (2004). *The blame machine: Why human error causes accidents*. Amsterdam: Elsevier Butterworth-Heinemann.

Wiegmann, D. A., & Shappell, S. A. (2003). *A human error approach to aviation accident analysis: The human factors analysis and classification system*. Aldershot: Ashgate Publishing Company.

World Health Organization. (2006). World alliance for patient safety. Available at www.who.int/patientsafety. Retrieved February 9, 2008.

Zahn, C., Hicks, R., Blanchette, C., Keyes, M., & Cousins, D. (2006). Potential benefits and problems with computerized prescriber order entry: Analyses of a voluntary medication error-reporting database. *American Journal of Health System Pharmacy*, *63*(4), 353–358.

Zhan, C., & Miller, M. R. (2003). Excess length of stay, charges, and mortality attributable to medical injuries during hospitalization. *Journal of the American Medical Association*, *290*(14), 1868–1874.

HIT MANAGEMENT RESEARCH AND THE TIP OF THE ICEBERG: SETTING A RESEARCH AGENDA – A COMMENTARY

Eric W. Ford and Nir Menachemi

In 2009, the Health Information Technology for Economic and Clinical Health Act (HITECH) was signed into law. This Act, part of the broader "stimulus" legislation, represents the U.S.'s largest investment in health information technology (HIT) to date. More importantly, it sets a vision and provides a plan intended to transform the U.S. health care system to a safer, more efficient place to receive care. To that end, the Act seeks to fundamentally change the path HIT applications' adoption and implementation was taking to ensure that "meaningful use" and interoperability are achieved. However, such bold and sweeping changes will not come without unintended consequences, and their broad scope makes measuring the new public policy's success a challenge.

HITECH made $27 billion in incentive payments available to providers interested in adopting, implementing, and "meaningfully using" certain HIT applications (e.g., electronic health records). Given this large investment in the nation's HIT infrastructure, the incentive payments also represent a natural experiment by changing the factors that influence HIT adoption by health care organizations and professionals. More importantly, health care

Organization Development in Healthcare: Conversations on Research and Strategies
Advances in Health Care Management, Volume 10, 313–317

ISSN: 1474-8231/doi:10.1108/S1474-8231(2011)0000010024

managers in organizations large and small will need to exercise leadership to align their organizations to the changing environment sparked by HITECH, as well as contribute to the overall plan of transforming the U.S. health care system. In many instances, administrators' efforts to achieve meaningful use will thrust them into clinical domains that have historically been the sole purview of health professionals (i.e., doctors, nurses, and pharmacists among others). Two chapters by Stefano Calciolari, and Patrick A. Palmieri et al., in the current issue of Advances in Health Care Management (AHCM) are particularly timely as the diffusion of HIT takes on a central role in many nations' health policy agendas.

The first chapter explores the implementation of specific HIT applications using three case studies drawn from various regions of Italy. The first case explores the use of tele-health to coordinate emergency care for neurology patients in clinics that do not have access to such specialists. The case's main finding is that building a network with effective health information exchange (HIE) for real-time events is a valuable addition to the overall quality of care available across the region. The second case study addresses the use of web-portals to promote care-coordination activities. The portals served both clinicians and consumers' needs. For clinicians, the portal created an online venue for seeking second opinions across the regional systems providers. For consumers, the web-portal allowed them to access educational tools and schedule appointments. The latter feature provided the most compelling storyline with nearly twenty percent of all appointments being made online in 2004. Clearly, such interfaces offer the possibility of creating a more efficient scheduling system. The last case study looked at the use of enterprise resource planning (ERP) to manage administrative functions in eight public hospitals located in the Lombardi region. In effect, the last case was comprised of eight minicases comparing the adoption of common HIT application while allowing the implementation process to be pursued in varying ways. The overall finding was that the new ERP system's success varied greatly depending on how it was implemented. Testing the process used to implement HIT applications in one region of a country prior to rolling them out nationwide is an interesting strategy for achieving a health system's priorities.

The second chapter deals with the potential for HITs to introduce *more* error types into the health care system. These electronically induced errors can come in two forms. The first type of error is best described using the old adage that: "Automating a flawed process only makes bad things happen faster." In other words, adopting HIT systems may serve to further solidify error-prone care practices if the implementation process is not coupled with an effective evaluation and modification of current workflows. The second form of care errors the authors describe are the new types of mistakes that can arise from using HIT systems. The seriousness of this possibility has been deemed significant enough for the Institute of Medicine (IOM) to begin a yearlong study of the problem starting in 2011 (Connolly, 2005). Therefore, it is conceivable that not only will implementing an HIT system mitigate existing sources of medical errors but may also introduce new sources of errors.

The purpose of the chapter by Palmieri et al. is to explore the unintended consequences of HIT use and propose a model for understanding the phenomenon. In particular, the potentially negative impacts on clinical outcomes (iatrogenesis) are explored within the context of the social, cultural, and administrative factors. The chapter then offers a set of management practices that can be used to address potential error sources during the transition process from adoption through implementation.

Both chapters, one broadly discussing unintended consequences of HIT adoption and the other looking very narrowly at the implementation of specific applications, provide a valuable backdrop for considering the research activities that might be pursued to make meaningful use a reality. As the U.S. health care system undergoes major changes stemming from HIT implementations, it is vital that timely and rigorous HIT research – particularly framed through a management lens – be available for health care managers and policy makers alike. Health management scholars provide a unique organizational-level perspective that an HIT research agenda should be developed around. Such an agenda should expand the work of Calciolari and Palmieri et al. to include studies that unleash the power of regional research, focusing not only on "best practices" but also on "worst-demonstrated practices" that may include technological iatrogenesis and the use of ineffective implementation strategies.

Additional research strategies that would help to identify and test "best-" and "worst-demonstrated practices" should also be considered. In particular, studies that look at environmental features, organizational structures, implementation processes, and performance outcomes are needed to provide a more complete model of HIT phenomenon. The case studies presented in the Italian paper controls for environmental features by looking HIT use in discreet regions. Such research provides a valuable "proof of concept," but may not provide an actionable model that other facilities can implement. Therefore, it is essential that research look across differing environmental conditions to identify where HIT innovations are more likely – and less likely – to be successfully implemented. However, the management literature provides very strong evidence that merely finding favorable environmental conditions is not enough to guarantee success. Rather, it is the fit between environments and organizational structures that managers should seek to achieve (Ford, Menachemi, Huerta, & Yu, 2010; Freudenheim, 2010).

Understanding how organizational structures impact HIT adoption is a critical feature for achieving meaningful use and avoiding the unintended consequences discussed in the electronic iatrogensis chapter. While it is possible for health care facilities of every stripe to have a common goal – delivering safe and effective care – not every hospital has the same wherewithal to implement HIT. In particular, it is likely that smaller facilities, such as the rural hospitals built with Hill-Burton funds, do not have the operational scale to employ dedicated HIT support staff that are critical to implementing HIT. Even relatively large, freestanding facilities may not achieve the purchasing power, economies of scale or coordination benefits that networked systems can bring to bear on HIT activities. In a similar vein, hospitals that are not tightly integrated with a physician group may not be able to get the "doctor buy-in" that has caused other HIT implementations to fail (Kazley & Ozcan, 2007). Therefore, it is critical that organizations' structural and design elements be integrated into HIT research. While having a better picture of how environmental and organizational fit influences HIT implementation is critical, it is still not enough to ensure that meaningful use will be achieved.

The third critical dimension to achieving successful implementations leading to meaningful use of HIT is the implementation process itself. The strategies that health care facilities use to adopt and implement HIT also play a critical role in determining success (Ford et al., 2010). Integrating this third dimension into the environment–organization fit paradigm would make important contributions to both the applied health care and theoretic management literature streams. While this would be an important addition, it does not achieve the ultimate goal of moving beyond "best-demonstrated practices" to the validated, "evidence-based management" (Rousseau, 2006) paradigm needed to ensure the meaningful use of HIT keeps pace with the emergence of new technologies over time.

The two chapters discussed earlier provide useful glimpse at the research field ranging from the purely theoretic to most granular level of applied studies. But the work presented herein and conducted to date is barely the tip of the iceberg. Below the surface of HIT research lies a large body of important topics that still need to be considered within the HIT and meaningful use contexts. Given the extraordinary investments being made in health care writ large and HIT in particular, far more work is warranted lest we sink valuable resources into an expedition that is traversing hazardous waters without a clear view to the other side.

REFERENCES

Connolly, C. (2005). Cedars-Sinai doctors cling to pen and paper. *The Washington Post*, p. A1.

Ford, E. W., Menachemi, N., Huerta, T. R., & Yu, F. (2010). Hospital IT adoption strategies associated with implementation success: Implications for achieving meaningful use. *Journal of Healthcare Management*, *55*(3), 175–188. Discussion 188–189.

Freudenheim, M. (2010). Panel set to study safety of electronic patient data. *The New York Times*.

Kazley, A. S., & Ozcan, Y. A. (2007). Organizational and environmental determinants of hospital EMR adoption: A national study. *Journal of Medical Systems*, *31*(5), 375–384.

Rousseau, D. M. (2006). 2005 Presidential Address: Is there such a thing as "Evidence-based management"? *The Academy of Management Review*, *31*(2), 256.

PART VI
SYSTEMS ISSUES

E PLURIBUS UNUM: USING GROUP MODEL BUILDING WITH MANY INTERDEPENDENT ORGANIZATIONS TO CREATE INTEGRATED HEALTH CARE NETWORKS

Angèle Pieters, Henk Akkermans and Arie Franx

ABSTRACT

*This chapter reports on an action research case study of integrated obstetric care in the Netherlands. Efficient and patient-friendly patient flows through integrated care networks are of major societal importance. How to design and develop such interorganizational patient flows is still a nascent research area, especially when dealing with a large number (*n > *3) of stakeholders. We have shown that a modification of an existing method to support interorganizational collaboration by system dynamics-based group model building (GMB) (the Renga method, Akkermans, 2001) may be effective in achieving such collaboration.*

Organization Development in Healthcare: Conversations on Research and Strategies
Advances in Health Care Management, Volume 10, 321–344

ISSN: 1474-8231/doi:10.1108/S1474-8231(2011)0000010025

Keywords: Health care; networks; group model building; organizational change; action research; interorganizational collaboration

Change processes in organizations do not always concern clear problems and solutions, a well-defined strategy and a step-by-step implementation to reach goals and objectives. Often problems are vague, different perspectives on problems and solutions exist, the direction of change is unclear, and the changes to be made are far-reaching. In such situations a developmental approach to change processes may be required (Boonstra, 2004), where solutions are looked for involving the members of the organization, and where the focus lies on behavior of individuals and social processes in groups.

One popular theory regarding planned organizational change is Lewin's (1951) three-step process of change: unfreeze, move, and freeze. In this process, unfreezing is necessary to overcome resistance to change. This resistance is a major topic in organizational development, because if not recognized and answered in the right way, it will lead to delays, blockages and even worse, complete project failure. Resistance is seen as a natural habit of people, such as fear of the unknown. However, it is also strengthened by a top-management, content-driven, top-down change approach. The result is a lack of interaction and cooperation between relevant stakeholders (Gravenhorst & Veld, 2004). In addition, the absence of trust between stakeholders creates adverse effects on their cooperation (Nooteboom, 2004), and thus on the outcome of an organizational change process.

The common-sense notion of making change a collaborative and interactive effort from the start is only relatively rarely practiced. By involving all parties and having stakeholders work together, resistance is decreased because interest groups are not treated as adversaries but as partners in change. Thus, change processes have to be designed in such a way that stakeholders work together instead of against each other (Gravenhorst & Veld, 2004). This chapter describes the design of an organizational change project that was characterized by a high level of participation of all stakeholders and by collective reflection, and, as a result, by increased trust, mutual understanding and collaboration between the stakeholders.

INTRODUCTION

The health care sector is a major industry in developed countries, representing more than 10% of the Gross National Product (Organization for Economic Co-operation and Development [OECD], 2011). At the same time, the health sector is facing many problems: rising costs, an aging population, more and more people suffering from lifelong diseases, among which obesity, and unsatisfactory quality (McGlynn, Adams, Hicks, DeCristofaro, & Kerr, 2003). For a long time, specialization, differentiation, and fragmentation were the main characteristics of the health care sector. As a result, patients are confronted with multiple care providers and disconnected care processes. This fragmented care leads to a suboptimal performance of the system in terms of costs, effectiveness, and quality of care. Chains of care processes need to be designed to fulfill the needs of the patient (Herzlinger, 2004). So, the health care sector is challenged to collaborate, to better coordinate demand and supply, and to provide more efficient care. One has to challenge the rigidity of the boundaries of existing organizations and explore intensifying collaboration with other organizations. Concepts used in this context are transmural care, shared care, integrated care, managed care, and disease management.

Much is known concerning (health care) networks. For example, the development of networks should combine both a bottom-up and a top-down approach (Axelrod, 1997; Akkermans, 2001). In the beginning, it is often not known what the structural and strategic characteristics of the network will be, for there are different configurations of networks possible (Nooteboom, 2004; Bazoli, Shortell, Dubbs, Chan, & Kravolec, 1999). And factors that contribute in becoming a successful network include: knowing each other, understanding each other's points of view, interests and convictions, and trusting each other (Boonstra, 2004). However, little has been written on *how* to build those networks and on *how* to foster collaboration, especially among a large number of stakeholders ($n > 3$). Thus, the objective of this chapter is: *How to develop health care networks, especially with a large number of stakeholders?*

This chapter reports on a case study concerning redesign of care processes by developing a health care network. In 2006 a project started in Tilburg, the Netherlands, aimed at improving the performance of the obstetric care system. This chapter describes the methods used and the design applied in more detail. Participants are the obstetricians of two hospitals and the midwives of 12 independent midwifery practices. The challenge of the project was how to motivate the stakeholders to participate in a joint project, how to foster collaboration between this large number of stakeholders, and how to make such a process manageable. The design of the project is based on an existing method (the Renga approach) for facilitating intra- and interorganizational network development, but had to be adjusted to cope with the large number of stakeholders.

The second section is a literature review of the development of (health care) networks. The third section describes the case setting, the Dutch obstetric care system and, in particular, the obstetric care system in Tilburg. The method – the Renga approach – which forms the basis of the project design is described in section four. The project design and the outcomes are presented in section five and six. Lastly, section seven comprises the conclusion.

LITERATURE REVIEW

The notion that networked firms are going to be the new dominant organizational form is increasingly taken for granted. Although no standard definition of this new organizational form exists, according to Tapscott (1996) essential elements include the following: it is a grouping of a number of semi-independent organizations, each with their capabilities and competencies, which collaborate in ever-changing constellations to serve one or more markets in order to achieve some business goal specific to that collaboration. In health care, different definitions of a network exist. A health care network can be defined as two or more health care organizations that have merged (Weil, 2001), or – a much broader definition – as a formalized cooperation between independent health care providers (Meiboom, De Haan, & Verheijen, 2004). Networks in health care are variously described by concepts such as Integrated Delivery Systems, transmural care, shared care, integrated care, managed care, and disease management (see e.g., Shortell, Gillies, & Anderson, 1994; Van der Linden, Spreeuwenberg, & Schrijvers, 2001; Campbell, Hotchkiss, Bradshaw, & Porteous, 1998; Miller, & Luft, 1994; Bodemheimer, 1999).

The interactions and interdependencies in networks are so complex that it is virtually impossible to control and design them centrally and hierarchically, as management theory has long believed. In such highly decentralized networks – according to complexity theory – coordination and order emerge bottom-up, rather than being forced top-down (Axelrod, 1997). Because there is no single locus of formal authority, power and influence replace the formal line and command, and communication, convincing and consensus building take the place of orders (Akkermans, 2001). Moreover, when developing interorganizational networks, it is often not known what the specific characteristics of the network will be, such as the number of participants, the strength of the ties between the participants, the legal form of a network, etc. (Nooteboom, 2004). Based on theories of organization behavior and industrial organization economics, Bazoli et al. (1999) identified three strategic/structural dimensions on decisions that have to be made: (1) differentiation, which refers to the number of different products/services along a health care continuum; (2) integration, which refers to mechanisms used to achieve unity of effort across organizational components; and (3) centralization, which relates to the extent to which activities take place at centralized versus dispersed locations.

Much has been written on various types of health care networks, with differences in the strategic/structural dimensions as described earlier. Lessons have also been learned regarding factors that contribute to (developing) a successful network, such as knowing each other, understanding each others' points of view, interests and convictions, and trusting each other (Boonstra, 2004). Also, historically good relationships, a shared vision, commitment from management, projects that have high priority, and having an energetic lead are mentioned in the literature (Woods, 2001). However, little has been written on *how to* foster these success factors and on *how to* develop health care networks.

One approach for developing such networks is using collaborative improvement models such as the Breakthrough Series (BTS) (Kilo, 1999). The BTS brings together groups of health care organizations that share a commitment to making major rapid system changes to specific aspects of their health care organization. Approximately 20–40 organizations participate in a 6- to 13-month program involving three 2-day learning sessions alternating with action periods (Wagner et al. 2001; Minkman, Schouten, Huijsman, & Van Splunteren, 2005). Although this approach seems promising (Pearson et al., 2005), some remarks can be made. BTS surpasses the individual case level and is brought into action on a wider level needing several participating regions or cases. Starting yourself is difficult; starting with several regions at the same time can be even more difficult. Also, one is only allowed to participate if one is willing to improve care processes and if project management resources are available at the start. In practice, these two conditions are not always easily fulfilled. In contrast to the development of Integrated Delivery Systems which is merely top-down oriented, the BTS is an example of a bottom-up approach (Shortell et al., 1994; Shortell, Gillies, Anderson, Erickson, & Mitchell, 2000).

Akkermans (2001) designed a facilitation approach to intra- and interorganizational network development that is aimed at, on the one hand, creating favorable conditions for spontaneous bottom-up emergence of successful network relations and, on the other hand, developing – from a top-down perspective – workable business processes in which to embed those network relations. This facilitation approach is based firmly on concepts of system dynamics modeling and process consultation or, to use the terminology of the system dynamics field, group model building (Vennix, 1996; Andersen, & Richardson, 1997). This generic facilitation style is embedded in a project design that lends itself especially well to collaboration between groups from different organizational units. This approach will be discussed in more detail in section four.

CASE SETTING

Obstetric Care in the Netherlands

Different models of obstetric care exist. For example, in the United States, the maternity system adheres strongly to the "medical model," with pregnant women being cared for by obstetricians within a medical, hospitalized setting. Almost on the other side of the spectrum we find the Dutch obstetric care system, which is based on the "social or midwifery model," stating that being pregnant and giving birth are healthy and natural events, physiological processes, involving no illness or disease.

The Dutch obstetric care system is a unique system, consisting of a first, second, and third echelon (Fig. 1). Women are assigned to an echelon on the basis of their initial risk. Normal, low-risk pregnancies are cared for in the first echelon (primary care) by independent midwifery practices. Complicated or high(er) risk pregnancies are cared for by the second and third echelon (secondary and tertiary care) by obstetricians and their residents who are employed in obstetric departments in hospitals. The risk a pregnant

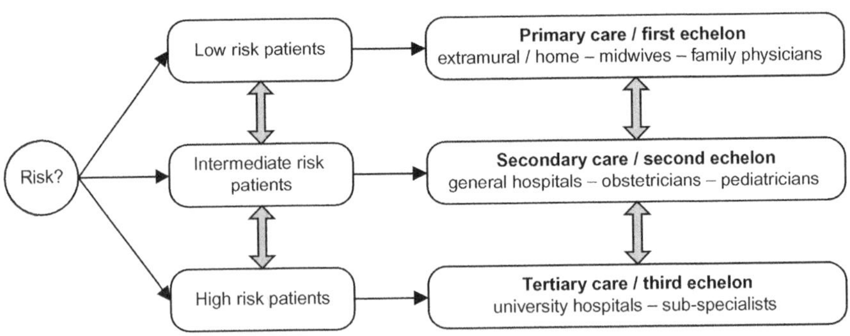

Fig. 1. Dutch Tiered Obstetric Care System.

woman faces during her pregnancy or during labor and delivery can change, resulting in a referral to another echelon. The risk and referral criteria are set up by the Royal Dutch Organization of Midwives (KNOV) and the Dutch Society of Obstetrics and Gynecology (NVOG). Birth is given at home (if medically permitted) or in the hospital.

The Netherlands count about 1900 midwives, 650 obstetricians and 465 obstetric active general practitioners (Wiegers, Van der Velden, & Hingstman, 2005). Midwives work in small organizations (midwifery practices) which employ on average 3.5 midwives or in hospitals (Wiegers et al., 2005). Obstetricians work in hospitals. In 2006 about 186,000 children were born in the Netherlands as a whole (Dutch Perinatal Registry, 2006). Insurance, which is obligatory for all inhabitants of the Netherlands, compensates all costs, although "normal" pregnant women who want to deliver at the hospital have to pay a modest sum themselves.

Although the Dutch obstetric care system is organized so very differently from other systems such as the one in the United States, it nevertheless appears to be working fairly well. For instance, the number of obstetric interventions is low compared to neighboring countries (Amelink-Verburg et al., 2007), and the Netherlands has one of the smallest number of caesarean deliveries in the world (14% compared to 30% in the United States) (Quickstats, 2005). However, the Netherlands is not leading the field concerning perinatal mortality (Mohangoo et al., 2008) which is widely regarded as an important indicator of the quality of obstetric care. And there are doubts as to the adequacy of risk selection of women with low risk of complications during labor (Reuwer, Bruinse, & Franx, 2009).

Possible explanations for the high perinatal mortality rates are found in the characteristics of women, such as ethnicity, smoking, age, twin births, obesities, and less prenatal screening (Achterberg, 2005). Among many other factors, the way the Dutch have organized obstetric care may be related to less technical effectiveness. Obstetric care is provided by different echelons, depending on the risk of a pregnancy. However, at the start of a pregnancy, it cannot always be accurately assessed whether the pregnancy will be of low, medium, or high risk. Often complications occur during pregnancies and women are referred to another echelon. For example, in 2002, 85% of the pregnant women started in primary care, whereas only 40% of the women gave birth in primary care. The others were referred to and taken over by secondary care (Anthony, Amelink-Verburg, Jacobusse, & Pal-de Bruin, 2005). Keep in mind that these numbers represent the number of women who are actually taken over. Data about the number of women that have consulted an obstetrician a few times during their pregnancy but who still remain under the care of a midwife are not counted. Thus, when adding that there often is a lack of coordination, cooperation and exchange of information between primary and secondary caregivers, the question arises whether the current organization of obstetric care is the most efficient, effective, and safe.

Obstetric Care in Tilburg

Tilburg is the sixth city in the Netherlands by count of its inhabitants (in 2006 a little over 200,000) and is located in the South of the Netherlands. Obstetric care for Tilburg and its nearby villages is provided by two hospitals, 1 in the North (NH) and 1 in the South (SH), and 12 midwifery practices (MP). Each midwifery practice has a preferred hospital, mostly for geographic reasons (Fig. 2). In 2005, the birth of about 4,500 children was supported by this system.

In 2006, a voluntary joint project was initiated by some obstetricians in the SH and researchers of the University of Tilburg. The overarching goal of

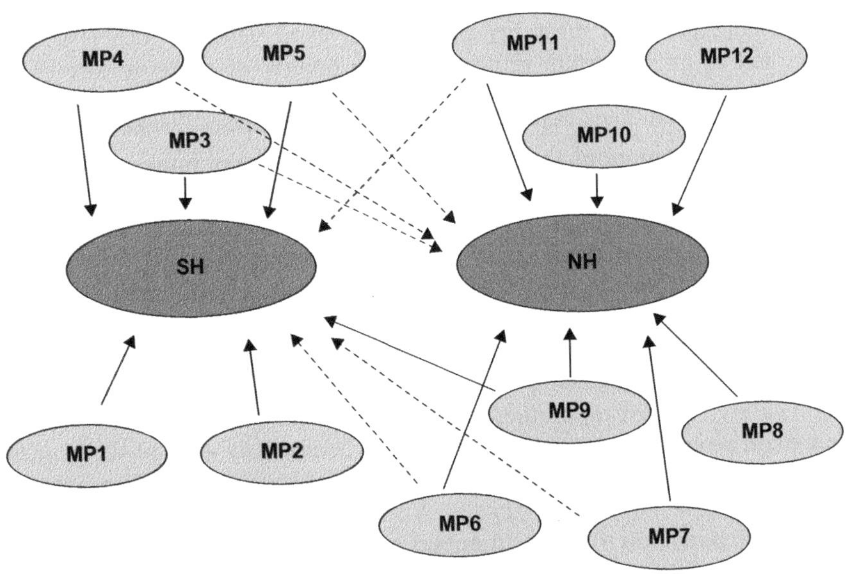

Fig. 2. Distribution of Midwifery Practices to the Hospitals.

the project was to improve the obstetric care process. Even though many different disciplines are involved in the obstetric care process, such as midwives, obstetricians, residents, general, obstetric and maternity nurses, pediatricians, ultra sound scan specialists and others, this project focused on obstetricians, and midwives since they are mainly responsible for the overall care process. However, although midwives and obstetricians communicated and collaborated in patient care, their relation was hampered by mutual distrust and misunderstanding. As a result, creating support and commitment was seen as one of the major conditions for the project to succeed.

METHOD

The design of the project is based on an existing method (the Renga approach) for facilitating intra- and interorganizational network development. This method will be discussed in subsections "Renga Approach" and "Group Model Building". In the subsection "Fit of the Renga Approach with the problem setting" we will discuss why this approach suits our project so well.

Renga Approach (Akkermans, 2001)

The Renga approach is a facilitation approach to intra- and interorganizational network development that is aimed at, on the one hand, creating favorable conditions for spontaneous bottom-up emergence of successful network relations and, on the other hand, developing – from a top-down perspective – workable business processes to embed those network relations in.

Renga Elements
The Renga approach has three essential elements: group model building workshops, combining process maps, and system dynamic modeling and simulation.

1. *Group model building workshops: group interaction and improvisation for trust and understanding*

Group model building workshops (see also next subsection) form an essential means for creating trust and mutual understanding between stakeholders in network development. The design of these workshops is aimed at achieving an atmosphere of open and trusting communication, in which people can say what they really think without having to worry about adverse impacts of their words. Having a group facilitator with an independent and nonmanipulative attitude in achieving such an atmosphere is therefore of major importance.

2. *Combining process maps: multiple levels of abstraction for seamless workflows*

Mental maps of the processes at stake are combined in three levels of abstraction. First, there are individual preparatory interviews (individual level). Then, there are company-by-company process-mapping workshops (company level). After that, these company process maps are combined and discussed in one or more plenary workshops (network level). The workshops utilize both a process view, using stocks-and-flow diagramming (Richmond, 1994), and a cause-and-effect perspective, using causal loop diagrams (Senge, 1990). Both views are essential in achieving a thorough understanding of the underlying structure and the resulting dynamics of the network in operation.

3. *System dynamics modeling and simulation: rules and rigor to appreciate counter-intuitive behavior*

System dynamics modeling and simulation provide the rules and rigor necessary for a careful analysis of the behavioral characteristics of the network in operation. It is one of the secret strengths of group model building that it makes the use of formal methods such as simulation much more acceptable to operational people and this also applies in the context of interorganizational networks. With the simulation model, different external developments and managerial policies can be evaluated and discussed, which can increase the analytic quality of the discussions considerably, without losing stakeholder ownership of the resulting recommendations.

Renga Project Phasing

When bringing the earlier described three characteristics together in a process, a Renga project phasing is visualized as in Fig. 3. A project starts

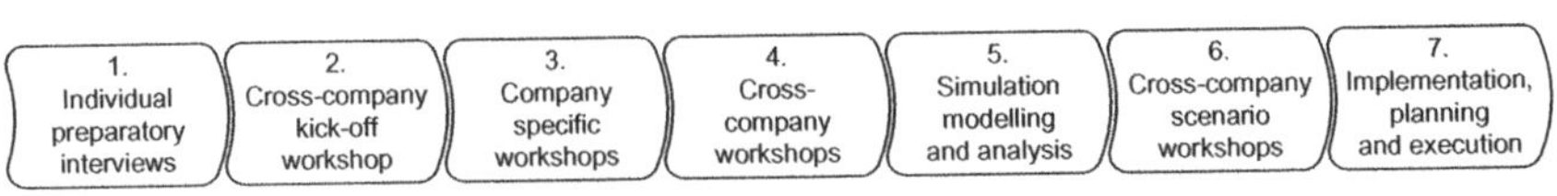

Fig. 3. The Renga Approach Project Phasing (Akkermans, 2001).

with interviewing representatives of the companies involved (step 1), followed by a cross-company kick-off workshop at which the findings are fed back and discussed (step 2). Next, more detailed work will be conducted in the company-specific workshops (step 3), followed by a one or more cross-company workshops, where all companies come together to present their work and discuss future activities (step 4). After that, detailed modeling and simulation is conducted (step 5), followed by cross-company workshops (step 6). Finally, implementation can be planned and executed (step 7).

Group Model Building

Every organization regularly faces strategic problems. These problems are often called messy problems, being characterized by different people holding widely dissimilar views of the situation and defining the problems differently (people having different "mental models" of the situation). These differences in opinion can give rise to lengthy and frustrating discussions, which is particularly the case when individual team members seem convinced that their perspective is correct and others must be wrong. Also, there is a risk of underperformance of the organization as a whole, caused by underachievement of teams (Vennix, 1996).

Group model building (GMB) assumes that people's mental models are limited by human information processing capabilities and that people have a strong tendency to think in terms of causal processes. As a result, people tend to think in simple causal chains rather than networks of related variables and it is rare for people to see more than one cause of a problem. Thus, when problems become more complex people will, by necessity, have a limited view of the problem (Vennix, 1996). Therefore, in a GMB project, one tries to elicit the hidden causal assumptions that all of us automatically hold, bring together different mental models of people involved, integrate these into a more complete representation of the problem, and define courses of action in which all team members will feel confident and to which they all feel committed. The goals of a GMB project can be described at three levels (Anderson, Richardson, & Vennix, 1997; Rouwette, Vennix, & Van Mullekom, 2002). Goals at the individual level are learning, mental model improvement, change in attitudes, change in behavior, positive reaction, and commitment. At the group level, the goals are mental model alignment, consensus and commitment to a decision, increased quality of communication, and creation of a shared language. At the level of the organization, system changes (doing things differently), and systems results (improvement of the problematic condition) are the main described goals.

GMB is a bundle of techniques mostly used to construct system dynamics models working directly with client groups on key strategic decisions. The primary goal of a system dynamics model is to enhance understanding of the system's behavior and to find robust policies to tackle strategic problems (Forrester, 1961, see e.g., also Vennix, Akkermans, & Rouwette, 1996; Senge, 1990; Sterman, 2000). GMB uses facilitated face-to-face meetings to elicit model structure and to engage client teams directly in the process of model conceptualization, formulation, analysis, and decision making (Anderson et al., 1997). In order to be able to use this method effectively, one has to be familiar with the system dynamics method, the way to set up a group model building project, and the way to facilitate the group model building process (Vennix, 1996). More information can also be found in Andersen and Richardson (1997).

Fit of the Renga Approach with the Problem Setting

The project this chapter reports on is characterized by four items. The Renga approach suits these characteristics well. First, improving care processes often implies making changes. However, before one can change something, one has to understand it. At the start of this project, neither it was known what all relevant variables were, nor their precise relationships. So it seemed obvious to opt for a breadth first search strategy; initially investigate a large number of variables and relations, and find out which of these appear to be the most significant (Akkermans, 1995). This is done by the group model building sessions. Second, we expected that the performance of the obstetric care system depends, among others, on the collaboration and communication between the different organizations. Collaboration and communication are formed by people's inner motivation. Therefore, it is interesting to look for those inner motivations, to investigate people's inner worlds, which requires close researcher participation. Close researcher participation is central to the Renga approach. Third, the project was initiated by only one of the actors in the region, the South Hospital. The other organizations involved (the North Hospital and the 12 midwifery practices) needed to be motivated to participate in this project together and they needed to discover that in order to improve the obstetric care system, collaboration is necessary. This is challenging because the two tiered system has been in place in the Netherlands for several decades. Primary care (i.e., midwives) and secondary care (i.e., obstetricians) are not used to close cooperation, to really getting to know each other. One of the main effects of GMB workshops is the creation of trust and mutual understanding among stakeholders in network development. A fourth and final characteristic of this project is that organizational development has to be seen both as a *bottom-up* and as a *top-down* process, which is facilitated by the Renga approach.

PROJECT DESIGN

In this section the design of the intervention is presented in detail. This design in based on the Renga approach. This is discussed in the subsection "General Project Design". The subsections "Phase A: Problem Analysis", "Phase B: Defining Improvements," and "Phase C: Implementing Improvements" discuss the three phases of this project in more detail: the problem analysis phase, the defining improvements phase, and the implementing improvements phase.

General Project Design

Project Phasing

The project phasing is based on the Renga approach. Overall, our project consisted of three phases. The first phase (A: problem analysis) corresponded to the first four steps of the Renga approach. The second and third phase (B: defining improvements and C: implementing improvements) corresponded to the sixth and seventh step of the Renga approach.

The Renga approach has been tested for a small number of participating organizations ($n = 4$). Because of the number of actors involved (2 hospitals and 12 midwifery practices) the Renga approach was adjusted, especially in the first four steps of the approach. There, a design was chosen whereby smaller groups work together and regular feedback was given to all actors involved in plenary sessions. Fig. 4 shows this process. In the first phase, two groups were discerned: Group 1 (the pioneer group) and Group 2. Group 1 consisted of the SH and three midwifery practices whose patients – if necessary – were predominantly referred to the SH for specialized care. Their findings in the problem analysis phase were promising, so they presented them in a plenary session to the NH and to the other nine

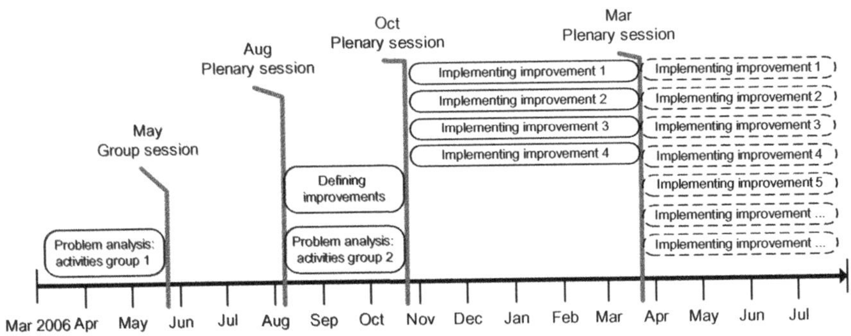

Fig. 4. General Intervention Design.

midwifery practices in the region. As a result, they also wanted to experience the same process. Group 2 was formed, consisting of the NH and three midwifery practices whose patients were predominantly referred to the NH. In addition, in the second phase of our project, the improvement proposals were defined in a smaller group, consisting of key representatives of obstetricians and midwives, and feedback was given in the plenary session. In theory, analyzing the problem and defining improvements should be done consecutively. However, in this project these activities were done simultaneously. The main reason for this was that Group 1 did not want to slow down and wait for some months to proceed with the process. They did not want to lose the momentum that was created in the problem analysis. Because of close researcher participation in all phases, the researcher supervised the whole project and, where necessary, bridges between these two phases could easily be built.

As you will notice, no simulation model has been made. Instead, the researchers and participants felt defining and implementing improvement options was the best way forward.

Project Activities

The different activities within the project were based on the Renga approach. The table below gives an overview of the activities in this project and how they suit the characteristics of the Renga approach as discussed earlier. The activities of our project are described in more detail in the following subsections.

Renga Characteristic	Our Project
1. Group model building workshops	Group model building sessions
2a. Combining process maps, individual level	Questionnaires
2b. Combining process maps, company level	Interview Group model building sessions
2c. Combining process maps, network level	Group session Plenary sessions
3. System dynamic modeling and simulation	–

Phase A: Problem Analysis

The problem analysis consisted for both Group 1 and Group 2 of the following activities: a questionnaire, an interview, a group model building session, and a group and/or plenary session(s). These will be discussed later in more detail.

The questionnaire was filled in by the obstetricians and midwives individually. It focused on the cooperation between midwives and obstetricians, and was a compilation of other questionnaires which study the existing cooperative situation of interfirm relationships (Johnston, McCutcheon, Stuart, & Kerwood, 2003; Humpreys, Li, & Chan, 2003). Twenty-four questions were asked, divided in five categories: transparency, trust, performance, power, and effort. Each question was rated on a 7-point Likert scale, where 1 = I strongly disagree, 4 = neutral, and 7 = I strongly agree.

The interviews were held on an organizational level; the hospital and the midwifery practices each had their own interview. The interviews lasted for about 2 h and focused on topics such as: What contributes to good cooperation? What contributes to bad cooperation? How do you notice the performance of the cooperation? The interviews were not recorded, but notes were made by two persons (the interviewer and the researcher) and the participants were given the opportunity to react to them.

In a group model building session the hospital and midwifery practices each focused on one problem which dominated their interview. Causal loops diagrams were used to disentangle the problems. The group model building sessions were not recorded, but notes were made by two persons

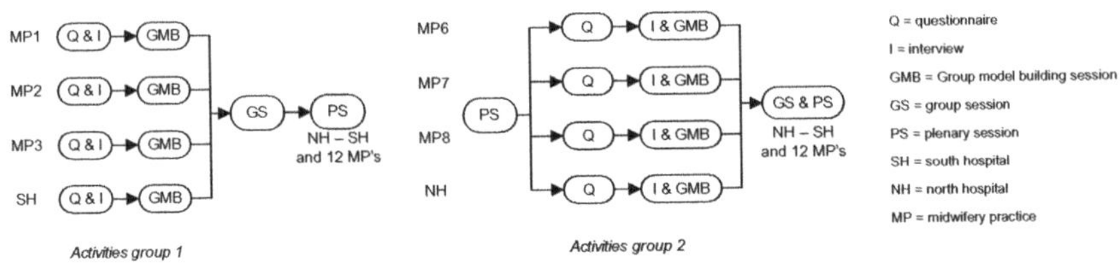

Fig. 5. Activities in Phase A. Problem Analysis.

(the facilitator and the researcher) and participants were given the opportunity to react to them.

Group 1 and Group 2 had a slightly different process, which is presented in Fig. 5. Group 1 started with two meetings with the researcher. In the first they filled in the questionnaire (Q) and had the interview (I). The second meeting was the group model building session (GMB). They presented their findings to each other in a group session (GS), and reported this session to the other hospital and midwifery practices in a plenary session (PS). As a result, Group 2 started with a plenary session, filled in the questionnaire and had their first meeting with the researchers where they were both interviewed and had their group model building session. For Group 1, the group session served as the cross company kick-off workshop (Renga, step 2) because it resulted in the commitment of the actors to continue with the project. For Group 2 (and for the group as a whole), the plenary session served as a cross company kick-off workshop.

Phase B: Defining Improvements

After the first plenary session two obstetricians formulated about 20 improvement proposals for the obstetric system in Tilburg, varying from low to high collaboration between obstetricians and midwives. Each proposal was formulated in the same format (see framework). These improvements were discussed in two sessions: first by four midwives, each from different midwifery practices, and later by four other obstetricians representing each hospital. Finally, a list of top four of improvements was compiled by looking at two criteria: easy to realize and urgency. "Easy to realize" because achieving results in the short-term motivates the actors involved and stimulates collaboration between them. "Urgency" because some improvements are necessary because of national developments, or because of just avoiding mistakes, misunderstandings, and unnecessary actions.

Format description of improvement
- description of the improvement
- problems which are dealt with
- unwanted consequences
- hypothesis why the improvement should work
- relation with other improvements
- necessary conditions
- advantages for obstetricians, midwives, assistants, pregnant women, care process, and final outcome of care
- needed efforts from obstetricians, midwives, pregnant woman, and management of the hospital

In the second plenary session these four improvement proposals were presented and project groups were compiled, each consisting of two obstetricians (one from each hospital) and two or more midwives (from different midwifery practices).

Phase C: Implementing Improvements

The project groups specified the improvements and, where possible, set up a pilot. Some topics could be realized easily, whereas others demanded more preliminary work. All actors involved were kept up to date by a newsletter which was sent once every two months. Every four months, until January 2008, plenary sessions were organized, where all actors involved were informed about the developments and where new improvement proposals were selected.

OUTCOMES

In this section the main outcomes of each of the three phases in this project – problem analysis, defining improvements, and implementing improvements – are presented.

Outcomes Phase A: Problem Analysis

The problem analysis consisted of different activities: questionnaires, interviews, group model building sessions, a group, and a plenary session. The results of each of these activities are discussed later.

Questionnaire

The questionnaire focused on the current relation between obstetricians and midwives. In general, both the obstetricians and the midwives rated the overall performance of the relationship above average. However, some remarks can be made. For example, in Group 1, the midwives trusted the obstetricians more than the other way round. Also, the midwives rated the contribution of the relationship to the quality of their work and to the service to their patients higher than the obstetrician do. Further, obstetricians and midwives perceived the responsibility for the relationships differently. The midwives saw this responsibility as an equally joint one, the obstetricians did not. It seemed that the midwives rely more on the obstetricians than vice versa. In Group 2, there were fewer differences in the perception of the relationship by midwives and obstetricians. It is striking that midwives as well as obstetricians of both groups rated the influence of the relationship on the costs as minimal. Further, the SH spoke less positively about the relationship with the midwifery practices than the NH did.

Interviews

The interviews focused on topics concerning the cooperation between obstetricians and midwives. Meeting each other often, having a shared vision on maternity care, and being familiar with each other's standards, tasks and competences, contributed, among others, to good operation. On the contrary, changes in staff, differences in power, bad communication, and the fear of "stealing each other's clients" did not contribute to good cooperation. The performance of the cooperation came to the surface among others in the number of conflicts, the number of irritations, the frequency of consultations, and the evaluation of patients.

Group Model Building

Although the interviews covered the same topics, each had a different emphasis reflecting the interests and annoyances of each participant. In a group model building session every group focused on a problem which dominated their interview. In total one process flow diagram and 11 causal loops diagrams were made. The principles of constructing the causal loop diagrams were quickly grasped by the obstetricians and midwives. Everybody appeared to engage readily with the technique and enjoyed the process of exploring their relationships. Below, as an illustration, a part of one of the diagrams is shown (Fig. 6).

Starting in the middle of the figure, good cooperation between midwifery practices (mp) results in more openness in the relation and to more respect for each other, resulting in greater mutual trust, which results in more cooperation (Loop 1). Also, as a result of good cooperation, midwifery practices are unified. Making appointments together with the obstetricians is easier. For example, this results in more openness according to the assignment of childbeds (pregnant women who deliver their baby under supervision of an obstetrician in the hospital often have their childbed at home under the supervision of a midwife). This again results in more trust and more cooperation (Loop 2). However, in Tilburg, the South Hospital has given some privileges to one midwifery practice. This results on the one hand in a competitive advantage for this midwifery practice, but on the

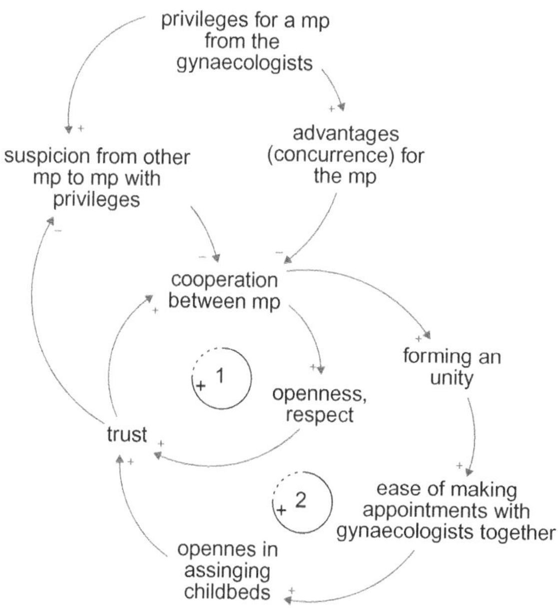

Fig. 6. Causal Loop Diagram from the GMB Sessions: Cooperation between Midwifery Practices.

other hand to suspicious behavior of the other practices. This does not attribute to the cooperation between the midwifery practices. However, trust has a diminishing effect on this suspicion.

Plenary Sessions
During the group and plenary sessions the participants were able to tell each other their views on their relationship and on the performance of the care processes by presenting their causal loop diagrams. In other words, they shared their mental models on their relationship and on their working together. As a result, the participants gained insight into how others work and think, into how others interpret behavior, and into what the implications are of acting in a particular way. Further, they learned – to a certain extent – to see their common world through the eyes of the other, to speak each other's language, and to look at the care process from the other's point of view. The participants of the group model building workshops mentioned that it was the first time they spoke together about their common world. Also, they were surprised one could look at the obstetric care system from an interorganizational point of view. After the second plenary session all midwifery practices and the two hospitals were motivated and willing to cooperate in order to improve obstetric care in the region together.

Outcomes Phase B: Defining Improvements

In total, 20 improvement proposals were written. These proposals connected to issues mentioned in the analysis phase, such as better knowing each other and each other's practices, enlarging trust and developing common policies. Most proposals were written on three levels (little, medium, and much collaboration) because the obstetricians expected midwives to be reserved about much collaboration. Surprisingly, midwives were very inspired by the proposals with much collaboration. The following four were selected by obstetricians and midwives by looking at the ease of realization and the urgency for the improvement: discussing pregnancies with a doubtful risk weekly, founding a joint organization for the prenatal screening for Down syndrome, organizing a joint education program, and developing a shared system for electronic patient records. It was not difficult at all to recruit obstetricians and midwives for the workgroups. During the plenary third session the participants agreed on detailing and implementing more improvement proposals. It concerned cooperation with pediatrics, uniform information material, preconception care, and suspicion of (child) abuse.

Outcomes Phase C: Implementing Improvements

In January 2008, the improvements were being implemented. Although some improvements such as the electronic patient record were not easy to implement, others have achieved some results. For example, the weekly discussion of pregnant women was visited on average by five different midwifery practices every week. The participants mentioned that speaking each other's language was improved, that they gained more insight in how others work and think, and that they know each other better both professionally and personally. In addition, several sessions (4 h) of the joint education program were organized. These sessions were attended by more than 50% of the obstetricians and midwives and were evaluated very positively on aspects such as content, chosen format, teachers, and importance. On the evaluation form an obstetrician answered the question "Have your learned something?" with: "I have not learned anything concerning the content, but I have learned how midwives work and think."

CONCLUSION AND IMPLICATIONS

Conclusion

Efficient and client-friendly patient flows through integrated networks are of major importance for public health. How to design and develop such intra-organizational patient flows is still a nascent research area. One of the research issues that needs to be addressed is how to foster collaboration and coordination between a large number of independent organizations, a situation which is typical for health care networks. This chapter has reported a status report on research in the Dutch health care sector in the area of obstetric care, the care for pregnant women and their newborn babies. We have shown that a modification of an existing method to supply interorganizational collaboration using system dynamics-based group model building may be effective. The case setting concerned obstetric care in the Tilburg region, which has 2 hospitals and 12 independent midwifery practices.

Implications

Those stemming from practice probably have experienced that different stakeholders often come from different backgrounds, have different cultures, seem to speak different languages, and see the world differently. Or, as Senge (1990) would call it: they all have different mental models. As we have seen in the introduction, these differences are likely to result in resistance to change. This chapter presents an approach – the Renga approach – with which stakeholders gain insight into these differences, make them explicit, and can then start overcome their effects. Drawing causal loop diagrams can be an inspiring, agreeable and yet concrete tool to see one's mental model expressed and to discuss those of others. As a result of this shared learning about the real world, better solutions can be designed to the (underlying) problems which caused the need for change. The idea is that in such participative approaches, implementation as a separate, sequential process is made redundant. If employees participate in the design process, then the results do not need to be implemented, simply because implementation is integrated into the change process itself (Levin, 2004).

However, although the approach described in this chapter focuses on the "unfreeze" and "move" phases of a change process, one cannot ignore the "freeze" phase, because otherwise people might end up reverting to the old situation, before the intervention. Or as Lewin (1951, p. 148) already formulated this over half a century ago: "Experience with leadership training had convinced us that the workshop setting is among the most powerful tools for bringing about improvement of skill in handling inter-group relations. Even a good and successful workshop, however, seems seldom to have the change to lead to long-range improvements in the field of inter-group relations. The individual who comes home from the workshop full of enthusiasm and new insights will again have to face the community, one of perhaps 100,000. Obviously, the changes are high that his success will not be up to his new level of aspiration, and that soon disappointments will set him back again. We are facing here a question which is of prime importance for any social change, namely the problem of its permanence."

REFERENCES

Achterberg, P. W. (2005). *Measuring up to the best? International differences in perinatal mortality*. Bilthoven: RIVM. (In Dutch).

Akkermans, H. (1995). *Modelling with managers. Participative business modelling for effective strategic decision-making*. Eindhoven: Eindhoven University of Technology.

Akkermans, H. A. (2001). Renga: A systems approach to facilitating inter-organizational network development. *System Dynamics Review*, *17*(3), 179–193.

Amelink-Verburg, M. P., Verloove-Vanhorick, S. P., Hakkenberg, R. M. A., Veldhuijzen, I. M. E., Bennenbroek Gravenhorst, J., & Buitendijk, S. E. (2007). Evaluation of 280000 cases in Dutch midwifery practices: A descriptive study. *BJOG*, *115*(5), 570–578.

Andersen, D. F., & Richardson, G. P. (1997). Scripts for group model building. *System Dynamics Review, 13*(2), 107–131.

Anderson, D. F., Richardson, G. P., & Vennix, J. A. M. (1997). Group model building: Adding more science to the craft. *System Dynamics Review, 13*(2), 187–202.

Anthony, S., Amelink-Verburg, M. P., Jacobusse, G. W., & Pal-de Bruin, K. M. van der. (2005). *De Thuisbevalling in Nederland 1995–2002, Rapportage over de jaren, 2001–2002 ("Home birth in the Netherlands. A summary over the years 2001–2002")*. Bilthoven: Stichting Perinatale Registratie Nederland. (In Dutch).

Axelrod, R. (1997). *The complexity of cooperation, agent-based models of competition and collaboration.* Princeton, NJ: Princeton University Press.

Bazoli, G. J., Shortell, S. M., Dubbs, N., Chan, C., & Kravolec, P. (1999). A taxonomy of health networks and systems: Bringing order out of chaos. *Health Services research, 33*(6), 1683–1717.

Bodemheimer, T. (1999). Disease management: Promises and pitfalls. *New England Journal of Medicine, 340*, 1202–1205.

Boonstra, J. J. (2004). *Dynamics of organizational change and learning*. Chicester: Wiley.

Campbell, H., Hotchkiss, R., Bradshaw, N., & Porteous, M. (1998). Integrated care pathways. *British Medical Journal, 361*, 133–137.

Dutch Perinatal Registry. (2008). *Obstetric care in The Netherlands 2006*. Utrecht: Stichting Perinatale Registratie Nederland.

Forrester, J. (1961). *Industrial dynamics*. Cambridge, MA: MIT Press.

Gravenhorst, K. B., & Veld, R. in 't (2004). Power and collaboration. Methodologies for working together in change. In: J. J. Boonstra (Ed.), *Dynamics of organizational change and learning*. Chicester: Wiley.

Herzlinger, R. E. (2004). *Consumer-driven health care*. Chicester: Wiley.

Humpreys, P. K., Li, W. L., & Chan, L. Y. (2003). The impact of supplier development on buyer-supplier performance. *Omega, 32*(2), 131–143.

Johnston, D. A., McCutcheon, D. M., Stuart, F. I., & Kerwood, H. (2003). Effects of supplier trust on performance of cooperative supplier relationships. *Journal of Operations Management, 22*(1), 23–38.

Kilo, C. M. (1999). Improving care through collaboration. *Pediatrics, 103*(1), 384–393.

Levin, M. (2004). Organizing change processes. Cornerstones, methods, and strategy. In: J. J. Boonstra (Ed.), *Dynamics of organizational change and learning*. Chicester: Wiley.

Lewin, K. (1951). Field theory in social science: Selected theoretical papers. In: D. Cartwright (Ed.), New York: Harper.

McGlynn, E. A. S., Adams, J., Hicks, J., DeCristofaro, A., & Kerr, E. A. (2003). The quality of health care delivered to adults in the United States. *New England Journal of Medicine, 348*(26), 2635–2645.

Meiboom, B., De Haan, J., & Verheijen, P. (2004). Networks for integrated care provision: An economic approach based on opportunism and trust. *Health Policy, 69*(1), 33–43.

Miller, R. H., & Luft, H. S. (1994). Managed care plan performance since 1980. *JAMA, 271*(19), 1512–1519.

Minkman, M. M. N., Schouten, L. M. T., Huijsman, R., & Van Splunteren, P. T. (2005). Integrated care for patients with a stroke in the Netherlands: Results and experiences from a national Breakthrough Collaborative Improvement project. *International Journal of Integrated Care, 5*, 1–12.

Mohangoo, A. D., Buitendijk, S. E., Hukkelhoven, C. W., Ravelli, A. C., Rijninks-van Driel, G. C., Tamminga, P., & Nijhuis, J. G. (2008). Higher perinatal mortality in the Netherlands than in other European countries: The Peristat-II study. *Nederlands Tijdschrift voor Geneeskunde, 152*(50), 2718–2727 (In Dutch).

Nooteboom, B. (2004). *Inter-firm collaboration, learning & networks. An integrated approach.* London: Routledge.

Organization for Economic Co-operation and Development (OECD). (2011). *OECD health data 2010.* Retrieved from http://stats.oecd.org/index.aspx?queryid=24862. Accessed on May 15, 2011.

Pearson, M. L., Wu, S., Schaefer, J., Bonomi, A. E., Shortell, S. M., Mendelm, P. J., Marsteller, J. A., Louis, A., Rosen, M., & Keeler, E. B. (2005). Assessing the implementation of the chronic care model in quality improvement collaboratives. *Health Services Research, 40*(4), 978–996.

QuickStats. (2005). Rates of cesarean deliveries-selected countries. *Birth, 35*(4), 336–337.

Reuwer, P. J. H. M., Bruinse, H. W., & Franx, A. (2009). *Pro-active support of labour.* London: Cambridge University Press.

Richmond, B. (1994). Systems thinking/system dynamics: Let's just get on with it. *System Dynamics Review, 10*(2–3), 135–158.

Rouwette, E. A. J. A., Vennix, J. A. M., & Van Mullekom, T. (2002). Group model building effectiveness: A review of assessment studies. *System Dynamics Review, 18*(1), 5–45.

Senge, P. M. (1990). *The fifth discipline. The art and practice of the learning organization.* New York: Doubleday Currency.

Shortell, S. M., Gillies, R. R., & Anderson, D. A. (1994). The new world of managed care: Creating organized delivery systems. *Health Affairs*, 46–64.

Shortell, S. M., Gillies, R. R., Anderson, D. A., Erickson, K. M., & Mitchell, J. B. (2000). *The evolution of organized delivery systems.* San Francisco: Jossey-Bass Publications.

Sterman, J. D. (2000). *Business dynamics. Systems thinking and modeling for a complex world.* Boston, MA: Irwin McGraw-Hill.

Tapscott, D. (1996). *The digital economy: Promise and peril in the age of networked intelligence.* New York: McGraw-Hill.

Van der Linden, B. A., Spreeuwenberg, C., & Schrijvers, A. J. P. (2001). Integration of care in The Netherlands: The development of transmural care since 1994. *Health Policy, 55*(2), 111–120.

Vennix, J. A. M. (1996). *Group model-building. Facilitating team learning using system dynamics.* Chichester: Wiley.

Vennix, J. A. M., Akkermans, H. A., & Rouwette, E. A. J. A. (1996). Group model-building to facilitate organizational change: An exploratory study. *System Dynamics Review, 12*(1), 39–58.

Wagner, E. H., Glasgow, R. E., Davis, C., Bonomi, A. E., Provost, L., McCulloch, D., Carver, P., & Sixta, C. (2001). Quality improvement in chronic in illness care: A collaborative approach. *Joint Commission Journal on Quality Improvement, 27*(2), 63–80.

Weil, T. P. (2001). *Health networks, can they be the solution?* Michigan: The University of Michigan Press.

Wiegers, T. A., Van der Velden, L. F. J., & Hingstman, L. (2005). *Behoefteraming verloskundigen 2004–2015 ("Need for midwives 2004–2015").* Utrecht: Nivel. (In Dutch).

Woods, K. J. (2001). The development of integrated health care models in Scotland. *International Journal of Integrated Care, 1*(3). (Online).

HEALTH CARE ORGANIZATIONS AS "PATIENTS": TRANSFORMING THE FUNDAMENTAL OD PARADIGM

Irwin M. Rubin

ABSTRACT

Hidden behind such frequently used phrases as "The system/policy requires …," "The organization has decided…" is one simple fact. Systems/policies don't drop from the sky etched in stone tablets and organizations don't decide anything. People make decisions and design systems and write policies. Embracing this fact increases the likelihood that the provision of health care emanates from a "care dealership" in contrast to a "car dealership." Ignoring this fact leads to less humane, less effective, and more costly health care. This chapter will challenge all of us concerned with caring for all of us – from Organizational Development (OD). Practitioners to CEOs to … to … all of us at some point in our lives – to step up to the need to transform our most basic paradigms. To remind ourselves that human beings give birth to, nurture, sustain, and care for that which we call an organization. In so doing, we will be able to begin to act from the premise that a health care organization is itself a living breathing human organism, a "Patient" in need of care. The quality of care we afford this "Patient" directly and

Organization Development in Healthcare: Conversations on Research and Strategies
Advances in Health Care Management, Volume 10, 345–365

ISSN: 1474-8231/doi:10.1108/S1474-8231(2011)0000010026

inevitably impacts the quality of care we are afforded as patients. Acting from this premise will transform all of health care, all "care dealerships" ... and potentially "car dealerships" as well. OD professionals, therefore, can propel us all to a fourth dimension of caring for all of us.

Keywords: Organization as a "Patient"; measuring Vital Signs; "Patient" care vs. patient care; transforming the cultural paradigm; a case study in transformation

OUR CHALLENGE

Imagine the following scenario. This is the third time in three months you've visited your Physician with the same presenting symptoms. Each time more detailed tests were done to get at the root causes of your problem and a new prescriptive protocol initiated, but to no effect, with the exception of a rise in your level of anxiety, frustration, and concern about your Physician's level of competence. Perhaps even the appearance of some new potentially iatrogenic symptoms. Your Physician, if you are fortunate, may begin to wonder if the "root" cause of the problem might not be the very paradigm she is using to diagnose the root causes of the condition.

The thesis of this chapter is directly analogous. A health care organization is a *Patient* – a living breathing human organism – that cares for patients (Rubin & Fernandez, 2006; Fraser, Rubin, & Wilson, 2005) It is a "care dealership," not a "car dealership." In the former, the treatment of people is related to the quality of the product, but their customers are not human beings in need of humane caring. In the latter, by contrast, the treatment of people is both the process and the content of the business (Rubin, 1992). As an inevitable result, the humane quality of the care the *Patient* receives will directly impact the humane quality of care the patient receives.

The hard empirical data unequivocally support (Rubin, 1999; Osatuke & Dyrenforth, 2006; Meterko, Mohr, & Young, 2004; Kaissi, Kralewski, Dowd, & Heaton, 2007; Stock, McFadden, & Gowen, 2007; Laschinger & Leiter, 2006; Brewer, 2006) this premise that poor *Patient* care is directly associated with more costly, longer length of stay, less safe, and even more lethal patient care. This confronts us as a profession with a vital question: "In what ways has this data found its way into the mainstream shape and form of our OD interventions?" If it hasn't, perhaps like the Physician noted above, we may need to "begin to wonder if the 'root' cause of the continuing problems our clients experience might not be related to the very paradigm we are using to diagnose and treat their illness."

TWO NEW CONCEPTS

In a car dealership paradigm, many patient care improvement efforts focus primarily on technical effectiveness (traditional quality assurance) and managerial efficiency (resource utilization). The transformational shift to viewing an organization as a *Patient* rests first, therefore, on embracing two heretofore unaddressed concepts. One is Behavioral Quality Assurance (BQA, for short) (Rubin & Inguagiato, 1990; Rubin, 1996a, 1996b, 2009) (Fig. 1).

BQA's singular focus is the day-to-day choices ALL of the staff make about how to behave toward one another. An organizational culture is the cumulative consequence of these choices. The complex web of interpersonal relationships, like the arteries and veins in our bodies, is the vehicle through which the culture travels and has its impact. BQA, in other words, begins around the Boardroom table – the theoretical source of the organization's heart and soul, the part of the body politic where the talking is intended to take its first walking steps – and trickles down throughout the entire *Patient*. Staff infections around the Boardroom table become as lethal as staph infections around the operating room table. Consequently, a consistent failure to ensure BQA's essential place among all three of the legs on the stool will leave the "attendings" – the organization's senior executives – open to charges of "managerial malpractice" in the care of their *Patient* (Rubin, 2004).

Let's look at a few examples of managerial malpractice, the second of our new concepts, in action. These examples are based on real experiences,

Fig. 1. The Three Pillars of Total Quality Management.

which I have pieced together to preserve anonymity. As you read them, I'd invite you to reflect upon situations in your own experience where interpersonal tensions between staff – at any level of the organization – distracted them or a colleague and might in some way have created a dynamic that ultimately put patients at risk or contributed to medical errors.

In example one, it's about 6:30 am Monday morning in any Big City Hospital, USA. Several upper-level hospital Administrators are arriving for work early. In spite of their yeoman efforts, the mountain of paperwork that sits atop their desks grows daily. Everyone is overworked and understaffed. Each person is met by a Security Guard at the Hospital entrance and given a letter announcing that, due to current economic pressures, their positions have had to be eliminated. They are walked to their respective desks, asked to pack up all of their personal belongings, and escorted back to the Hospital entrance. As they leave, their Security Badges are taken away. They have been down-sized!

The rumors of this heretofore well-kept secret action ("We didn't want to create undue panic and anxiety," the CEO said when asked to explain her preemptive strike!) spread like poison ivy throughout the entire organization. Sometime later a Security Guard happened to wander past the entrance to the Operating Room (OR), perhaps heading for the men's room. At the same instant a newly hired Intern was about to administer a vitally important injection to a patient, he caught a glimpse of the Guard out of the corner of his eye. In that split second of distraction, either a near miss occurred (unlikely to be reported in the fear driven cultures of most organizations these days!) or an undeniable sentinel event occurred … as was true in this case.

The required root cause analysis (RCA) confirmed that the new Intern was asked to inject local anesthesia – Lignocain. He went to the box where it was stored, checked the drug, took the vial, and was about to load it into the syringe but he dropped it. He went to the same box, read the box, and took the next vial, but didn't read it. It looked same and was in the same box … and the Security Guard was passing by! The patient died of cardiac arrest. He had injected a dangerous drug – Suxamethonium. The RCA will conclude that a case of medical malpractice occurred, and to be sure that is a *partial truth*. The question of how the Suxamethonium (dangerous drug) was in Lignocain box would be investigated in detail. Drug manufacturers will be told about two vials looking alike and told to change them. Other vitally important steps will be taken to strengthen the technical effectiveness leg of our stool. But there is another *equally important* truth, which we will address shortly.

In example two, Sally has just joined Hospital Y as its VP of Risk Management. She is attending her first Executive Team meeting. About a third of the way through the meeting, she becomes aware that the CEO,

Mark, frequently interrupts people before they seem to be finished speaking. When John, the VP of HR, and one of the quieter members gets cut off yet again, Sally lifts her hand slightly off the table and says to Mark, very calmly; "Mark, I'm not sure John has finished his point yet. John?" The resulting sphincter-tightening anxiety is palpable!

As the meeting breaks up, Sue, the VP of Finance – and one of the organization's veterans – asks Sally if she has a minute to chat. The essence of Sue's message is that the "espoused open-door, honest communication policies aside" the kind of behavior that Sally just exhibited could become career-limiting or worse, a resume-generating event!

At the same moment as Sue is "socializing" Sally as to "how things work around here," imagine that a physician in the Hospital is *making it perfectly clear* that the Nurse who just questioned one of his actions was stepping out of line! Seconds later, they carry this bad blood into the Emergency Room (ER) where they have less than 30 seconds to take the actions needed to prevent a Code Blue from becoming a brain-dead vegetable (Knaus, Draper, Wagner, & Zimmerman, 1986).

Let's combine the two examples. If you were a provider worried about perhaps getting down-sized, might it be just a slight bit easier to get distracted at the wrong moment? If you were a nurse and you had gotten a mere fleeting glimpse of the label on the second vial and the doctor in question was the one who had just *made himself perfectly clear* to you, would you dare to mention the possibility of a wrong vial? Maybe ... if pigs could fly!!!

Make no mistake about it; examples like these are happening worldwide as we speak. Thousands of e-mails cross paths daily on just one Patient Safety Listserve and the overwhelming majority have only to do with technical effectiveness. Yet the whole truth goes unnamed and therefore undiscussed. To uncover the whole truth, equally detailed RCAs need to be done into the human culture of the organization, the *Patient* organism. These kinds of RCAs will uncover a mountain of examples of managerial malpractice. That's right! Managerial malpractice not medical malpractice. It is the unspoken root cause of many examples of medical malpractice symptoms that are (a) costing untold millions of dollars, (b) contributing to avoidable safety errors, and (c) taking the lives of patients (Jewell & McGiffert, 2009; Studer Group).

NEW DIAGNOSTIC AND TREATMENT TOOLS

Conducting RCAs of the health of the *Patient's* human culture, of the extent to which everyone is being held accountable for their part in ensuring BQA, will require a reframing of existing OD diagnostic and treatment tools and the creation and use of others. The three, which follow, along with case examples of their use, are drawn from my own practice.

(1) The Vital Signs Assessment Tool (VSAT)

Untold thousands of times weekly, the following scene takes place. *Dr. Mary Carlson enters the ICU room to check on her patient, Mr. Stromberg. She and her support team – the RN on duty, a consulting specialist, and the Resident Attending – gather at the foot of Mr. Stromberg's bed. Dr. Carlson is handed a clipboard. In a moment's time, she and her treatment team will get a snapshot of Mr. Stromberg's Vital Signs. Any sources of concern indicated by these vital signs will receive immediate prescriptive attention, including the possibility of ordering more intensive diagnostic tests to see what's driving the desired norms out-of-kilter. If all is well, the current treatment process is likely to continue as planned. Dr. Carlson and her team will then move on to the next patient on their agenda.*

Similarly, a CEO and Senior Management Team are the "Attendings" – the "provider team" in charge of their *Patient*. Like Dr. Carlson and her provider team, they, too, need to be able to gather around the Boardroom table, pick up a "clipboard," and in a moment's time, get a snapshot of their *Patient's* human vital signs, and take appropriate action.

The VSAT, therefore, seeks to tap into symptomatic measures of the holistic health of the organization. Its focus is the organization's mind, body, and spiritual condition – its heart and soul. The VSAT (see Fig. 2) is a single two-sided page (thereby taking less than a few moments to complete) having five questions.

Question 1, referred to as "Anxiety About Organizational Competence," taps into the extent to which the members of the organization have confidence in the quality of care they provide. A score of "Very likely to" on this question means when the "luck of the draw" is involved, the employees of the organization would feel quite anxious about the care "a loved one" of theirs would be receiving. Conversely, a score of "Very unlikely to" means they would have virtually no anxiety about who would be on duty if a loved one of theirs arrived for care while they, personally, were not there to watch over them.

Question 2, referred to as "Attractiveness of Job," speaks about the extent to which employees would feel motivated to encourage a very dear friend to consider taking a job with the organization.

VITAL SIGNS OF CULTURAL HEALTH

A health care organization is a human organism, a "patient", if you will. It requires the highest level of patient care humanly possible. Indeed, there is clear evidence to prove that patients will receive lower quality care if the "patient organization" is not cared for. The brief five (5) item questionnaire which follows, is designed to provide information vital to assessing how well your organization is caring for itself. For each question on both sides of the page, please **CIRCLE** the response options most reflecting your own perception.

1. Imagine you are away on a vacation. You call home to say hello and are told that a loved one of yours is being rushed to ________________ with a life threatening illness. On the five point scale below, how likely would it be that one of the prayers that flash through your mind would be of the form: "God, I hope, so-and-so (a particular person or persons) is not on duty when they arrive."

A	b	c	d	e
Very likely to	Likely to	Somewhat likely to	Somewhat unlikely to	Very unlikely to

2. Imagine that a very dear friend is considering applying for a job at ________________ and this person is highly motivated and very achievement-oriented. If this friend asked you for your honest opinion about their decision, which of the following would most likely reflect your advice? Without a moments hesitation, I'd say:

A	b	c	d	e
"Go for it!"		"You could do worse."		"You'll end up being sorry!"

3. According to Webster's, to verbally abuse is to "speak insultingly or harshly **to or about** someone." In other words, it is even verbally abusive "to speak insultingly or harshly" about another person who isn't even around to hear it, not to mention "speaking insultingly or harshly" to their face (and into their heart.) How many times in the last month have you been personally verbally abused by a colleague and or overheard a colleague verbally abuse someone else (patient or colleague.)

A	b	c	d	e
Not once	Once or twice in the last month	Once per week	More than once per week	Almost daily

Please turn over and complete the last two questions

Fig. 2. Vital Signs Assessment Tool.

4. When the fear of being honest and direct grips an organization, the organization experiences a "hardening of the arteries" and communications become stifled. People choose to say nothing challenging, particularly to their managers, and to their physician or nurse colleagues: "I don't want to rock the boat and get myself into trouble." They talk about people behind their backs, not face-to-face. Using the scale below, how would you rate the degree of open, honest, and direct communications at ________________?

- **a)** Most people are very fearful of speaking up.
- **b)**
- **c)** Some people are willing to hear the truth, but you have to be very careful to **pick and choose.**
- **d)**
- **e)** Two-way communications always flow freely and openly.

5. Integrity is a vital element of any patient's total wellness, particularly their spiritual strength. In an organizational context, integrity boils down to the extent to which senior managers and supervisors live the organization's mission and values. "Walking the talk" brings slogans and words on plaques to life. Using the scale below, how would you describe the extent to which senior managers and supervisors at ________________ are "walking their talk?"

- **a)** They are all "walking their talk."
- **b)** They are making a sincere effort to "walk their talk."
- **c)** It's still a "mixed bag"—some are trying, some are just going through the motions.
- **d)** They are still just "talking the walk."
- **e)** The rhetoric, the talk, is still badly misaligned with the walk.
- **f)** I don't know the mission and values of the organization.

Thank you for your openness and honesty.

Fig. 2. (Continued).

Question 3, referred to as "Degree of Interpersonal Toxicity," speaks directly about the issue of verbal abuse that is beginning to get the front-and-center attention it deserves (Cook, 2000).

Question 4, referred to as "Degree of Fear of Being Open," in patient-related terms, speaks about the onset of a "hardening of the arteries."

Finally, Question 5, referred to as "Degree of 'Walking the Talk'," speaks about the issue of organizational integrity.

A case study

This case study involves a 260-bed hospital located in a rural community. With 1,000 FTEs, most of whom are members of very strong unions, the hospital represents the largest employer in town. During an already scheduled personal visit to each and every Department (for another reason), the CEO personally invited employees to complete the instrument. As a consequence, 500 employees returned usable responses to the VSAT. (A likely Guinness record!)

The current state of this organization's culture of human health is reflected by their Vital Signs in Table 1.

Almost half (45%) of the employees would be "somewhat to very likely" anxious about who would be on duty if, while they were unavailable themselves to "oversee the process" a loved one of theirs needed to be rushed to the hospital with a life-threatening illness. Looking at it from the other end, only one-third of all the hospital's employees (34%) would be "very unlikely" to experience any anxiety as to who their loved one needing care would get by the luck of the draw.

Of particular significance and relevance is the fact that the entire sample of 500 included subsets of responses from each of 23 of the hospital's key departments: OB-GYN; OR; ER; Laboratory; Surgery; Admitting and Business Office; Housekeeping; Dietary; Maintenance, etc. While there were occasional differences among the many possible pair-wise comparisons, for example, between the ER and, say, Housekeeping, it was the overall similarity that was most impressive, and *predictable*.

A person who mopped up the hallway floor was therefore just as likely on average to feel anxious about the quality of care available by the luck of the draw, as was someone who worked directly where blood samples were being drawn ... or a Senior Executive.

Why "predictable?" The VSAT is designed to tap into the organization's physical and emotional bloodstream. Trying to get a pulse rate from feeling a person's big toe instead of one of their major arteries is

Table 1. Vital Signs of Organization Employees.

1. *Anxiety About Organizational Competence*	
(A) Very likely to	12%
(B) Likely to	8%
(C) Somewhat likely to	34%
(D) Somewhat unlikely to	21%
(E) Very unlikely to	34%
2. *Attractiveness of Job*	
(A) "Go for it!"	63%
(B)	20%
(C) "You could do worst."	10%
(D)	3%
(E) "You'll end up being sorry."	3%
3. *Degree of Interpersonal Toxicity*	
(A) Not once	22%
(B) Once or twice in the last month	33%
(C) Once per week	15%
(D) More than once per week	16%
(E) Almost daily	14%
4. *Degree of Fear of Being Open*	
(A) Most people are very fearful of speaking up	17%
(B)	10%
(C) Some people are willing to hear the truth, but you have to be very careful to pick and choose	56%
(D)	8%
(E) Two-way communication always flow freely and openly	9%
5. *Degree of "Walking the Talk"*	
(A) They are all "walking their talk"	4%
(B) The are making a sincere effort to "walk their talk"	28%
(C) It's still a 'mixed bag' – some are trying, some are just going through the motions	48%
(D) They are still just "talking the walk"	11%
(E) The rhetoric, the talk is still badly misaligned with the walk	7%
(F) I don't know the mission and values of the organization the talk is still badly misaligned with the walk	1%

ludicrous. But, a blood sample drawn from anywhere in the human body will yield the same vital signs because all of it flows through the same heart. The same is true for the health of an organization's human culture.

Responses to Question 2 confront us with the "golden handcuffs" syndrome where employees, because of stock options and other benefits, often feel as if they are prisoners in an unrewarding situation. Almost two-thirds of the hospitals' employees would, "without a moments hesitation," tell a "very dear friend" to seek employment in the very same hospital where they are "somewhat to very likely" to feel anxious about the quality of care afforded to "a loved one."

When we turn to Question 3, the potentially toxic impact of this psychological schizophrenia now sounds like the following scenario: "Come to work here and you're virtually guaranteed a job with great benefits. In return for that security, you will however have to be prepared to pay two 'small prices.' One, expect to be verbally abused, and/or hear a colleague be verbally abused, on average, *at least* once per week. Two, expect to be worried about who would be on duty to care for a loved one of yours with an unexpected life-threatening illness."

The parallels between the extent of verbal abuse and the fear of being open are distinct. Fifty-six percent of the employees report being willing to be no more than selectively open. It would be safe to assume that they would be "very careful to NOT pick and choose" from among the 45% who regularly verbally abuse them or others in their presence.

That fully 75% saw at least some sincere efforts among senior managers and supervisors to "walk the talk" was seen as a sign of progress in organizational integrity.

So what did they do? Sadly there was no Hollywood ending to this story. In the face of an imminent visit from the Joint Commission (TJC), formerly the Joint Commission on Accreditation of Healthcare Organizations (JCAHO), and counter to my counsel, all "healing therapies" were put on hold for several months. A massive organization-wide campaign was initiated to have the *Patient* look/sound/feel as presentable and healthy as possible, that is, to hide the VSAT data and its implications. A JCAHO score of 95% was greeted with a deep sigh of relief. The CEO was so excited he asked for a second VSAT sample. Against my better judgment we did so. As I expected, and he refused, in spite of my counsel to believe would be the case, the data looked much worse.

Because an organization's culture begins at the top, the VSAT data predict the following. Among the group of seven who made up the Senior Management Team, the following culture – by statistical definition – existed. Over 80% felt some significant degree of caution about being freely open. Almost 50% had experienced or observed (or been the perpetrator!) some form of verbal abuse in the past week. An equal number would be "somewhat to very likely" anxious about who, by the luck of the draw, would be caring for a loved one of theirs who had a life-threatening illness.

So it was decided, by the same pseudo-consensus modality that had plagued them for years, to tackle the consequences of their vital signs data by themselves. The use of outside help to support the culture change effort was therefore canceled.

Another messenger was killed. An action perfectly consistent with their disease. An action guaranteed to further exacerbate their disease.

(2) The Organizational Excellence Survey (OES) (http://www.temenosinc.com/sitebody/diagnosing_organizational_culture/index.htm)

If you were a physician, and the clipboard in front of you read: *temperature = 104; pulse rate 180 over 110; psychological signs of regular abuse and low self-confidence* and you choose to do nothing, there would be absolutely no question you'd be guilty of flagrant medical malpractice. You would be expected to (a) take action to reduce the immediate threats and (b) to do further extensive and intensive testing to identify underlying root causes.

In response to this need in *Patient* organizations, Temenos has developed the OES. The complete OES comprises 48 specific, observable, and, therefore, measurable behaviors. They are derived from the empirical studies noted earlier that document the hard bottom-line correlation between the health of the organization's human culture and the quality of care patients will receive. They are the causal behaviors underlying the VSAT vital signs symptoms and carefully researched to represent the behavioral tools essential to the creation and maintenance of a healing-oriented human culture. Furthermore, while it is useful for health care organizations to formulate and agree upon a set of core values – respect, caring, etc. – it is equally essential to keep in mind that those values cannot be managed. Only behaviors can be managed (www.temenosinc.com; Rubin & Inguagiato, 1991a, 1991b).

Because of its exhaustive and very focused nature, the OES is a more "invasive" diagnosis. If the VSAT is akin to a body scan, the OES is akin to an MRI. Like the VSAT, it is also administered anonymously. Representative samples of employees share their perceptions on two questions: (1) How important is the specific behavior being treated *Currently*; and (2) How important that behavior *Should Be* treated in the future in order to create an excellence healing-oriented organizational culture.

The % *Should Be* score *minus* the % *Currently* score yields a Delta (Δ). The bigger the Delta (Δ), the greater is the discrepancy between the organization's self-defined standard of behavioral excellence – the height of the bar – and their current level of achievement. A small sampling of the Deltas (Δ) diagnosed in two different health care organizations appears below.

Behaviors and Δs in Two Organizations	A	B
Focus on "What we can learn from this mistake?" and not on "Who is to blame?"	60	90
Gracefully accept feedback.	47	85
Admit our mistakes.	57	81
Apologize for our mistakes.	47	77
Pay careful attention without interrupting when people are trying to make a point.	28	82
Remain patient and receptive when someone disagrees with or challenges our point of view.	47	84

The underlying lack of health in Organization B, relative to that in Organization A, is clear. It begins with an apparently relatively innocuous condition – being cut off when trying to make a point, particularly when said point is at odds with someone else's. The toxicity gets more severe with a marked tendency to avoid both admitting and apologizing for mistakes. Fully understandable when the typical response to a mistake is to seek someone's head to cut off. Little wonder that feedback is avoided and defended, but not accepted gracefully (Rubin, 1998). (Three months after the organization's senior management reacted with defensive denial to the feeding back of all the OES results, the "canarys stopped singing." They suffered a severe strike among their nursing staff!)

Given this inherent and purposeful difference in specificity and "intrusive intensity" into the *Patient's* culture, the two instruments are designed to serve very different needs. After an extensive baseline picture is obtained, the VSAT is designed (not unlike those tools that many organizations use to track how well they are doing with their customer service efforts) to be used to secure periodic snapshots of the health of the organization's human culture. The OES, by contrast, is designed to be used less frequently to guide the design and implementation of more long-term systematic treatment processes.

PUTTING THE PIECES TOGETHER: A SECOND CASE STUDY IN PROCESS

In mid-2000, Paul Sokoloff, Director of Performance Consulting, began facilitating a journey at Carondelet Health Care in Kansas City, MO, aimed at enabling the *Patient* to transform itself (Sokoloff, 2006). Embarking on a process of BQA was, he notes, a natural extension of their mission: "Carondelet Health consists of Catholic organizations dedicated to the healing ministry of Jesus Christ. Our commitment to human dignity compels us to provide compassionate quality care for body, mind, and spirit, with a special concern for the poor. We are responsible stewards serving the needs of all people from conception to death."

The process they are following, while subject to the turbulent and ambiguous ups and downs of health care today, is built around several of the key elements discussed earlier. Step one was to revisit their vision and values. The CEO and Executive VP of Mission personally conducted employee focus groups with over 400 staff. The result was a vision of Service Excellence and a set of core values of Integrity, Compassion, and Unity ("Yes," as Sokoloff notes, "ICU").

However, consistent with our premise those values cannot be managed, only behavior can, he goes on to note: "While values, assumptions, and beliefs guide us, I believe it is more fruitful to talk about behavior. How people actually behave determines the culture of an organization … it is in this realm of interpersonal relationships that the culture gap in organizations is most glaring. It is the most critical, yet the most difficult gap to close. This is because it is not a matter of knowledge, but of taking what most people consider to be common sense (treating patients and each other with dignity, respect and caring), and making it common practice."

Embracing the fact that culture and behavior are synonymous, as Carondelet did, carried a vital corollary. No change in culture can be presumed to have taken place without a measurable shift in the normative pattern of day-to-day choices people make about how to behave toward one another. Step two, therefore, involved the administration of the OES in September 2001.The results of the OES survey identified 14 behaviors that had Deltas of greater than 70%. A sampling of the 2001 results appears below.

OES Behavior	2001 Δ (%)
Tell people what we like about what they are doing.	91
Express our appreciation when someone does something well.	68
Remain patient and receptive when someone disagrees with or challenges our point of view.	76
Tell one another clearly what we want from one another.	89
Use well-reasoned arguments to support our proposals.	65
Apologize for our mistakes.	81
Tell people what we don't like about what they are doing.	70

The "prescriptive therapies" Carondelet continues to call upon to treat itself as a *Patient* are varied and evolving. However, several have been consistent. One is providing employees with the skills needed to seek, give, receive, and process feedback. Two is access to a web-based *non*-anonymous relationship calibration tool. This tool, called The Behavior Minder™ is, by design, built around exactly the same 48 specific behaviors at the core of the OES (Rubin & Campbell, 1997, 2006; http://www.temenosinc.com/sitebody/the_behavior_minder/index.htm). Why? Because the OES Deltas as they exist *Currently* are the result of the day-to-day choices people made about how to behave toward one another. The only way the culture will grow to become as the *Patient* feels it should be is if people begin to make different day-to-day choices. In other words, BQA is to *Patient* care what continuous quality improvement (CQI) is to patient care. Both are totally dependent on the quality of the feedback available.

In June 2004, the OES was readministered. A snapshot of those results appears below.

OES Behavior	2004 Δ (%)
Tell people what we like about what they are doing.	60
Express our appreciation when someone does something well.	44
Remain patient and receptive when someone disagrees with or challenges our point of view.	48
Tell one another clearly what we want from one another.	61

OES Behavior	2004 Δ (%)
Use well-reasoned arguments to support our proposals.	41
Apologize for our mistakes.	58
Tell people what we don't like about what they are doing.	58

While *no* item had a Delta higher than 70% after 4 years, and there was *no* item that had a higher Delta than in the previous survey, there is still much to be done. Many key behaviors, while their Deltas did not increase, also did not enjoy anywhere near the dramatic decrease observed by some items, for example, like "Tell people what we like about what they are doing" (from a Delta of 91 to 60), and "Remain patient and receptive when someone disagrees with or challenges our point of view" (from 76% to 48%). While continuing their commitment to the two prescriptive therapies noted above, recent efforts have expanded to include vital steps to integrate BQA into the very fiber of the *Patient's* physical, emotional, and spiritual backbone.

Included in these efforts is working to integrate BQA into Carondelet's performance management system by making the process a part of every manager's assessment and development. "Each year," Sokoloff notes, "as part of the performance review process, managers send out The Behavior Minder questionnaires and develop leadership goals based on the feedback they have received .... In addition, the assessment process for leadership has been reworked. Instead of an evaluation that is a year-end review, we have implemented a process that includes goals and measures tied to the strategic plan (and reflective of BQA), and that is part of a larger on-going process that includes planning, coaching and periodic reviews."

WHERE THE BUCK STOPS ... AND *PATIENT* CARE BEGINS

Painful as it is, we must return briefly to the issue of managerial malpractice in the care of the *Patient*. For if we don't, the following "hypothetical" front page of the *New York Times* article looms ominously on the horizon.

> Irrefutable evidence in a landmark malpractice suit points the finger of blame in a patient's death at the heartlessness of the organization's senior executives. The nationwide implications could be cataclysmic. Unidentified sources reported that Dr. Joshua Caliban, world-renowned surgeon, founding father and CEO of Care Corporation of America (CCA), the fifth largest health care provider in the nation,

> called a closed doors meeting late yesterday afternoon. All of the power brokers of Chicago's legal, business, health care and insurance industries were in attendance. While the media lined up outside CCA's boardroom door sounding like vultures cackling in anticipation, a heated discussion was taking place focused on CCA's accountability in the death of a patient. Just before a deadly silence seemed to envelop the boardroom, Dr. Caliban's voice was heard booming above the rising din: "Unless you all agree to accept my proposal, at 5:30 today, Care Corporation of America will be entering a plea of guilty as charged of managerial malpractice in the death of a patient."(Rubin & Boden, 2006)

Embracing the fact that a health care organization is itself a *Patient* in need of care means that Senior Executives are organizational "Attendings." As a consequence, they bear the same accountabilities and responsibilities as do their physician colleague attendings: (1) First do no harm and (2) first heal themselves. A failure to live up to this organizational equivalent of the Hippocratic Oath leaves them open to accusations of being organizational hypocrites ... or worse!

Take a moment if you'd like to assess your potential for managerial malpractice liability by answering the 10 questions below. Does your physician and nonphysician staff march to the *same* behavioral code of conduct? Can some of your highest producing physicians "get away" with behaviors not tolerated from other staff? Etc.

Managerial Malpractice Liability Quiz (http://www.managerialmalpractice.com/Managerial%20Malpractice/pmml/pmmlquiz.htm).

We have one common Behavioral Code of Conduct for everyone.	T F
Our Behavioral Code of Conduct is enforced without "favoritism."	T F
Everyone gets a performance review at least yearly.	T F
Both technical and interpersonal competencies impact performance ratings.	T F
Feedback is direct and face-to-face versus anonymous and averaged.	T F
We have "dead messengers" in some of our closets.	T F
We have big "undiscussed elephants" on some of our meeting room tables.	T F
We know that "staff infections" are as potentially lethal as "staph infections."	T F
We know that the culture in the Boardroom filters into the treatment room.	T F
We view our organization as a human entity, a "*Patient* in need of care."	T F

A tall order? Absolutely! Don't be the least bit surprised if Banathy's prediction of the self-talk running through your head sounds something like the following: "Be a realist." "There are too many constraints." "We have to show results quickly." "You are chasing dreams." "It would never work." "We have no time for it." "It will cost too much."

While acknowledging these familiar to-be-expected statements of compromise and rationalization, he also lays the challenge at our feet. "At times of dynamic, revolutionary and continuous societal changes and transformations, anything less than the design of an ideal system and a continuous pursuit of the ideal leaves us behind. Anything less is a waste of time. The ideal system could be revolutionary, but the journey toward it can be evolutionary. Nothing less than the ideal is worth the effort" (Banathy, 1996).

THE IDEAL

Given the enormity of the task, we need to remind ourselves of the benefits to be reaped by transforming our fundamental paradigm, to focusing our profession on helping our clients to treat their organizations as *Patients* in need of the most humane and compassionate care humanely possible. While doing so will help the organization to better market its product, that motivation is defensive and ignores two vitally *more important* underlying reasons. One of these is offensive – in the sense that doing so will improve the quality of care *Patients* can deliver to patients – their reason for existence.

To provide a context for the second of the even *more important* reasons, I need to share a story. I was blessed to have Douglas McGregor, author of the timeless *The Human Side of Enterprise* (McGregor, 1985) as a faculty advisor and then colleague at MIT. As Doug lit up his pipe, a sure sign that something profound was to be released by his heart, the small group of Doctoral students in his presence sat in silent anticipation. While the date and time have long since left me, I hope the essence of what Doug said never does. He was feeling bad and wondering whether or not he was actually having any real impact on his clients. A moment of shocked silence was followed by a defensive chorus of "But what about the number of people who've read about Theory X and Theory Y, the number of places you've lectured around the world, etc." Waiting patiently as he did until the din died down, he went on to explain, and I'm paraphrasing from an aging memory. "What bothers me here," he said, touching his own heart, "is that I make the argument to my clients in extrinsic terms. Treat people well and, as a consequence, they will produce for you. When what I really believe," pointing to his heart again, "is that the reason why we should treat people well is intrinsic, because we are all miracles of our one Creator. I don't think my clients would listen to me if I spoke to them in those terms."

By transforming the fundamental OD paradigm from which we work with health care organizations to helping them to see and treat themselves as *Patients* in need of care, we will be helping to remind ourselves of the essential oneness of human development with organizational development. As "car dealerships" look to "care dealerships" for ways to manage and lead their organizations, the health care industry – and the profession of OD (Rubin & Nicoll, 2002) – will have the opportunity to contribute to the health of the nation.

NOTE

Of the 2000 or so sentinel events recorded by the VA in 2007, almost 70% were attributed to "poor communication between nurses and physicians." The data on abusive interactions – where abusive equals the kinds of uncaring interactions between physicians and nurses, and between and among nurses themselves is also just beginning to bubble to the surface in tsunami proportions. So much so that JCHO's new NPSG for 2009 requires that every health care organization have a plan in place to handle unprofessional or inappropriate behavior. The operational definition of what this means is left up to each institution, as is a plan for handling the consequences of falling outside whatever norm is set.

REFERENCES

Banathy, B. H. (1996). Designing social systems in a changing world (p. 288). New York. Available from Amazon.com

Brewer, B. B. (2006). Relationships among teams, culture, safety and cost outcomes. *Western Journal of Nursing Research*, *28*(6), 641–653.

Cook, J. (2000). O.R. Scorn. Nursing Management, September.

Fraser, S. W., Rubin, I. M., & Wilson, T. (2005). *Caring matters: Every day tales for healing organisations*. West Sussex, UK: Kingsham Press.

Jewell, K., & McGiffert, L. (2009). To err is human – To delay is deadly, May. Consumers Union.

Kaissi, A., Kralewski, J., Dowd, B., & Heaton, A. (2007). The effect of the fit between organization culture and structure on medication errors in medical group practices. *Health Care Management Review*, *32*(1), 12–21.

Knaus, W. A., Draper, E. A., Wagner, D. P., & Zimmerman, J. E. (1986). An evaluation of outcome from intensive care in major medical centers. *Annals of Internal Medicine*, *104*(3), 410–418.

Laschinger, H. K. S., & Leiter, M. P. (2006). The impact of nursing work environments on patient safety outcomes. *Journal of Nursing Administration*, *36*(5), 259–267.

McGregor, D. (1985). The human side of enterprise: 25th anniversary printing. New York: McGraw-Hill Irwin.

Meterko, M., Mohr, D., & Young, G. J. (2004). Teamwork culture and patient satisfaction in hospitals. *Medical Care*, *42*(5), 492–498.

Osatuke, K., & Dyrenforth, S. (2006). Civility in VA hospitals relates to costs and performance indicators. Paper presented at the 114 Annual Convention of the American Psychological Association, New Orleans, LA, August 10.

Rubin, I. M. (1992). Total quality management: Care dealers vs. car dealers. *Physician Executive Journal of Management*, *18*(5), 15–20.

Rubin, I. M. (1996a). *Behavioral quality assurance: The information highway's new lane*. Honolulu: Temenos Inc.

Rubin, I. M. (1996b). Transforming organizational cultures: Simple as ABC. The 1996 Annual: Volume 2 Consulting. Pfeiffer & Co.

Rubin, I. M. (1998). Feedback: The key to true collaboration. *Healthcare Forum Journal*, *41*(3), 32–36.

Rubin, I. M. (1999). Interpersonal economics: How the "Soft Stuff" affects hard bottom lines. *Health Forum Journal*, *42*(5), 42–44.

Rubin, I. M., & Nicoll, D. (2002). Organization transformation: OD's new growth challenge. *OD Practitioner Journal of the Organizational Development Network*, *34*(2), 34–40.

Rubin, I. M. (2004). Managerial malpractice and patient safety: What's the connection? In: M. Hatlie & B. J. Youngberg (Eds), *The patient safety handbook*. Boston: Jones and Bartlett.

Rubin, I. M. (2009). Clinical engineering and managerial malpractice: What's the connection? *Journal of Clinical Engineering*, *34*(4), 210–213.

Rubin, I. R., & Boden, T. W. (2006). *Dying for compassion*. Honolulu: Temenos Inc.

Rubin, I. R., & Campbell, T. J. (1997). The ABCs of effective feedback: A guide for caring professionals. San Francisco: Jossey-Bass. November.

Rubin, I. R., & Campbell, T. J. (2006). *Having it both ways: The ABCs of win-win relationships*. Honolulu: Temenos Inc.

Rubin, I. M., & Fernandez, C. R. (2006). *My pulse is not what it used to be: The leadership challenges in health care*. Honolulu: Temenos Inc.

Rubin, I. M., & Inguagiato, R. (1990). Behavioral quality assurance: A transforming experience. *Physician Executive Journal of Management*, *16*(5), 30–33.

Rubin, I. M., & Inguagiato, R. (1991a). Training excellence: An organizational approach. *Physician Executive Journal of Management*, March.

Rubin, I. M., & Inguagiato, R. (1991b). Changing the work culture. Training and Development, July.

Stock, G. N., McFadden, K. L., & Gowen, C. R. (2007). Organization culture, critical success factors, and the reduction of hospital errors. *International Journal of Production Economics*, *106*(2), 368–392.

Studer Group. Leadership Malpractice: Does Your Organization Have the Symptoms? Unpublished manuscript.

Sokoloff, P. (2006). Practicing what we preach. Health progress. *The Catholic Health Association of the United States*, *87*(1).

SUSTAINING HIGH PERFORMANCE: DYNAMIC BALANCING IN AN OTHERWISE UNBALANCED SYSTEM

Jason A. Wolf

ABSTRACT

As Ovid said, "There is nothing in the whole world which is permanent." It is this very premise that frames the discoveries in this chapter and the compelling paradox it has raised. What began as a question of how performance is sustained, unveiled a collection of core organizational paradoxes. The findings ultimately suggest that sustained high performance is not a permanent state an organization achieves, but rather it is through perpetual movement and dynamic balance that sustainability occurs.

The idea of sustainability as movement is predicated on the ability of organizational members to move beyond the experience of paradox as an impediment to progress. Through holding three critical "movements" – agile/consistency, collective/individualism, *and* informative/inquiry *– not as paradoxical, but as active polarities, the organizations in the study were able to transcend paradox, and take active steps to continuous achievement in outperforming their peers. The study, focused on a collection of hospitals across the Unites States, reveals powerful stories of*

Organization Development in Healthcare: Conversations on Research and Strategies
Advances in Health Care Management, Volume 10, 367–384

ISSN: 1474-8231/doi:10.1108/S1474-8231(2011)0000010027

care and service, of the profound grace of human capacity, and of clear actions taken to create significant results. All of this was achieved in an environment of great volatility, in essence an unbalanced system. It was the discovery of movement and ultimately of dynamic balancing that allowed the organizations to in this study to move beyond stasis to the continuous "state" of sustaining high performance.

Keywords: High performance; paradox; health care; sustaining performance; dynamic balance

SUSTAINING AS MOVEMENT

> All things change, nothing is extinguished … . There is nothing in the whole world which is permanent. Everything flows onward; all things are brought into being with a changing nature; the ages themselves glide by in constant movement.
>
> – Ovid

As Ovid said, "There is nothing in the whole world which is permanent." It is this very premise that frames the discoveries in this chapter and the compelling paradox it has raised. What began as a question of how performance is sustained, unveiled a collection of core organizational paradoxes. The findings ultimately suggest that sustained high performance is not a permanent state an organization achieves, but rather it is through perpetual movement and dynamic balance that sustainability occurs.

The idea of sustainability as movement is predicated on the ability of organizational members to move beyond the experience of paradox as an impediment to progress. Through holding three critical "movements" – *agile/consistency, collective/individualism,* and *informative/inquiry* – not as paradoxical, but as active polarities, the organizations in the study were able to transcend paradox, and take active steps to continuous achievement in outperforming their peers. The study, focused on a collection of hospitals across the United States, reveals powerful stories of care and service, of the profound grace of human capacity, and of clear actions taken to create significant results. All of this was achieved in an environment of great volatility, in essence an unbalanced system. It was the discovery of movement and ultimately of dynamic balancing that allowed the organizations to in this study to move beyond stasis to the continuous "state" of sustaining high performance.

THE POSSIBILITY OF PARADOX

> Why is it that organization theorists should be concerned with the issues of paradox? What insights does it offer to the understanding of organizations that are not available or have not been available though the existing "nonparadoxical" perspectives? For us, the answer to these questions is quite simple: *paradoxes are important because they reflect the underlying tensions that generate and energize organizational change* (italics added)... A focus on paradox, therefore, moves us away from the concept of organizations as static systems coping with problematic environmental fluctuations through deviation counteracting processes to a concept of organizations as continually dynamic systems that carry the seeds of change within themselves. (Ford & Backoff, 1988, p. 82)

In examining the idea that sustainability itself may actually be grounded in action or movement, we are called to examine the paradoxical nature of organizations themselves. While there is now a greater recognition of the importance of paradox in understanding the complexity of organizational performance (Marsh & Macalpine, 1999; Pascale, 1990; Peters & Waterman, 1982), paradox as a concept unto itself carries many challenges and stigma in current management thinking. Much of the focus of contemporary theory construction is still biased toward the side of permanence, order, and stability (Poole & Van de Ven, 1989). Little has been addressed in looking at the tensions or oppositions (paradoxes) in organizations. All too often investigations of complicated organizational phenomena are focused on linear solutions and achieving equilibrium (Quinn & Cameron, 1988), either ignoring contradictions or identifying one extreme as good and the other bad in order to resolve the issue. This seems to suggest that there is still a general discomfort with the idea of, and feeling experienced when, facing paradox.

This avoidance of, and attempt to resolve, paradox seems to generally permeate organizations as well. While acknowledging paradox exists, many continue to suggest paradox is something to be "managed" (Morgan, 1997; Peters & Waterman, 1982) or "addressed" (Van de Ven & Poole, 1988). In contrast as paradox has become increasingly prevalent in organizational studies (Lewis, 2000; Poole & Van de Ven, 1989; Quinn, 1988; Quinn & Cameron, 1988), it has also presented itself as an effective means by which to explore what is taking place in organizations (Luscher, Lewis, & Ingram, 2006).

In recognizing paradox, we are exposed to and can more effectively explore the complexity and ambiguity of organizational life (Cameron & Quinn, 1988). In exploring a model for sustaining high performance, paradox presents a powerful means to reveal the dynamic factors involved.

Paradox itself can serve as a viable alternative strategy of theory building (Poole & Van de Ven, 1989). In looking for organizational tensions or oppositions, we can stimulate the development of broader, more interesting (Bartunek, Rynes, & Ireland, 2006; Davis, 1971) theoretical concepts. While understanding paradox does not necessarily solve all problems, it does create the potential for new possibilities (Luscher et al., 2006).

Paradox presents the "inevitable struggle of opposites" (Morgan, 1997, p. 294). If we are to lead successful change, namely transformational change in organizations, managers must be skilled in managing the tensions that arise. Morgan (1997) suggests two steps in managing paradox. The first is recognizing that both dimensions of the contradictions usually have merit. This dialectical view allows for the potential to embrace both sides of the paradox. "Paradox cannot be successfully resolved by eliminating one side" (1997, p. 294). The second step is to suggest ways that capture the value of the dual tensions while minimizing the conflict. This is not conflict avoidance, but rather finding new perspectives in which to frame the dialectical nature of paradox.

Instead of attempting to reduce the tension of paradox or rationalize its existence, we should use paradox to generate insight and change. The linear models under which we tend to frame organizational action do a great disservice to the complex organizations of today (Lewis, 2000). Instead, to capitalize on paradox, organizations must use "the inherent tensions to one's advantage rather than ignoring or resolving them" (Fiol, 2002, p. 655). Fiol (2002) suggests there is a tendency to engage in a process of "deparadoxification," which she believes is exemplified by the tendency of research to avoid or attempt to resolve tensions by focusing on some middle ground. This overlooks the essence of a paradox; its grounding in the dynamic and distinct tensions of polarities and not necessarily some halfway point between them.

While it is also widely recognized that the paradoxes raised in organizational life are unavoidable, little has been offered on how they may actually support or even enable the sustainability of organization vitality and performance. It is in the idea of transcending paradox (Pascale, 1990, Lewis, 2000), not simply managing it, that we can begin to explore a new way to experience and exist with paradox as a regular element of organizational life. If sustainability is potentially based on the paradoxical nature of the movements discovered, we need to be willing to accept the very nature of paradox we look to avoid.

> The rising intricacy, ambiguity, and diversity of organizations place a premium on researchers' abilities to think paradoxically: to live and even thrive within the plurality

> and changes of organizational life and help practitioners do likewise. Building this capacity requires confronting our own defenses—the desire to over rationalize and oversimplify the complications of organizational life—and learning to explore the natural ebb and flow of tensions. (Lewis, 2000, p. 774)

It may then be paradox itself that best supports our ability to both survive and thrive in an environment of constant change. Paradoxes both energize change and move us beyond the view of organizations as static systems (Ford & Backoff, 1988). In doing so, the potentiality of movement is raised, for if we deny the presence of paradox or are simply stopped by it, we restrict the very movement an organization can make. Ultimately we need to look at the idea of transcending paradox (Lewis, 2000; Pascale, 1990) in which we see the elements of paradox not as roadblocks, but rather as potential conduits for sustaining organizational performance and discovering greater possibility.

THE RESEARCH PROCESS

The study was based on the longitudinal examination of performance for a set of 12 hospitals across the United States. Over a seven-year period, it was discovered that nine were able to sustain performance on a set of high performance measures, while three did not. This lead to the central question: *What supports the sustainability of high performance?* The research process followed a qualitative approach (Cresswell, 2007; Glaser & Strauss, 1967; Strauss & Corbin, 1998) and was grounded in the ideas of generative theory (Gergen, 1978) that closely aligns with this exploration of potentially paradoxical concepts. Instead of substantiating "truth," generative theory looks to "unseat the comfortable truths of wide acceptance" (p. 1357).

The study was based on 41 interviews conducted at the 12 hospital locations. Interviews at the sustaining facilities were held with the CEO, longest-tenured executive, longest-tenured staff member, a director or manager with tenure from at least 2000, and a staff member with tenure from at least 2000. The interviews were conducted using a semistructured interview protocol (Rubin & Rubin, 2005), digitally recorded and transcribed resulting in almost 900 pages of data.

Using the conventions of grounded theory (Glaser & Strauss, 1967; Strauss & Corbin, 1998), a comprehensive process of open and axial coding was conducted and the outcomes confirmed via a multirater validation. The findings were then compared with those of four research partners to enrich the interpretive process. Once codes were identified (over 1,200 raw codes initially), a review of the data was conducted to categorize and identify key themes. The initial code count was reduced to 128 initial categories that were then grouped into 24 supercategories capturing the main concepts developed in the study. The supercategories were then consolidated into 10 key themes. After additional review, the 10 themes were refined into three core concepts, framed around nine key actions and representing three active polarities – the three movements of sustaining high performance.

THE DISCOVERY

The findings in this study were drawn from hundreds of stories shared by participants in the hospitals studied. While this chapter does not share an extensive number of the actual stories, it provides the compelling and powerful messages they conveyed through the three movements of sustaining high performance. Each movement is comprised of three key actions (Table 1) that represent what the sustaining high performers revealed as critical to their ability to achieve ongoing performance. The movements and key actions are not items to simply be checked off. They are actions that must be taken on relentlessly day-after-day. Sustaining performance is a never-ending journey that requires great stamina, resolve, and a commitment to these fundamental actions.

The first movement, *agile/consistency*, represents the culture, or consciousness, of the organization. It is both the focus on purpose and a balanced commitment to progress that provides people the ability to move toward moments of anxiety, but without fear. This movement represents the

Table 1. The Three Movements and Nine Key Actions in Sustaining High Performance.

Movement	Key Actions
Agile/Consistency	Acting with clarity of purpose
	Going above and beyond
	Challenging the status quo
Informative/Inquiry	Caring about our people
	Seeking input and sharing information
	Walking the talk
Collective individualism	Committing to who
	Connecting and caring
	Acting with ownership and autonomy

capacity to engage in organization efforts and participate in guiding organizational outcomes not as contradictory to purpose, but rather as contributing to cause.

The first of three key actions under *agile/consistency* is *acting with clarity of purpose*. The data showed these organizations to have a strong sense of collective self and organizational pride supported by a sense of personal connection to the organization and the contributions people could make. This is supported by the second key action, *going above and beyond*, which represents the ability of individuals to do what it takes to create peak experiences for customers and for one another. One CEO annually challenges his staff to list what achievements they will strive for in the year ahead. The goals, such as "Best Place to Work," "Magnet Status," or the Baldridge Award, are taken on as critical commitments aligned with the purpose of the organization. This is reflected in the significant number of times participants referred to their facility as striving "to be the best."

The third key action is *challenging the status quo*. The ability to challenge the status quo is reinforced by an environment that supports people's efforts to try new things. Most importantly, it is the ability to do so with the knowledge that mistakes are not career-ending, but rather the discoveries they lead to (positive or negative) are seen as organizational gifts. This belief, that it is far better to fail trying than not to do at all, represents the very idea of movement. Following a consistently clear purpose, while maintaining the agility to alter course, trying new ideas and taking on new endeavors is one key movement in sustaining performance.

The second movement, *informative/inquiry*, represents the important influence of leadership in sustaining organization performance. This movement focuses on the critical role of leadership in sustaining high performance. This is not leadership as simply characterized by traits or styles such as transformational or visionary, but rather it is in the constancy of actions from leadership at all levels in the organization. One of the most resilient of the sustaining organizations in the study had a change in CEO two times over the course of the six years examined yet maintained their results. Leadership is not necessarily about the individual, but rather about how the fundamentals of leadership are applied in the organization.

The first key action is *caring about people*, which focuses on sincere interest in and respect for people across the organization. This fundamental action carries great weight in encouraging the engagement of people in supporting performance. The second action, *seeking input and sharing information*, is more than delivering communication. It represents the consistent effort to reach out to people in the organization for their ideas, concerns, and contributions. Most critical as the data suggested is the informal communication process in which leadership invests the time to personally connect with people, while gathering a broad collection of information from people across the organization. The third key action is *walking the talk*. This may be the core of effective leadership in sustaining high performance. The data suggest that the impact of leaders doing what they say, of living their words through their actions, captures the very essence of the simple yet powerful nature of the movements in sustaining high performance. It is in walking the talk that commitment is realized and respect is delivered. It is also where commitment to and respect for leadership is earned.

The third movement, *collective/individualism*, represents the powerful element of people in the organizations. This movement represents the polarities of ensuring the right people are part of your organization; people who are aligned with, understand, and are committed to the organization's purpose and direction; people who can serve as strong individual contributors, but who also recognize that in spite of individual strength they can most effectively contribute by using their individual strengths in powerfully collaborating across individual and organizational boundaries. This engages us in the systemic perspective of organizations that while they represent a collection of individuals, it is the organization that provides the framework for accomplishment. The idea of collaboration does not diminish individual contribution, but rather expands organizational capability.

The first key action, *committing to who*, is grounded in the idea of getting the right people on board, but it is not only the attraction and acquisition of talent. It also takes us to the next level of our commitment to each of those individuals with an investment in developmental opportunities. *Connecting and caring* is the next key action and is about providing the opportunity for people in the organization to connect with one another, weave a network (that many in the study referred to as "family") that is supportive even in the face of critical work demands. This action is about ensuring someone's basic needs are met, not as mandatory management action, but rather from a groundswell of collegial support. This is not to suggest that every individual will embrace one another in any organizational setting, but the data shows sustaining high performance is solidly grounded on the level of care shown for and among people across the organization, from outreach in moments of crisis to celebrations in moments of joy. The support for and encouragement of personal connection has a profound effect on the sustaining of performance.

The last of the key actions is *acting with ownership and autonomy*. This is the freedom and ability of members of the organization to make significant decisions at the point of contact. These actions come from people who feel they are not at risk for doing the wrong thing and given the opportunity continuously do what is right. Decision hierarchies may be necessary for significant expenditures or fundamental strategy shifts, but providing the space for individuals to make contributions through their daily interactions and individual decisions without the fear of retribution or punishment plays a significant role in supporting the movement of *collective/individualism* and its role in sustaining high performance.

This overview of findings represents the themes discovered through the many stories shared by people across the facilities in the study. They signify a consistency in commitment, clarity in purpose, and a focus on action that is reflective of the importance of dynamic movement versus static characteristics. The movements and key actions represent an active picture of daily life in these facilities. The data ultimately suggest that it is the connected nature of these movements and key actions that has allowed these facilities to face paradox and distinguish themselves as sustaining high performers.

TRANSCENDING PARADOX: MOVEMENT AND DYNAMIC BALANCE

Schumacher (1977) takes us one step closer in engaging with rather than being stopped by paradox, framing it as one of two distinct types of problems organizations face. Convergent problems are those that are solvable based on logic or single solution responses. This would be the selection of one key action as our sole means to achieve outcomes. Single solution responses fall short of providing the comprehensive actions organizations need today to survive the continuously changing terrain.

The "paramount attribute characterizing organizations that have the capacity to adapt successfully (to turbulent times) is the presence of paradox" (Cameron, 1986, p. 545). It is this capacity, to capitalize on the presence of paradox, which is fundamental to achieving and sustaining high performance. Yet, this is exactly what most organizations fail to do. They instead maintain a mindset of convergent problem solving, looking for the single solution or "appropriate response." A world of constant, transformational change and in particular the chaotic ever-changing environment in health care requires a dynamic perspective in which single solutions no longer work. Operating with this management philosophy is like simply bringing a watering can to a forest fire; it exemplifies an unmistakable underestimation of the complexity of the situation and the dynamism required in the response.

Perhaps the strongest step the sustaining high performers take is in facing the challenge of paradox and choosing to recognize the very paradoxes they face. They seem to understand that organizations are nothing less than dynamic entities that live in a world wrought with paradox. While this stops most, the sustaining performers' willingness to be in motion and take on simultaneous, complementary actions holds the key to their success.

The counter to the convergent problems facing organizations are divergent problems (Schumacher, 1977), that is, problems that are not easily quantifiable or verifiable and do not seem to have a single solution. While a convergent mindset leads to the mindset of either contradiction or extremism, divergent problems take on a different quality, leading to higher levels of thinking where one can begin to hold opposites not as conflicting, but as complementary. Ultimate divergent problems, such as paradox, cannot be avoided; rather they can be transcended.

Pascale (1990) challenges the management principles of the day, warning us of the complacency of organizations in today's business environment. He suggests that with operational excellence seemingly an end unto itself, organizations have the tendency to believe they have "achieved" performance and in essence, stop moving. This seems to present a contradiction in the face of the turbulent organizational environments where standing still is actually falling behind.

To overcome this, organizations must have the willingness to take a bold step into the fray, to address paradox head on and in doing so transcend (Pascale, 1990; Lewis, 2000) its ominous drag and thrive in its potential. In transcending paradox, the tensions of opposites shift from dualities (either/or) to polarities (ends of a continuum). Interactions shift from either/or to and/also, moving beyond static state to dynamic tension.

Central to the consciousness and shared spirit experienced in the sustaining high performers is their ability to hold this tension. They do so by being in action and moving between the poles of the paradoxes that support their success. This is "dynamic synthesis" (Pascale, 1990, p. 53), taking on a new mindset of embracing paradox versus the prevailing mindset caused by tending toward one end of the continuum or the other. It is finding the ability to be in state of dynamic balancing. Beyond paradox, long-term survival is dependent on the balancing of polarities and being in dynamic action (Quinn and Cameron, 1988).

In follow-up interviews focused on addressing the effects of the three movements and the polarities they represent, a selection of the original interviewees were asked how they experienced the movements in their workplace and how these movements potentially affected daily work and organizational outcomes. The participants' responses did not deny the experience of tension but rather as one respondent acknowledged, "Tensions do show up, but we embrace them and have to own them directly." This person suggested that in fact she saw the ability of members of her facility to manage the tension as a critical "way of being."

Another participant supported this observation, adding that inherent tensions were addressed by engaging people at all levels in the organization. When asked how this was accomplished, she used the example of the movement *collective/individualism* as not only a polarity held by the organization but also the means by which it was addressed. She suggested that while individual efforts and collaboration may seem contradictory, it was committing to having the best people, the ongoing focus on caring and connecting, and the sense of ownership that supported staff in working together that enabled her facility to transcend the potential paradoxes they faced.

A facility CEO added that the potential tension posed by the pull between the two ways of being represented in each movement was not experienced as a contradiction, but rather, "they are complementary and provide invigorating, vibrant opportunities." This perspective validates in practical terms the suggestion of Pascale (1990) that, "what have heretofore been regarded as hardships (owing to their paradoxical nature) or chronic sources of aggravation to managers are, in fact, the wellspring of organizational vitality" (p. 52). He adds, "Polarities provide an ongoing vehicle for sustaining constructive disequilibrium" (p. 52). This constructive disequilibrium is a product of the actions of the organizations themselves. In being in constant movement in the nine key actions, these organizations have been able to develop a shared consciousness and spirit, supported by leadership action, culture, and the people that comprise the organizations. The elements of the three movements themselves have provided the capability for the organizations to transcend paradox and find a place of constant action, shared spirit, and dynamic balance.

The idea of "transcending" paradox shifts the thinking about paradox from convergent problem solving to a reframing of the tensions inherent in paradox; contradictions become complementary and integrated polarities. The link between potentially opposing forces (Smith & Berg, 1987) instead allows for dynamic movement and an oscillation between two continuous poles. This transcendent link is what releases the individual, group, and organization into a space of movement, into the ebb and flow between the polarities. In continuously balancing change and stability, collectivism and individuality, and informing and inquiring, these organizations take on sustaining themselves as movement. "The steering of a viable course requires that opposites ... be balanced dynamically" (Ford & Backoff, 1988, p. 88). It is this idea of dynamic balance, the art of balancing, in which we find the true possibility of transcending paradox.

> We stand in turmoil of contradictions without having the faintest idea how to handle them: Law/Freedom; Rich/Poor; Right/Left; Love/Hate—the list seems endless. Paradox lives and moves in this realm; it is the art of balancing opposites in such a way that they do not cancel each other but shoot sparks of light across their points of polarity. It looks at our desperate either/ors and tells us they are really both/ands—that life is larger than any of our concepts and can, if we let it, embrace our contradictions. (Mary Morrison cited in Smith & Berg, 1987, p. 3)

THE ART OF BALANCING

Embracing our contradictions describes the art of balancing taking place in each of the three discovered movements. The movements remain in a constant state of adjustment and oscillation (Smith & Berg, 1987) following "the inherent pulse of nature" (Guerra, 2005, p. 136). It is in this pulse between polarities where we find the answer to our search for what supports the sustainability of high performance.

In the model, balance is not a state to be achieved, but rather it is continuous, transformational, and dynamic change (Marshak, 2004; Woodman, 1993). It is not movement with the intention of achieving equilibrium, which many would suggest equates to the death of a system (Bertalanffy, 1950; Blegen, 1968; Katz & Kahn, 1966). Rather, it is the "maintenance" of a steady state of nonequilibrium (a seemingly paradoxical statement in its own right) that requires the constant art of balancing. Much like breathing, where one cannot inhale, without exhaling, or exhale without inhaling, it is the combination of both polarities in each movement that enables the sustaining of performance.

This idea of wholeness of actions and perpetual balancing challenges much of Western philosophical and management thinking. Polarity and duality in Western thinking has us see opposites as contradictory, disconnected or unrelated. Polarity in the context of Eastern philosophy, as represented in the principle of Yin-Yang, has us experience the existential interdependence of the dual aspects of one unity (Coward, 1996; Karcher, 1999; Marshak, 1993; McGregor, 1960; Sun, 1999). This is an important distinction seen in the sustaining high performers. They had the inherent ability to hold this interdependence and live in each of these dynamic balances managing, for example, with *collective/individualism*, the ability to ensure strong individual contribution, while supporting work through powerful collaborative actions.

In his investigation of Yin-Yang and management, Sun (1999) introduces three pairs of characteristics that specifically support the polarities represented by the movements in the sustaining high performers. The first, "co-existence and unity," provides the framework for the whole. While each concept is unique, they are not distinct. Without one, the idea of the whole disappears. The second, "change and exchange," provides for the interaction of the polarities. Although one may be the guiding process for a while, they will invariably shift roles over time. Environmental factors, organizational choice, and other circumstances all influence these shifts. The third, "balance and harmony," leads us again to the art of balancing. While Tao is about the achievement of harmony, we should not mistake this for equilibrium. This resulting "balance" would render the polarity and in essence the organization itself lifeless. Instead harmony is about the constant interchange and relationship between opposing poles. It is about movement.

> Thus being long lasting does not mean being in a fixed or definitive state. Being fixed and definitive, a thing cannot last long. The way to be constant is to change according to circumstance. (I Ch'eng as cited by Marshak, 1993, p. 402)

A METAPHOR OF MOVEMENT REDUX

While sustaining by its definition is "the act of maintaining" (Random House Unabridged Dictionary, 2006), it is the focus on sustaining as the "act of moving" that the findings seem to suggest. If we accept that standing still at today's pace of change is falling behind, we are already shifting to a mindset of movement. But the participants in the study did not talk of change for the sake of change, and the motivation for their movements did not seem to be simply keeping pace with others. In fact, there was little discussion in the data about planned change programs or initiatives. In asking people if their facility made a decision to intentionally change and become a "high performing facility," almost every subject responded that they did not. Instead they spoke of the continuous effort to align key ideas, supported by key leaders, and enacted by key people.

This is an interesting discovery. Most people said they did not undertake an intentional change program, yet the stories they shared show a pattern of intentionality in their decisions and actions to be the kind of health care facilities they hoped to become. Rather than talking about what these facilities achieved in sustaining their performance as a decision to change, they simply made a decision to act, to be in movement toward a "state" they believed was not an end point, to take on a continuing journey.

The participants revealed in their words that high performance was not a destination, and in fact may not even have been a goal. Rather, it was about moving forward, or as one subject said "we can't stop here!" These words and the many others shared by the participants in this study are representations of actions that together paint a picture of movement represented by the interplay of the three movements: *collective/individualism*, *agile/consistency*, and *informative/inquiry*.

A MODEL FOR SUSTAINING HIGH PERFORMANCE

Based on this discussion, a model for sustaining high performance is grounded it in a fundamental understanding of the power of an almost unconscious, continuous, transformational (Marshak, 1993; Tushman & O'Reilly, 1996; Weick & Quinn, 1999; Woodman, 1993) and morphogenic (Marshak, 2004) change process; incorporated with an understanding of the relational nature (Gergen, 1999; Gergen & Walter, 1998; Homans, 1951/1992) of humanness and a consideration of dynamic balance (Bertalanffy, 1950; Blegen, 1968; Evans, 1992; Guerra, 2005; Katz & Kahn, 1966; Smith & Berg, 1987); and the potential for unity in polarity (Durlabhji, 2004; Karcher, 1999; Marshak, 1993; Sun, 1999).

In pulling these elements together, it is possible to move past the frontiers of typical change paradigms (Kuhn, 1962) and beyond the typical thought processes of bureaucratic management models (Morgan, 1997; Weisbord, 2004) into the generative realm of theory development (Gergen, 1978). The result is the symphonic connection of the three movements, *collective/individualism, agile/consistency, and informative/inquiry*, as individual polarities linked in a state of ongoing interaction and dynamic balancing.

As represented in the model (Fig. 1), each movement maintains the unity of its own "trilarity" of key actions, while contributing to the overall whole.

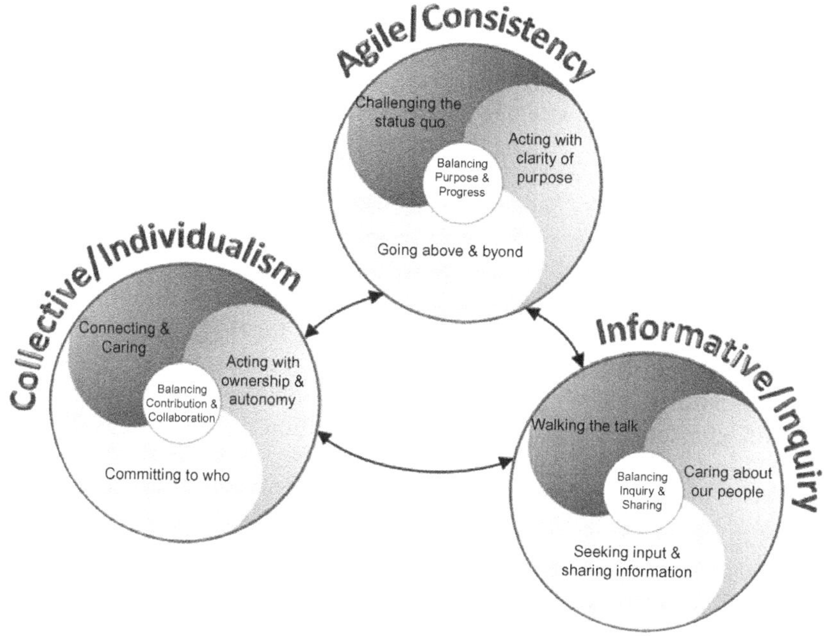

Fig. 1. Model for the Sustaining of High Performance.

Each part of the model represents movement and the continuous balancing of polarities. The data show the power of *collective/individualism* (people) enables strong individuals to interact and collaborate in powerful ways. The strength of *agile/consistency* (culture) provides unwavering purpose and the ability to rapidly respond in a moment's notice. The reach of *informative/inquiry* (leadership) supports an internal dialogue that not only informs but also continually learns and supports the very ability of its counterparts to operate most effectively.

Central to the model is that the movements coexist and are in a mode of continuous action. While at times one movement or another may ebb and flow, it is only together that they are effective in sustaining high performance. As one subject said, "We can't really have one without the others if we are going to be successful." As with the understanding of the Yin-Yang, it is through the complementary nature of the movements and the interconnectedness of their individual strengths that the system gets its power and the potential exists for the sustaining of performance.

The model is grounded in the challenges posed by paradox in organizations. It is supported by the potential that there is more that can be accomplished than simply managing paradox. If we shift perspective and begin to look at these extremes, not as contradictory impediments, but as polar complements, we reframe the ability for organizations to address these seemingly conflicting issues. It is a shift in organizational consciousness, driven by a focus on key actions. It is recognizing that transcending paradox is about a willingness to be in a state of continuous balancing and disequilibrium.

The elements of the model, the three movements of sustaining high performance, provide a framework of possibility for the subject facilities to do just that. As one CEO injected, this is not "rocket science," it is rather about intentional action and the willingness to hold the key actions found in the data as a central part of what the organization does every day.

> When we transcend a paradox there is often a quality of obviousness that produces a shock of recognition. No longer held captive by the old way of thinking, we are liberated to see things we have known all along, but couldn't assemble into a useful model for action. (Pascale, 1990, p. 110)

SUSTAINING HIGH PERFORMANCE AND DYNAMIC BALANCING

In developing a model of sustaining high performance, there is a new awareness that the language and organizational discourse of past tense with "-ed" words such as achiev*ed* or sustain*ed* no longer meets the needs of measuring performance in an environment of constant change. The data provide a sense that the subject facilities did not reach an end point but rather were engaged in a continual process of becoming (Tsoukas & Chia, 2002). The active tense prevails with "-ing" words such as sustaining and ultimately balancing. As the data show, "excellence is not a fixed state ..." (Quinn, 1988, p. 23).

Perhaps, though it is the subjects themselves that say it best. As these care providers tackle an environment every day that constantly pushes them from one extreme to the other, to either/or, and to a state of achievement versus achieving, these sustaining facilities have found a way to bring dynamic balancing and movement to an otherwise chaotic and unbalanced system. As one subject said at the close of an interview, "You absolutely cannot just sit back and say well we've achieved 'x' and that's good enough ... we just keep trying to raise the bar." Two other subjects led the group in agreement during a focus group, adding:

Subject A: *We have to keep moving. Just because we got to this point doesn't mean we can slack off.*
Subject B: *Never!*

REFERENCES

Bartunek, J. M., Rynes, S. L., & Ireland, R. D. (2006). What makes management research interesting, and why does it matter? *Academy of Management Journal*, *49*(1), 9–15.

Bertalanffy, L. V. (1950). The theory of open systems in physics and biology. *Science*, *3*, 23–29.

Blegen, H. M. (1968). The system approach to the study of organizations. *Acta Sociologica*, *11*(1–2), 12–30.

Cameron, K. S. (1986). Effectiveness as paradox: Consensus and conflict in conceptions of organizational effectiveness. *Management Science*, *32*(5), 539–553.

Cameron, K. S., & Quinn, R. E. (1988). Organization paradox and transformation. In: R.E. Quinn & K. S. Cameron (Eds), *Paradox and transformation: Toward a theory of change in organization and management* (pp. 1–18). Cambridge, MA: Ballinger.

Coward, H. (1996). Taoism and Jung: Synchronicity and the self. *Philosophy East & West*, *46*(4), 477.

Cresswell, J. W. (2007). *Qualitative inquiry and research design: Choosing among five approaches* (2nd ed.). Thousand Oaks, CA: Sage.

Davis, M. S. (1971). That's interesting!: Towards a phenomenology of sociology and a sociology of phenomenology. *Philosophy of the Social Sciences*, *1*(2), 309–344.

Durlabhji, S. (2004). The tao of organization behavior. *Journal of Business Ethics*, *52*(4), 401–409.

Evans, P. A. L. (1992). Balancing continuity and change: The constructive tension in individual and organizational development. In: S. Srivastva & R. E. Fry (Eds), *Executive and organizational continuity: Managing the paradoxes of stability and change* (pp. 253–283). San Francisco: Jossey-Bass.

Fiol, C. M. (2002). Capitalizing on paradox: The role of language in transforming organizational identities. *Organization Science*, *13*(6), 653–666.

Ford, J., & Backoff, R. (1988). Organizational change in and out of dualities and paradox. In: R. E. Quinn & K. S. Cameron (Eds), *Paradox and transformation: Toward a theory of change in organization and management* (pp. 81–121). Cambridge, MA: Ballinger.

Gergen, K. J. (1978). Toward generative theory. *Journal of Personality and Social Psychology*, *36*(11), 1344–1360.

Gergen, K. J. (1999). *An invitation to social construction*. London: Sage.

Gergen, K. J., & Walter, R. (1998). Real/izing the relational. *Journal of Social & Personal Relationships*, *15*(1), 110.

Glaser, B. G., & Strauss, A. L. (1967). *The discovery of grounded theory: Strategies for qualitative research*. Hawthorne, NY: Aldine de Gruyter.

Guerra, D. (2005). *Super performance: New profound knowledge for corporate leaders*. Houston, TX: Old Live Oak Books.

Homans, G. C. (1992). *The human group*. New Brunswick, NJ: Transaction Publishers.

Karcher, S. (1999). Jung, the tao, and the classic of change. *Journal of Religion & Health*, *38*(4), 287.

Katz, D., & Kahn, R. L. (1966). *The social psychology of organizations*. New York: Wiley.

Kuhn, T. (1962). *The structure of scientific revolutions*. Chicago: The University of Chicago Press.

Lewis, M. W. (2000). Exploring paradox: Toward a more comprehensive guide. *Academy of Management Review, 25*(4), 760–776.

Luscher, L. S., Lewis, M., & Ingram, A. (2006). The social construction of organizational change paradoxes. *Journal of Organizational Change Management, 19*(4), 491–502.

Marsh, S., & Macalpine, M. (1999). The search for reconciling insights: A "really useful" tool for managing paradox. *Journal of Management Development, 18*(7/8), 642.

Marshak, R. J. (1993). Lewin meets Confucius: A review of the OD model of change. *Journal of Applied Behavioral Science, 29*(4), 393–415.

Marshak, R. J. (2004). Morphing: The leading edge of organizational change in the twenty-first century. *Organization Development Journal, 22*(3), 8–21.

McGregor, D. (1960). *Human side of enterprise*. New York: McGraw-Hill.

Morgan, G. (1997). *Images of organization* (Rev ed.). London: Sage.

Pascale, R. (1990). *Managing on the edge: How successful companies use conflict to stay ahead*. New York: Simon and Schuster.

Peters, T. J., & Waterman, R. H. (1982). *In search of excellence: Lessons from America's best-run companies*. New York: Harper & Row.

Poole, M. S., & Van de Ven, A. H. (1989). Using paradox to build management and organization theories. *Academy of Management Review, 14*(4), 562–578.

Quinn, R. E. (1988). *Beyond rational management: Mastering the paradoxes and competing demands of high performance*. San Francisco: Jossey-Bass.

Quinn, R. E., & Cameron, K. S. (Eds.). (1988). *Paradox and transformation: Toward a theory of change in organization and management*. Cambridge, MA: Ballinger.

Random House Unabridged Dictionary. (2006). New York, NY: Random House, Inc.

Rubin, H. J., & Rubin, I. S. (2005). *Qualitative interviewing: The art of hearing data* (2nd ed.). Thousand Oaks, CA: Sage.

Schumacher, E. F. (1977). *A guide for the perplexed*. New York: Harper & Row.

Smith, K. K., & Berg, D. N. (1987). *Paradoxes of group life: Understanding conflict, paralysis, and movement in group dynamics*. San Francisco: Jossey-Bass.

Strauss, A., & Corbin, J. (1998). *Basics of qualitative research: Techniques and procedures for developing grounded theory*. Thousand Oaks, CA: Sage.

Sun, H. (1999). Yin-Yang theory and its implications for management. *International Journal of Management, 16*(3), 439.

Tsoukas, H., & Chia, R. (2002). On organizational becoming: Rethinking organizational change. *Organization Science, 13*(5), 567–582.

Tushman, M. L., & O'Reilly, C. A. (1996). Ambidextrous organizations: Managing evolutionary and revolutionary change. *California Management Review, 38*(4), 8.

Van de Ven, A., & Poole, M. S. (1988). Paradoxical requirements for a theory of organizational change. In: R. E. Quinn & K. S. Cameron (Eds), *Paradox and transformation: Toward a theory of change in organization and management* (pp. 19–63). Cambridge, MA: Ballinger.

Weick, K. E., & Quinn, R. E. (1999). Organizational change and development. In: J. T. Spence, J. M. Darley & D. J. Foss (Eds), *Annual review of psychology* (Vol. 50, pp. 361–386). Palo Alto, CA: Annual Reviews.

Weisbord, M. R. (2004). *Productive workplaces revisited: Dignity, meaning, community in the 21st century*. San Francisco: Jossey-Bass.

Woodman, R. W. (1993). Observations from the field of organizational change and development from the lunatic fringe. *Organization Development Journal, 11*(2), 71–74.

LEARNING TO THINK SYSTEMICALLY ABOUT HEALTH CARE SYSTEMS: A COMMENTARY

Jonathan King

The following three articles form a sequence of sorts in addressing changes required in our prevailing health care organizations, changes of a magnitude comparable to F.W. Taylor's "scientific management" revolution at the beginning of the 20th century as we seek to "transform the fundamental O.D. paradigm." All three are based on case studies. And each has its own prescription: three "movements" each with three "key actions" for "constructive disequilibrium"; three "essential elements" for "integrated networks", and five "dimensions of key day-to-day behavioral practices."

The first article focuses on *how* to build networks among health care organizations. Sounds familiar enough since much has been written of late about the significance of networks. For example, check out the first chapters of Gladwell's *The Tipping Point* (2000). The fact that it's still on the NY Times top 10–15 best seller list 10 years later attests to the perceived and widespread relevance of networks. However, as the authors point out, "little has been written on how to foster these success factors and on how to develop health care networks." It's probably no surprise that top-down and bottom-up collaboration is crucial to developing such networks in the first place. And it's probably not too difficult to guess what "success factors include" – for example, knowing each other, understanding each others points of view, interests and convictions, trusting each other. Along these

Organization Development in Healthcare: Conversations on Research and Strategies
Advances in Health Care Management, Volume 10, 385–388

ISSN: 1474-8231/doi:10.1108/S1474-8231(2011)0000010028

lines, it probably wouldn't hurt were you to (re)read Covey's chapter on seeking first to understand in his *The 7 Habits of Highly Effective People*.

Of particular interest are the results of jointly constructed causal loop diagrams that both illustrate *systemic* problems and thereby help those involved to transcend "blame games." Anyone familiar with Barry Oshry's workshops or his book, *Seeing Systems: Unlocking the Mysteries of Organizational Life* (1995), will immediately recognize the power of the "Renga approach."

However, referring to Kurt Lewin's justly famous recipe for organizational change – "unfreeze, change, refreeze" – the article concludes that even effective workshops still face the daunting challenges of "refreezing" desirable changes into day-to-day behaviors.

The second article begins by offering the compelling metaphor of a health care organization as a "Patient" whose job it is to care for "patients." Those familiar with the sheer power of metaphor in all walks of life will appreciate both the way this metaphor "resonates" – makes sense – and its stark contrast to the machine metaphor shot through our dominant methods of inquiry, the ways we organize ourselves, the ways we talk and the ways we behave toward one another. Thus, the major argument of this article is that our day-to-day behaviors toward one another determine the culture of an organization. And the diagnostic tools offered by the author speak directly to this key reality of organizations.

Thus, it is no surprise that one of the five questions on the VSAT (Vital Signs Assessment Tool), addresses the "Degree of 'Walking the Talk'." Sounds familiar. One of the criteria used by military historians to determine the greatest all-time military leaders – that is, Alexander, Napoleon, and Washington – is the degree to which they "walked the talk" with the result that their men would follow them anywhere.

The final article – "Sustaining High Performance" – lays out the basic challenge. We must literally learn to transcend "problem solving" in both the ways we think and the ways we organize ourselves such that we "sustain" processes of "constructive disequilibrum." Good terms! Those familiar with research on "corporate creativity" will therefore find much that is familiar in this article.

Stuart Kauffman has recently made a similar and instructive claim. And Kauffman is worth quoting.

> Economists have so far not been able to offer much help to firms trying to be more adaptive. Although economists have been slow to realize it, the problem is that their attempts to model economic systems focus on those in market equilibrium or moving toward it. They have drawn their inspiration predominantly from the work of physicists

> in this respect (often with good results, of course).... We do not yet know what makes some systems more adaptable than others, but research on complexity has yielded some clues ... Too much control freezes the system into limited configurations; too little causes it to wander aimlessly. Only systems that hover on the border between order and chaos exhibit the needed general stability and capacity to explore the universe of possible solutions to challenges. ... Not surprisingly, most economists have so far resisted these ideas. Yet there can be little doubt that learning to apply these lessons from biology to technology will usher in a remarkable era of innovation and growth. *Scientific American* (October 16, 2006).

If you find this first article challenging – in a constructive sense – then I would encourage you to read *Natural Capitalism.* Google the authors first. You will be impressed. The book offers a wide variety of examples illustrating what they term "whole systems thinking" characterized by "multiple parameters of value." Or, as I once had a chance to ask Amory Lovins, "Could the subtitle of your book be "Transcending Business and Environment Trade-offs"? He replied, "Absolutely." And this is precisely what the first article is after – constructive disequilibrium in organizations through viewing problems as opportunities, through transcending the either/or of paradox. Thus, one of the author's "key movements" includes a dialectical process between the supposed either/or of collective and individual.

You can also read precisely the same arguments offered by Russell Ackoff via Jamshid Gharajedaghi, in *Systems Thinking: Managing Chaos and Complexity*, especially the subsection 'Multidimensionality" in "Part 2 System Principles." In short, the author is in good company.

After reflecting on all three articles, one is also struck by the obstacles facing attempts to "update" health care organizations. First, while so-called "complexity theory" is addressing shortcomings of our traditional linear, analytic, quantitative scientific method, there is much that needs to be done. For example, while it is proper to speak approvingly of interdisciplinary research and teaching, guess what? It is still the exception, not the rule, in our universities. Second, and related to the first, is what Chris Argyris has for years termed "defensive thinking." Only the last article takes a serious stab at addressing this obstacle, one Argyris has found is especially prevalent among "highly qualified people" – that is, MD's, PhD's, CEO's. You might also reread the next-to-last paragraph where McGregor speaks of "intrinsic motivation." Then thumb through Gallup's twenty-plus year research on why such motivation still remains the exception rather than the rule. The title is instructive – *First, Break All the Rules.* Worse, there is growing evidence that people revert to blame games when faced with complexity unless they are "emotionally prepared." Yet the very notion of "emotional intelligence" is anathema to traditional science.

In short, we still have much to learn about the nature of obstacles to the proposals offered in these articles. Hundreds of years of "machine-age thinking" have left us quite a legacy to transcend. There are, for example, further issues concerning the effects of building and office design on both our behaviors and thoughts. And there is also strong evidence that "extrinsic" motivation – read top-down, carrot-and-stick – acts as a self-fulfilling prophecy.

If all this seems a bit overwhelming as it does to me, then reread, as I did, the two paragraphs near the end of the second article starting with "A tall order?" They are inspiring.

CONCLUDING REMARKS

WELL-BEING REVISITED

As we challenged you at the outset, our hope with this book was to do more than inform you. Rather we hope that it will catalyze you to think and act in transformational ways as you address the complex, yet delicate world of healthcare. The tapestry of ideas presented on these pages pulls you through multiple perspectives and healthcare venues big and small. They address revised views on common practice, reframe long-standing management principles, and push at the very edge of how we can continue to make healthcare a healthy and vibrant organizational experience.

As healthcare providers help those looking to heal, so can (and should) Organization Development (OD) scholars and practitioners work to help the organizations they work in or with find and/or sustain their vitality and strength. OD work in healthcare plays a unique role of a "healing" practice working with a healing profession. But the research and discoveries that are shared within these pages are not simply about the practice of OD but about the implications of organizational life that influence the way in which healthcare experiences are delivered every day.

PRINCIPLE AND PROGRESS

This book provides a frame for viewing and understanding the constitution and function of organizations within healthcare and the unique challenges they face. Accordingly, these institutions represent evolving, conditional narratives holding inspiring vignettes of progress, and principle. Woven within these complex narratives are the desires of an evolving human species searching for meaning, purpose, and redemption. OD as a profession and calling has a unique opportunity to focus and direct the energy, passion, and commitment in a way, which sustains the practitioner and those she serves.

The chapters within this book reflect a stimulating mix of interrelated forces influencing the trajectory of organizations and the people within them. We primed the pump of purpose by posing a life support question concerning the genesis of organizational purpose – mission statements – early in the work. This examination draws attention to the potential for mission statements to act as points of potential engagement for healthcare practitioners seeking connection to a deeper sense of belonging. These deep-seated existential antecedents provide the platform for leaders to build cultures of connection, common purpose, and meaning. The power of relationships and teams in impacting both positive and disruptive environments sheds light on the issue of the need for healthy leaders who can engender collaborative work. Information technologies role in underpinning our work brings a 21st century view toward healthcare's migration into a highly interconnected world, amplifying our sense of interconnectedness and interdependence. As such, this book reflects a landscape of principle and progress – an ever-shifting panorama of planned and unplanned change. In doing so this brings us back to our hope that you not find an "answer" within these pages, but more so you discover your own reason to be in action in a world of constant motion.

SUSTAINING OD'S "ETHIC OF THE STREET"

OD's richness emerges from the diverse and complex disciplines that have tended to its introduction and execution over the past 70 years. Driven by a sincere desire to affect positive change within organizational life, practitioners took their cue from the fields of psychology, sociology, philosophy, economics, industrial psychology, labor relations, human resources, education, and management. Accordingly, a pluralistic lexicon has evolved and is manifest in the language and practice of the OD practitioner and student. As such OD appears as a ready and open platform designed to embrace the complexity of communities within the healthcare world. This openness invites movement and energy toward diverse thinking and application of OD ideas and protocols – a diversity that can at times appear obscure and opaque.

At the same time, this diversity fuels the potential and ability for the OD "personality" to find greater synergy to its relative context. This adaptive capacity may in fact contain what is both sacred and profane within our profession – a flexible paradigm built to recognize and address the complexity of systems seeking pleasurable equilibrium while simultaneously ushering systems toward potentially painful yet generative disequilibrium. It is this dynamic balancing that reminds us that we never stop moving and also provides us the ability to be present in an environment of chaotic change.

So how does the practitioner move (and ultimately thrive) within this fluid environment, tending to humanistic desires and traditions while engaging and blending rigor within research and method? It may require a broad ethic designed to ensure a course of consistency within the rich history while seeking the unknown or less traveled. The temptation may arise to recast or rename our effort to more closely sync with the context to which OD finds its energy and purpose. However, our ethic must sustain our profession to ensure that we evolve our capacity to utilize the tools and resources crafted along the way while maintaining our sense of ecological and contextual intelligence – that sense about the environments in which we work that support the meaning and purpose we seek.

OD can build on our seemingly paradoxical human desires and motivations for inclusion and independence, discovery and exploitation, as well as our universal need for meaningful work. As such, our ethic can seek to create and sustain what Manfred Kets de Vries (2001) describes as the "authentizotic" organization – organizations designed to engender trust and reliance while affirming life. Cultivating life-affirming organizations through connection to mission, through the application of individual competence, and through the empowerment of individuals to make a difference can bring health and hope to our work and those we serve. It also provides a framework for adaptation of the work of OD in the healthcare setting.

BUILDING ON THE ACCUMULATED WISDOM

In many ways, OD reflects the diverse population it seeks to serve. Capturing the gains offered by those who have come before us requires a "faith" in what is possible. The authors and chapters within this book reflect the accumulation and utilization of years of wisdom. As OD has evolved from an examination and interpretation of individuals and teams within organizations, to the discernment and understanding of broader systems and principles, there remains a deeply rooted commitment to the importance of cultivating and supporting healthy organizational ecologies that engender healthy outcomes.

The world of "work" will continue to evolve, impacted by internal and external conditions, demands, and "elements," reflective of the evolution of both the individuals and communities that our organizations serve. David

Whyte (2001), in offering his testament to the marriage of identity and meaning work, noted that

> … we must assume a certain shape that puts us in conversation with the elements; we must cultivate a kind of faith in the moving energies around us and the way they to come to our aid, give us lift, no matter our circumstances or difficulties.

Leveraging our lessons learned while remaining open to the potential of what life may hold seems to speak to the faith required – the idea that what is possible remains to be seen, within ourselves as scholars and/or practitioners, within OD as a profession, and within our work of ensuring expanding health of the very healthcare systems we serve.

Jason A. Wolf
Heather Hanson
Mark J. Moir

REFERENCES

De Vries, M. K. (2001). *The leadership mystique: Leading behavior in the human enterprise*. Prentice Hall Publishing.

Whyte, D. (2001). *Crossing the unknown sea: Work as a pilgrimage of identity*. The Berkley Publishing Company.

Printed and bound by CPI Group (UK) Ltd, Croydon, CR0 4YY

16/09/2026

14963402-0003